SHAW 11

The Annual of Bernard Shaw Studies
Volume Eleven

Fred D. Crawford, *General Editor*

SHAW
AND
POLITICS

Edited by

T. F. Evans

The Pennsylvania State University Press
University Park, Pennsylvania

Shaw and politics / edited by T. F. Evans.
        p.   cm. — (Shaw : v. 11)
   Includes bibliographical references.
   ISBN 0-271-00733-8
   1. Shaw, Bernard, 1856–1950—Political and social views.
2. Political plays, English—History and criticism.   I. Evans, T.
F.   II. Series.
PR5366.A15 vol. 11
[PR5368.P6]
822′.912—dc20   90-47974
                                                                      CIP

It is the policy of The Pennsylvania State University Press to use acid-free paper for the first printing of all clothbound books. Publications on uncoated stock satisfy the minimum requirements of American National Standard for Information Sciences—Permanence of Paper for Printed Library Materials, ANSI Z39.48–1984.

Note to contributors and subscribers. *SHAW's* perspective is Bernard Shaw and his milieu—its personalities, works, relevance to his age and ours. As "his life, work, and friends"—the subtitle to a biography of G.B.S.—indicates, it is impossible to study the life, thought, and work of a major literary figure in a vacuum. Issues and men, economics, politics, religion, theater and literature and journalism—the entirety of the two half-centuries the life of G.B.S. spanned was his assumed province. *SHAW*, published annually, welcomes articles that either explicitly or implicitly add to or alter our understanding of Shaw and his milieu. Address all communications concerning manuscript contributions (in 3 copies) to Professor Fred D. Crawford, General Editor, *SHAW*, Dept. of English, Central Michigan University, Mount Pleasant, MI 48859. Subscription correspondence should be addressed to *SHAW*, Penn State Press, Suite C Barbara Building, 820 North University Drive, University Park, PA 16802. Unsolicited manuscripts are welcomed but will be returned only if return postage is provided. In matters of style *SHAW* recommends the *MLA Style Sheet*.

Contents

T. F. Evans

INTRODUCTION: THE POLITICAL SHAW

At the beginning of the second act of *Man and Superman,* there is a brief exchange on political themes between Tanner, his friend Octavius, and his chauffeur, Straker. Tanner warns the would-be literary man, Octavius, not to start Straker on political economy because "he knows all about it and we don't." He goes on to explain, "You're only a poetic Socialist, Tavy: he's a scientific one."[1] The lines carry a deeper resonance than their significance in the play itself. First, Shaw was always more concerned with political economy than with politics in the general sense of the word. Second, the remarks underline the gulf that Shaw always found between those who, like Tavy, thought of themselves as poets and dramatists without any deep concern for the nature of the society to which their art and literature ought to make some contribution and those who, in contrast, thought of art and politics as indissolubly linked. Shaw himself might be held to have begun as a "poetic" socialist who made himself into a "scientific" one. In strictness, however, neither adjective can be applied without a great deal of qualification or explanation.

Shaw was a socialist, of some kind, throughout the whole of his adult life. In common with many others on the political Left, he seems to have spent more of his time pointing out the errors in policy and practice of those who were theoretically on his own side rather than the opposing Right, but in this he closely resembled the members of religious factions that sometimes appear to find much greater satisfaction in drawing attention to the errors of members of other sects than in pointing out the paths of error being followed by nonbelievers. What distinguished Shaw from other politically inclined writers is how he combined both his political and artistic interests and activities.

The well-known story told by William Archer of his initial meeting with Shaw embodies the essential truth. He first glimpsed Shaw in the reading room of the British Museum with two large volumes spread out before him on the desk: "Karl Marx's *Das Kapital* (Volume 1, in French), and an orchestral score of *Tristan und Isolde.*" Archer added that he did not then know "how exactly this quaint juxtaposition symbolised the main interests of his life."[2] Whether as journalist and critic in his earlier days, or later when he established himself as primarily a dramatist, Shaw was always to combine to an unrivaled extent his literary interests and activities on the one hand and, on the other hand, the closest absorption, practical and theoretical, with the means by which humanity organized itself into societies and managed and governed those societies. Indeed, such a word as "combine" fails to emphasize the true nature of Shaw's joint concerns. For him there was no such thing as art separate from politics or politics separate from art. It may be a useful form of short-hand, but the very term "the political Shaw" must have about it something incomplete and therefore misleading.

Nevertheless, it can be useful to look at Shaw primarily from the political point of view and to try to assess, however loosely, the extent to which his concern with political matters did dominate his life and the part that it played in his artistic creation. Tanner warns Tavy not to start Straker on political economy, not politics more generally. For Shaw, the terms were interchangeable. In fact, while he was for long periods deeply absorbed in political economy, he never had a great deal of time for politics in the limited sense, whether that might mean theories of government or an examination of the day-to-day occupation of party maneuvering or like dealings in Great Britain. For these, Shaw had only a withering contempt. What interested him was the way in which society might be organized in the best interests of all. In a review of *Three Plays for Puritans* in 1901, the novelist Arnold Bennett wrote that Shaw was "the indefatigable champion of social justice, not because he has a passion for social justice but because he has an intellectual perception of it."[3]

Yet, this is a difficult argument to sustain. To refer to Shaw as an "indefatigable champion of social justice," not because he has a passion for social justice but simply because he has an intellectual perception only, is to reduce social justice to pure mathematics or a subtle series of maneuvers in which human motives or concerns play no part. To return to the antithesis in the exchange from *Man and Superman,* it cannot be contended that there was in Shaw himself nothing of the "poetic Social-ist," one who is attracted by the emotional or aesthetic appeal of socialism rather than by the merely practical or scientific. To Shaw, such men as Shelley, Ruskin, and Morris were, at different times, among his most influential teachers. To him, Ruskin was not merely an influential critic of art, Shelley not merely a great lyric poet, Morris not merely a master of art and design. All three looked forward to a new order of society.

Shaw always professed to have become a socialist as a result of the influence of others. It is clear that his socialism was a broad river fed by different tributaries. After his death, an admirer, but by no means an uncritical one, summed him up. This was R. Palme Dutt, a Marxist, in an obituary: "He was a Marxist and an anti-Marxist, a revolutionary and a reformist, a Fabian and a despiser of Fabianism, a Communist and a crusader against super-tax."[4]

Shaw paid tribute to an early teacher, Richard Deck. He had met Deck in 1880 and took lessons in French from him, but, in addition, Deck introduced his pupil to other subjects, including the ideas of Proudhon, the French socialist with his ringing declaration that "Property is theft." Of more immediate importance, said Shaw, Deck "helped to prepare me for Henry George's 'Progress and Poverty,' which I read in Sept.–Oct. 1882, and which made me an enthusiast for 'Nationalization of Land.' "[5] Shaw heard Henry George speak at the Memorial Hall in Farringdon Street, London, on 5 September 1882. Paradoxically, George was not a socialist himself, and Marx spoke of him with scorn as a defender of capitalism. Nevertheless, from the day of the meeting and his subsequent reading of the book, Shaw realized the importance of "the economic basis" of society and of human existence itself, and the path of his entire life was given its direction. Shortly after this he went on to read and study Marx and to concentrate on mastering economics. At about this time, Archer found Shaw reading Marx in the British Museum. From then on, Marx became an important part of Shaw's life. He wrote in 1887 a long review of *Das Kapital* in the *National Reformer,* the weekly paper of the National Secularist Society.[6]

The review was printed in three parts in successive issues of the paper. It is more than eight thousand words long. To Shaw, as he declared in the opening paragraph, the book, first appearing twenty years before but only recently published in England, was "revelation." He contends, "He that believeth is a true 'scientific Socialist:' he that believeth not is a middle-class self-seeker, a *bourgeois,* an exploiter of labor, and most likely a police spy." After such a beginning, it comes as something of a surprise that Shaw spent a great deal of the article pointing out where Marx went wrong. Of course, he paid him expansive tributes. Marx, according to Shaw, "keeps his head like a God. . . . The thread of history is in his hand." After reading Marx, said Shaw, students of "the dismal science," however erudite they might be, can never be the same. Nevertheless, the extraordinary impression made by Marx, declared Shaw in a lofty tone, does not depend on the soundness of his views but more on "their magnificent scope and on his own imperturbable conviction of their validity." He went on in a long section of the review to point out the fundamental error in Marx.

This took him into a long discussion of Marx's labor theory of value. In very rough terms, the theory is that the value of anything produced consists of the equivalent of the cost of the labor required to produce it. Shaw dissented from this theory and accepted instead the view of the English academic Stanley Jevons. Jevons differed from Marx by declaring that value was determined not by the cost of labor in production but, at the other end of the scale, as it were, by reference to the utility value of the article to the ultimate purchaser. Jevons, who was as much an academic logician and mathematician as he was an economist, was certainly no socialist either, but Shaw decided that he had the truth of the matter in him and always clung to the Jevonsian theory of value as opposed to the labor theory of Marx.

Not surprisingly, this led to some criticism from the Left, as indicated in the obituary memoir by Palme Dutt, in which the writer declares that "the science of Marx was a closed book to Shaw" and asserts that he

> boggled at the first schoolboy's elementary conundrum over the theory of value, gave up the attempt to think a little further and master the key which unlocked the secrets of the laws of locomotion of capitalist society, and preferred to settle down with the tenth-rate platitudinous commonplaces of a Jevons or a Marshall, without realising that he had thereby theoretically capitulated to the capitalism which his emotions detested.[7]

There may well be some truth in this harsh comment, but Shaw, no matter how he differed from Marx on questions of faith, doctrine, or theory, declared at the end of the long *National Informer* review that he "never took up a book that proved better worth reading than *Capital*." It was "the extraordinary picture of modern industrialism which gives the book its main force and fascination." It was the devastating criticism of nineteenth-century capitalism combined with the visions of a better world that he found, or was to find, in the writings of Shelley, Ruskin, and Morris that, despite Shaw's labors in the field of political economy, tended to make him, in Tanner's terms, as much a poetic as a scientific socialist.[8]

The orthodox Socialists and economists of the extreme Left thought Shaw was wrong. In a memorable phrase later to be used by Lenin, his contemporaries who looked for an immediate revolution thought of him as "a good man fallen among Fabians." The Fabian Society had been founded in 1883, and Shaw read the Society's first tract, *Why Are the Many Poor?*, in 1884. The Society appealed to his intelligence and to the need for socialism to make inroads among the intelligentsia of the middle class. Despite the contradiction inherent in Shaw's contempt for orthodox public-school and university education and his being seduced by the classical reference in the name of the Society, he was at once attracted by the idea of a group that, by means of intellectual argument, would succeed in permeating those sections of society in which real power lay. Shaw had already shown himself a great joiner of societies, and he had established himself in such bodies as the Zetetical Society and the Dialectical Society, as well as in such nonspecifically political bodies as the Shelley Society. In all of them, he had developed his powers of exposition and elucidation and his quite remarkable skill as a controversialist, a quality which was later to lead the historian A. J. P. Taylor to describe him as "the greatest arguer there has ever been."[9] As a member of the Fabian Society and, more particularly, as a member of the "Fabian Triumvirate," a loose alliance between himself and the Webbs (Sidney and Beatrice), he made a contribution to the development of the Left in Britain and, indeed, to the pattern of British society that, despite many vicissitudes, may still be seen to have its effect today.[10]

In inception, the Fabian Society was not a political body in the limited sense of the word—it did not set itself up in opposition to either of the two great parties, the Conservatives and the Liberals. Its aim was to permeate. To this end, it sought to cultivate the leaders and the best brains of both parties (or of none) and, by a process of rational argument and persuasion founded on research and publication, to bring them round to accept the need for basic reform and a new structure for the economy and society. Beatrice Webb was a skillful research worker; Sidney Webb, trained in the civil service, was, in Shaw's words, "the ablest man I ever knew" and an expert draftsman and explainer of political programs. Shaw's great contribution was his flair for publicity and his matchless skill as orator and platform performer, combined with the literary gifts which were put at the disposal of the Society in writing essays and pamphlets and in editing the work of others.

If the 1880s were the decade in which Shaw's political orientation was finally settled, the 1890s were the decade in which he did most of his concentrated political work, chiefly in the Fabian Society. He acted as a kind of general editor for such works as *Fabian Essays*, which appeared in 1889 and which, comprising not only contributions from other pens, but a long introduction by himself and two additional essays on the economic basis of socialism and the transition to socialism, represented one of his most sustained pieces of political writing. For well over a decade, he continued to write and speak regularly for the Fabian Society, and one remarkable feature of his activity at this time was that it was not concentrated on such domestic subjects as, for example, that covered in his booklet *The Common Sense of Municipal Trading*, but extended beyond the boundaries of these islands in his concern for the international aspects of the growth and development of socialism, particularly in its relationship to Britain's imperial responsibilities. The statement issued by the Society entitled *Fabianism and the Empire* impresses not simply as a lucid exposition of a view on an intensely difficult and controversial subject, but perhaps more so because it was produced by Shaw after reading 134 contributions by members of the Society to distill a statement which was accepted as the combined view of the entire Society.

A book which provides an admirable conspectus of Shaw's thoughts on politics and economics during the period of his life when he was most actively concerned with these subjects is *The Road to Equality*, a collection of previously unpublished lectures and essays, edited by Louis Crompton and published in 1971. The ten pieces included were written between 1882 and 1918. The first, "Our Lost Honesty," is the text of a lecture given to the Bedford Debating Society under the chairmanship of the Reverend Stopford Brooke. This was on 22 May 1884, very shortly before Shaw joined the Fabian Society. Briefly, his theme is the effect of capitalism on normal standards of honesty. Even more than in many of his other writings on political and economic themes, this piece develops the relationship between (to use again the formulation in Tanner's remarks to Octavius) the "poetic" and the "scientific." More striking still than the structure of Shaw's argument is the witty tone of voice in which it is expressed. One outstanding example will illustrate this. Shaw presents in his opening a comparison and contrast between the highwayman of old and the present-day capitalist. The highwayman brought romance and color into life, and his existence could be justified economically because, among other things, he gave employment to large numbers, from horse dealers to hangmen. In the course of his activities, he ran enormous risks. Shaw asked, "Will anyone pretend that the risks of the holders of the London and North Western Railway stock are comparable to these? Yet we not only hang the highwayman and reward the shareholder, but we sometimes allege that we reward the shareholder for his risk."[11]

Succeeding lectures include reflections on various different aspects of politics. The last and longest item is the text of a Fabian Society lecture given by Shaw in May 1918. After the cataclysm of the war, Shaw looked at "The Climate and Soil for a Labor Party," but because it covers a wider scope than this title might imply, the editor has called it "Socialism and Culture." The lecture is an odd blend of optimism and pessimism. Nothing could be the same again, but Shaw wanted changes to be fundamental and organic. Thus, he looked for a transformation in the essential economic structure of society rather than for mere political juggling. As in later writings, he recognized the importance and legitimate aspirations of the trade unions but had some misgivings about the precise role that they were to play.

Shaw's activity as a political pamphleteer, general crusader, and persuader during the 1890s would have been remarkable even if it had not been accompanied by other significant work on his part. His activity is even more worthy of praise since, during these years, he embarked on that other career which was to represent his greatest claim to outstanding distinction in the world of the stage and literature. In 1892, his first play, *Widowers' Houses,* was performed, and, by the end of the century, he had written nine more plays. That, almost without exception, they failed to attract any great attention is of less importance than that Shaw had now found the means of expression in which he was ultimately to have the greatest effect on the reading and theatergoing public. In addition, for three years, Shaw was a regular dramatic critic, writing a long article each week for the *Saturday Review.* As with the regular music criticism which he had written earlier, first for the *Star* and then for the *World,* Shaw's comments on plays and players were likely to be interspersed with observations on the political or economic situation of the day.

For Shaw, life was never divided into separate and distinct compartments. In a bogus interview which he purported to give to the correspondent of the *Star,* and which was published as part of the advance publicity for *Widowers' Houses,* he declared that the play was, in reality, a lesson in political economy and that he could not guarantee success unless he was allowed to have a blackboard on stage at one point, the better to teach that lesson to the audience. When the play was first published in book form, Shaw concluded his Preface by trying to have it both ways, as it were. The play, he declared, was not only "a work of art as much as any comedy of Molière's is a work of art," but it also dealt with "a burning social question and is deliberately intended to induce people to vote on the Progressive side at the forthcoming County Council election in London."[12]

With this publication, and with the appearance in two volumes of *Plays Pleasant and Unpleasant* in 1898, Shaw began the practice of publishing his plays with long prefaces. These were designed not, as suggested by some unkind critics, to instruct prospective members of the audience what to think about the plays before they saw them in the theater, but rather to explain the background of the ideas from which the plays had sprung. Thus, there is more overt discussion of politics and economics in the prefaces than in the plays themselves, and no assessment of Shaw as a political writer can ignore the direct contribution that the prefaces make, as contrasted with the indirect contribution to the controversies of the plays themselves.

It was also in the 1890s that Shaw took his first steps as a politician in practice as well as in theory. He participated in local government, and his letters during this period give evidence of the amazing way in which he was able, at the same time, to pursue the parallel careers of playwright and vestryman, or councillor. Eyebrows were raised among some of Shaw's fellow dramatists at what they considered the unliterary content of some of his plays. Shaw defended himself with spirit. To one he explained that his plays, far from being born out of an inward-looking concern with the theater itself and essentially theatrical values, had been written in the afternoons after mornings spent in council meetings, listening to "h-less orators," a comment which was saved from being patronizing by its truth.[13] He had earlier told William Archer when the latter had criticized *Widowers' Houses* that he had collected rents and philandered widely, in contrast to the limited experience of Archer. He concluded by dismissing his friend as a "sentimental Sweet Lavendery recluse."[14] The jibe was double-barreled. As well as taunting Archer with having no experience of the real world, he managed to relate this to Archer's admiration for the nonpolitical dramatist Pinero by using the title of one of his sentimental comedies, *Sweet Lavender*.

Another critic to whom Shaw replied with spirit was Henry Arthur Jones. Jones was also a successful dramatist of the day and ranked with Pinero as a pillar of the "serious" drama of the 1890s. Nobody tried harder to be a great playwright than did Jones, and Shaw praised his work much more than that of Pinero, although Pinero won greater admiration from other critics and the public. Shaw thought more highly of Jones because he tried to direct some of his works to genuine society itself rather than to the specialized hothouse of what Pinero referred to in *The Second Mrs. Tanqueray* as "this little parish of St. James's." Yet Jones thought that Shaw was not enough of a literary man and too much of a politician. Shaw replied. He was a politician, he explained crisply, because he believed in efficiency and did not concern himself merely with narrow abstract "literary" values. It was because he was a politician that he could go to the heart of matters which left other dramatists mouthing platitudes. In other words, it was because he was a politician that his plays were about something, and therefore better plays.[15]

Shaw's active career in politics as a member of an elected body lasted for six years. In 1897 he was elected as vestryman of St. Pancras, and he served until 1903. In 1906, he was defeated in an election for the London County Council. If the 1890s have been described as the years of his most active concern with the Fabian Society, it is not to be supposed that he gave up involvement with politics thereafter. Even though in the early years of the new century, from 1901 with *Man and Superman* to 1914 with *Pygmalion*, he was deeply immersed in the theater, writing (and often producing) ten plays which rank with his most important work, as well as others of lesser value that are nevertheless clever and entertaining, he continued to contribute to the work of the Fabian Society by providing pamphlets, lectures, essays, articles, and general advice to all. He drafted election manifestos and programs, advised candidates, and took part in countless meetings of committees and other bodies. He played a leading part in defending the "Old Gang" of the Society against a spirited attack by H. G. Wells. While the merits of the controversy are still a matter for discussion, it was Shaw's power of argument and his matchless platform personality that discomfited the petulant Wells and finally carried the day. Yet Shaw was not merely of value to the Society when at the center of the stage. His work in preparing *Fabianism and the Empire* is a most striking example of his great contribution to the Society. Edward Pease, its secretary, wrote that "Bernard Shaw has accomplished many difficult feats, but none of them, in my opinion, excels that of drafting for the Society and carrying through the Manifesto called *Fabianism and the Empire*."[16]

In some flights of fancy from time to time, Shaw would consider himself as remote from the preoccupations of ordinary life. "My kingdom was not of this world," he once said. "I was at home only in the realm of my imagination, and at my ease only with the mighty dead."[17] He was never further from the truth. In his work for the Fabian Society and in his political activity generally, he was never simply the literary man who had strayed by accident into politics. Poetic socialist he may have been, but he always had an eye not so much to what was theoretically desirable as to what was practically possible, to what could be done and what, therefore, should be done. Thus, in a Fabrian election manifesto in 1892, he advised the workers how to vote to secure the election of the best candidate or, if all the candidates were bad, to see that the least bad was elected. (There were no Labour candidates at this time.) Shaw advised firmly against any sulking if an elector's whole program could not be adopted: "Every working man must try to get as much of the Labor program as he possibly can staked in his constituency at the election; but if he only succeeds in getting half-an-inch of it staked, he must vote and agitate for that half inch as resolutely as if it were the whole."[18]

On another occasion, Shaw expressed himself with some force on the need for compromise in politics. He castigated Joseph Burgess who, after refusing to compromise in an election, lost:

> When I think of my own unfortunate character, smirched with compromise, rotted with opportunism, mildewed by expediency, blackened by ink contributed to Tory and Liberal papers, dragged through the mud of Borough Councils and Battersea elections, stretched out of shape with wire-pulling, putrefied by permeation,

worn out by 25 years pushing to gain an inch here or straining to stem a back-rush there, I do think Joe might have put up with just a speck or two on those white robes of his for the sake of the millions of poor devils who cannot afford any character at all because they have no friends in Parliament. Oh, these moral dandies! these spiritual toffs! these superior persons! Who is Joe anyhow that he should not risk his soul occasionally like the rest of us?[19]

While Shaw managed to combine the two activities of playwright and politician, bringing energy to the discharge of either task to an extent that would have involved full-time commitment on the part of anyone else, his concern for politics during this period did not end with his work for the Fabian Society, nor indeed with his campaigning against the censorship of plays, which also took up a great deal of his time. An idea that was widespread at one time and, indeed, survives today, is that Shaw's plays were merely propagandistic or proseletyzing in intention. They were concerned to illustrate political problems, but in personal and dramatic rather than in directly crusading terms. Thus, the interest in "dirty money," involving as it does fundamental questions about the individual's integrity and his or her relationship to society, had intense personal relevance and power in the limited dramatic sense, as well as having the more lasting effect of, it was hoped, persuading those who had seen the play to think more deeply about the social implications that it suggested. Thus, the question, merely momentary in its theatrical interest, of whether Trench, in *Widowers' Houses,* should take the money of the wealthy landlord, Sartorius, or whether Major Barbara in the later play should, in effect, connive at her wealthy father's buying the Salvation Army, would lead to the fundamental question of whether the whole of society should be radically transformed.

In the years after the 1914–18 war, with his local-government period well behind him and never to be resumed, and no longer an active member of the Fabian Society, Shaw's direct concern with the political world may have declined, but his interest continued to be as lively and provocative as ever. This showed itself in articles, lectures, letters to the press, and continual private discussion with friends and acquaintances concerned with the Labour movement. During this period, he made three principal statements on the politics of the time. The longest were *The Intelligent Woman's Guide to Socialism and Capitalism* and *Everybody's Political What's What?*. These two treatises, published in 1928 and 1944, respectively, were attempts by Shaw to set down, in reasonably manageable form, the basis of his political faith and his advice on how the aspirations of that faith could be converted into an effective program of political reform of government and management of the economy. They were written with outstanding lucidity and, even today, when changes in society cannot fail to affect the unfolding of Shaw's argument, the force of his prose makes the exposition of complicated problems still fascinate readers because of his control of the subject and the combined vigor, polish, and wit of his rhetoric.

The third exposition of socialist principles which Shaw published in this period was an article contributed to the supplementary volumes of the *Encyclopaedia Britannica* published in 1926, "Socialism: Principles and Outlook."[20] An unusual note is struck at the beginning. Shaw states directly that socialism, in its simplest and most direct form, consists of the abandonment of private property (although not of personal property) and its transformation into public property. What is unusual and novel in Shaw's exposition is the forthright declaration that "a complete moral *volte-face*" is involved in the total transformation of beliefs, policies, and practices that is required. In Shaw's vocabulary, the words "moral" and "immoral" had always had special connotations. When he declared himself to be a consciously and deliberately "immoral" playwright, he was trying to shock his readers by suggesting that there was in his attitude something of impropriety or even indecency. In fact, he was seeking to convey that morality was not a question of right and wrong, or otherwise of ethical values, but simply a question of what society was prepared to accept. However, when he uses the world "moral" in the *Encyclopaedia Britannica* article, he employs it in the ethical rather than the customary sense. His attitude here is not far from that in the peroration to *The Intelligent Woman's Guide* when, explaining that what he submits is the true meaning of the term "lady," he defines the real lady as the person who gives more to her society than she takes from it.[21] In this article, Shaw tended to combine and, possibly, to confuse the idea of political and economic organization with that of personal and social rectitude.

The article, which is less than four thousand words long, begins with a fairly familiar explanation of Shaw's analysis of the development of capitalism and the type of society that emerged in the nineteenth century, first in Britain and then in other developed countries. He lays special emphasis on the cardinal position of private property in a capitalist system and the importance attached to "the play of free contract and selfish interests . . . no matter what anomalies it may represent." There is an explanation of the growth of the rentier class, the middle class that grows as an ancillary to the possessing classes, and of the way in which lower elements of society become supporters of those whom they would be expected to oppose, simply because, being parasitic on those others, they have to recognize that, to a large extent, their own well-being must depend on the continuing prosperity of those who are already much better off than they themselves. At the same time, competition among employers frequently has the effect of causing overproduction, and there follow cycles of "booms" and "slumps," when continuing employment cannot be guaranteed to the "proletariat." It is remarkable how closely some of this refers to developments more than half a century after the words were written. In addition, Shaw analyzes the extent to which the nominal owners and therefore directors of large concerns have to employ middle-class managers, rather on the lines of Mangan, presented in *Heartbreak House* as something like a Napoleon of industry who, while admitted in the government as "a practical business man," is kept going by his traveling expenses alone. Here, too, Shaw was able to foresee the growth of a "managerial" society.

"The end of the first quarter of the 20th century," contends Shaw in his *Encyclopaedia Britannica* essay, "finds the political situation in Europe confused." He thought it threatened dangerous remedies and the abandonment of previously sacrosanct institutions of parliamentary democracy. Writing before the advent of Hitler in Germany, he mentions coups d'état and dictatorships in Italy, Spain, and Russia. The loss of faith in capitalism and the realization of the decline of "the moral plausibility of capitalism" were nevertheless not balanced by "the gain of any widespread or intelligent faith in socialism." Not surprisingly for one who would later depict disillusioned trade unionists in the characters of Boanerges in *The Apple Cart* and old Hipney in *On the Rocks,* he had no faith in trade unionism as the answer to the questions posed by capitalism. Crisply, he sums up with the comment that "the trade union driving force aims at nothing more than capitalism with Labour taking the lion's share."

In 1938, there appeared the first and most uncompromising criticism of Shaw on the grounds that, while he attacked the capitalist system from a professedly socialist standpoint, he did not, in effect, propose any serious or substantial change in the system. Thus, Christopher Caudwell (Christopher St. John Sprigge) devoted to Shaw the first essay in a compilation of pieces on representative writers and thinkers, *Studies in a Dying Culture.* The essay on Shaw was called "A Study of the Bourgeois Superman." Briefly, Caudwell's thesis is that Shaw, while understanding the nature of capitalist society and, because he had read Marx, able to "attack destructively all bourgeois institutions," was never able to give an effective and satisfactory answer to the question of what should be done. While he showed in such works as *Widowers' Houses, Mrs Warren's Profession,* and *Major Barbara* the iniquity of "tainted money," he compromised, resisted the idea of "proletarianism" which he had found in Marx, and "adhered to Fabianism with its bourgeois traditions and its social respectability."[22]

A second writer, Erich Strauss, in *Bernard Shaw: Art and Socialism,* published in 1942, also criticized Shaw from, apparently, the standpoint of a convinced Marxist.[23] In the preface to the book, Strauss explained that his study of Shaw had turned out differently from what he had originally intended. He had begun with the idea of illustrating the gradual abandonment of socialism by Shaw the dramatic artist, as distinct from Shaw "the theoretical Socialist." He had found that the book did not proceed in that way. Instead he discovered that all Shaw's work, dramatic as well as nondramatic, was dictated and shaped by his socialism, but that, as Strauss went on to show in the book, there was a gradual disillusion with some aspects of Shaw's socialist faith and a feeling that it would not work in practice. According to Strauss, therefore, Shaw's dissatisfaction with what attempts had been made to introduce socialist solutions to the problems of Britain and of the world led him to confuse an indictment of capitalist democracy with attacks on the essential nature of democracy itself. This caused him to look with increasing favor on the emerging dictatorships of the interwar years, to sound warnings in *The Apple Cart,* and to express the ideas of the old trade unionist, Hipney, in *On the Rocks:*

> Adult suffrage: that was what was to save us all. My God! It delivered us into the hands of our spoilers and oppressors, bound hand and foot by our own folly and ignorance. It took the heart out of old Hipney; and now I'm for any Napoleon or Mussolini or Lenin or Chavender that has the stuff in him to take both the people and the spoilers and the oppressors by the scruffs of their silly necks and just sling them into the way they should go with as many kicks as may be needful to make a thorough job of it.[24]

The attitude of Hipney goes some way toward justifying Strauss's original idea that Shaw the dramatist had abandoned socialism, but Shaw, when he read the book and wrote to the young author about it, did not take up this aspect of the matter. He complimented Strauss on his book but noted that he had fallen into the error of identifying the statements of characters with their creator's own ideas. Thus, he said,

> As a Socialist it is my business to state social problems and to solve them. I have done this in tracts, treatises, essays, and prefaces. You keep asking why I do not keep repeating these propositions and principles Euclidically in my plays. You might just as well ask me why I don't wear my gloves on my feet or eat jam with a spade. And when you make all these thoughtlessnesses the basis of a tragedy of ambition (a blind lust which I have never felt in my life), disappointment, failure and despair, your book gets out of

all relation to the facts, much more to the poetry of my life and work.[25]

A third book, in which Shaw's political position was criticized from roughly the same standpoint as the previous two, was published in 1950, the year of Shaw's death. This was the Marxist Alick West's "*A Good Man Fallen among Fabians.*" His title was the well-known aphorism that Lenin used to sum up his idea of Shaw's political views. In accordance with that opinion, West, as the two previous writers had done, commended Shaw's acceptance of Marx's analysis and criticism of the way in which capitalism had developed during the nineteenth century, but felt that he had failed to take his views to their logical conclusion of espousing and advocating a full assault on capitalism in order to destroy it and to replace it by a fully Socialist or Communist system.

West's attack on Shaw comes to a climax in his analysis of *Major Barbara,* the last play with which he deals. He finds Shaw's dramatic art most impressive in the way the second act shows Undershaft, the munitions manufacturer, as the embodiment of the capitalist system, in direct contrast to the values of the spirit personified by his daughter, Barbara. Unfortunately, in his opinion, Shaw destroys the force of his drama by giving Undershaft a contradictory double role. He is not simply the embodiment of all that is worst in nineteenth- and twentieth-century capitalism, against which Shaw launches eloquent criticism in the preface to the play. He is also made a kind of hero or savior because of his power to destroy capitalism with the benevolent "welfare-statism" of his policy toward his employees in the model village community surrounding the factory visited by Barbara and the other characters in the final act. Shaw justifies this by giving Undershaft the statement that poverty is the worst of all crimes and all ills and that the first duty of everyone is to combat it, both on his own account and, insofar as he can, for the benefit of others.

For West, "neither in the play *Major Barbara* nor in the preface will Shaw face the fact that it is the working class that must have the power to use against the capitalist class." Shaw, in West's view, was right to dream of a socialist future, but he would not take the step of advocating or supporting a full revolutionary move toward that future. Thus, "Shaw's compromise with capitalism, his ridicule of the true idealist as well as of the false, is the logic of his Fabianism, of his abandonment of the hope of socialism as he had dreamed it. It is the defeated admission that his vision is an impractical dream. But it is not the vision itself."[26] For West, as for others of his particular cast of political outlook, Shaw was a good man and right in essence, but his goodness (that is, the acuteness of his political vision) failed to have the right practical effect because he fell among Fabians.

There are two other important aspects of the political Shaw. The first concerns the personal application of his general approach to political themes in the plays. It was his habit, and in this he was probably not very different from other literary artists, to model characters in his plays on real people. Some of the identifications are well known: Sidney Webb was the model for Bluntschli in *Arms and the Man,* and T. E. Lawrence (of Arabia) was the model for Private Napoleon Alexander Trotsky Meek in *Too True to be Good.* A fascinating gallery might be made up of the portraits of twentieth-century prime ministers who appear in his plays.[27] Admittedly, neither Balfour nor Asquith is clearly recognizable in the composite Balsquith in *Press Cuttings,* but both Asquith and Lloyd George are caricatured with some penetration as Lubin and Joyce Burge, respectively, in *Back to Methuselah.* Neither Bonar Law nor Baldwin came into Shaw's focus, but he seized on the many-sided personality of Ramsay MacDonald to create the prime minister Joseph Proteus in *The Apple Cart,* the real-life model for whom was immediately apparent to everyone who saw the play, with the single exception of MacDonald himself. Chavender in *On the Rocks* and Sir Orpheus Midlander in *Geneva* make up a composite picture clearly based on Sir Austen Chamberlain, who, in fact, never became prime minister although holding other high offices, including that of foreign secretary, the position of Sir Orpheus in *Geneva.*

Perhaps the single and most important conclusion that emerges from this portrait gallery is of Shaw's conviction that the burden placed on prime ministers is ridiculously excessive, combining as it does the immensely demanding task of supervising the entire business of government with the requirement for regular attendance at sittings in the House of Commons. As Chavender puts it, "I was in the House yesterday until three in the morning; and my brains are just so much tripe."[28] Shaw made it clear that he did not consider the holders of the most important office in the country as anything but capable men; it was simply his view that impossible demands were made upon them. King Magnus in *The Apple Cart* was clearly the most able man in the country, but he had time to be so, and his energies were not sapped by the demands of the party game. This cannot be taken too far, of course. Magnus, as Charles II in *"In Good King Charles's Golden Days"*, may have represented Shaw's ideal of the philosopher-king, but neither could serve as the model for an effective ruler in late twentieth-century conditions.

The second important aspect relates to Shaw's deeper thoughts on the development of Western society.[29] There is very great irony in looking into the subject of Shaw and politics at the beginning of the last decade of the century, when the hold of Socialism (or Communism) over a considerable part of central and eastern Europe is disappearing. Indeed, it is possible to go further. Taking a broader view, it could be argued that the nineteenth century, following the American and French revolutions, was a period of the advance of society in contrast to, if not at the expense of, the individual. Shaw, born in the middle of the century, was able to take his part in the various political movements of the time which pointed in the direction of the nonconservative regimes of the twentieth century in, for example, the Britain of Labour governments, the America of the Franklin D. Roosevelt years, and the extreme Socialism or Communism of those countries where the experiment is now being rejected. The latter part of the present century has thus seen movement in the direction opposite to that of a hundred years ago. Yet, the position is by no means so simple. When Shaw went to Russia in 1932, he spoke of Lenin as having instituted a great experiment in social organisation and added that "if that experiment in social organization fails, then civilization falls, as so many civilizations have fallen before."[30] Shaw did not live to see the end of Stalin, whom he praised with such unqualified superlatives, and, of course, he did not foresee the present collapse, or near collapse, of the Lenin-Stalin experiment and the efforts being made by Gorbachev to bring the state back to life. It is unlikely that he would have been too greatly disturbed. He was nothing if not evolutionist. As, at the end of *Back to Methuselah*, he could see the whole of human life and the entire race as an experiment which could fail and be replaced by another experiment, so he could envisage one political experiment failing and being replaced by another.

Yet his assessment of the development of human society was always optimistic. He had what he called a religious sense, "to be working for things outside yourself," and he would have applied himself to helping to build a world out of the wreckage. Indeed, in the present circumstances, it is not hard to imagine him working, not for a return to a totally unbridled market economy, but for a third force. This would combine the best of individual-centered capitalism and the best of society-centered Socialism, in much the same way that Ibsen foresaw a new force emerging from the conflict between the elements represented by the antagonists in *Emperor and Galilean*. The synthesis would be truly egalitarian, or even Marxian, in its technical and philosophical development.

Thus, despite Shaw's most enthusiastic championing of the Soviet experiment, to prove him wrong in this respect is not to establish that the whole of his political thinking should be rejected. Shaw always condemned the way in which capitalism tended to usher in an idolatry of richness and idleness which inverted previous ideas of social morality. His views have been echoed most impressively in the recent past by a writer who, while not paying any direct debt to Shaw, is the most Shavian in style and content of modern commentators on economic problems—John Kenneth Galbraith. He has remarked on the decay beneath the prosperous surface of some of the outwardly successful Western economies. In his words, "While the only evident remedy under socialism is to move towards the market, so the only possible solution for us is a larger, more compassionate role for the state."[31] At the same time, as Shaw's plays continue to hold the stage for their unique combination of sound sense and witty fun, so may some of his politico-economic writings, touched as they are by much of the same blend of gaiety and intelligence, still command interest and attention.

Notes

1. *Man and Superman, Collected Plays with Their Prefaces,* ed. Dan H. Laurence (London: Max Reinhardt, 1970–74), 2: 519.

2. William Archer, *World* 963 (14 December 1892), 14.

3. Arnold Bennett, *Academy* (February 1901), p. 127.

4. R. Palme Dutt, "George Bernard Shaw," editorial in *Labour Monthly* (London) 32. no. 12 (1951).

5. *Bernard Shaw, The Diaries 1885–1897,* ed. Stanley Weintraub (University Park: Penn State University Press, 1986), I: 23.

6. *National Reformer* (London), 7 August 1887, p. 84.

7. Dutt.

8. Before settling upon Socialist as his political label, Shaw passed through a phase in which he thought of himself as an anarchist. This is examined in *From Radicalism to Socialism: Men and Ideas in the Formation of Fabian Socialist Doctrines, 1881–1889* by Willard Wolfe (New Haven and London: Yale University Press, 1975). This aspect of the subject is dealt with also in a concise but informative essay, "Shaw and Anarchism: Among the Leftists," by Richard Nickson in the *Independent Shavian* 26, nos. 1–2 (1988). This issue of the *Independent Shavian* also includes a reprint of "What's in a Name?" by Shaw, which first appeared in the Boston weekly *Liberty* (11 April 1885), the first publication in the United States of anything by Shaw. His thesis is that "we shall never get rid of slavery until we have got rid of authority." Writing some years before he abandoned anarchism and wrote his pamphlet *The Impossibilities of Anarchism* in 1888, Shaw refers to two types of socialists, anarchist and collectivist, and explains that

> the Collectivists would drive the money-changers from Westminster only to replace them with a central administration, committee of public safety, or what not. Instead of "Victoria, by the Grace of God," they would give us "the Superintendent of such and such an Industry, by the authority of the Democratic Federation," or whatever body we are to make our master under the new dispensation.

9. A. J. P. Taylor, *Politics, Socialism and Historian* (New York: Stein and Day, 1952), p. 131.

10. A full study of the relationship between Shaw and the Webbs has yet to be written. It would provide illumination of both personal and political value. Beatrice was frequently

exasperated with Shaw, as may be seen from the comment in her *Diary* for 13 July 1913, a fairly representative sample of her displeasure:

> We are unhappy about Shaw. About five years ago I thought he was going to mellow into deeper thought and feeling, instead of which he wrote *Fanny's First Play*. He used to be a good colleague, genuinely interested in public affairs and a radically kind man. Now he is perverse, irate and despotic in his relations, and he is bored with all the old questions. And the quality of his thought is not good . . . poor and petulant reasoning, the lack of accuracy, logic and dignity.

Not six months later, however, she wrote on 4 December 1913,

> GBS is making an effort to keep in with the Fabian Society and ourselves and he has attended every one of our six public lectures and taken the chair twice. Also he has been most kind in doing things for the Fabian Society, he no longer writes for the *New Statesman*, though he is quite friendly and asks whether we want more money.

The Diary of Beatrice Webb, ed. Norman and Jeanne MacKenzie (London: Virago Press and the London School of Economics, 1984), 3: 190–91.

11. Bernard Shaw, *The Road to Equality: Ten Unpublished Lectures and Essays, 1884–1918*, ed. Louis Crompton (Boston: Beacon Press, 1971), p. 8.

12. Preface to 1893 Edition, *Widowers' Houses, Collected Plays with Their Prefaces*, 1: 46.

13. Letter to Ellen Terry, 28 May 1897, *Collected Letters*, ed. Dan H. Laurence (London: Max Reinhardt, 1965), 1: 770.

14. Letter to William Archer, 14 December 1892, *Collected Letters*, 1: 373.

15. Letter to Henry Arthur Jones, 24 December 1894, *Collected Letters*, 1: 461.

16. Quoted in Michael Holroyd, *Bernard Shaw: The Pursuit of Power, 1898–1918* (London: Chatto & Windus, 1989), p. 44.

17. Preface to *Immaturity* in *Prefaces by Bernard Shaw* (London: Odhams Press, 1938), p. 680.

18. Bernard Shaw, *The Fabian Election Manifesto*, Fabian Tract no. 40 (London: Fabian Society, 1892), p. 14.

19. Quoted in Hesketh Pearson, *G. B. S.; A Full Length Portrait* (New York and London: Harper & Brothers, 1942), p. 156.

20. *Encyclopaedia Britannica*, 13th ed. (New York, 1926), 31: 572–75.

21. *The Intelligent Woman's Guide to Socialism and Capitalism* (London: Constable, 1928), p. 463.

22. Christopher Caudwell, *Studies in a Dying Culture* (London: John Lane, Bodley Head, 1938), p. 14.

23. Erich Strauss, *Bernard Shaw: Art and Socialism* (London: Gollancz, 1942), p. 108.

24. *On the Rocks, Collected Plays with Their Prefaces*, 6: 719. This speech may be compared with that of Lord Summerhays in *Misalliance* when he tells Tarleton that "to make Democracy work, you need an Aristocratic democracy. To make Aristocracy work, you need a Democratic aristocracy." *Misalliance, Collected Plays with Their Prefaces*, 4: 169.

25. Letter to Erich Strauss, 4 August 1942, *Collected Letters* (London: Max Reinhardt, 1988), 4: 633.

26. Alick West, *"A Good Man Fallen among Fabians"* (London: Lawrence and Wishart, 1950), p. 133.

27. In a letter to Molly Tompkins, 19 October 1924, Shaw wrote very disparagingly of British politicans following a general election: "For sheer coarse savage bloody-mindedness it would be hard to beat the orations of Birkenhead, Lloyd George and Churchill. For good sense, unaffected frankness and educated mental capacity give me Trotsky all the time." *To a Young Actress*, ed. Peter Tompkins (London: Constable, 1960), p. 78.

28. *On the Rocks, Collected Plays with Their Prefaces*, 6: 637.

29. With the greater attention that he paid to international affairs, the later years of his life saw some diminution in Shaw's concern with domestic developments (although *Everybody's Political What's What?* is an important exception). He did write the occasional newspaper article, however, and a good example of his comment on topical developments was in relation to the social-insurance plans produced by Sir William Beveridge in 1944. See "What Would Marx Say about Beveridge?" written in connection with the sixtieth anniversary of the death of Marx, *Daily Herald* (10 March 1943). For a lucid commentary on Shaw's political development in his later years, see Edmund Wilson, "Bernard Shaw at Eighty," in *The Triple Thinkers* (London: John Lehmann, 1952), p. 158.

30. Dan H. Laurence, ed., *Platform and Pulpit* (London: Hart-Davis, 1962), p. 217.

31. J. K. Galbraith, "Assault on Ideology," *Weekend Guardian* (London), 16–17 December 1989, p. 16.

Bernard Crick

SHAW AS POLITICAL THINKER, OR THE DOGS THAT DID NOT BARK

Why is Shaw so ignored by my colleagues? I ask myself this question as a political philosopher with an interest in the history of ideas. He is not ignored by some literary scholars, but he is by academic political philosophers and by most historians of modern British politics.

This may seem in this volume an inept attempt at a weak Shavian paradox. Shaw ignored! Well, perhaps I should bluntly say, not taken seriously. Any political history or history of ideas that mentions the Fabians mentions Shaw, but usually only a mention it is. *The Labour Party's Political Thought: A History* by Geoffrey Foote (an otherwise excellent book) has only four minor references to Shaw.[1] He tells us in thirteen lines, not wholly accurately, that Shaw attempted to convert the early Fabian Society to Marx but was himself converted to Jevons's theory of economic value. Foote devotes a more substantial paragraph to Shaw's defense against the anarchists of the Fabian theory of the state. He notes that the Fabians "dabbled in eugenics, with Shaw proposing in his play *Man and Superman* that national suicide could be averted only by scientific breeding" and that "Shaw eventually became disillusioned with parliament, and was to praise the national efficiency inculcated by Stalin and Mussolini" (why does he spare the references to Hitler?)[2]

Political philosophers ignore him. I am not aware of a single article on Shaw by an academic political philosopher; the gap in Britain between the academic and the general intellectual (which I am sure is greater than in the United States and Canada) is shown at its widest. Shaw was, after all, the most famous and prolific political intellectual of his time. But the suspicion remains with many scholars that he was mainly famous for being famous, into which he put so much successful effort over such a long time.

The influence of the Webbs on British politics and social policy is acknowledged, even by those who detest it. But if every schoolboy knows that Shaw often said that they were the brain and he their megaphone or mouthpiece, only a schoolboy would take that at face value. Did he not have a mind of his own! When years afterward Shaw told Lady Londonderry, "All I could do for Webb was to beat the drum in front of his booth, as he could not master that useful instrument himself," his tone is of comic mock-modesty, and no one should doubt that such a drummer with a tone-deaf master will beat out some dominant rhythms of his own. Yet the actual influence of Shaw himself is either doubted or thought to be so difficult to assess that scholars shy away from the problem, fearful of making fools of themselves by trying to sort out what he really meant amid all the comic welter of sometimes provocative, sometimes defensive, badinage. And there is the awkward problem of how much of Shaw's political beliefs we can read into his plays. Do we take even the major assertions of a play literally, or as pointing to a Ph.D. doctor's dilemma? I first read Geoffrey Foote's summary of *Man and Superman* above with some unease, now with some disagreement.

Even those who recognize Shaw's great influence as a propagandist and publicist seem wary of assessing his ideas. Robert Skidelsky in writing on Shaw and "The Fabian Ethic" makes the important general point that "the heart of the Fabian ethic was an overwhelming sense of public duty."[3] This distinguished them both from the religious, with their duty to God, and from the "New Lifers," with their duty to, or obsession with, self. But having made this general point, Skidelsky remains, as far as ideas are concerned, on a level of generalities, and the rest of the essay returns to the historian's familiar task, albeit with skill and wit, of establishing "connections," personal connections. (I am sometimes puzzled whether modern historians simply see this as their only proper task as historians, or whether they actually believe that all ideas are simply a product of personal loyalties and interests—a kind of disease of liberalism.)

Michael Holroyd, even, fights shy of assessing Shaw's political ideas, indeed of taking them seriously. His approach is fundamentally reductionist, not in an economic sense, of course, but in a psychological one. He showed his hand early in the entry for Shaw in *Makers of Modern Culture:*

> The Fabian Society became Shaw's new family and his socialist reforms a means of changing society so that no child should have to go through the sort of upbringing that he had endured. Believing himself to be unloveable, he made out of Collectivism a weapon against individualist romantic propaganda. . . .
> He believed that he had inherited from his parents incompati-

ble qualities which he must reconcile within himself. . . . From this process emerged his concept of the Life Force which is not a symbol of power but a unit of synthesis.[4]

Small wonder that Holroyd called the first volume of the biography *The Search for Love*.[5] The passage just quoted shows that Holroyd or his publishers did not adopt that question-begging title partly to promote the book, as some reviewers naughtily hinted. It had long been his theory. But the evidence he advances (leaving aside that none of it was new, something masked by the lack of footnotes and sources)[6] shows that he may not merely have been overinterpreting, but also making, on balance, the wrong interpretation: the book could be as plausibly called on the evidence he himself presents "The Search for Ideas" or "The Search for Identity (through ideas)." As a young man Shaw tried out different ideas even more energetically than he did different women, and the advantage of ideas over women was that they could be synthesized, for nothing was entirely wasted: even synthesized into a theory of evolution and creativity by sexual selection.

Holroyd obviously has little sympathy with rationalist humanism: that one adopts ideas by a process of reasoning. Ideas are simply rationalizations of psychological drives or traumas (or of economic self-interest, say others). The true intellectual historian can only say "sometimes," not always; and *never* for a person's entire ideology—there are too many variant doctrines on offer at any given time, and too many broken homes that do not throw forth a genius. The historian of ideas has to look at the intellectual context, not merely the social context, much less only the family history of the person concerned. The trouble with purely psychological explanations in biography, as Richard Ellmann once argued, is that they are perfectly reversible: an individual was molded by childhood experiences, or reacted violently against them (what Karl Popper called "the fallacy of psychologism").[7] It makes a good story either way, but the relation to historical truth remains problematic.

This psychologism makes it easy for Holroyd to bypass any serious discussion of Shaw's political ideas. To explain how he held them is always more important than what they are. In the encyclopedia article he even said that "Shaw's socialism . . . *invades* many of his plays" (my emphasis). There is a whiff in Holroyd of the old-fashioned English man of letters who wants politics and literature kept firmly apart. Now to some extent this foreshortening or separation is necessary in any biography of comprehensible size. But Holroyd makes it worse by actually mocking serious political discussion, or rather by retelling Shaw's own later comic accounts of what it was like and misrepresenting how seriously he must have taken the issues at the time.

Annie Besant in 1886 forced a confrontation between Fabians of anarchist persuasion and the collectivists:

> At the end of some high-pitched speeches, a mixed Fabian and SDF team that included Annie Besant, Shaw and John Burns . . . routed by forty-seven votes to nineteen the anarchists, led by William Morris and Mrs Wilson, who had argued that the inevitable compromise and concession of parliamentary politics would poison the well, obscuring socialist principles and hindering socialist education throughout the country. An immediate outcome of this rowdy debate was a notice from the manager of the hotel informing the society that further meetings could not be accommodated there. After an interval in a church, Sydney Olivier arranged for later functions to be held at Willis's Rooms which, decked with silver candelabra and patrolled by liveried footmen, were famous as the least expensive, most aristocratic, meeting-place in London.[8]

That is very funny, and probably an excellent and concise summary of the minority argument; but what—may one ask?—did the majority argue? One suspects (and without the missing references few readers can tell) that Holroyd's narrative is very close to some account by Shaw himself—too close perhaps and too uncritical, in effect trapped in Shaw's "sure, it was all a joke" badinage. Almost every autobiographical statement by Shaw is for some present effect or polemic at the time he wrote; and they all need dating and putting into context to judge their truth for the time relative to which they nominally refer (and again, without references, few readers can tell). And his adopted persona was not, after all, the Clown, but the Wise Fool. However comically he might have delivered his speech against the anarchists at that meeting, wrapped up in it must have been a deadly serious argument if he thought that, had the vote gone the other way, the Fabian Society as he knew it would have been at an end.

To be fair to Michael Holroyd, he ends that same chapter with a comment on William Morris's review of the *Fabian Essays* that clearly identifies the tension between the personal and the political, neither subsumed in the other:

> Morris and Webb were more than friends to Shaw: they were his political mentors. Morris was a great man and Webb a great brain; Morris a hero for all time and Webb a man of the time. Shaw wanted to unite the applied arts with the social sciences and use Webb's logic to circumvent Morris's sense of history. But as Morris's review of Webb's essay makes clear, they were two heralds beckoning Shaw in different directions. So Shaw continued speak-

ing of the Fabians with two voices. His most persistent voice aggran-
dized the Fabian achievement. The other voice sounded his despair
that they had not achieved more. . . . He turned to the one and
then to the other: and eventually he turned to the Soviet Union.[9]

Leave aside for the moment the last sentence, which is glib and too
simple—it needs the word "too" added, for one of the problems with
taking Shaw seriously as a thinker rather than as a popularizer of utter
genius is that he never gave anything up; yet there is another way of
looking at "different directions" rather than as political and philosophical contradictions arising from personal loyalties. The historian of ideas
is familiar with very similar problems, such as occur famously in Rousseau. Can, with "contextual charity," his contradictions between individualism and collectivism, between romantic and austere classical values, be
explained away empathetically; or must these contradictions, with "contextual clarity" (confound it, that's what the fellow actually said), be
exposed rigorously? Well, people say what they say and write what they
write, but at different times and in different circumstances and to be
understood by different audiences. Statements can presume or imply
different time scales. This is particularly characteristic of progressive
thought. If you believe that the future will not resemble the past and will,
indeed, be better, then there need be no absolute contradiction between
visionary and tactician. Both are needed. Could we imagine a good (or
even a better) society without either Webbs or Morrises? There can be
Machiavellian utopians, so long as time scales are distinguished;[10] and
there is no particular reason why philosophers should be impractical (as
Michael Oakeshott and F. H. Bradley have reminded us, the mind
ranges through many different levels of experience or modes of being).[11] The economist will distinguish between short-term, middle-term,
and long-term factors, and the theologian between things of this world
and of the next; but the essayist, the satirist, and the entertainer may
deliberately juggle with and confuse them, partly for fun ("laughter,"
said Hobbes, "is a sudden glory") and partly to stimulate new thought by
desanctifying conventions (*Pickering:* "Have you no morals, man?" *Doolittle;* "Cant afford them, Governor. Neither could you if you was as poor as
me."). In this sense Shaw is a speculative thinker, more in the tradition of
Socrates and Voltaire than of the great system builders like Hegel, Marx,
and Herbert Spencer. The process of thought is almost as important as
the content.

   And the content? Let me now look at what a few academic students of
politics, who have been brave enough to try to include Shaw in their
narratives, think important about his ideas.

One of the most impressive achievements of British political scholarship in our time is W. H. Greenleaf's *British Political Tradition,* of which three volumes have so far appeared and a fourth is to follow. Greenleaf is a disciple of Oakeshott, about whom he has written; in a broad sense he is of conservative persuasion. He has done what the Master and other disciples have mainly talked about, written an actual account of a tradition of politics, not simply a philosophic justification of tradition. And in looking at the full complexity of the tradition, his objectivity as well as his width of reading is awesome. He quotes Shaw sixty years later telling Kingsley Martin how he helped Webb sweep the "Perfect Lifers" and "all the nonsense and Bohemian anarchism" out of the early Fabian Society. And he quotes Shaw as saying that he put thoughts of the New Jerusalem aside in favor of a thorough understanding of the theory of rent and the sanitary regulations of a London borough. Instead of the "scramble for private gain," the Fabians sought "the introduction of design, contrivance and coordination" in the conscious pursuit of "collective welfare." But Greenleaf cautiously notes that "if recent commentary has properly indicated the ethical basis or undercurrent of early Fabian thought," yet Webb at the time was saying that the main effort of the English socialist movement "was to bring about a society infused with collectivist principles and techniques."[12] Greenleaf is right at least to remind us of the ethical undercurrent, and perhaps he takes Shaw's renunciation of New Jerusalem for free public lavatories for women a little too literally. Several of the great plays tell a different story, not only *Man and Superman.* Anyway, saints need not be unsanitary. On different time scales both preoccupations are compatible, or, if that sounds too socialist a methodology or hermeneutic for Greenleaf, then like Oakenshott or F. H. Bradley he might better construe them as on different levels of experience. Shaw's denunciation of bohemianism should have sounded critical alarm bells. That's either the pot calling the kettle black or should remind the reader, as any good tailor or couturier knows, that there are many shades of black. He too gets sucked into Shaw's wholehearted heroic rhetorical exaggeration.

Greenleaf is on firmer ground when characterizing Shaw's elitism. He quotes from Shaw's Fabian tract *Socialism and Superior Brains: A Reply to Mr Mallock* that always and everywhere—in this he agreed with the Tory Mallock—"the few will . . . organize the many."[13] Shaw was an elitist. Of that there is no possible doubt, no possible doubt whatever—except about what kind of elitist he was. Greenleaf fails to note that unlike Mallock, and like Major Barbara's evolutionary mate, Adolphus Cusins, he does think it necessary to educate the masses. Perhaps one day in the Life-Forced future when there is equality of income, imposed by the public-spirited and dedicated elite, and when the palpably unfit Snobby

Prices (the Snopeses of Cockneydom) have been bred out or contracepted into genetic sterility, there will be virtual equality of ability. And, unlike Mallock again, Shaw says this on Labour movement platforms even. Greenleaf notes that he assured the trade unionists on behalf of the Fabian Society that extreme devices of democracy were undesirable and reassured them that the "organized, intelligent and class-conscious Socialist minority" must not be placed at the mercy of the unorganized and apathetic rabble of electors and routine toilers.[14] The word "organized" may have convinced the brothers that they were of the Elect. (The socialist historian Eric Hobsbawm has said that one of the difficulties of socialism, even in its Communist form, was that it was always in practice a doctrine of the skilled worker.)

In the same passage, however, Greenleaf notes "the extreme and provocative tone" of the Shavian formulation in "Sixty Years of Fabian Socialism" when he says, first, that the elite should be selected by experts, not by popular vote, and, second, that "under Socialism social misfits should be 'painlessly liquidated' and that those who are not able 'to prove their social solvency' should be made to do useful work or be put to death." Greenleaf wisely ruminates that

> one never really knows with Shaw whether he means exactly what he says or is simply trailing his coat. Certainly this particular expression of opinion is the *reductio ad absurdum* of that alliance between eugenic selection and benevolent despotism that Shaw always favoured.[15]

But I put it to my fellow political philosopher that "*reductio ad absurdum*" is subtly wrong. Mr. Dooley once said that every time Andrew Carnegie gave away a library, he gave away himself in a speech. But Shaw was not giving himself away; he surely picked his words deliberately, even if, by the time he did, they were grossly insensitive. So something like "clownish melodramatic exaggeration" might fit it better, or simply call it "Shavian dramatic hyperbole." And while "benevolent despotism" is all right, "enlightened autocracy" would be better (these two terms mean something different in the history of ideas). Certainly Shaw and Webb's elite was programmed to work *through* the existing system—permeation as the tactic and the "inevitability of gradualism" as the theory. Again Greenleaf himself notes this when he quotes from Shaw's Preface to the 1908 reprint of *Fabian Essays:*

> In 1885 the Fabian Society, amid the jeers of the catastrophists, turned its back on the barricades and made up its mind to turn heroic defeat into prosaic success. We set ourselves two definite

tasks: first, to provide a parliamentary programme for a Prime
Minister converted to socialism as Peel was converted to Free
Trade; and second, to make it easy and matter-of-course for the
ordinary respectable Englishman to be a Socialist as to be a Liberal
or a Conservative.[16]

Yet Shaw himself can mislead the reader by such a hearty contrast,
helpful though it was to the Fabians, between revolution and permeation. For to him, if hardly to Sidney Webb, even permeation was part,
cosmically a small part, of the unfolding of evolutionary progress and
the Life Force, moving toward an eventual perfected or fully realized
human nature. Beatrice Webb was to confide to her diary that "religious
ends and scientific methods are indivisible if mankind is to rise above the
brute battle for life."[17] It could even be argued that if socialism has
revolutionary ends, it had best adopt political and evolutionary means.

Stanley Pierson in his *British Socialists* is a rare historian to take seriously, but not uncritically, Shaw's philosophy of history.[18] There have
been more studies of popular religious or quasi-religious movements
from American than from British scholars (such a book as Ian MacKil-
lop's *British Ethical Societies* [1986] is rare). Pierson quotes Shaw as saying
that had it not been for Webb, he "might have been a mere literary wise-
cracker like Carlyle and Ruskin," but more clearly than Greenleaf he
demonstrates that Shaw never gave up, even when he was beating the
Fabian drum, a belief in the special role of the imaginative artist. "He
began to construct a personal religion or mythology" convinced that the
secularists and the scientists had failed to explain "the mystery of consciousness." And Shaw, says Pierson, looked not to Darwin but to Samuel
Butler's argument that "man's mind disclosed the presence of a cosmic
force working through evolution;" and he says that Schopenhauer and
Nietzsche also influenced Shaw in this—he could have mentioned Bergson, too.[19] He is surely right. And the road to this conclusion is a bold but
clearheaded use of Shaw's plays, as well as his strictly political and polemical writings. A play cannot demonstrate an author's conclusions with
finality (unless it is a very bad play), but it can demonstrate his or her
main concerns: what the author thinks is relevant. Certainly it cannot be
said of Shaw that he raises more questions than he answers. He, or his
characters, answers everything, often with different answers. But his
seriousness and originality as a political thinker should be judged by the
questions he asks rather than by the dramatically arresting but varying
answers he gives.

Man and Superman is, of course, Shaw's great testament to his evolutionary ethic and contains one powerful *speculation* about the nature and role
of elites. Pierson quotes Sidney Webb, writing to Pease: "I have just read

Shaw's Don Juan play and I do not admire it at all."[20] Small wonder. But there is also the view of Cusins as he prepares to share the Undershaft money and power with the former Major Barbara: "I want a democratic power strong enough to force the intellectual oligarchy to use its genius for the common good." That sounds more like a power for democracy than a democratic power; but this speculation is back closer to Sidney and further from Beatrice. However, on balance, Pierson is right to say that "Shaw's desire for a more radical transformation of society was evident in his treatment of two phenomena which the Fabians tended to ignore—power and religion."[21]

Shaw treats power and religion as, respectively, the means and the ends of Creative Evolution: the Black Girl will find that her god is perfected man, or at least a very greatly improved model. And the powerful means to that end will be a new elite, whose members will be part artist and part engineer—part Octavius Robinson and part Henry Straker. But in forcing us to face, however much we talk about democracy, that there will always be elites of some kind, an author can get trapped in his own rhetoric. Strictly speaking, Shaw was presenting elites as a disciplined and dedicated "order," and it should follow that the members of such elites, like aristocrats or army officers, exercise a broad equality among themselves; collectively they are a hierarchy when facing other ranks and orders, but internally they are a fraternity. Yet Shaw's fascination with, intellectual generosity toward, and misreading of Hitler, Stalin, and Mussolini, together with his lack of interest in their parties, is undeniable and regrettable. In 1933 he addressed the Fabian Society off the cuff and out of the back of his bursting head:

> Herr Hitler—a very remarkable, very able man. . . . But I cannot agree with Hitler on every point . . . I think he is the victim of bad biology and of a bogus ethnology. . . . Now let us look at Signor Mussolini. What has he built up? He is trying to build up in Italy what he calls a corporate state . . . I approve of that, because it is precisely what the Fabian Society wants. . . . Now let us come to another interesting gentleman whose personal acquaintance I have had the pleasure of making—Stalin. . . . Now Stalin is a nationalist exactly like Hitler. He does not fall back on the world revolution, but understands that he has to have Socialism in Russia, which is quite big enough for him to look after without troubling himself about Socialism in Edinburgh, or anywhere else.[22]

In some ways he lapsed back to thoughts and concepts stirred by Carlyle: great men, not even dedicated elites, as the real catalysts of history. It can not have escaped Shaw's attention entirely that each of his three heroes, however temporary their stand on his empty pedestal, could have rather short ways with surviving fellow leaders of the elite from the early days of the struggle. Shavian dramatic hyperbole (hereinafter called SDH) seems an appropriate rhetorical device when talking about evolution and the Life Force but less so when talking about the great dictators: the trouble with them, which Shaw did not realize in time, was that they meant exactly what they said about the need to eliminate the unfit and the unsocial; they were not joking.

Let us see how well SDH worked in the advocacy of the third side of the triangle of G. B. S.'s political philosophy: equality. In the last twenty-five years academic philosophers have written many books and articles on the concept of equality, and broad positions are taken, more or less for and more or less against. But none of them makes any substantial reference to Shaw.[23] Now, of course, they write for a different audience using more rigorous, academic conventions of argument. Shaw addressed intellectuals and the self-educated whose only university was the free public library (the audience that Dickens, Mark Twain, H. G. Wells, and Orwell have written for). In Shaw's day, few intellectuals were found in or dependent upon universities, and even in our happy times one could exaggerate the intellectualism of university teachers: many are more concerned to build and maintain disciplinary barriers than to communicate widely through the free play of ideas. Great issues are more often debated in novels, plays, or minority-time television "talking heads" shows than in seminars. But the academic political philosophers regularly devour the views of other past figures who had little or no lasting connection with universities: say Hobbes, Locke, Rousseau, Mill, Tocqueville, Marx, and perhaps Simone Weil. But the historian of ideas must look at the general preconceptions or dominant concepts or paradigms of an era wherever they are best expressed.

When Shaw put the case for a literal equality of income and outcome, not of opportunity (a view put forward by no other known socialist thinker since Gracchus Babeuf), he forced his audiences into mental movement, challenging them to come back with criteria for differentiation or to define what they meant by such concepts as "an equal society," "a radically more equal society," and "an egalitarian society." He began an address to the National Liberal Club on 1 May 1913 (the May Day holiday for radical labor), "When I speak of 'The Case for Equality' I mean human equality; and that, of course, can only mean one thing: it means equality of income. It means that if one person is to have half-a-crown, the other is to have two and sixpence."[24] And he rattles on with a spectacular defense of this impossible position (impossible if taken literally—what if I use a penny of the half-a-crown, as William Cobbett once advised poor immigrants, to sow mustard seed, but then begin to sell it at profit as superior to the chemically doctored manufactured stuff?). But he is plainly fishing for stock responses in discussion.

A Mr. Richard Whiteing rose to the bait and evidently put the familiar case that cultured human beings need more. First, Shaw hits him on the head with an idealized distinction (appropriate to the audience) between the "real gentleman" and the "sham gentleman." The real gent is dedicated to public service: "my ideal . . . shall be to strive to give to my country in return more than it has given me; so that when I die my country shall be richer for my life." But sham gent says, "I want a handsome and dignified existence; but a less handsome and dignified existence is good enough for other people." Shaw concludes, "If any man wants a better life, he should not seek that life for himself alone, but should attain it by the raising of the general standard of life."[25] That is an impressive moral argument and rings true, even if it is scarcely a justification for his opening claim for literal equality of income—unless that claim is seen not as a program for the next government but as a Platonic ideal or standard or as the telos of Creative Evolution.

In *The Intelligent Woman's Guide* he repeats the literal argument. His summary of the contents of chapter 26, "The Diagnostic of Socialism," includes, "Many professed Socialists are so because they believe in a delusion called Equality of Opportunity, and would recant if they discovered that Socialism means unconditional equality of income for everyone without regard to character, talent, age or sex." And the text robustly asserts that it is "quite possible and practicable, not only momentarily but permanently. It is also simple and intelligible. It gets rid of all squabbling as to how much each person should have." But the main thrust of his argument is in fact aimed at achieving a classless society, and "the best test of that," one which must be supported by "every device of taxation of income, restriction of inheritance and the like," is simply "intermarriageability": social policy has "no other object than to keep the entire community intermarriageable."[26] At the National Liberal Club he had wrapped this up with comic badinage, not needed for intelligent women: he was not saying that every National Liberal must marry everyone else, nor need find everyone else equally attractive, nor that men and women under socialism would not say "no" far more often than "yes," especially in relation to marriage. All he was saying, he protested, was that only in a fully egalitarian society would social objections never be put in the way of a couple who wanted to marry.[27] That must have been close to his auditors' experience.

Intermarriageability is in fact a very shrewdly chosen indicator of class prejudice or classlessness, revealing a masterly "sociological imagination." And it is a cogent way of showing, as in his old arguments with the suffragettes, that full female emancipation needs not merely the vote but, at least, a radically more economically equal and ethically egalitarian society. (I now realize that I was unconsciously taking a leaf from the Master's book in my book, *In Defence of Politics,* when I used "death" in the same form of counterfactual argument: *if* the life chances [that is, expectation of life] of any social group were equal to any other, we would know that we were in a classless society—there is a perfect correlation between mortality statistics and social class.)[28] Even gaining the vote was a delusion of progress when unenlightened women continued to vote for men: therefore Shaw advocated "the coupled vote" to gain equal numbers in elected assemblies—an elector should only be able to vote on one ballot for a man and a woman combined.

However, *The Intelligent Woman's Guide* makes clear that equality will be reached by leveling up to the income that is needed to sustain the professional elite who will guide and inspire the transition; the project is not leveling down.[29] And this is spelled out in some detail in 1945 in one of his very last newspaper articles, "How Much Do We Need?" An arithmetical division of the national income cannot be immediate. A basic income must be imposed large enough to produce the professionals needed to run a modern society, whom he estimates to be about 10 percent of the population. What is left will be distributed: "from this point progress towards equality of income must depend on increased production." During the transition "the thinkers and directors" will be "sufficiently paid, and the rank and file underpaid." All increases in national wealth must be used "to raise the family incomes of the rank and file until they, too, can afford the privacy, the leisure, the culture, and all the other amenities and opportunities which the basic income commands."[30] I make no comment on the validity of this: whether in socialist terms it would simply entrench a new technocratic elite, or whether it demands an amount of regulation and control that would, indeed, convince many of us that the market is a lesser evil ("market socialism"?). I simply wish to establish what his view really was, a kind of realism: Rome could not be built in a day, but nonetheless there is a vision of a New Jerusalem. I think this combination was early Fabianism, Sidney Webb notwithstanding. SDH masked an unusual synthesis of idealism and realism, and it was well designed to do just that.

My lament has been for the neglect of Shaw by my fellow academics in politics and modern history. But as early as 1925 there was a book, *Contemporary Political Thought in England* by Lewis Rockow (an historian at the University of Oregon), which gave Shaw a significant role in a cast that already included Hobhouse, Graham Wallas, Laski, Russell, and Cole.[31] He did this by adding to ten chapters on clearly certifiably serious political thinkers one on Wells, "The Governance of a Utopia," and two last chapters on "The State in Literature" dealing with drama and the novel. Shaw dominates the drama. Rockow summarizes his main themes well: equality in distribution, the public-service elite guided by and guiding the Life Force of Creative Evolution, and eugenics.

We must always make a hard conceptual leap to the context of the time, before Hitler's racism and the Holocaust discredited the whole speculation. Rockow, before all this, sagely noted that "the subject of eugenics includes two separate questions, one of ends and one of means." As regards ends, Shaw did *not*, Rockow argues, advocate a uniform pattern of a perfected humanity—what will emerge in better conditions is uncertain, will not be uniform, and is a matter of trial and error. And the means are largely through economic equality, which will increase the chances of intermarriage among the most talented: sexual attraction was a better form of natural selection than social snobbery. "Some undesirable types he would exclude entirely from parentage, and the more extreme cases he would send to the lethal chamber." But Rockow concludes, perhaps surprisingly but I think justly, "Shaw's discussion of eugenics, if we omit some Shavian exaggerations, is moderate and helpful." Can we omit "the lethal chamber"?[32] On my analysis of Shaw's use of dramatic hyperbole in political speculation, I think we can—with contextual charity. But after the Holocaust and the Killing Fields? At least such language should not be used again even in humor in discussion of public policy; it must be contextualized as "in literature." We see what he meant, but it would not be easy to read Swift's *Modest Proposal* with tolerance, let alone relish, if during the great famine the Irish poor had practiced cannibalism on their own children.

Rockow was wise to adopt the method of approaching Shaw through his drama. For in the plays it is obvious that SDH is at work and, as a literary strategy, usually or often works well. And the plays are obviously "Shavian." The exaggerations can be more easily discounted than in books, tracts, and speeches, but the substance of his views on what is overwhelmingly important in personal life and social relations cannot get lost—as it can in the badinage of his nonfiction, all written with the free use of the first person, thus tempting (from Holroyd and others) endless reductionist commentary about "connections" or the childhood psychological roots of political ideology. "Shaw," concluded Rockow, "is doing valiant service in educating the public mind."[33] That was indeed his intent. And his method was to encourage speculation: most of the dogmatism was provocation and deliberate exaggeration.

This is not to say there were not blind spots, or that his political doctrines constitute a complete philosophical system. The common man of Rousseau, Kant, Wells, Orwell, and the American Jeffersonian tradition can hardly be expected to sit around waiting for the elite to become perfected and then to perfect him. He must be up and about as a demo-cratic citizen. Ross Terrill sadly comments, in his sensitive study of per-haps the greatest of the English socialist thinkers, R. H. Tawney, that "it is a commonplace that the democratic component of socialist theories which claimed to be democratic has had an uncertain career. Not only at the hand of communists but also of Fabians like Shaw and Labour Party intellectuals like Laski."[34]

Shaw through his strategy of SDH forced people to put counter-arguments against literal equality, so it was probably intended to benefit a more discriminatory, relative equality, certainly an egalitarian ethos and morality. The philosopher John Rawls has argued that while "equal-ity" is not a clear or definable moral standard for social policy, yet all inequalities of rewards, goods, and power must be capable of being justified as contributing to the greater benefit of the least advantaged and must be attached to positions or offices open to all under fair condi-tions of equality of opportunity.[35] But they must in fact be justified. The presumption is that all such inequalities have to be challenged publicly. The boot is on that foot. And Shaw did much of the kicking where it most hurts, outside the academy. And he might have have relished the Rawlsian paradox that "toward equality!" may not be a categorical im-perative but that "no unjustifiable inequalities!" is. Sometimes double negatives, or the negation of the negation, are as helpful as satire.

Notes

1. Geoffrey Foote, *The Labour Party's Political Thought: A History*, 2nd ed. (London: Croom Helm, 1986), pp. 25, 28, 30, 32.

2. Ibid., p. 30.

3. Robert Skidelsky, "The Fabian Ethic," in Michael Holroyd, ed., *The Genius of Shaw* (London: Hodder and Stoughton, 1979), p. 113.

4. Michael Holroyd, "Shaw," in Justin Wintle, ed., *The Makers of Modern Culture: A Biographical Dictionary* (London: Routledge & Kegan Paul, 1981), p. 475.

5. Michael Holroyd, *Bernard Shaw: The Search for Love, 1856—1898* (London: Chatto & Windus, 1988).

6. Holroyd, ibid., p. 467, explained that he would print his sources separately for scholars after the publication of his third volume. In a correspondence in the *Times Literary Supplement* (28 October 1988 ff.), I objected strongly to this procedure, first on general grounds that it inhibits scholarly criticism and, second, because Shaw wrote so much about himself and so jokily that the reader needs to be able (since Holroyd quotes and para-phrases Shaw so much) to judge why, on what occasion, and for what effect Shaw was recalling and retouching the past. Also, in preparing this article, I have realized how heavily Holroyd has relied on certain key sources—Stanley Weintraub's edition of the

shorthand diaries, *Bernard Shaw: The Diaries;* Dan H. Laurence's four volumes of *Collected Letters;* Lloyd J. Hubenka's edition of Shaw's essays and platform lectures, *Bernard Shaw, Practical Politics;* Margot Peters's *Bernard Shaw and the Actresses* (which in fact deals with all Shaw's women friends); and B. C. Rosset's *Shaw of Dublin.* Doubtless, conventional acknowledgments will be made in due course. Holroyd's lack of important new findings perhaps tempted him into overinterpreting his material, sparing readers Shaw's often conflicting accounts of his own past states of mind and motives, but giving intelligent readers (who else?) no opportunity to judge for themselves.

7. See "On the Difficulties of Writing Biography and of Orwell's in Particular," in Bernard Crick, *Essays on Politics and Literature* (Edinburgh: Edinburgh University Press, 1989), pp. 117–32.

8. Holroyd, p. 182.

9. Ibid., pp. 189–90.

10. See Bernard Crick, *Socialist Values and Time* (Fabian Tract no. 495) (London: Fabian Society, 1984), pp. 35–38, and *In Defence of Politics,* 2nd ed. (London: Penguin Books, 1982), pp. 236–41.

11. See Michael Oakeshott, *Experience and Its Modes* (Cambridge: Cambridge University Press, 1933) and F. H. Bradley, *Appearance and Reality,* 2nd ed. (Oxford: Oxford University Press, 1959).

12. W. H. Greenleaf, *The British Political Tradition,* vol. 2, *The Ideological Heritage* (London: Methuen, 1983), pp. 366–67.

13. Ibid, p. 360.

14. Ibid., p. 369.

15. Ibid.

16. Ibid., p. 378.

17. Norman and Jeanne MacKenzie, *The Diary of Beatrice Webb* (London: Virago, 1984), 3: 367, entry for 17 September 1920.

18. Stanley Pierson, *British Socialists: The Journey from Fantasy to Politics* (Cambridge, Mass.: Harvard University Press, 1979).

19. Ibid., pp. 102–5.

20. Ibid., p. 107.

21. Ibid., pp. 109–10.

22. Bernard Shaw, *Practical Politics: Twentieth Century Views of Politics and Economics,* ed. Lloyd J. Hubenka (Lincoln: University of Nebraska Press, 1976), pp. 234–37. These quotations are from a verbatim report of the lecture "The Politics of Unpolitical Animals" given to the Fabian Society in December 1933.

23. A good bibliography for the "equality" debate and controversy is in Barry Hindess, *Freedom, Equality and the Market* (London: Tavistock, 1987), pp. 168–72.

24. Shaw, *Practical Politics,* p. 122.

25. Ibid., pp. 137, 143–44.

26. Bernard Shaw, *The Intelligent Woman's Guide to Socialism, Capitalism, Sovietism and Fascism* (London: Pelican Books, 1937), pp. 16, 478–79.

27. Shaw, *Practical Politics,* pp. 134–35, 140.

28. Crick, *In Defence of Politics,* pp. 223–35.

29. Shaw, *Intelligent Women's Guide,* pp. 477–79, a substantial qualification of splendid bombast on pp. 99–102, where the case for equality is stated in absolute terms (always, in Shaw, if one is patient, looks hard enough, both principle and practice appear).

30. Shaw, *Practical Politics,* pp. 242–43, from the *Observer,* 13 August 1944.

31. Lewis Rockow, *Contemporary Political Thought in England* (London: Allen & Unwin, 1925), pp. 266–75.

32. Ibid., pp. 271, 273.

33. Ibid., p. 274.

34. Ross Terrill, *R. H. Tawney and His Times: Socialism as Fellowship* (London: André Deutsch, 1974), pp. 270–71.

35. John Rawls, *A Theory of Justice* (Cambridge, Mass.: Harvard University Press, 1971), pp. 101–8.

Stanley Weintraub

BERNARD SHAW BESIEGED: POLITICAL PROGRESSES TO OXBRIDGE, 1888–1892

On 18 February 1888, an Irish school dropout named Bernard Shaw, who had never spent a day in college and considered the British Museum's domed and arc-lighted reading room his university, took the five o'clock train from King's Cross, en route to Cambridge. His journalism as music and art reviewer for two London papers, plus occasional writing for others, kept him just sufficiently solvent to be able to afford to lecture at no fee on socialist issues wherever in England anyone would have him, and he averaged, in season, three lectures a week—often two on Sunday.

At King's College, Cambridge, he was to talk on "Socialism: Its Growth and Necessity," a subject upon which he could improvise variations with eloquent ease from a few notes on index cards. The arrangements for the weekend visit had been made by Nathaniel Wedd, then twenty-four and a Fellow of King's, who combined classical studies with the secretaryship of the fledgling Cambridge Fabian Society. Small and chunky, and making up in pugnaciousness what he lacked in size, Wedd would still be regarded in Cambridge as a dangerous radical a decade afterward when he became E. M. Forster's tutor. (Even later, when he had become a dedicated Tory, he remained blasphemously anticlerical.)

No one met Shaw at the train—he was not important enough for that—but he had directions to Wedd's lodgings at 3 Peas Hill. There he had tea with Wedd—having something other than tea, which he eschewed—and went off with his escort to the New Lecture Room at King's, where his talk was scheduled for 8:15. In the chair was the popular, although preposterously pompous, Oscar Browning, at fifty-one a university lecturer in history with ambitions to transform King's, if not Cambridge, into a gentlemanly Athens. Had Shaw a snobbish nerve in his body it would have been stroked by Browning's introduction and by the expression of thanks afterward by Herbert Somerton Foxwell, a Cambridge-trained economist who, at forty-nine, was professor of political economy at University College, London. Shaw's own credentials were far more informal: he had read a lot, and thought a lot, especially on trams and trains.

In the audience, other than students, were Sedley Taylor, a senior Fellow at Trinity; Alfred Marshall, a senior Fellow at St. John's and professor of economics; and even Brooke Foss Westcott, who at sixty-three was Regius Professor of Divinity and a Fellow of King's. When the discussion simmered down, Foxwell led Shaw off to the King's rooms of another and younger Fellow, Charles Waldstein, who would receive his doctorate in literature later in the year. There the three sat and talked until one-thirty, when Shaw's voice, soothed earlier by threepence worth of jujubes he had bought to assist his public speaking, finally gave out.

After sleeping in rooms in College arranged for by Wedd, Shaw had breakfast the next morning in the rooms of George Walter Protheroe, an historian of Germany who at forty had taken on the task of translating Leopold von Ranke's *Weltgeschichte*. Protheroe, who, like Waldstein, would eventually be knighted, then took Shaw on a walking tour of the colleges, ending back at King's at the rooms of Goldsworthy Lowes Dickinson, where they were to lunch. Dickinson, at twenty-seven six years younger than Shaw, was a Fellow at King's who would spend a career there as a lecturer in political philosophy. Appropriate to the affability he always exuded, he preached a liberal Hellenism predicated upon his faith in reason, decency, and the assumed triumph of Socratic discussion over disparate views, an outlook he would dramatize in his briefly influential book *A Modern Symposium* (1905).

Wedd was there too, and when lunch was over and Shaw had to begin thinking about his train for Liverpool Street Station, Wedd, on behalf of his local Fabians, handed his guest a sovereign for his expenses. Shaw returned to his rooms to leave twopence for his bedmaker and went on to the railway station, where he bought a third-class ticket to London. There was still a long day ahead, with the tube and trams to follow. He was to lecture, at eight o'clock, at the Deptford Liberal Club on "The Limits of State Socialism." It was, after all, a Sunday.

The next day he mailed ten shillings ninepence—change from his sovereign—back to Nathaniel Wedd. He charged only his expenses and had kept the costs down by traveling third class.

Nearly a year later Shaw was back. It was 9 February 1889, and Wedd had asked him to talk on "The Economic Basis of Socialism," the subject of his piece in *Fabian Essays*, which he was editing for release later in the year. He had first turned Wedd down since he was to speak to the Brixton Liberal Association that Sunday (the next day). But that had been moved foward into January. For Shaw, a Sunday without lecturing dates was not a Sunday at all.

This time Dickinson was on the platform at Cambridge to greet Shaw and take him to his rooms for tea. Then it was off to the familiar lecture room, where again Oscar Browning handled the introduction, and Shaw spoke with passionate intensity about the necessity of socialism and the perfectibility of men. Still, there was little evidence of enthusiasm for his subject among the undergraduates, who, it might be assumed by the skeptics in the audience, had come out to see an offbeat London personality now often in the daily and weekly newspapers. Perhaps, too, they were intimidated by the presence in the chair of Oscar Browning. They raised no questions, and Shaw was escorted back to Dickinson's rooms, although Dickinson himself was nowhere to be seen. Instead, Nathaniel Wedd and Arthur Berry, who would take his master of arts degree that year, appeared in charge, and, Shaw noted in his diary, a lot of other young men were there, with whom he talked until midnight.

Listening was G. C. Moore Smith, later a Cambridge professor, who for two years had been keeping a commonplace book of conversations which he felt were worth recording. Impressed by the contrast between Shaw's reputation as a fiery radical and his "mobile face which when animated radiates a lighthearted Irish insouciance," Moore Smith concluded that "nothing could be less like the conspirator, or fanatical revolutionist, than the freedom with which he pokes fun at his own cause and his fellow Socialists. He is a delightful talker without doubt."

Not all of Shaw's poking was intended in fun, for he was in Cambridge on Fabian missionary activity, and he demolished the pretensions to validity as socialist organizations claimed by rival radical groups. Even his beloved William Morris—a father figure—came in for negative appraisal, Shaw suggesting that Morris's Socialist League branch would not survive its patron and his financial sponsorship. H. H. Hyndman, Shaw added, was also thought of by supporters as impoverishing himself in the cause of socialism, which he preached, said Shaw, with more invective than efficacy; however, in actuality Hyndman had lost more money speculating in electric-lighting ventures. Christian socialism, said Shaw disarmingly, turning to a more moderate variety, is the form, via its interest in land nationalization, "in which Socialism can best be served to the middle-class religious people. The Fabian Society consists to a great extent of people who are antireligious."

When the talk turned to Shaw's nonpolitical writings, one of the men observed that he had heard that Shaw had published a novel, and he wondered how much money it had earned. Shaw confessed that he had made nothing from his fiction. Someone asked whether a novel taken by the circulating libraries might bring the author as much as £30. "Oh, more than that," said Shaw; "a novel must be *very* good if it only makes £30."

After the students dispersed, Berry took Shaw down to the Cam to see the river by moonlight and then to the rooms in which he was to spend the night. As they were looking over the sleeping arrangements, Wedd and Dickinson returned, having been away for all of Shaw's remarks. His diary recorded no comment about the apparent discourtesy, only that he slept poorly in the "strange bed," which was too short for his six-foot frame, "though I was warm enough."

The next morning (a Sunday) he took the 10:20 train back to London, to Liverpool Street Station. He was to speak at a mass meeting in Hyde Park to protest the Irish Coercion Bill that afternoon, and he had time only to buy a sweetmeat in lieu of lunch. When the tumultuous rally was over, he walked to the National Liberal Club with H. W. Massingham, Belfort Bax, Clement Shorter, and H. H. Hyndman, all of whom had been in the park, and chatted with them over a cup of cocoa before he had to rush off to Limehouse, where that evening he was to lecture to a Social Democratic Federation meeting. After that there was still his music review for the *Star* to write, his first under the nom de plume of Corno di Bassetto. At home at Fitzroy Square, he sat over his copy until one in the morning. It was all a far cry from the cozy undemanding atmosphere of Cambridge.

Although Oxford was closer to London, Shaw was not to visit there to speak until three years later. "Mr. Bernard Shaw, the well-known Socialist, who has been on a visit to Oxford," the *Times* reported on 23 February 1892, "was, late on Saturday night, the victim of a practical joke on the part of some undergraduates." Like many collegiate pranks, the incident went beyond being a joking matter. As the report described the affair,

> Whilst a meeting was being held in the rooms of Mr Best, in the new buildings of Magdalen College, which face the High Street, the outer door was screwed up, and it is said that cayenne pepper was heated in the vicinity, and a most unpleasant odor produced, whereupon those who were present discovered that they had all been made prisoners. When an attempt was made by some to escape by letting themselves down from the windows a copious supply of dirty water was poured from above. Ultimately the attention of the authorities was attracted by the uproar, and the inhabitants of the room were liberated shortly before midnight.

Shaw had been invited by a student group at Magdalen to talk on socialism. Still without fee, and often as frequently as three or four times a week, he had continued to speak to laboring and left-wing audiences, outdoors and indoors, rain or shine. Recalling a pleasant day the year before when, on a Fabian proselytizing tour of Oxfordshire towns, he had been put up by a Christ Church lecturer in law, Frederick York Powell, Shaw had accepted the undergraduates' invitation. Powell, whose fervent socialism would not be a barrier to his becoming Regius Professor of Modern History (a post he held from 1894 until his death, at fifty-four, in 1904), stood aside to permit the students to arrange things; but, advertised in a handbill as "The Working Day," the formal Sunday lecture at the Oxford Reform Club seemed likely to be of little interest to young men never anticipating even a day's blue-collar employment. Shaw expected a few earnest youths, and a few more curious about the Irish heretic from London.

He had taken the train to Oxford on Saturday afternoon, 20 February, occuping his time en route trying to devise a clever inscription for the flyleaf of a copy of his new *Quintessence of Ibsenism,* which he was going to give to a friend. At the station he was met by William Hines, a one-time chimney sweep who had become a Fabian Society stalwart and local trade-union organizer. Hines took him to York Powell's for supper, then past Corpus Christi and Merton to Magdalen College. Never one to make a fuss about accommodations, Shaw expected to be put up cheaply and informally, accepting an offer of overnight lodging in the rooms of Thomas A. V. Best, the student organizer of the Sunday lecture. Later Sir Thomas Best, a Colonial Office administrator who would govern the Falkland Islands, Leeward Islands, Trinidad, and Malta, Shaw's host was an affable, ambitious young man well thought of by friendly dons like Powell.

En route to Magdalen that evening, Shaw assumed that he would find that Best had gathered a few students in his rooms for "a mere chat on things in general," he noted in his diary, "but when I arrived there were about 15 or 16 undergraduates assembled; and I was called on for a lecture. An opposition party outside screwed us up and wrecked the adjoining room. It threatened to be a very serious business, but I got out at last with a whole skin."

The laconic entry failed to tell the whole story, but, in better humor the next day, Shaw wrote up the experience for the *Pall Mall Gazette,* which published the story the day before the *Times*'s downplayed account appeared. Couched in heavy irony, Shaw's report was captioned "Revolutionary Progress at Oxford":

> Sir,—Will you be so good as to allow me to use your columns to thank the members of Magdalen College, Oxford, for the very enthusiastic reception which they have just accorded to the first Socialist who has ever lectured within their walls? The greatest

difficulty with which a public speaker has to struggle is the tendency of the audience to leave before the conclusion of his remarks. I therefore desire especially to thank the thoughtful and self-sacrificing body of undergraduates who voluntarily suffered exclusion from the room in order that they might secure the door on the outside and so retain my audience screwbound to the last syllable of the vote of thanks. I desire to explain, however, that I do not advocate the indiscriminate destruction of property as a first step towards Socialism, and that their action in entirely wrecking the adjoining chamber by a vigorous bombardment of coals, buckets of water, and asafoetida [a resinous gum which exudes an odor of garlic and onions], though well-meant, was not precisely on the lines which I was laying down inside. Nor, though I expressed myself as in favour of a considerable extension of Communism in the future, did I contemplate the immediate throwing of all the portable property in the lobby into a common stock, beginning with my own hat, gloves, and umbrella. Not that I grudge these articles to Magdalen College, but that I wish them to be regarded as an involuntary donation from myself to the present holders rather than as having been scientifically communized.

Speaking as a musical critic, I cannot say that the singing of the National Anthem which accompanied these modest beginnings of revolution was as successful as that of "Ta-ra-ra-boom-de-ay," which one of my friends within the room kindly supported, at the general request, by a pianoforte accompaniment. It is injurious to the voice, I may add, to sing in an atmosphere rendered somewhat pungent by the projection of red pepper on a heated shovel.

I need not dwell on the friendly care which was taken not to unscrew the door until our proceedings were entirely over. I wish to say, however, that we should not have incommoded our friends by crowding the staircase had not the rope formed of two blankets by which we originally intended to proceed from the apartment directly into the open air, unhappily given way under the strain of being energetically steadied at one end by the outside and at the other by the inside party. There was really no danger of friction igniting the blankets, so that the pains of the detachment posted at an upper window to keep them drenched with water were unnecessary. The gentleman who rendered me a similar attention from the landing above as I descended the staircase also wasted most of his moisture through infirmity of aim; but his hospitable desire to speed the parting guest was unmistakable.

Although my admirers mustered in such numbers that there were at least three times as many persons outside the door as inside (including a don), I am credibly assured that if I had lectured in Brasenose my reception would have been still more overwhelming; and I quite believe it. I was the more overcome, as I visited Magdalen under the impression that I was to pass a quiet hour chatting with a few friends, and had no idea until I arrived that I was expected to address a meeting or that my advent had aroused so deep an interest.—Yours truly, G. Bernard Shaw.

The leader of the student "rag," Shaw learned later, was Simon Joseph Fraser (1871–1933), who had succeeded his father in 1887 as fourteenth Baron Lovat. His next raiding mission would be at the close of the decade, when he would raise and command the Lovat Scouts in South Africa in the Boer War.

The first recorded outcome of Shaw's letter was his receipt of a new tall hat "With best wishes, from three Oxford ladies who admire Mr. Shaw." He wore the hat and filed away the letter. Then early the next month came an eight-page handwritten letter with a Magdalen address, dated 5 March 1892. The notepaper with the college name was unofficial in appearance—as if it could have come from any shop on the High Street. Since Shaw knew little about Oxford, and the letter had a condescending (yet guiltily embarrassed) tone suggesting a pompous undergraduate explaining away behavior he thought worth little more than a mild rebuke, almost certainly Shaw did not realize that the writer with the air of unreality was a youngish don—three years older than Shaw—who was president (head) of Magdalen. A minor poet and classicist, he would become vice-chancellor in 1906, professor of poetry in 1911, and a knight in 1914.

My dear Sir,

I should have written to you before, but that I have had since some difficulty in obtaining your address. I was inclined indeed to write to you originally just after the affair here, was especially after reading in the *Pall Mall Gazette* your very witty and I will say very generous letter, but I did not do so for this reason. In the first place I thought I would really be making too much of the affair. Officially it had been dealt with by the Dean and a certain measure of penalty dealt out to offenders against law and order and as the case had not been brought before the higher court I did not wish to interfere. Unofficially I gathered that both sides among the undergraduates were satisfied and wished it to be treated as a joke. Though perhaps a somewhat excessive joke. Beside that, I always think that formal apologies from a third party seem a little hollow.

The reason of my writing you is that I am informed that you left the College minus a "hat gloves and umbrella." Now that I think is quite improper and although you, as you amusingly convey in your letter, may be willing to leave that matter an unimportant incident, yet I feel that it leaves the College under an obligation or debt which ought not to remain. I should be obliged therefore if you would kindly let me know if this is really the case and that any or all of these articles or anything else belonging to you is still missing.

And now that I am writing I hope that you will allow me though somewhat late to say that I am extremely sorry that you should have received any rude treatment or been put to any serious inconvenience within the walls of my College. I trust from what I gather that as far as you yourself were concerned this would fairly explain what happened.

Anything like a Socialist meeting held in their College against their liking might I think seem to many undergraduates a natural opportunity for a challenge & an anti-demonstration & a certain amount of practical joking and horseplay in the form in which such a demonstration too easily takes. But I think the joking part, though your letter treats it very kindly, was carried a good deal too far and became a very "mauvaise plaisanterie."

I am not inclined to be a Socialist myself, being unwilling to sink my own individuality, and finding my chief interest in the individuality of others, but I think there is an immense deal which may be luminously discussed and advantageously approached from this side of Socialism and Platonism. I ought not to be afraid of Communism. As a matter of courtesy I wish my young friends had treated the Socialists as Plato proposed to treat the poets. Anointed them with myrrh instead of water and conducted them festively to another college.

To close this long letter then I hope you will allow me to express my regret and add that as a matter of fact that none of our men had anything to do with an attempted disturbance which I understand took place at Woodstock.

Believe me to be

Yours very truly

T. Herbert Warren

Before Shaw had even found the time to write the letter to the *Pall Mall Gazette* which would only mildly embarrass Warren, York Powell had been to his rooms to carry him off to the fencing club, where two of the men who had been trapped at the evening talk—George Cooke, professor of Hebrew and canon of Christ Church, Oxford, and Dayrell

Crackanthorpe, a Merton undergraduate and brother of future *Yellow Book* contributor Hubert Crackanthorpe—were fencing. To Shaw's astonishment, Powell went over to Monsieur Goudourville, the instructor, and asked that their guest be given an impromptu lesson. Having been an amateur boxer, Shaw had some idea of how to defend himself; and he had proven his agility the night before. He parried and thrust with Goudourville, to prove he could do it, until the others decided that it was time to go. Shaw had another talk to give.

Later, at the Reform Club, he was introduced by Godfrey Benson, Liberal politician and litterateur, who would become M.P. for Woodstock in the general election the following July. Then only twenty-eight, Benson (who would become the first Lord Charnwood) was then better known as the brother of actor-manager Frank Benson. Since he wanted Shaw to put in a few good words for him at Woodstock, Benson paid his debts in advance with a few choice encomiums, after which Shaw delivered one of his semi-improvised exhortations, from a few notecards, on the need for the humanizing and equalizing beneficence of socialism.

Dinner afterward, at Balliol, was a formal affair, with old Benjamin Jowett, the Master, and his colleagues. Primed for the occasion with stories of Jowett's erudition and charm, Shaw remained unimpressed. Jowett, then seventy-five, had been Regius Professor of Greek since 1855 and was translator of Plato, Aristotle, and Thucydides, but to Shaw, recalling the event two years later (a year after Jowett's death), the Master of Balliol had been only "an amiable gentleman, stupendously ignorant probably, but with a certain flirtatious, old-maidish frivolity about him that had, and was meant to have, the charm of a condescension from so learned a man." It was perhaps unkind, but Shaw was sensitive indeed, especially after the Saturday-night incident, to anything which smacked of Oxbridge condescension. He was well aware that the assorted dons and fellows—and, even, undergraduates—would not have invited an Irish-born school-leaver who had never been inside a public school had he not already achieved an enviable reputation despite the absence of such advantages. And the condescending response from the presiding dignitary at Magdalen was yet to come.

That Sunday night Shaw sat up late talking to Powell at Christ Church and then slept (at Powell's) very well, in contrast to the night before. The next day he was to lecture nearby, at the Town Hall in Woodstock. While wandering about Powell's study and looking into his books that Monday morning, and working on the proofs of his music column he had brought with him, he was interrupted first by Hines, who was to escort him to Woodstock, and then by Cooke, who came in with a warning that a second attempt by Oxford students to "rag" Shaw was being rumored in the colleges.

Unperturbed, Shaw left five shillings as a tip to Heath, York Powell's scout, and went off for a walk, and to visit the museum and local acquaintances, before going to the railway station. It was only when on the train with Hines that he observed "half a dozen undergraduates or so . . . disguised as farmers and equipped with sticks as for a disturbance." But Oxford students, however attired, blended in poorly with real farmers, and Shaw's audience in any case was large and friendly and forewarned.

The "farmers," Shaw noted in his diary, "were completely cowed by my supports; and the meeting came off all the better for the fun of chaffing them." But despite Herbert Warren's almost-penitent letter, no gloves or umbrella were returned or replaced, and Shaw would remain convinced that undergraduate life was the road to immaturity, with Oxford coming off worse than Cambridge. In *Buoyant Billions*, a play completed when he was nearly ninety-one (in 1947), he had a character boast, "I would have you to know that I am a Master of Arts of the University of Oxford, the centre of all the learning in the universe. The possession of such a degree places the graduate on the highest mental plane attainable by humanity."

"How did you obtain that degree, sir?" the Oxonian is asked.

"By paying a solid twenty pounds for it."

When Shaw returned to Oxford in March 1914, just before the opening of his *Pygmalion,* this time to lecture on "The Nature of Drama," the event was nonpolitical and the crowded Saturday evening audience very different from the one on a Saturday evening in 1892. Possessing no academic degrees, not even a twenty-pound M.A., the maker of plays introduced himself as one "here in the capacity of a tradesman." We do not know whether the Professor of Poetry was present.

A Note on Sources

Shaw's letter to the editor of the *Pall Mall Gazette,* "Revolutionary Progress at Oxford," appeared in the issue of 22 February 1892, p. 3. T[homas] Herbert Warren's eight-page apology, and the anonymous note from "three Oxford ladies who admire Mr. Shaw," are in BL Add. Ms. 50512. The diary extracts are from *Bernard Shaw, The Diaries 1885–1897,* ed. Stanley Weintraub (University Park: Penn State University Press, 1986). The original diaries are in the London School of Economics and Political Science. Moore Smith's commonplace book was extracted from by Douglas Hamer in "Some of Shaw's 1889 Political Opinions," *Notes and Queries* (September 1966), pp. 343–44. Shaw's comments on Jowett are from his "Religion of the Pianoforte," *Fortnightly Review,* February 1894.

James Woodfield

SHAW'S *WIDOWERS' HOUSES:*
COMEDY FOR SOCIALISM'S SAKE

Shaw's own statements, and commentaries on his work, tend to leave the impression that his first play, *Widowers' Houses,* came into being mainly because of William Archer and J. T. Grein, who, in 1884 and 1892, respectively, provided the initial plot of "Rheingold" (based on Augier's *Ceinture Dorée)* and the subsequent impetus for its completion.[1] Had this been the whole case, it is most unlikely that Shaw would have made any further attempts to court the dramatic muse because, as he records in Appendix I to the play, the first production was vilified by many critics on several counts, and the chances of his profiting in any way from the theater were remote. Its true genesis is much broader. *Widowers' Houses,* which Shaw began in 1885, was not his first attempt at dramatic writing: in 1878 he had begun "a profane Passion Play" in blank verse, soon abandoned.[2] In 1888 he entered into a collaboration with the Norwegian H. L. Braekstad on an English version of sections of Ibsen's *Peer Gynt,* which, after some sporadic efforts, was "indefinitely postponed," and in 1889 he began working on a "comedy of intrigue called *The Cassone,* with characters based on the Archers, the Charringtons and himself."[3] It was never completed, but did contain the seeds of *Candida.*

Such dabbling in drama was to be expected from a writer who, since boyhood, had been "intoxicated" by music, books, and theater (Holroyd 69). In Dublin he had been steeped in the eloquent, heroic style of the Theatre Royal, admiring above all the operatic Barry Sullivan. In London, much of his theatergoing was to the opera in his capacity as music critic, but he also regularly sampled the full range of dramatic offerings from the Lyceum to the Alhambra, as his diary reveals. His fascination with theater included a fascination with stage performers, notably the actresses Janet Achurch (Mrs. Charles Charrington) and Florence Farr. He met the former in 1889 at a dinner to celebrate the English premiere

of *A Doll's House,* in which she played Nora, and the latter the following
year, becoming her dramatic elocutionist and lover.

Through Archer, Shaw had already "discovered" Ibsen, and after the
premiere Ibsen's work aroused sufficient interest for the Fabian Society
to invite Shaw to give a lecture on it in a series entitled "Socialism in
Contemporary Literature." The lecture was given at the St. James's Restaurant on 18 July 1890 and subsequently expanded for publication in
1891 as *The Quintessence of Ibsenism* (without, of course, the chapter "The
Technical Novelty in Ibsen's Plays," added in 1913 and more relevant to
Shaw's dramaturgy than to Ibsen's). Shaw may have lacked the "hands-
on" experience in the theater that characterizes most successful playwrights, but in other respects he was well positioned in 1892 for launch-
ing a career as a dramatist.

Shaw's five somewhat tedious novels precede his first play, but one
looks in vain in them for scenes and dialogue that prefigure the dramatic
genius; their rambling profuseness cries out for the discipline of the
dramatic mode. What one does find in the novels are the forerunners of
later characters and attempts to work out in fiction the ideas that were
fermenting in Shaw's mind during the period and were to inform the
whole of his dramatic output, notably socialism, vitalism, and the destruction of ideals—all subsumed in the ultimate of "world-betterment." The
most important of these with respect to *Widowers' Houses* is his socialism,
an examination of which is essential to a full appreciation of the play, not
only for its impact on a Victorian audience but also for its presentation to
a modern one.

In *Sixteen Self Sketches* Shaw recalls his stint in a Dublin real-estate
office (one of his tasks was to collect rents): "I took not the slightest
interest in land agency; but I laid up a large stock of observations which
became useful when Henry George explained their political significance
to me."[4] When he came to London in 1876 and discovered the most
appalling squalor and poverty, he added to that store and was inevitably
drawn into the orbit of first the radicals, then the socialists. Archer's
story of seeing Shaw in the British Museum Library with a copy of *Tristan
und Isolde* in one hand and Marx's *Capital* (the French version) in the
other, and Shaw's flirtation with Marxian revolutionary orthodoxy, have
tended to find the inspiration for Shaw's brand of socialism in Marx.
However, before encountering Marx, Shaw had "cut his teeth on classic
liberalism . . . and had thrived on the literary classics of social protest"[5]
—that is, theories emanating from the Enlightenment and developed
earlier in the nineteenth century by Bentham, Mill, Spencer, Ruskin, and
Carlyle. The basis of the radical approach was

> a faith in individual autonomy and self-determination and a belief
> that the fullest development of the moral and intellectual capaci-

ties of every person could be achieved only within an atmosphere of freedom from external coercion or restraint . . . [with] the economic corollary . . . that every individual should have as his property the fruits of his own labour. (Wolfe 5, n. 3)

The radicals charged that "the existence of privileged and propertied classes—'idle' and 'wasteful' from their very nature—was a moral evil" (Wolfe 8). Socialism emphasized theories of collectivism, envisaging a new social structure; of surplus value, arguing that under capitalism working men were robbed of the value they produced to sustain a leisure class of idle rentiers; and of poverty, holding "that *the misery of the slums was a direct consequence of the affluence of the leisure class of capitalist rentiers,* expanding as that class expanded, and could only be abolished by abolishing that class" (Wolfe 12, emphasis added). Reviewing the intellectual and religious context of London after 1860, Holroyd observes that

> a new urgency had entered the progressive movement, reinforced by those who, in the aftermath of Darwinism, had merged personal sin with social guilt and transferred their service to God into a duty to the community. (Holroyd 124)

Socialism, with its emphasis on moral ends and social values, became a substitute faith for those who had lost the certitudes of traditional religion. The spectrum is wide, the details confusing, the boundaries between theories and movements fuzzy with overlapping emphases: Shaw sampled the whole range of offerings to distill his own brand.

After "haunting" meetings for several years, Shaw made his first public speech at a gathering of the London Zetetical Society in October 1880: his experience led him to vow "to join the Society; go every week; speak in every debate; and become a speaker or perish in the attempt" (*Self Sketches* 57). Another turning point in his development came when he attended a lecture on 5 September 1882 given by an American politician and economic theorist, Henry George, "apostle of Land Nationalization and Single Tax" (*Self Sketches* 58), from whom

> he derived . . . not just a theory but a Weltanschauung and a new cause to which he could commit himself. . . . "robbery" of unearned increments became Shaw's battle cry, blending the Georgian Law of Rent with Proudhon's view of property as theft. (Wolfe 119)

After this lecture, he "plunged into a course of economic study . . . became a Socialist and spoke from that very platform on the same great subject, and from hundreds of others as well" (*Auto* 114).

In 1883, Shaw first heard an address by H. M. Hyndman, an educated and wealthy man dedicated at first to the radicalism of the 1870s, who founded the Democratic Federation in 1881 (renamed the Social Democratic Federation in 1884). Anticipating the Fabians, Hyndman at first appealed to the educated middle class to take the lead in bringing about a peaceful transition to socialism through state management and advocated permeation of radicalism with socialist ideas. However, his attitudes began to shift, and in a letter to Henry George (c. 1882), he declared,

> As I go through the courts and lanes of this city . . . [and] watch the capitalist class grinding hours on hours of unpaid toil out of the half-starved women and half-starved men, I feel that no bloodshed, no anarchy, no horror conceivable could be worse for the mass of people than the existing state of things. (Cited in Wolfe 78, n. 3)

From this point on, the Federation was to adopt a Marxist, militant approach, directing its appeal toward the working class. Shaw became associated with it through his friendship with William Morris, a member of its executive council. When a schism developed within the Federation between Hyndman and his supporters, with their extreme collectivism and absolute faith in Marxist doctrine, and Morris, who "advocated a form of Radical-individual utopianism" (Wolfe 132, n. 48), it is not surprising that Shaw followed Morris. Looking back more than sixty years later, Shaw condemned Marx's *Capital* for not being "a treatise on Socialism: it is a jeremiad against the bourgeoisie . . . addressed to the working class; but the working man respects the bourgeoisie, and wants to be a bourgeois" (*Self Sketches* 49). He even took an anarchist position to define his opposition to Hyndman, and withdrew his application to join the Federation

> on discovering the newly founded Fabian Society, in which I recognised a more appropriate *milieu* as a body of educated middle-class intelligentsia: my own class in fact. Hyndman's congregation of manual-working pseudo-Marxists could for me be only a hindrance. (*Self Sketches* 59)

The genesis of the Fabian Society was in a group called the Fellowship of the New Life, formed in London in 1882 under the leadership of Dr. Thomas Davidson, an inspiring Scottish teacher of ethics. The basic aim of the Fellowship was to bring about social melioration by perfecting the individual. Despite the utopian aspirations—with echoes of Pantisocracy and Brook farm trancendentalism—many members became dissatisfied,

and a split developed between the dedicated disciples who pursued Davidson's goal of ethical perfection and those who sought social influence
and action. The latter, Shaw explained, "modestly feeling that the revolution would have to wait an unreasonably long time if postponed until
they personally had attained perfection, set up the banner of Socialism
militant" (*Auto* 129).

The name of the new group, which first met on 4 January 1884, was
devised by Frank Podmore after Fabius Maximus, the Roman general
who opposed Hannibal by waiting and striking at the most opportune
moment. The early aims of the Society were to "EDUCATE, AGITATE, ORGA-
NIZE . . . [toward] a tremendous smash-up of existing society, to be succeeded by complete Socialism" (*Auto* 132). It was composed of middle-
class intellectuals conscious of the responsibility of the educated and of
the possible consequences of the extended franchise to working men.
The Fabians quickly abandoned their idea of a "smash-up" of society and
concentrated on the following aims:

1. Extension of democracy and the improvement of the machinery of democratic government [including women's suffrage].
2. Extension of government powers to improve community welfare (especially the welfare of the working class).
3. Positive government action to promote equality [e.g., in educa-
   tion].
4. Other miscellaneous items [e.g., Irish home rule].[6]

A cardinal principle of this form of evolutionary socialism was the "permeation" of existing democratic institutions by individual socialists. In
rejecting the class war of Marxism and asserting that reform must come
through the enlightened cooperation of all classes, the Fabians were
clearly following the English radical tradition. In the 1908 Preface to
Fabian Essays (1889), Shaw declared,

> We set ourselves two definite tasks: first, to provide a parliamen-
> tary program for a Prime Minister converted to Socialism . . . and
> second, to make it as easy and matter-of-course for the ordinary
> respectable Englishman to be a Socialist as to be a Liberal or
> Conservative. [7]

The Fabians were an essentially middle-class group, not a party, an
intellectual aristocracy dedicated to unselfish efforts toward the reconstruction of society. These efforts were backed up by the gathering of
solid statistical and social information, with which the names of Sidney
and Beatrice Webb are forever associated, and self-training (the David-

son legacy) for the propagation of their gospel. Fabian activities between 1884 and 1892 included group discussions, especially at the Hampstead Historic Society, the publication of tracts based on careful research (including polemics from an easily recognized pen), lectures and attendance at public meetings, establishment of a Fabian Parliamentary League, and sponsorship of a conference on nationalization of land and capital. *Fabian Essays* (1889) was one of the most important and influential publications. Shaw was editor and contributed two sections, one on the economic basis of socialism, the other on the transition to social democracy. A footnote reports that "in the year ending April 1889, the number of lectures delivered by members of the Fabian Society alone was upwards of 700" (*Fabian Essays* xxxix).

Land and property ownership, the near-monopoly of a privileged class, had long been a prime target of reformers. In 1873, noting the "gigantic incomes" of the Grosvenor, Portland, and Portman estates in London that were "still swelling," John Stuart Mill expressed the nub of the issue when he demanded why "this increase in wealth, produced by other people's labour and enterprise . . . [should] fall into their mouths while they sleep, instead of being applied to the public necessity of those who created it?" (cited in Wolfe 62). In addition to the protests against economic "theft" through ownership, there was a growing agitation against the social aspects, particularly the burgeoning slums that plagued the major cities. Public awareness of the appalling conditions in most urban centers, especially London, was significantly enlarged in 1883 by publication of *The Bitter Cry of Outcast London*, by the Reverend Andrew Mearns, which, in the words of a subsequent royal commission, caused "a tremendous sensation and thrill of horror throughout the land."[8]

Mearns catalogued more than the physical conditions: the London "rookeries" were breeding grounds for immorality—prostitution, violence, murder, drunkenness, and incest. There were church and other charitable organizations in the slums attempting to counter immorality, but Mearns insisted that living conditions had to be improved before the moral and spiritual issues could be addressed. For the Victorians, it was but a short step from the awareness of rampant sin at the heart of their own society to a sense of guilt and of responsibility for the society that created such conditions.

Proof that the public conscience had been touched was the establishment of the Royal Commission on the Housing of the Working Classes by Gladstone's government in 1884. One member of the group was Edward, Prince of Wales, who, with his friend Lord Carrington, had actually visited the slums of Clerkenwell and St. Pancras disguised as a laborer, "witnessing scenes of deprivation and misery that filled Edward with indignation."[9] Establishment of the commission and release of its report added impetus to the steady stream of publications on urban conditions (including Dickens's articles in *Household Words*) which had been flowing since the 1840s.[10] There was some official action: slum-clearing projects were undertaken in London, Liverpool, and Birmingham; the Torrens (1868, 1877) and Cross (1875, 1879) acts, aimed at improving housing for the poor, were passed after considerable debate; and the Housing Act (1890) gave important powers to the London County Council (created in 1888) in particular. By the beginning of the last decade of the century, both Chamberlain's Liberals and Salisbury's Conservatives were voicing the same concerns as radicals and socialists of all stripes: much like the issue of the environment today, "the slums [were] a subject with which every intelligent person was familiar" (Wohl 11).

The question of slum landlordism lay at the heart of the problem of property ownership and its attendant economic and social evils. The issue, and its topicality, combined with Shaw's personal experience in politics, literature, and the theater, provide a context for the transformation of 'Rheingold' into *Widowers' Houses*. When Shaw began working on Archer's material for a conventional well-made play, his problem was how to adapt a worn, ramshackle vehicle to bear the freight of his social message. It is not surprising that he "perversely distorted it into a grotesquely realistic exposure of slum landlordism,"[11] given the incompatibility of theme and form, nor that when he returned to complete the third act "the very qualities which made it impossible for ordinary commercial purposes in 1885 might be exactly those needed by the Independent Theatre in 1892" (*PU* 13)—that is, those possessed by the "new drama" of social realism. The climate of the times had shifted, both politically in the topicality of the issue and theatrically because of productions of Ibsen on the London stage and the emergence in Europe of theaters "free" from censorship or commercial constraints—notably the *Freie Bühne* and the *Freie Volksbühne* in Berlin and *Théâtre Libre* in Paris—and committed to the criticism of morality, society, and institutions.

The challenge Shaw faced was how to present the "new drama," with its focus on real personal, social, and political issues, on a stage where they had been conspicuously absent—or worse, falsified—for so long. His solution was to use conventional dramatic modes, drawing his audience in by starting with a form to which it was accustomed, then manipulate plot, character, and even the genre to make his statement. In adopting such a strategy, Shaw was not only following in the footsteps of the master, Ibsen, whose tight plotting bears all the hallmarks of the well-made play, and whose use of melodrama places him in a century-old tradition, but also, in accordance with Fabian tactics, exploiting materials to hand to influence the predominantly middle-class theater audience.

Lenin described Shaw as "a good man fallen among Fabians," implying that his socialism was diluted by the association. Alick West takes this
description as the title for his book, which "endeavours to show how
good an artist Shaw is, and how it harmed him that he fell among
Fabians."[12] The extent to which the affiliation weakened his artistry
raises the whole question of the relationship between art and propaganda. West obviously agrees with Lenin, so it may be assumed that he
also considers Shaw's art to be socialist propaganda diluted by Fabian
influence. He argues that Shaw "began to write plays because through
the drama he wished to arouse for the fight against capitalism those
emotions of the people which Fabianism could not stir" (West 70), and he
maintains that the plays in fact criticize Fabianism. Another Socialist
critic, Erich Strauss, contends that "every phase of Shaw's dramatic work
was determined by his experience as a socialist" (West 6), and that his
socialism is a constructive force in his artistic work. This stance is little
more than application of the commonplace that an artist's work is condi-
tioned by his or her experience. An obvious third view is that the propaganda spoils the plays. Each position invites questions concerning the
relationship, or reconciliation, in Shaw between his artistry and his didacticism: to what extent does the one serve or undermine the other?

Charles Carpenter identifies *Plays Unpleasant* as "propaganda plays"
which form part of "the ground-clearing phase of Shaw's evolutionary
programme"[13] aimed, in Shaw's words on Ibsen, at "sharpshooting at the
audience, trapping them, fencing with them, aiming always at the sorest
spots in their consciences."[14] The "forensic" drama thereby undermines
conventional ideals and prepares the way for the introduction of emanci-
pating ideas. Such plays, Shaw claims, "are capable of hurting us cruelly
and of filling us with excited hopes of escape from idealistic tyrannies, and
with visions of intenser life in the future" (*Quintessence* 182). Shaw has been
accused of using his characters in *Widowers' Houses* as mechanical vehicles
of propaganda. However, West claims he does not employ them to show
conditions in the slums, but uses the conditions-in-the-slums theme to
reveal his characters. In fact, his characters are mechanical to the extent
that they are stock comic figures, but Shaw's desire to explain social phenomena through real human beings, although not fully realized in his first
play, does result in the creation of three main characters who are at once
socially representative and individually credible.

As their role-defining names indicate, the characters in *Widowers' Houses*
are clearly in the comic tradition: "Trench" has a heavy sound which
suggests that his initial "*rather boyish*" manner overlies an unappealing
stodginess (he also digs himself a "trench" from which there is no escape);
"Blanche" conveys purity, but with the duality of whiteness through which
it also has unpleasant connotations; "Sartorius" echoes Carlyle's *Sartor*

Resartus, the tailor retailored, his *"imposing style"* clothing the antithesis of a gentleman; "Cokane" proclaims Cockaigne, the fabulous land of luxury and idleness, signifying what he represents; and "Lickcheese" is a grotesque name that defines his toadylike "lickspittle" nature.[15] Meisel places the cast firmly within nineteenth-century convention:

> the leading couple are supported by Sartorius, a Heavy Father; Cokane, a Walking Gentleman in the tradition of the stage swell; Lickcheese, a Low Comedy vulgarian; a Chambermaid of the comic-pathetic variety; and a Utility waiter and porter.[16]

Trench is an eligible bachelor whose lack of fortune is well compensated for by his aristocratic connections. His natural desires to acquire both mate and money—preferably in one move—are well matched by those of Blanche, who has the cash but desires a mate and the prestigious connections her own parentage has failed to provide. As hero and heroine, their relationship follows an archetypal comic pattern: boy meets girl; they fall in love at first sight; plans for their union are disrupted by a blocking circumstance; they separate and pine; fortuitous events bring them together to fulfill the promise of marriage; and the mating game is completed. Bernard F. Dukore notes that Trench is not a typical romantic comedy hero because he is weak-willed, foolish, and cowardly, and that Blanche is not a conventional ingenue but a callous and brutal virago.[17] However, these aspects of their natures are not evident initially. In outline, the expectations of conventional romantic comedy are fulfilled. The other characters duly play their appointed comedy roles. Sartorius, representative of the older generation, is not directly a blocking parent—in fact, he approves and encourages the union; however, he does fill the blocking role to the extent that it is his "tainted money" that comes between the lovers. As a self-made, nouveau-riche man of property, his desires are to consolidate his position in society and to see his daughter well married (his strong family affection for Blanche is a redeeming feature that offsets his moral "villainy")—again, preferably in one move. Lickcheese is a parasitic, wily slave, or "Vice," who manipulates the three main characters, a function shared by Cokane, who is primarily buffoon.

The Wagnerian motif in the original title and the Rhine setting of Act I invite comparisons with the music drama *The Rhine Gold*, particularly the Shavian analysis, in *The Perfect Wagnerite*, of the Ring cycle as a socialist myth: Trench/Alberic, the dwarf, discoverer of "gold" on the river rather than in it, who acquires the gold and thereby becomes both a master of slaves and a slave to his possession; Cokane/Mimmy, the maker of a magic helmet for his brother, Alberic: Sartorius/Wotan, the god whose desire for a castle enslaves the giants; Blanche/Freia, the promised prize; and Lickcheese/Loki, the schemer. As with all such analogies, the equations are more suggestive than exact: larger forces are at work. This dimension is not apparent until part way into the second act, although there are a few hints in the predominantly comic Act I.

An 1892 audience would feel at ease in the opening scenes. It would recognize the stock characters, including comic foreigners ignorant of or mangling the English language, and respond good humoredly to familiar themes of mating and marriage, class differences and social climbing, and the education of the innocent. The somewhat creaky plotting might invite unfavorable comparison with "the sons of Scribe," but a dramatist must be allowed his donnée to get his piece off the ground, even at the risk of stretching probability and coincidence. That hero and heroine should meet on a river cruise and instantly fall in love is in the high realm of the probable; that they should then, apparently by chance, arrive at the same hotel and within a few moments become engaged while parent and friend, surprisingly ignorant of the budding relationship, take a lightning tour of a local church, is stretching both coincidence and probability; that the father has a connection to the hero through his aunt stretches both even further. However, this is the stuff of comedy, particularly the well-made-play variety, a perception reinforced by the light tone, amusing dialogue, and brisk pace.

Shaw keeps the play firmly in the comic realm throughout Act I, particularly in the business of the letter, and leaves his audience expecting an obstacle to the marriage from Lady Roxdale. Act II opens in September, the season confirming the probability of a low point in the lovers' relationship. It then introduces the "servile" rent collector Lickcheese, who gives the comedy an unexpected "blue-book" turn with the intrusion of a world far from comic. As indicated above, an 1892 audience could not have been unaware of the horrifying reality represented by the landlord and his lackey. Therefore, when Lickcheese explains that "one pound four for repairs" was needed for "the staircase on the third floor . . . [which] was downright dangerous" (*PU* 55), he recalls familiar descriptions, such as that of Mearns:

> You have to ascend rotten staircases, which threaten to give way at every step, and which, in some places, have already broken down, leaving gaps that imperil the limbs and lives of the unwary. You have to grope your way along dark and filthy passages swarming with vermin. (Wohl 58)

The reported complaints of the Sanitary Inspector and the clergyman intensify the sour note, with the hollow indignation of Sartorius, and his arbitrary dismissal of Lickcheese, confirming the suspicion that his gentlemanly poise masks a ruthless nature. An audience accustomed to the well-made-play formula, in which nothing is irrelevant to the plot, would be puzzled by this apparently unrelated scene because it is outside the framework of comedy where Act I placed it. Thematically, the possibility that Sartorius's money is tainted has been introduced earlier by Cokane, whose gentlemanly scruples remind Trench that it would "concern your family to know how the money was made. . . . Sartorius might be a retired burglar for all I know" (*PU* 47). Meisel notes that in romantic comedy, "though the alliances between classes nearly always involved a barter of rank and money, the disdainful pride of the stage aristocrat often took the form of a scrupulosity about the origin of money" (Meisel 162).

With the arrival of Trench and Cokane, the play returns briefly to the comic mode, but the audience would be even more puzzled by the failure of the older generation, in the person of Lady Roxdale, to oppose the marriage and would be wondering about the precise direction of the plot. While the three men are congratulating one another, Lickcheese has continued to lurk on stage, rather like Lady Windermere's fan waiting to be noticed. After Sartorius has left, he intrudes on Cokane and Trench with his account of the source of Sartorius's money, again shifting the tone away from the comic to the "unpleasant." Shaw now transposes the play to a different frame of reference: romantic interest is supplanted by a discussion of "blue-book" sociology, and romantic motives give way to economic considerations. It is now Trench who is being educated through a series of discoveries, and the audience is presented with a dramatized lecture on the morality and economics of slum landlordism. Trench adopts a righteous tone, recognizing it as "a damnable business. . . . Ive seen it all among the outpatients at the hospital; and it used to make my blood boil to think that such things couldnt be prevented' (*PU* 61). He takes the noble stance, telling Blanche, "I have resolved not to take any money from your father" (*PU* 65), but refusing to explain. This refusal, and her misinterpretation of his "secret," are comic in pattern, but the scene is soured by the previous exchange, her unladylike speech, and the feelings which render her "*white with rage*" (*PU* 66).

The climax of Act II is not the parting of the lovers because of the misunderstanding, as romantic comedy would have it, but occurs after Sartorius has demolished Trench's "sentimental notion" (*PU* 70) regarding Sartorius's income and revealed Trench's complicity as mortgage holder. As in Ibsen, not only is the inheritance tainted, but the corruption it represents is all-pervasive. In response to the dazed Trench, who exclaims "Do you mean to say that I am just as bad as you are?" Sartorius explains: "If, when you say you are just as bad as I am, you mean that you are just as powerless to alter the state of society, then you are unfortunately quite right" (*PU* 72). The "biter bit" inversion underlying Trench's realization of his own complicity in slum landlordism is essentially comic, as is the reversal he undergoes from assertive moralist to "*a living picture of disillusion*" (*PU* 72). The Old King has triumphed over the New King contender in a classic agon when, in an Aristophanic comedy, "the tone becomes most serious due to the gravity of the political and social themes"—even the buffoon is present and contributes.[18] The agon

> ends in the crisis and turning-point of the play, reverses the situation of the adversaries, and leads not to an academic resolution, but to all the rest of the action that follows. Above all, it is . . . organically related to the final marriage in which the victor is bride-groom, the triumph of the new God or new King. (Cornford #9)

But for the fact that it is the loser who becomes the bridegroom, this description fits *Widowers' Houses* perfectly. Shaw's blend of Aristophanic and romantic comedy makes the crucial issue of Act II the recognition of shared guilt. The wider implications from the propagandist's point of view—the term "rent" in Fabian economics is not confined to property, but generalized to include all unearned income—are obvious: to what extent is every member of the audience guilty of such profiteering and complicity?

The disillusioned Trench departs, leaving Sartorius to explain to Blanche that the marriage is on again, but before he has a chance, Shaw introduces another surprise in Blanche's scene with her maid. Her forward behavior in the hotel scene, when she manipulates Trench into a marriage proposal, and her display of temper earlier in Act II identify her as "unladylike" and prepare for the scene, but is it gratuitous? In the portrayal of character, it is unnecessary because that has been established; in the development of plot it makes no contribution; but in the service of socialist propaganda it is a crucial scene because it demonstrates the master-slave relationship which exists between capitalist-exploiter and worker-victim. Tyson says that between 1892 and publication in 1898, Shaw modified the maid's character to replace her original "truculence and dislike for Blanche, by a *love*—no less—for her exacting and violent mistress"[19] This change improves the characterization without altering the message. In particular, Blanche is the indulged product of the most vicious form that exploitation takes: slum landlordism. Her selfish nature and refusal even to recognize the economic and social conditions on which her wealth and comfort are based reflect the inhumanity and sin of the society of which she is representative. Without this demonstration, her refusal to contemplate her humble origins or the facts concerning her father's business revealed in the "bluebook" she picks up (*PU* 84–85)—"I hate the idea of such things. I dont want to know about them' (*PU* 86–87)—would appear mere petulance: with it, inhumanity becomes manifest. When the play returns to the romantic question of marriage after the scene with the maid, it comes as no surprise that she refuses to "marry a fool" who has "played fast and loose with [her]" (*PU* 76–77).

The comfortable domestic scene that opens Act III counterpoints the lingering image of slum conditions carried forward from the previous act, but the winter mood is reflected in the manner in which Sartorius and Blanche *"are sitting glumly by the fire"* (*PU* 78). She is clearly fretting over Trench, but in her pride she hotly denies it. Nevertheless, comic reconciliation is clearly in the wind. Lickcheese enters transformed from parasitic "Vice" into melodramatic stage villain: evening dress, fur-lined overcoat, silk hat, even waxed and pointed mustache. His sudden change in fortune has not changed his function as exposer of the crimes of capitalism: he has discovered how the system can be milked through compensation (provided one has the benefit of inside information), and he seeks the cooperation of Sartorius, who in turn needs that of Trench. Cokane and Sartorius present the proposal to Trench as a matter of "duty . . . to put those abominable buildings into proper and habitable repair" (*PU* 88). Whatever his moral weaknesses, Trench has acquired some attributes of the Shavian realist:

> TRENCH. . . . as I understand it, Robbins's Row is to be pulled down to make way for the new street into the Strand; and the straight tip now is to go for compensation. . . . It appears that the dirtier a place is the more rent you get; and the decenter it is, the more compensation you get. So we're to give up dirt and go in for decency.
> SARTORIUS. I should not put it exactly in that way; but—
> COKANE. Quite right, Mr. Sartorius, quite right. The case could not have been stated in worse taste or with less tact. (*PU* 89)

This exchange also illustrates that just as Blanche has a dual function as heroine of a romantic comedy (albeit with aspects of the virago and femme fatale) and as corrupted representative of an immoral society, Cokane serves a similar duality: on the one hand, as "Billy," his appearance, *"affected manner,"* and mechanical speech mark him as buffoon in the comedy; on the other, as Mr. William de Burgh Cokane, he is a representative aristocrat in the didactic scheme. His major concern as

Trench's companion is to "make a true gentleman of [him]" (*PU* 42), and he is constantly lecturing the headstrong young man for his "bad taste" and lack of "principle." As the exchange indicates, tact and hypocrisy are one and the same for Cokane. To him, and to the class he represents, social forms and appearances are more important than such values as truth and sincerity: that the role of buffoon is combined with that of "Vice" is no accident.

Shaw's scorn for all that Cokane, Sartorius, and Lickcheese stand for is implicit in the apparently plausible, but specious, self-indicting arguments they employ in their attempt to win over Trench, who is reduced to a state of *"consternation,"* snarling like a cornered animal. However, he lacks the moral conviction to oppose them, and the wily Lickcheese, sensing that it will take little to tip the moral scales, suggests including "a bit of romance in [the] business" (*PU* 92), and the play is set to return to the comic mode: how can the hero maintain his moral integrity, win the girl, and secure a fortune?

That this conventional expectation will not be met in a conventional manner is indicated by Trench's sulky agreement with the suggestion that he should wait for Cokane and Lickcheese to see him home after they have finished their business with Sartorius. This engineers the opportunity for Blanche (who, as Lickcheese obviously guesses, is listening at the door) to return and prepares for another reversal. The scene is far from the conventional noble commitment of hero and heroine. She is *"provocative, taunting."* Realizing that *"all this ferocity is erotic"* he responds by showing *"a faint grin of anticipated victory"* (*PU* 95) and playing hard to get, forcing her to throw herself at him. As in the first scene, she is the aggressor, the manner this time more unpalatable to Victorian tastes, and the "unpleasantness" of the scene is compounded by the awareness that he is the victim of her predatory sexual passion rather then the male conqueror he considers himself to be. This adds the spice of irony to a situation that has, in its basic pattern, returned to archetypal comedy, a pattern proclaimed by the embrace of the lovers, the closing of family and social ranks as Trench declares he will "stand in, compensation or no compensation," and the adumbrated *komos* as the five players, arm in arm, *exeunt* harmoniously to supper.

The comic structure is used to match the propagandist's message: once launched in the comic mode, the play arouses expectations that the lovers will triumph over blocking elements, the hero (as Archer proposed) "throwing the tainted treasure of his father-in-law, metaphorically speaking, into the Rhine" (*Prefaces* 699), the villains being defeated or reformed, and social ranks closing in a final reconciliation. As indicated, to a large extent these expectations are met, but with Shavian inversions that are comic in form yet didactic in effect. When Trench returns in Act III, his boyish self has died to be replaced by a "*coarsened and sullen*" (*PU* 88) man whose innocence has been transformed into cynicism. He is reborn in the arms of Blanche, as his "delight" demonstrates, a comic reversal that leads to moral reversal when he throws in his lot with the villains, who, in another inversion of expectation, are neither defeated nor reformed. A further Shavian inversion is that the comic pattern is maintained by having the pair integrated into society, as imaged in the concluding linking of arms, but into a society that has been defined as corrupt. The irony is of a satiric order, but Shaw stops short of satire—which would demand ridicule—in order to incriminate both his characters and his audience. The lovers have become knowing but uncaring accomplices of the villains. Blanche has undergone no change, but the audience will perceive Trench's acceptance of the economic realities of his position as a betrayal of his moral scruples, as ignoble capitulation and conformity. The effect on the members of the audience is that, on the one hand, they derive pleasure and satisfaction from seeing the triumph of the vital force, while, on the other, they have the pleasure soured by the capitulation and the satisfaction qualified by moral condemnation of a social evil for which, in their aroused consciences, they must share responsibility.

The main issue for Shaw is not an exposé of slum landlordism itself, nor the need for action to bring about changes, because the issue was already in the public arena. The facts being known, his "didactic object . . . [was] to bring conviction of sin—to make the Pharisee who repudiates Sartorius . . . recognize that Sartorius is his own photograph" (*Auto* 271), and similarly to recognize that Trench is a reflection of his own capitulation and complicity. As Shaw himself pointed out, the play "is, on its bluebook side, a sample . . . of one of the most familiar, popular, and firmly established *genres* in English dramatic literature" (*Prefaces* 708). The difference is that, rather than deal with the issues directly and seriously from the outset, he first establishes a conventional comic form and then proceeds to manipulate it with both comic and noncomic inversions, reversals, and ironies. Critics have labeled the result in various ways. After discussing the play as melodrama, as well-made play, as romantic comedy, and as satire, Dukore concludes that in the end it comes closest to "tragicomedy" in that no new society crystallizes around the young couple, but the reverse occurs and the comic pattern is inverted because of the triumph of "dark forces." However, "the point . . . is not that the triumph of dark forces gives *Widowers' Houses* an unhappy ending but that it prevents a purely happy ending" (Dukore 30). Valency sees the play as "*comédie rosse*,"[20] following the naturalist mode of the *Théâtre Libre*. Morgan regards the final scene as a "parody of romance," with a satirical effect that creates revulsion.[21] That established critics should find it difficult to provide a clear label would not surprise Olsen, who identifies Shaw's

> favorite overall device . . . [as] *suspense of form. . .*, [which] consists in keeping the audience uncertain as to *what kind of a play* they are witnessing. . . . [Its use] implies a systematic attack upon all the conventional . . . emotional and moral responses of the audience . . . [and] subverts the . . . context in terms of which people react to a play. . . . It undermines the very foundation of their emotions and moral judgements.[22]

By throwing the audience off balance through the disruption of their theatrical expectations, Shaw both prepares for and intensifies the impact of the disturbing content: expectation, emotions, and moral judgments are churned by the Shavian plow to facilitate the sowing and rooting of Shavian ideas.

In a pithy statement, Eric Bentley describes Shaw as "a concrete moralist, a master of parable, who has worked out for the presentation of his protestant pragmatist morality a new dramaturgy."[23] This "new dramaturgy" is initially a matter of exploiting theatrical forms ready to hand to present a parable that is primarily romantic comedy. Such exploitation inevitably leads to parody and, being an attack on the evils of society, to the inclusion of satiric elements and to a depiction of dark forces that undermine the comic ending. The chief weakness of *Widowers' Houses* is the lack of any positive social or moral assertion: it presents the problem but no solution, no moral or social alternative. Trench has to decide whether to accept the system or refrain from profiting by it, and the possibility of opposing it exists only outside the framework of the play. As propagandist, Shaw could be defended on the grounds that his intention is to disturb, and that he succeeds in doing so, but as an artist, he is guilty of not presenting a sharply defined conflict in the very area he considers central. As Fabian, Shaw sticks to the individualism dear to the British radical tradition, rejecting the class basis of Marxism and its concomitant tendency to regard people in the mass, and placing the social conflict within his characters. Trench is not called upon by an anarchist to burn down tenements, but to make a moral decision, one that each member of the audience must make: the battle for social justice is first lost or won within the individual—the principle of Dr. Davidson and the New Life—and the plays are weapons in the Fabian armory. Let Shaw have the last word:

> The current respectability of today is nothing but a huge inversion of righteous and scientific order weltering in dishonesty, use-

lessness, selfishness, wanton misery and idiotic waste of magnificent opportunities for noble and happy living. . . . Evil is enormously worse than we knew, yet it is not eternal—not even very long lived, if we only bestir ourselves to make an end of it. (*Fabian Essays* 27)

Notes

1. See Preface to Bernard Shaw, *Plays Unpleasant* (Harmondsworth: Penguin, 1946), p. 12, and Preface to *Widowers' Houses* in Bernard Shaw, *The Complete Prefaces* (London: Paul Hamlyn, 1965), pp. 699–700, for accounts by Shaw and by Archer. Alan S. Downer, "Shaw's First Play," in *Seven Critical Essays*, ed. Norman Rosenblood (Toronto: University of Toronto Press, 1971), pp. 3–24, notes that Eden Greville credits Grein with scheming to have Shaw write a play for his Independent Theatre. Subsequent references to *Prefaces* appear in the text.

2. Bernard Shaw, *Shaw: An Autobiography, 1856–1898*, ed. Stanley Weintraub (New York: Weybright and Talley, 1969), p. 82. Subsequent references to *Auto* appear in the text.

3. Michael Holroyd, *Bernard Shaw: The Search for Love, 1856–1898* (London: Chatto and Windus, 1988), p. 278. Subsequent references to Holroyd appear in the text.

4. Bernard Shaw, *Sixteen Self Sketches* (London: Constable, 1949), pp. 30–31. Subsequent references to *Self Sketches* appear in the text.

5. Willard Wolfe, *From Radicalism to Socialism: Men and Ideas in the Formation of Fabian Socialist Doctrines, 1881–1889* (New Haven: Yale University Press, 1975), p. 115. Subsequent references to Wolfe appear in the text.

6. A. M. McBriar, *Fabian Socialism and English Politics, 1884–1918* (Cambridge: Cambridge University Press, 1962), p. 25.

7. Bernard Shaw et al., *Fabian Essays in Socialism* (1889) (London: George Allen & Unwin, 1948), p. xxxiii. Subsequent references to *Fabian Essays* appear in the text.

8. Andrew Mearns, *The Bitter Cry of Outcast London* (1883), ed. Anthony S. Wohl (Leicester: Leicester University Press, 1970). p. 12. Subsequent references to Wohl appear in the text.

9. Kinley E. Roby, "Strap Street to Robbins's Row," *Shaw Review* 18 (January 1975), p. 2.

10. Other noteworthy publications include James Greenwood, *A Night in the Workhouse* (1866); George Sims, *How the Poor Live and Horrible London* (1889); William Booth (founder of the Salvation Army), *Life and Labour of the People of London* (1889) and *In Darkest England and the Way Out* (1890); G. Haw, *No Room to Live* (1900); Seebohm Rowntree, *Poverty: A Study of Town Life* (1901); and Jack London, *The People of the Abyss* (1902).

11. Bernard Shaw, *Plays Unpleasant* (Harmondsworth: Penguin, 1946), p. 12. Subsequent references to *PU* appear in the text.

12. Alick West, *"A Good Man Fallen among Fabians"* (New York: International, 1950), p. v. Subsequent references to West appear in the text.

13. Charles A. Carpenter, *Bernard Shaw and the Art of Destroying Ideals* (Madison: University of Wisconsin Press, 1969), p. 13.

14. Bernard Shaw, *The Quintessence of Ibsenism* (New York: Hill and Wang, 1957), p. 183. Subsequent references to *Quintessence* appear in the text.

15. Rev. E. Cobham Brewer, *The Dictionary of Phrase and Fable* (1894) (London: Galley Press, n.d.) is illuminating: a "Trencher-Knight. A table knight, a suitor from cupboard love"; "White Ladies [*Les Dames Blanches*]. A species of fée in Normandy" who ask travelers to dance: "if they receive a courteous answer, well; but if a refusal, they seize the churl and fling him into a ditch where thorns and briars may serve to teach him gentleness of manners." Diderik Roll-Hansen, "Sartorius and the Scribes of the Bible: Satiric Method in *Widowers' Houses*," *Shaw Review* 18 (January 1975), p. 5, argues that the name Sartorius suggests that he is "eager to conform, not only by being well-dressed and well-spoken, but also . . . by accepting the prestige pattern of a snobbish late-Victorian society." The "de Burgh" in Cokane's full name echoes that of Jane Austen's archaristocrat in *Pride and Prejudice,* Lady Catherine de Bourgh, reinforcing his role as representative of that class.

16. Martin Meisel. *Shaw and the Nineteenth-Century Theater* (Princeton: Princeton University Press, 1963), p. 27. Subsequent references to Meisel appear in the text.

17. Bernard F. Dukore, *"Widowers' Houses:* A Question of Genre," *Modern Drama* 17 (1974), 27–32. Subsequent references to Dukore appear in the text.

18. Francis M. Cornford, *The Origin of Attic Comedy,* ed. Theodor H. Gaster (Gloucester, Mass.: Peter Smith, 1968), #10, #8. Subsequent references to Cornford appear in the text.

19. Brian F. Tyson, "Shaw Among the Actors: Theatrical Additions to *Plays Unpleasant,*" *Modern Drama* 14 (December 1971), 268; Tyson's emphasis.

20. Maurice Valency, *The Cart and the Trumpet: The Plays of George Bernard Shaw* (New York: Oxford University Press, 1973), p. 79.

21. Margery M. Morgan, *The Shavian Playground: An Exploration of the Art of Bernard Shaw* (London: Methuen, 1972).

22. Elder Olsen, *The Theory of Comedy* (Bloomington: Indiana University Press, 1968), pp. 122–23.

23. Eric Bentley, *The Playwright as Thinker* (New York: Meridian Books, 1946), p. 126.

Norman Buchan, M.P.

SHAW AND PARLIAMENTARY DEMOCRACY: A PARLIAMENTARIAN'S VIEW

By no means the least of the teasing paradoxes of Shaw's politics is that the only feasible vehicle to bring about the socialism he argued for, parliamentary democracy, was an institution he treated with total contempt and, when offered the chance, refused to enter. As a further irony, he was one of the ten people brought together to found the Labour Representation Committee. This was the origin of the Labour party, the expression of socialism within Parliament throughout the twentieth century. But, unlike some of the other parodoxes which both delighted and dismayed his contemporaries, this one was deeply held and, in a curious way, was perhaps the logical link between the apparent polarity of his Fabianism and his support for Stalin.

This might suggest a simple rejection of practical politics altogether, a desire rather to become merely a theorist and prophet. Nothing could be further from the truth. On the contrary, he was concerned, from the very beginnings of his association in the burgeoning socialist fervor of the 1880s, with the need to establish, to create practical and representative labor and socialist organization and to secure for it representation in Parliament. The paradox is deep indeed.

An early choice which Shaw had to make was between throwing his lot in with the Fabians or with the Social Democratic Federation (SDF). This was a much narrower choice than it now seems. It was not the Marxism of the SDF that put him off. On the contrary. Marxism was both politically and intellectually respectable to most radicals of the Left—as it was to become in Britain for a period in the 1930s—and perhaps even more widely than only on the Left. Shortly after the death of Marx, the ultrarespectable Arthur Balfour, later to become Conservative prime minister of Britain,

addressed a conference at which he "paid unexpected tribute to the intellectual powers of Karl Marx." At the same conference, Shaw typically
delivered "a fine apologia for burglars as compared with landowners and
shareholders." The bizarre image of a Margaret Thatcher or a George
Bush being even present on such an occasion, or in such company, perhaps emphasizes how far orthodoxy in political life has grown terrified of
being shaken by ideas. (And if further confirmation is needed on the
question of the then-comparative respectability of Marx, we find it in the
curious folk memory of the British socialist movement. The only facts still
universally remembered about the leader of the Marxist SDF, H. M.
Hyndman, are that he habitually wore a silk top hat and morning dress
and that he played briefly in first-class cricket!)

Shaw was bowled over by Marx. He told Hesketh Pearson that *Das
Kapital* "had a tremendous efect on him. . . . It had converted him to
socialism, turned him into a revolutionary writer, made him a political
agitator, changed his outlook, directed his energy, influenced his art,
[given] him a religion and made a man of him!" Thus, it was not the
question of Marxism that caused him to reject the SDF. In fact, he
discovered when he returned to the SDF "full of the new gospel" that
"not a soul there except Hyndman and myself had read a word of Marx."

The real reason was what would now be called sectarianism, the seemingly inbuilt tendency to split and split again of all those groups who
believed that they alone knew the true way forward. The SDF betrayed
the symptom to a finely-tuned degree. Marx had thundered against the
sects from the start. He was in favor of the broadest possible alliance of
labor organizations and working-class groups, whom he tried to weld
together in the First International. His successors were rather different.
By the time Shaw came to join the SDF as a candidate member, it had
already lost Eleanor Marx, along with Dr. Aveling and William Morris.
That, as well as the apocalyptic theory that the centenary of the French
Revolution in 1889 would inevitably bring in the new dawn of the Socialist Revolution, was too much for Shaw. He later said,

> I remember being asked how long it would take to get Socialism
> into working order. I replied that a fortnight would be ample for
> the purpose. When I add that I was frequently complimented on
> being one of the more reasonable socialists, you will be able to
> appreciate the fervour of our conviction, and the extravagant
> levity of our practical ideas.

Shaw turned from the SDF to the Fabians. At the time this seemed a
strange alternative. It was new, it was tiny, it was equally ferocious in its
socialism. Its initial tract proclaimed,

Must workers continue in their misery whilst professors and politicians split straws and wrangle over trifles?

While Capital is in the hands of the few Poverty must be the lot of the many.

. . . [You must] sweep away this blind idol of Competition, this misuse of Capital in the hands of individuals.

All fairly fustian stuff, in the style and mood of the times, and then,

You who live dainty and pleasant lives, reflect that your ease and luxury are paid for by the misery and want of others! Your superfluities are the parents of poverty. Surely all humanity is not burnt out of you by the gold your fathers left you!

Now, as Margaret Cole points out, most of this could have been written by any of the radical groups from the Chartists onward. Why, then, did it appeal to Shaw?

Hesketh Pearson suggests that it was the name that attracted him since it suggested an educated group. Michael Holroyd proposes that the beauty of the title to Shaw was that it could be used to mean anything. More significant, surely, was the direct appeal made by the Society to the humanity and understanding of the upper and middle classes. Already much of the leadership throughout the movement (Hyndman or William Morris, for example) came from there. Shaw's decision to join the Fabians, he said, "was guided by no discoverable difference in programme or principle, but solely by an instinctive feeling that the Fabian and not the Federation would attract the men of my own bias and intellectual habits who were then ripening for the work that lay before us."

And he was quick to begin that work. In addition to his role as a member of the Fabian Society, he entered local government, although, if he is to be believed, with much less eagerness than Sidney Webb showed:

I had nothing to do with it. I addressed no meetings. I took no steps. I did what I could to provoke the wirepullers to drop me. No use; the Moderates rallied round me, the extra candidates were bullied into withdrawing; and I was elected without a contest on a compromise which enabled both sides to claim me.

There he learned that local government could be effective. And by comparison it sharpened his view about the ineffectiveness of existing parliamentary democracy, a view that was strengthened rather than diminished with the years.

Curiously, indeed paradoxically for such an enthusiastic political polemicist, theorist, propagandist, it was precisely the lack of all this in local government that filled him with enthusiasm. What he found galling and distressing was not the expected troglodyte attitude of his fellow vestrymen and councillors. That he could deal with, and indeed he often found unexpected support for sensible causes on all sides. It was the poverty of the local councils, the lack of resources for local services, that depressed him. He saw in it practical socialism, regardless of party. What was a bridge built by the community but socialism? What were communally provided water, electricity, street markets, public hygiene, but socialism?

So he had unexpectedly found great joy in his stint in local government. For six years, despite all his strictures on its drudgery and scathing comment on his fellow councillors, he had valued the experience. It had been enormously time-consuming but also immensely worthwhile. This was not really paradoxical. Nothing pleases the political theorist more than the chance of actually *doing* things. Parliament is full of back-bench members who now mope frustrated in the corridors of power, but who had formerly been councillors with concrete achievements to their credit, real things they could actually see and point to and say, or at any rate know, "I brought that about," whether it was a health center, a new school, or a well-built housing project. In contrast to local government, achievement of that kind in Parliament is possible only by becoming a minister. That in a sense is the ultimate corruption of parliamentary democracy—as well as its justification.

Shaw had a more comprehensive rejection of the parliamentary process. He attributed the success of local government to its lack of "the Party System." Councils were elected for a fixed term. No adverse vote could precipitate a local election. In addition, local governments operated by a system of committees. Problems were argued through in a practical and—says Shaw—usually nonparty way. Committee decisions were then put to the full council to be accepted or rejected. Whichever way, the council continued. Cross-party decisions could be made without the world coming to an end. As a consequence, sensible choices were usually made, and made quickly.

What a contrast, said Shaw, to Parliament. There, decisions were based on the party system, and in *Everybody's Political What's What?* he wrote a brilliant burlesque of its mythical origins to prove it. It featured William III and the Earl of Sunderland. In despair, William asks for advice:

> I am at my wits' end. I am expected to do everything for everyone. And I am expected to do it without money and without a standing army. . . . I'm going to shake the dust of England off my feet unless you can show me a way of making Parliament do what I tell it to do.

And Sunderland replies,

> I cannot do that; but I can show you a way to prevent Parliament
> from doing anything at all except vote your revenues and stave
> off the next election as long as possible.

Sunderland proposes the simple solution that the King should always
choose his cabinet from the largest party in the House. The consequence
of this has been that the fear of precipitating an election, with the possible loss of their own seats, ensures that the majority-party M.P.s will
always vote for the Government. In turn, the Government will avoid
taking any drastic action, however desirable, for fear of upsetting the
proverbial applecart and thus perfectly fulfill Sunderland's promise.
"Compare," said Shaw in *Everybody's Political What's What?*, "the sterility
of Parliament in everything but postprandial oratory with the extension
of municipal socialism by the municipalities, where there are no cabinets,
no royal selection, no general election except at immovably fixed dates;
in short, no possibility of the Party System."

It is not surprising that, with this view of the place, Shaw should have
rejected it for himself. The paradox to be explained is why then he
should have argued, organized, and worked for Labour representation
in Parliament at all. One reason is that, contempt for it or not, he rejected even more strongly the possibility of successful revolution. The
easy dispersal by London police of a huge crowd during the march on
Trafalgar Square on Bloody Sunday, 13 November 1887, had disabused
him of that. *"We skedaddled,"* he wrote to William Morris: " . . . it was the
most abjectly disgraceful defeat ever suffered by a band of heroes out-
numbering their foes a thousand to one."

Of course in some ways his attitude to Parliament can easily be explained. It was in part simply a straightforward intellectual rejection;
there was, and is, a good deal to be contemptuous about. Even today, for
example, the new system of select committees can find it impossible to
get information the government is determined to conceal. Neither Water-
gate nor Irangate could easily have happened in Britain. But if either
had, the British Parliament would never have been able to expose it. The
British government remains the most secretive in the Western world. In
his day Shaw, too, had good reason for contempt.

There is more truth than mischief in his comment in *On the Rocks:*
"Have you noticed," says the Duke of Domesday, "that though in our
great British constitution there is a department for everything else in the
world almost—for agriculture and health and fisheries, for home affairs
and education, for the Exchequer and the Treasury and even the

Chiltern Hundreds—we have no department for thinking?" And in the
Preface to *Heartbreak House* he says,

> From what is called democracy no corrective to this state of things
> could be hoped. It is said that every people has the Government it
> deserves. It is more to the point that every government has the
> electorate it deserves; for the orators of the front bench can edify or
> debauch an ignorant electorate at will. Thus our democracy moves
> in a vicious circle of reciprocal worthiness and unworthiness.

But in the prefaces no less than in the plays we must watch for the
teasing paradox.

What is consistent in Shaw is the imperative of the intelligence, of
reason. Therefore, there is an inevitable arrogance. Applied to politics, it
emerges as elitism or worse. On the one hand, as with the Fabians, it
leads to a desire to teach, to plan, to apply reason to social change—and
to be appalled by human frailty when reason alone has failed.

Explaining his initial fascination with Marx, Shaw said that Marx "appealed to an unnamed, unrecognised passion—a new passion—the passion of hatred in the more generous souls among the respectable and
educated sections for the accursed middle-class institutions that had
starved, thwarted, misled and corrupted them from their cradles." This
is generously said—and meant. But the very impatience to alter things—
which he could do, in however small a way, in local government—could
also lead to the apparently necessary acceptance of the rule of the intelligent few. The confidence of the Fabians in their earlier policy of
permeation—the ability to influence through reason without the need to
engage directly in open political struggle—also left them prey to the
belief that when an elite took power, then the way forward could be
achieved. Shaw viewed Mussolini and (to a lesser extent) Hitler in their
very early days as people who had grown tired of the blockage on the
road to progress imposed by the delays, the pettiness, the mindless selfishness of much of parliamentary democracy. In addition, the Webbs
and Shaw perceived—and for the same reason—Stalin's Soviet Union in
the same light. "In Russia," said Shaw, "they have many cabinets, including a cabinet of thinkers at the top. In Britain we have one cabinet, of
talkers, who haven't got time to think."

This was at the heart of the great Wells-Shaw controversy in the pages
of the *New Statesman and Nation* in 1934, a controversy which continued
week after week from October right up to the end of the year. Entering
into the fray were figures like Maynard Keynes, Ernst Toller (the German playwright, then a fugitive in Britain), and Julian Bell and Ralph
Fox (both writers to be killed later in Spain, fighting with the Interna-

tional Brigades). It is almost a microcosm of the intellectual Left of the period, and important for that reason. Fifty years afterward three questions, all of them now almost impossible to comprehend in their urgency, yet all of them crucial to an understanding of the period—and to an understanding of Shaw—stand out.

Left thinking at that time was almost dominated by the question of the Soviet Union. Was it socialist or not? Was it a new democracy or the old tyranny writ large? Was it final vindication, the rational world of the Fabians made flesh? The Webbs had no doubt. They went. They saw. They were conquered. They glimpsed their own image in it. It was, they said enthusiastically, a New Civilization. Shaw also visited the U.S.S.R.—in the unlikely company of Lady Astor. The "dictatorship of the proletariat" he interpreted as a form of extended municipal-committee system, organized under a proper benevolent despotism. He had, after all, in the Preface to *The Apple Cart*, qualified Lincoln. Government of the people—yes. Government for the people—yes. But government by the people—a thousand times no! "The people cannot govern. The thing is a physical impossibility . . . it is only a cry by which demagogues humbug us into voting for them. . . . [After all] it is much easier to write a good play than to make a good law. And there are not a hundred men in the world who can write a play good enough to stand daily wear and tear as long as a law must."

Wells, too, had just returned from Moscow. More important, he had also recently visited the United States. The *New Statesman* of 27 October 1934 printed his long report of his conversation with Stalin. His main theme was that the world had changed. The same problems facing the Soviet Union were also facing the U.S.A.—and both countries were applying, or needed to apply, the same solution: "Today the capitalists have to learn from you, to grasp the spirit of Socialism. What is taking place in the United States is a profound reorganisation, the creation of planned, that is socialist, economy."

Wells rather treated any transition from Rockefeller, Morgan, and Ford to socialism as a kind of inevitable natural phenomenon. Stalin politely but firmly demurred. He was, after all, a revolutionary Communist. (Indeed, after what we now know about him, he emerges all the more strangely in Wells's account as an astonishingly urbane, patient, and tolerant character!) "Without getting rid of the capitalists, without abolishing the principle of private property in the means of production, it is impossible to create a planned economy."

There developed an almost comic earnestness on the part of Wells as he gently tried to explain to Stalin that he did not *quite* understand how things were *really* developing in the U.S.A. and that this was all rather like the development Stalin was planning in the Soviet Union. It was a bizarre description of what was happening in both countries and displayed a naïveté almost beyond belief. The more Wells tried to press his case, the more bizarre it became. Stalin was wrong about capitalists, he said. Yes, it was true that "old Morgan only thought about profit; he was a parasite on society, simply; he merely accumulated wealth. But take Rockefeller. He is a brilliant organiser; he has set an example . . . worthy of emulation. Or take Ford . . . we should strive to combine all the constructive forces in one line as much as possible."

Stalin, like a kindly old tutor talking to a sophomore, replied: "It seems to me, Mr. Wells, that you greatly underestimate the question of political power, that it entirely drops out of your conception. . . ." And, in another kindly seeming intervention, he corrects Wells's English history. After all, Stalin had commented, the old system in England had not changed of itself: "did it not in fact require a Cromwell to crush it by force?" No, interjected Wells: "Cromwell operated on the basis of the constitution and in the name of constitutional order." Stalin replied, "In the name of the constitution he resorted to violence, beheaded the King, dispersed Parliament, arrested some and beheaded others!" Throughout—speaking to Stalin—Wells repeated his central argument that the "class war" was now old-fashioned if not, indeed, at an end, that both Soviet and Western societies were moving inexorably without fuss toward the same gentle, harmonious end.

The interview ends with Wells impressing upon Stalin the need for a P.E.N. Club in Russia: "It insists upon free expression of opinion—even of opposition opinion. I hope to discuss this point with Gorki. I do not know if you are prepared yet for that much freedom. . . ." Stalin was not impressed: "We Bolsheviks call it 'self-criticism.' It is widely used in the USSR"!

The comedy of all this was not lost on Shaw. And, he says, "I suspect it was not lost on Stalin. . . . Wells does not listen to Stalin. He only waits to begin again when Stalin stops. He thinks he knows better than Stalin all that Stalin knows. He has not come to be instructed by Stalin, but to instruct. . . . Stalin gives Wells a lucid elementary lesson in post-Marxian political science. It produces less effect on Wells than water on a duck's back."

As well he might, Shaw takes up Wells's main point that the organization methods of a Rockefeller or a Ford in industry (along with the New Deal measures of Roosevelt) will inevitably move their world toward the new socialist order. Shaw gives the obvious answer, echoing Stalin:

> whether these deliverers are to be apostles or energetic parvenus, there is no denying Stalin's proviso that they cannot change the world until they obtain political power. Also unless they have a Communistic ideal for which they care more than for any per-

sonal advantage to themselves they will use their power to ra-
tionalise Capitalism instead of to destroy it.

The problem with Wells, he said, is that "he thinks that Capitalism is
not a system but a chaos. He never made a greater mistake." And then,
the seemingly ultimate paradox for a socialist:

> Capitalism on paper is the most systematic and thoroughly rea-
> soned of all the Utopias. It was its completeness and logic as a plan
> for getting the optimal social result from the institution of private
> property that reconciled humane thinkers like De Quincey, Austin,
> Macaulay, and the Utilitarians to it, in full view of its actual and
> prospective horrors, before Socialism became conceivably political.

He went on to define what he called the real issue: "It is between private
property with its automatic privileged distribution and public property
with deliberately enforced equal distribution."

"I have long been laughed at in Russia," he says in the *New Statesman*
on 3 November 1934, "as a good man fallen among Fabians; but the two
old hyperfabian Fabians, Webb and Shaw, have stuck to their guns like
Fox [during the Fench Revolution] whilst the sentimental Socialists have
been bolting in all directions from Stalin, screaming, like St. Peter, 'I
know not the man.'" He ends with the mock-Shavian suggestion that
they should all invite Stalin to the next dinner of the P.E.N. Club.

Fifty years afterward much of the comedy has turned black. The joke
is as much on Shaw as on the purblind and burbling egotism of Wells
in his uncomprehending encounter with the monstrous Stalin. There
are phrases that haunt these old columns of the *New Statesman*. Shaw
observed,

> Wells might have reminded Stalin that the Bolsheviks were car-
> ried to victory by the great peasant-soldier class, bent to a man on
> private property in its most extreme form of peasant proprietor-
> ship. Ever since, Stalin and his colleagues have been engaged in
> the great task of exterminating these peasants and replacing them
> by cultured industrialists. Now it is not a paradox to say that this
> policy has the enthusiastic support of its more intelligent vic-
> tims. . . . Stalin has a trenchant pen and can put controversial
> opponents on the spot as effectively as Kulaks.

Later, Shaw said that "Stalin is a man who will get things done, including,
if necessary, the removal of Trotsky and the World Revolution from the
business of the day."

Well, yes again. He was pretty effective in both removal jobs. History has not dealt kindly with either Wells's or Shaw's assessment of Stalin. Even as he talked with Wells, the dictator was plotting either the assassination of Kirov or how he was to exploit it. It was this event, it will be recalled, that largely set in train the purges, the gulags, the deaths. It was this event, too, that caused the young poet John Cornford (who also died in Spain) to write, "Today is overturning yesterday's settled good." And even as Shaw was writing, lightly and unknowingly, about the kulaks, millions of them were dying from forced starvation. It is the most tragic of ironies that while Shaw used the word "exterminated" metaphorically, Stalin's actions were ensuring its literal application. We are not gloating, therefore—or sneering—from the easier vantage point of another fifty years of history. Nor is it simply the rustle of dead leaves. There are lessons to be learned!

Shaw and the Webbs were not alone in seeing the U.S.S.R. as the new civilization. The coming of Hitler and the rise of fascism sharpened the sense that people had to choose which side they were on. To many on the Left, and not only Communists, the Soviet Union was a workers' state: free, socialist, and democratic. And a few years afterward their view was seemingly endorsed by what was happening in Spain. The rustle of dead leaves brings awkward whispering echoes. But what was different about Shaw was that he supported the U.S.S.R. to a large extent precisely *because* he sensed that it was not a democracy in the classic sense. It was not quite *Man and Superman,* or Lamarck, or *Back to Methuselah*—but at least it practiced the rule of the doers and thinkers!

Old Hipney and Sir Arthur Chavender, the prime minister, come together in *On the Rocks.* "Adult suffrage," says Hipney, "that was what was to save us all. My God! It delivered us into the hands of the spoilers and oppressors, bound hand and foot by our own folly and ignorance." Hipney is now for anyone who will take them all "by the scruffs of their silly necks and just sling them into the way they should go." And Sir Arthur says that he is not going to stand for election to Parliament again. Nor is he going to take to the streets: "I am not a man of action, only a talker. Until the men of action clear out the talkers we who have social conscience are at the mercy of those who have none. . . ."

This, then, is the irony, that one of the ten men who met to organize the need for Labour representation in the House of Commons, and one who believed passionately both in the justice and in the intellectual rightness of socialism, had contempt for the only democratic institution which could bring it into existence.

Shaw never properly grappled with this. After all, those who have worked in the system know that much of his criticism is justified. He suggested, and only half ironically, that a proper system could do in thirty days what it would take a British Parliament thirty years to achieve. It can certainly be wearisomely long—legislation tends to be! But, curiously, that is not the main problem. Britain found itself at war with Germany in 1939 through a five-minute speech by Neville Chamberlain on a Sunday morning. We set off for the Falklands endorsed by a Parliament recalled for a Saturday-afternoon debate. The faults of the British Parliament are manifold. Delay is not necessarily one of them. Indeed, it is the weapon of the Opposition rather than of the Government. Opposition members play a full part in exploiting the rules of the House in order to delay the passing of legislation which a government wants but which the minority in opposition is determined to expose or change.

The real problem is not that majority government in the House of Commons has too little power to act, as Shaw thought, but that it has too much. To that extent, his criticism of what he called the party system is exactly right: the majority party *will* support its own government in almost any action if the alternative is to bring the opposing party into power. The two main parties in Britain are not analogous to the Republicans and the Democrats in the United States. For one thing, the executive is not separate from the legislature. The occasional uniting of members of Parliament, crossing party lines in order to oppose the executive, is therefore inevitably rarer than in the United States Senate or House of Representatives.

More important, in Britain the parties have much more deeply based ideological differences. At the present time (1990), this is even more starkly obvious. Mrs. Thatcher has introduced an ever-more ideological approach to government, with "radical" policies of the extreme Right. But in any case, and paradoxically, Shaw as a socialist seeking massive change should have supported a smashing of any tentative cross-party consensus. The use of the party system which he so despised would have been the necessary corollary of securing socialist representation in Parliament.

It is not therefore the nature of Parliament which has prevented Labour governments from introducing full-blooded socialism. It is rather a lack of will as they realized the domination of the opposing faction in the organs of public opinion. That, of course, could only have been countered by building up a sufficiently large body of support outside Parliament to create a favorable public opinion. From this arose Shaw's keenness to support the creation of a Labour organization dedicated to socialism, and resolved to secure representation in Parliament, even given his contempt for the working of that organization.

He had, therefore, confused Parliament with democracy, of which it is only a part. His dislike of the part spilled over to a kind of contempt for the workings of democracy itself. He thought that the effectiveness of municipal government could be replicated in Parliament. But Parliament is not simply concerned with detailed practical decisions of whether to build here or to build there. It is concerned with concepts, with choices therefore affecting the nature of society, with ideas, with values. Shaw almost assumed that the coming to power of a government—how he did not explain, but presumably by an election—would settle all that. We could then get on with the simple practical things, presumably, as we did in St. Pancras Vestry. He therefore wrote little about the reform of Parliament; when he did, it was to seek to reshape it into the form of the committee system he had found and practiced as a vestryman: "We need in these islands two or three additional federal legislatures, working on our municipal committee system instead of our Parliamentary Party system." Elsewhere, he argued in support of the plan of the Webbs to replace Parliament by two parliaments, one political and the other social, and he extended their proposition to a number of "separate and specialised authorities." Indeed, the "more we have, the more the escape from the ridiculous One Man One Vote of the Party System to the democratic ideal of One Subject One Vote" (the St. Pancras Vestry again). In the Preface to "*In Good King Charles's Golden Days*" he advocated the coupled vote, which would make it obligatory for each citizen to vote for both a man and a woman, thus ensuring equal representation of the genders in the House of Commons.

Therefore, this is the supreme paradox, that with all Shaw's great and genuine commitment to socialist equality, his willingness to accept the massive and necessary upheaval that would cause, his recognition of the injustice and crippling nature of contemporary capitalism, his amusement that Wells could somehow see in Ford and Rockefeller the creators of the kind of society he had fought and lectured and argued for, his deceptive simplicity of language and wit, his devastating use of paradox upon teasing paradox to make others see his truth—that with all that, he should himself see the effective instrument of change only in the shape of a vestry or a borough council.

How did this happen? It was surely because he mistook the nature of socialism. He saw it as an economic phenomenon, the social ownership of wealth and the production of wealth, and with it equality of income. But the classic socialists, and especially Marx, from whom he learned so much—or, at any rate, by whom he was inspired so much—said that it was about something more. Its final purpose was to maximize individual freedom. Because Shaw forgot that, or failed fully to understand it, he also failed to see the prime importance of political democracy as a crucial and necessary element in socialism. It was a mistake made by many impatient to end the injustices of capital. At the moment of writing, Gorbachev is wrestling with the consequences of that failure in the Soviet

Union. Shaw viewed government as a matter of necessary efficiency. He saw the inefficiency of Parliament. He could not reconcile the two.

Other rich paradoxes come to mind. The Labour party that Shaw helped to bring into existence in order to achieve socialism remains the alternative party of government, and a victory by the Labour party in a general election is the only way by which the firm hold of the Conservatives on power can be broken. It will then be the task of the Labour Government to use the parliamentary system so much despised by Shaw to bring about changes in society of which he might have approved. It may be a more ironically amusing paradox still that a woman prime minister has been one of the most effective in recent years in employing the parliamentary machine to bring about the changes in society she wanted. Shaw may well have disapproved strongly of the moves since 1979 designed to set back the development of the "welfare state" and to make the rich richer and the poor poorer, but the admirer of Joan—and Stalin—might well have had more than a crumb of admiration for a woman prime minister of the quality of Mrs. Thatcher.

Leon H. Hugo

BRITONS, BOERS, AND BLACKS: BERNARD SHAW ON SOUTH AFRICA

Feelings in the Fabian Society about the Anglo-Boer War ran high. The choice was between supporting the British imperialist policy in South Africa as a just and necessary cause and denouncing it as an act of blatant piracy. As the secretary, Edward Pease, recalled with some emotion, "the controversy . . . reached an intensity which those who cannot recollect it will find difficult to believe."[1] Shaw was determined not to stand by while the Society split over the issue, least of all, as he wrote to Pease, while it declared itself on a point of nonsocialist policy.[2] He apparently made up his own mind about the matter and succeeded in making it a point of socialist policy in no time at all. "[A]lmost in favour of the war," Beatrice Webb said of him three weeks after the conflict had broken out, when she was still dithering in great perplexity; other members of the Executive, including Olivier, were "desperately against the war", and Sidney Webb, abandoning his neutral position, was unenthusiastically plumping for the imperialist cause.[3]

As this was the less-than-united stance of the Executive, Shaw appears to have decided to promote the proimperialist point of view on his own initiative, arguing that it would be through capitalist imperialism that the interests of socialism would best be served. His letters to fellow socialists, Fabian and otherwise, suggest a personal rather than an officially sanctioned campaign and give the impression that he took the lead in defining the Fabian attitude, with others on the Executive and in the Society at large gradually falling in behind him. Anyone with the requisite vision and words at his command will find himself in this position, and Shaw used his armory of words to precise and calculated effect. Admonitory, exhortatory, chiding, and cajoling, he often seems rushed and flippant. But a strong sense of conviction pervades his remarks, and his awareness of the historical process gives the flippancy a characteristically oracular ring.

He viewed imperialism with Shavian skepticism. "Imperialism is, like all the other isms, a mere shibboleth," he informed Beatrice Webb, a trifle unnecessarily;[4] but in the circumstances imperialistic rule was the lesser of two evils, far more likely than two independent Boer republics to establish and maintain global civilization at a level where socialism would be able to permeate it. The Transvaal and Free State republics promised the very opposite. Shaw wrote to fellow Fabian Edward Rose when the crisis in the Society was at its height and Boer victories in the field were sending British forces reeling:

> Suppose the Boers lick us, which seems eminently possible at this moment. Well, the inevitable sequel will be the integration of South Africa in a great Afrikander Republican State, into which any recalcitrant colony will be forced by civil war if necessary, like the American Confederates. If this is to be, it will be; but the new state will inevitably become a great centre of capitalism like the United States. . . . The notion that it will be a more humane or just solution . . . seems to me absurd. . . .[5]

Allowing that the historical process is slow, this was a remarkably accurate forecast. The Boers lost the war, but they were victorious in the sense that in 1910, eight years after the Peace of Vereeniging, the two former Boer republics (the Transvaal and the Orange Free State) and the two British colonies (Natal and the Cape) became a union with Dominion status. Britain itself cleared the ground for the formation of Shaw's feared confederation. Since then Afrikaner nationalism has been an increasingly dominant force in South African politics because the Afrikaners outnumber English South Africans by about two to one. The vote of the Uitlander (the usually English-speaking immigrant), the denial of which by the Transvaal president, Paul Kruger, had been an ostensible cause of the war, was secured, but this made no decisive difference to the balance of white power in the country. Everything else that Shaw foresaw has also slowly come about. As British imperialism receded from the subcontinent, Afrikaner nationalism, increasingly ascendant since 1931 when the Statute of Westminster granted full sovereign rights to the country, steadily advanced to fill the power vacuum. It was only a matter of time before Shaw's specific fear, a powerful capitalist "Afrikander Republican State," should be formed, as it was in 1961, outside the British Commonwealth. (That it did not become an even greater confederation is due entirely to the whims of history: in 1922 Southern Rhodesia [Zimbabwe] voted against incorporation in the union, largely because of fears of Afrikaner domination; and German South West Africa [Namibia], which became a mandated territory administered by the union during the 1914–18 war and increasingly a fifth province of the union since then, has only recently [March 1990] become an independent state.) Capitalism, tempered by nationalization (of roads, transport, hospitals, and other services), has been the economic creed firmly endorsed by English commercial interests since union, while the ban on Communism, imposed in 1950, was lifted only in 1990. If the economic muscle of this southern African "confederation" is a far cry from that of the United States, it is considerable by African standards, and its military muscle—Shaw's other fear—makes it the dominant power of sub-Saharan Africa, if not of the whole continent.

The question whether continued British imperialism would have made any difference to the history of the region (assuming that it would have wished or been able to contain Afrikaner nationalism for a further half-century), and specifically whether it would have led eventually to the realization of a Socialist bloc, is perhaps not as imponderable as such questions usually are. The history of postimperial countries north of the Limpopo River—Zimbabwe, Tanzania, Zambia, and others—shows imperial capitalism to have been superseded by Marxism to an extent that would probably have pleased Shaw, although he may well have deplored the neglect in these countries of the Fabian principles of gradualism and efficiency. Given that full adult suffrage would have been established before a final British withdrawal from South Africa, a similarly Marxist regime could conceivably have developed in that country. It may do so yet.

As for imperialism proving a "more just or humane solution," Shaw spelled out the obverse on more than one occasion. Writing to G. F. McCleary, a fellow Fabian, on "war as wasteful, demoralising, unnecessary, and ludicrously and sordidly inglorious in its reality," he makes clear why, refusing to distinguish between fallacious "rights" and "wrongs," he cannot be pro-Boer: ". . . I dont believe anything that the Boer believes, and dont believe that his pet institutions can ever produce anything but sordid misery for the mass of mankind. . . ."[6] In a letter to the radical non-Fabian H. M. Hyndman, he goes further:

> Now Kruger is more than a moralist: he is a prophet of Jehovah, who is morality deified. The tide in the affairs of men came to Kruger after the [Jameson] Raid, when he had a respite sufficient to found his Republic to all eternity by playing the statesman. But he had no statesmanship. He saw that the Outlander was morally the inferior of the Boer. He proceeded to assert the supremacy of the moral man, and to arm himself for its defence by military force. To this day he has no word to say except that God, who implanted that instinct in him, will make it victorious in battle.

> ... I perceive that Jehovah and Mammon must fight it out.
> And as Mammon can be developed into a Socialist power in pro-
> portion as men become Socialistically minded, whereas Jehovah
> makes any such change of mind impossible, and stands for the
> false categories of moral good and evil in nature, and conse-
> quently for implacable war, punishment, enmity, aggression &
> repression between men, my sympathies are with Mammon, his
> instinctive greed for gold & diamonds being far less dangerous
> than the reason and virtue which, on the moralist system, makes
> Man, as Mephistopheles says, beastlier than any beast. Jehovah is
> mighty; for he has his chain on men's minds.[7]

Not even Shaw, for all his frequently uncanny vision, could have known
that this characterization of Kruger and his intransigent theology would
hold true for Afrikaner Calvinist nationalism a half century later; nor
could he have foretold the tragic destiny this intransigence has forced on
the country—although, as we shall see, he came close to observing this in
the 1930s.

Shaw repeated similar arguments in a rather frantic and disputatious
article in the *Clarion* a month after writing to Hyndman. His main thrust
here was that the war had caused socialists to desert the cause and rally
behind either the Conservatives or the Liberals. He insisted that he had
remained a true socialist and that his support of the war was prompted,
not by capitalist beliefs, but by adherence to socialist principles.[8] The
Clarion's columnist on contemporary affairs, "The Whatnot," responded
with a heavily sarcastic comment on Shaw's long-winded way of talking
"Absolute Nonsense."[9] There were also rebuttals by three other-thinking
socialists, who were at one in sympathizing with Kruger and in denouncing British imperialism and Shaw. "Socialists have ceased to take Mr
Shaw seriously," Walter Crane announced, and accused him of suffering
an attack of the " 'New Imperialism'—which seems going round like
measles." A. E. Fletcher asked whether a "more muddled product of the
human brain had ever sent [him] wondering" and said that if Shaw's
socialism could approve of the "brigandage" being committed in South
Africa by British imperialism, "so much the worse for his Socialism."
Frank Colebrook suggested that the article was a Shavian joke but agreed
to play along with Shaw to show him up for his droll wrongheadedness.[10]

Shaw's answer, a considerably more balanced, temperate, and therefore more trenchant piece of writing, appeared in the same paper three
weeks later:

> The three writers have done their best; and no man can do more.
> But ... they have stated no case except the Liberal case. ... Mr

Fletcher seems to think that the first backwoodsman who shoots a native, fells a tree, and stakes out a claim above the gold, has an eternal right, he and his heirs for ever, to hold it against all the world and enjoy the lion's share of the gold that other men dig from it. That is good private property doctrine, but it is not Socialist doctrine—quite the reverse. . . . Our policy is clearly one of extension, integration, organisation, consolidation, "parliament of man and federation of the world."[11]

There was, of course, no persuading those who did not wish to be persuaded, so Shaw and the Fabians went their way while other socialists went theirs. There was also no end to criticism of Shavian-Fabian policy. Chesterton had a go at sundry "Fabian Futilities" a few months later when trying to draw out Sidney Webb on the question of socialism's "moral force." Shaw replied that the proper moral force behind socialism was "the economic force which expresses itself in personal and political morality in an intense hatred of social waste and impatience of social incapacity." To him the "most disgraceful fact" of the Anglo-Boer War, what made him "feel savage," was that "we have killed our own men by thousands because we had not the energy and capacity enough to boil or distil their drinking water."[12]

The foregoing represents Shaw's letter and newspaper campaign before the publication of *Fabianism and the Empire* in October 1900. A good deal of what he said to fellow Fabians and to the public at large filtered down into the pamphlet, so much of it, in fact, that it is possible to see the letters and the articles as the seedbed of the pamphlet—a working out in draft of what would finally become official Fabian policy as "edited" by Shaw.

This is no more apparent in *Fabianism and the Empire* than in the statement in favor of capitalist imperialism, which offered a better opportunity than the Boer republics for the growth of socialism. Shavian, not Fabian, thinking produced this paradox. Indeed, that such literal-minded people as the Webbs, Pease, and other members of the Executive should have settled on this line of argument provides yet another indication, one is tempted to believe, that it was Shaw's powers of persuasion in committee (and in his letters) that carried the day.

The text of *Fabianism and the Empire* contains several echoes from the letters and the *Clarion* articles. There is this: "if we were beaten, the victorious Boers would be forced, whether they desired it or not, to make their work sure by uniting South Africa in an independent Afrikander Federation."[13] And this:

the fact remains that a Great Power . . . must govern in the interests of civilization as a whole; and it is not to those interests that such mighty forces as gold-fields, and the formidable armaments that can be built upon them, should be wielded irresponsibly by small communities of frontiersmen.[14]

Fabianism and the Empire was given out as having been "edited" by Shaw; it was to be seen therefore as a collective product expressing collective Fabian opinion. "Civilization and the Soldier," which appeared three months later in the January 1901 issue of the *Humane Review*, was palpably Shaw's and Shaw's alone. It is a "Shavianism and the Empire" in which he foresees the decline of the empire and Britain as a world power unless—so the future author of *Man and Superman* asserts—it radically alters its political thinking. In *Fabianism and the Empire* he made a good deal of the civilizing influence an enlightened imperial policy could bring to bear on the lesser developed regions of the world. In "Civilization and the Soldier" he makes a good deal of the singularly uncivilized policy being pursued in various outposts of empire, South Africa in particular, by the soldier (the agent of empire), whose job it is to kill and destroy. Discussing the extent to which a general will go to avoid defeat, ignoring "civil statesmanship," committing "any atrocity," Shaw discusses the British commander-in-chief in South Africa, Lord Roberts:

> this clever, shrewd, rather kindly old soldier, our idolised "Bobs," when left in an enemy's country dependent on a flimsy railway line of communication as long as from Paris to St Petersburg, loses every feeling except dread of having that line broken, and orders that whenever it is attacked, the farmhouses for miles round shall be solemnly burnt.
>
> There are two ways of regarding this step. It is clear to the non-military mind that to burn a Boer militiaman's farm when you have failed to shoot him is to convert him into a desperado with nothing to lose and an unpardonable injury to avenge. It is to give your civilian enemy the cardinal soldierly qualification of homelessness. It is to ruin the country you have just declared part of the Empire. It is to provoke the one real danger to the British Empire in the South African situation: the danger of a general rising of the Cape Dutch under the influence of a wave of indignation. It is to force the Home Government, which you have just saved by your victories, to capitulate at the first brush with the Opposition. . . . That is the general human point of view.
>
> But from the military point of view, it is simply war reduced by the brute force of facts from the visions of Jingo romance to its own real essence, which is, destruction of the enemy.[15]

Shaw characteristically adds a comment from the theatrical point of view:

> We still, however, retain our sense of the sacredness of a lady's bedroom. When we burn a farm, and the lady of the house asks where she is to sleep, we convey her to the nearest town and take rooms for her at a hotel. And so our melodrama, after all our expenditure in red fire and real blood, ends as comic opera.[16]

He did not waste time on the personalities involved in the conflict, although he did occasionally allow himself a sweepingly dismissive, usually caustic, comment. His observations on Kruger and Roberts have been noted. Joseph Chamberlain, the colonial secretary, was "not so black as he is painted,"[17] no doubt because of the relief work he had done among the poor in Birmingham. Cecil Rhodes, usually seen as the master planner of British capitalist imperialism in Africa, was "an Afrikander out-and-out" who had tried to foment an insurrection in the goldfields and had proved himself only a degree less stupid than his henchman in the enterprise, Leander Starr Jameson.[18] Alfred Milner, Chamberlain's high commissioner in South Africa, to many South Africans the personification of British perfidy, merits one contemptuous comment which must surely have raised a sarcastic cheer from all pro-Krugerites: "Sir Alfred Milner is, I think, the most representative Englishman now living; and Sir Alfred Milner reminds me of nothing but the most hopeless type of schoolmaster."[19] (Beatrice Webb, on the other hand, was not able to separate the issue from the personalities, Chamberlain's in particular. He, after all, was the man who had declined to marry her. She saw Kruger's republic as an anachronism ["that remnant of seventeenth-century puritanism"] but could not get over the "unsavoury . . . doings of our own people in the Transvaal—an underbred business." She was "mortified" that she could not think well of Chamberlain, whose methods, she wrote, were "vulgar and tricky.")[20]

Shaw's comments on the Anglo-Boer War are interesting as much for what he did not say as for what he said. He did not make any public statement about the infamous concentration camps, started by Roberts and extended by Kitchener. He would certainly have known about them. Nearly forty years later, writing to Nancy Astor about Labour policy regarding Hitler, he warned that there should be no mention of concentration camps "because it was we who invented them"[21]—an unfortunate remark in the circumstances. The concentration camps in South Africa were tent "cities" on the open veld into which Boer women and children were herded after their farms had been razed and where nearly 28,000 died because of the unsanitary conditions. Shaw would have seen all this as a logical development of Roberts's scorched-earth policy—of the soldier's carrying out his brief to defeat the enemy while neglecting the most elementary demands of "civil statesmanship."

Nor did Shaw say much about the native population among whom this ostensibly "white man's war" was waged. He mentions the blacks once in passing in a letter to George Samuel: "Now let us face the facts. Two hordes of predatory animals are fighting, after their manner, for the possession of South Africa, where neither of them has, or ever had, any business to be from the abstractly moral, the virtuously indignant Radical, or (probably) the native point of view."[22] The blacks come in for similarly parenthetical treatment in *Fabianism and the Empire*, where, as Patricia Pugh points out, they would not have been mentioned at all but for Wallas's criticism of the draft text.[23] The facts that both sides, particularly the British, used the blacks in the war as menials and combatants, that Kitchener interned 116,000 of them in sixty-six "native" concentration camps where 15,000 died, and that their political aspirations were ignored at the Peace of Vereeniging in 1902—that, in short, the blacks were exploited and suffered—simply did not count. To the policymakers, to the Fabians, to every colonial power of the time, they were, in what has become the most notorious line Kipling ever penned, "lesser breeds without the Law." The provision of a just but unambiguously authoritarian administration—the "white man's burden"—was due them, but nothing else.

Thirty years were to pass before Shaw again turned his eyes toward South Africa. This was in 1932 and 1935, when he and Charlotte visited the country. General J. B. M. Hertzog, a former Boer commander, founder of the National party, and prime minister in 1932, was informed of Shaw's pending visit and wrote him a courteous, if slightly anxious, letter:

> I have been informed by our High Commissioner in London, Mr F. C. Watson, that out of consideration for me and the many worries which presumably are troubling me, or should trouble me, you have decided not to do anything that will disturb the peace with me!—I hope, however, you will allow me to extend to you and Mrs Shaw a very hearty welcome to South Africa, and to wish you a very pleasant stay in our midst. If at any time I can do anything which can be of any assistance to you or to Mrs Shaw, it will be a pleasure to do so.[24]

Shaw obligingly did nothing to disturb the peace, and he and Hertzog, who entertained Charlotte and Shaw at a reception at his official residence, got on remarkably well, probably because they agreed that South Africa should not go off the gold standard, a red-hot issue of those depression years.[25]

The political situation at the time was fluid. Imperialism had lapsed into history, and Afrikaner nationalist aspirations, although steadily ascendant through the 1920s, were being held in squabbling check by strong postimperial loyalties to the British Crown. The political aspirations of the "black proletariat"—as Shaw referred to the blacks—were, like those of Afrikaner nationalists, not a critical question. This is not to say they were of no account. Black political awareness was in its infancy, but the groundswell of discontent was evident to anyone who cared to pay attention to the protests of such groups as the African National Congress. The white parliaments of the 1930s admitted this by denying it; that is, by passing legislation that entrenched racial segregation and anticipated apartheid twenty-five years before it became declared government policy. Shaw would observe all this during his two visits to the country.

He had the blacks very much in mind when he landed at Cape Town for his first visit. His initial question, when met on board ship by members of the Cape Town Fabian Society, was whether blacks had trade unions, and in his first interview he spoke about them again.[26] The effect the Great Depression was having on unemployed labor troubled him. It created "an appalling problem. . . . When you have 'poor whites' up against black men with a lower standard of living, what can you do with them [i.e., the blacks]? Simply drop them in the water?" (At the end of his visit, having seen some "poor whites" at close quarters in Knysna, he suggested that they rather than the blacks should be "dropped in the water.")[27] Later in the interview, in the context of Christianizing the blacks, he said, "We do not know that the next civilization may not be a black civilization. There is a danger in the natives taking their Christianity with intense seriousness, because they will find out their teachers only profess to be Christians. The best thing would be to develop their intelligence and make them sceptics." He would develop this theme a few weeks later in *The Adventures of the Black Girl in Her Search for God*.

What he saw of the customary division of the races along "master-servant" lines and the unhealed breach between English and Afrikaners disturbed him. He wrote to Emery Walker,

> This place is full of sunshine, long days, and darkies to do all the work. The gardens and old Dutch Peter de Hooghe interiors are enchanting; but the social problems—poor whites competing for unskilled labor jobs with a black proletariat which can live on next

to nothing, with no pensions nor unemployment insurance, and
race war between Dutch and English—are insoluble. . . .[28]

He broadcast a message to South Africa on the eve of his departure
from Cape Town, reverting to an argument he had used thirty years
before, in 1902, when the question whether women should influence
their menfolk to stop war had briefly engaged his attention. Then he had
given the *Free Lance* a letter on the subject[29] and had written to Clement
Scott, "The truth is that a slave State is always ruled by those who can get
round the masters; that is, by the more cunning of the slaves themselves. . . . No fascinating woman ever wants to emancipate her sex: her
object is to gather power into the hands of Man, because she knows that
she can govern him."[30] This was the paradox he developed as the main
theme of his broadcast address, which was that he had found South
Africa to be a "Slave State, . . . and that, too, the very worst sort of Slave
State," where the slaves manipulate their masters, making them incapable of doing anything themselves, reducing them to mental as well as
bodily dependence on the slaves. There was only one option to the
"slave-master"—dedication to "the higher work," by means of which he
would justify his status and earn the gratitude and admiration of his
"slave." It was either this or the collapse of the system. "If white civilization breaks down through idleness and loafing based on slavery . . . then,
as likely as not, the next civilization will be a negro civilization."[31]

Shaw's thinking is in transition here. There is still some adherence to
the old Fabian (and imperial) notion of the responsibilities of white
"civilization" to black "non-civilization"—acceptance of the system there-
for, with the proviso that white "civilization" had to justify its superiority
to survive. At the same time, there is again the strong suggestion that
black "civilization" was a possible, a probable, and a by no means inferior
alternative. When Shaw created his Black Girl a few weeks later in
Knysna after the motor accident that confined Charlotte to her bed, he
committed himself to this course and conceived a twentieth-century "noble savage" pursuing her own road to "salvation." By Shavian definition
this means full consciousness of self, which implies awareness of the
political self, which implies in turn a commitment to realizing a new
"civilization." This would be a black-Shavian "civilization," bearing in
mind that the allegory ends in a Voltairean garden with the Black Girl
married to a redhaired Irishman. That she and her redhead produce a
number of "charmingly coffee-coloured picaninnies" is a clear indication
of the trend of Shaw's thinking.

The Black Girl's confrontation with the Caravan of the Curious during
her quest has Shaw rejecting the colonial myth of white supremacy and
the benefits this was supposed to confer on subject races. The ethnologist

of the expedition repeats Shaw's theme that the next civilization will be black: "The white man is played out. He knows it, too, and is committing suicide as fast as he can." The Black Girl endorses this when she repudiates white colonial exploitation backed by guns and the corrupting capitalist ethic that underpinned it:

> But nothing will satisfy your greed. You work generations of us to death until you have each of you more than a hundred of us could eat or spend; and yet you go on forcing us to work harder and harder and longer and longer for less and less food and clothing. You do not know what enough means for yourselves, or less than enough for us. . . . This must be because you serve false gods. You are heathens and savages. You know neither how to live nor let others live. When I find God I shall have the strength of mind to destroy you and to teach my people not to destroy themselves.[32]

In rejecting imperialism the Black Girl asserts black consciousness and black power, which are clichés of African politics today. She is, however, declaring herself a full thirty years before London, Paris, and Brussels recognized the winds of change which were blowing through Africa and more than sixty years before Pretoria began to wilt under the blasts of bitterness and anger. Shaw's political vision was like his plays—years ahead of public comprehension, and therefore unpopular and frightening. White South Africa breathed more easily when he left.

Shaw and Charlotte returned in 1935 and spent three quiet weeks in Durban. He was in need of a rest and asked to be spared public appearances, but, being Shaw, he was up and about a good deal. He made it his business to meet A. W. C. Champion, a prominent black activist of the 1930s and 1940s, calling on him at the African Workers' Club because Champion, the racial laws being what they were, could not call on him at his hotel. He attended a public meeting to listen to Edward Roux, a prominent member of the South African Communist party, and, on another occasion, "discussed the Grey Shirt movement with its Natal leader."[33] He met members of the Zulu people for the first time and was greatly impressed by them; he must have seen them as more than justifying his 1932 forecast about a black civilization.

The Great Depression had forced Hertzog and Smuts to form a coalition government. This did not mean parliamentary accord, and the "native" legislation then being debated aroused the usual acrimony. Shaw kept silent, but could only have been disturbed by what, when the bills were passed by a huge majority in 1936, amounted to an endorsement of white supremacy. He would also have read about the right-wing splinter group led by D. F. Malan, the future "prophet" of apartheid, whose creed was an intensified Afrikaner nationalism. During the Anglo-Boer War Shaw had foretold the demise of Krugerism with the emergence of such enlightened Afrikaners as Cronwright Schreiner and others, but Krugerism, he must have realized when in South Africa in the 1930s, was far from played out. All he allowed himself in public, however, was a mild remark that it "savoured of impertinence" for a white parliament to organize the black majority within a specific legislative system[34] and a reminder that he had written *The Adventures of the Black Girl* for "the advantage of the Boer."[35]

Mussolini was about to embark on his Abyssinian adventure at the time. Shaw prepared a short statement, never used, on the implications of this belated incursion into colonial expansion. It was, he said, time for Africa, by which he meant white as well as black Africa, to rally to the cry of "Africa for the Africans" and—here Shaw gives clear evidence, if any was still needed, of his rejection of imperialism—"turn out the greedy dogs of Europe."[36] Once again he was anticipating a call that swept across the forests and savannas of the continent a quarter century later. He repeated these views during his last interview before embarking and, turning to South African affairs, criticized the heirs of Krugerism, whose continuing reliance on the Bible and tendency to "keep running away from civilization" made them as little able to manage a modern state as Kruger had been. Discussing white-black relations, he recommended the abolition of legislative barriers between the races and of the vote:

> If the native were more intelligent he would see that it was no good fighting for the vote. He would be more concerned in seeing that the white vote should go.
>
> If it takes you thirty years to do what could be done in thirty minutes, you may find yourselves in the position one day of having to do in thirty minutes what you should have done in thirty years. And that will entail a lot of bloodshed and cutting of throats. . . .
>
> Yes, I can see you people in a pretty mess before you get everything cleared up.[37]

One would have thought this prophecy, perilously close to fulfillment today, sufficient valediction and warning to a country which had disturbed him profoundly. But it was not like Shaw to leave matters unresolved. He had first thought, when writing to Emery Walker, that the problems were "insoluble" but then suggested a solution in *The Adventures of the Black Girl*. During this last interview he put it that racial fusion was a way out of the dilemma. Back in London a few weeks later, he declared himself more fully on this theme in a self-drafted interview in the *Daily Telegraph:*

MARRIAGES OF WHITE AND BLACK
Startling Plan by Mr Shaw

Means of Peopling South Africa
"Too Much Sun for Light Skins"

Mr Bernard Shaw has returned home from South Africa an advocate of inter-marriage between the white and black inhabitants.

By this means, he suggests, the white population of South Africa can solve the vital problem on which, in his view, its very existence depends. . . .

He has come back tremendously impressed by the extraordinary pleasantness of the climate. But it is the wonderful sunshine which is creating the danger.

CAN WHITES SURVIVE?

"The question," he said, "is beginning to arise whether white people can survive in these places. I do not mean that you die of the climate—you don't.

"The question is whether your descendants will breed. . . . South Africa does not fill up. It is not a question of birth control, because many people there are desirous to have children but they do not have them.

"I suppose it may be there is too much sunshine for people with white skins. The probable remedy for them is to darken their skins.

"This means, in South Africa, by marrying Bantus."

"Would not such an idea be highly repugnant to white people?" I asked.

"Well," replied Mr Shaw, "there are a great many half-breeds. . . .

"In South Africa the mixture of the two colours may provide the solution to the problem. It is not a question of black and white. In the first place there is no such thing as a white man on the face of the earth: the Chinese call us the pinks, very properly.

"The Zulus are a markedly superior type of person, and all attempts to keep them in an inferior position seem to break down before the fact that they are not inferior. Certainly when you see them working you wish you could see British workmen working that way."

Mr Shaw suggested that the problem was not confined to South Africa, but extended to a very large part of the African continent.

"People," he said, "are speaking glibly now about giving the Germans back their colonies. There is Abyssinia on which Musso-lini is thinking of laying his hand.

"You may parcel the country out among the European powers, but at the back of it one day Africa will say, 'None of you will have it.' Africans, whether Afrikander, black, white or anything else, will see that Africa belongs to the Africans and not to so many competing European powers.

"There may be mixture of blood, and so on, but the native has a good deal of capacity: in the long run it may be seen that he has the capacity to live in Africa and the others have not."[38]

Typically, Shaw gives his solution to the problem a basis in natural history. Genetics now tells us that his premise—that the climate was inimical to the natural growth of the white population—was false; he should rather have given the theory to a member of the Caravan of the Curious in *The Adventures of the Black Girl* as an example of the balminess of European scientific thinking. But genetics was scarcely a developed science in those days and one may forgive him his lapse, particularly if— as the *Daily Telegraph* suggested in its third leader the next day—Shaw's "purpose was rather to provoke discussion than be practical."[39] The interview provoked not so much discussion as violent protest, almost entirely by South Africans living in London, who wrote that to "South Africans pride in blood purity [was] paramount," that the idea of inter-marriage was as "repugnant" to blacks as to whites, and that "the native mind" was "a few thousand years behind the European in develop-ment."[40] The editorial response, firmly dismissing the idea of racial fu-sion, invoked "scientific realism" as insisting upon the necessity of "keep-ing up the white population." It asserted that the future development of the country depended on the energy of the whites, pointed to the United States, where the tendency was to more rigid segregation of the races, and, in sum, sketched an exemplary picture of racial attitudes of the day. When Shaw's interview was reported in South Africa, his stock fell to zero.

As usual, Shaw could see a good deal farther than his contemporaries. Having rejected imperialism and foreseeing the future conflict between Afrikaner nationalism and black nationalism, he came to the conclusion that reconciliation in interbreeding was the only possible solution. He was saying, in his way, "Make love, not war." Time, which is patient, has not yet tested his predictions to the full or put his solution to the proof. As South Africa moves into the 1990s, the options—war or love—seem evenly divided.

Yet, even as this article was being written, changes, as far-reaching as they were unexpected, began to be made. A new president of the Republic, F. W. de Klerk, instituted a series of reforms with the ultimate object of bringing the system of apartheid to an end. At the beginning, the ban on the African National Congress was lifted, and the long-imprisoned Nelson Mandela was released. It is too early to make definite pronouncements, but it is possible to say that, as Shaw's forecasts about the future of the country in his letter of 14 December 1899 proved remarkably accurate, so, too, his thoughts on the possibility of an ultimately interracial community may turn out to have been not very wide of the mark.

Notes

My thanks are due to Burridge Spies, Professor of History, for casting his expert eye over this text and for his helpful suggestions.

1. Edward R. Pease, *The History of the Fabian Society* (London: Cass, 1963), p. 135.

2. 30 October 1899. *Collected Letters, 1898–1910*, ed. Dan H. Laurence (London: Max Reinhardt, 1972), p. 115.

3. *The Diary of Beatrice Webb*, vol. 2, *1892–1905: "All the Good Things of Life,"* ed. Norman and Jeanne MacKenzie (London: Virago, in association with the London School of Economics and Political Science, 1983), pp. 164–69.

4. 30 July 1901. *Collected Letters, 1898–1910*, p. 234.

5. 14 December 1899. *Collected Letters, 1898–1910*, p. 119. Shaw wrote this letter in the middle of the British "Black Week," when they lost three-thousand men killed, wounded, or taken prisoner, and when four generals in four separate major engagements distinguished themselves by their incompetence in the face of a grimly determined enemy. The Boers failed to follow up their victories, and the British, hurriedly changing their high command and sending reinforcements to South Africa, were soon able to wrest the initiative from them. Shaw's fear that the Boers, if victorious, would form a confederation like that of the United States (outside the empire) is remarkably similar to that of the colonial secretary, Joseph Chamberlain, who preferred to envisage another Canada (inside the empire).

6. 24 May 1900. *Collected Letters, 1898–1910*, p. 169.

7. 28 April 1900. Ibid., pp. 161–62.

8. *Clarion* (London), 26 May 1900, 161: 5–6; 162: 1–2.

9. Ibid., 2 June 1900.

10. Ibid., 9 June 1900, 177: 4–6; 178: 1.

11. Ibid., 30 June 1900, 201: 5–6.

12. *Daily News* (London), 7 October 1901, 4: 5. Sixteen thousand British soldiers died of

disease during the war, many more than were killed in action. Shaw had more than ample cause for feeling "savage."

13. *Fabianism and the Empire: A Manifesto by the Fabian Society*, ed. Bernard Shaw (London: Grant Richards, 1900), p. 27.

14. Ibid., p. 23.

15. "Civilization and the Soldier," *Humane Review* (London) 1 (January 1901), 308; reprinted in *SHAW* 9 (University Park: Penn State University Press, 1989), 99–112.

16. Ibid., p. 311. Shaw, usually so skeptical, and highly critical of the censorship exercised by the War Office at the time, was taking this palliating snippet of misinformation in too great trust. No "lady of the house" was ever taken to "the nearest hotel." She and her children were allowed to gather their personal belongings and were then bundled off to the nearest concentration camp.

17. In a letter to George Samuel, c. 26–30 December 1899. *Collected Letters, 1898–1910*, p. 125

18. Ibid., p. 124.

19. "Civilization and the Soldier," p. 313; reprinted in *SHAW* 9 (University Park: Penn State University Press, 1989), 99–112.

20. *The Diary of Beatrice Webb, 1892–1925*, pp. 164–65.

21. *Collected Letters, 1926–1950*, ed. Dan H. Laurence (London: Max Reinhardt, 1988), p. 540.

22. c. 23–24 December 1899. *Collected Letters, 1898–1910*, p. 122.

23. Patricia Pugh, *Educate, Agitate, Organize: 100 Years of Fabian Socialism* (London: Methuen, 1984), pp. 79–80. The relevant passage in *Fabianism and the Empire* (pp. 15–16) is "We are no longer a Commonwealth of white men and baptised Christians: the vast majority of our fellow-subjects are black, brown, or yellow. . . . We rule these vast areas and populations by a bureaucracy as undemocratic as that of Russia. And if we substituted for that bureaucracy local self-government by white traders, we should get black slavery, and, in some places, frank black extermination, as we have had in the 'black blocks' of Australia. As for parliamentary institutions for black races, that dream has been disposed of by the American experiments after the Civil War."

24. Bernard Shaw Papers, Add. Ms. 50520, British Library.

25. The leader of the Opposition, General Smuts, was strenuously preaching "off gold." When he and Shaw met, Shaw told him that this would be economic suicide. Smuts was not impressed.

26. *Cape Times* (Cape Town), 12 January 1932, 9: 1–2.

27. *Cape Argus* (Cape Town), 18 March 1932, 11: 8. Shaw's actual words on this occasion were "What you want to do is shoot your poor whites—every one of them. You should also shoot many of your rich whites."

28. 5 January 1932. *Collected Letters, 1926–1950*, p. 274.

29. *Free Lance* (London) 3 (25 January 1902), 429.

30. January 1902. *Collected Letters, 1898–1910*, p. 260.

31. The full text appeared in the *Cape Times* (Cape Town), 8 February 1932, 9: 1–2; 10: 2–3. It was reprinted in the *Shavian* (London), no. 16, October 1959. Lengthy excerpts were reprinted in my "Upset in a Sun-Trap: Shaw in South Africa," *SHAW: The Annual of Bernard Shaw Studies*, vol. 5, ed. Rodelle Weintraub (University Park and London: Penn State University Press, 1985), 159–61.

32. *The Black Girl in Search of God and Some Lesser Tales* (London: Constable, 1934; repr. 1954), pp. 52–55.

33. *Natal Witness* (Pietermaritzburg), 24 May 1935, 6: 6–7. Champion was one of the leaders of the (nonwhite) Industrial and Commercial Workers' Union, later Natal President of the A.N.C. The Communist party of South Africa, although highly vocal in the

1920s and 1930s, was never more than a fringe group: its main support would have come from the blacks, who were, however, denied political rights. It was declared an "illegal organisation" in 1950. The Grey Shirts were a short-lived fascistic, anti-Semitic group of the 1930s. Shaw was obviously testing the restless political waters at several points.

34. *Natal Witness*, 10 May 1935, 1: 6; 9: 6

35. *Cape Argus* (Cape Town), 24 May 1935, 14: 3.

36. Bernard Shaw Papers, Add. Ms. 50698, British Library.

37. *Cape Times*, 25 May 1935, 12: 6.

38. *Daily Telegraph* (London), 11 June 1935, 11: 7.

39. Ibid., 12 June 1935, 14: 3.

40. Ibid., 12–15 June 1935.

Patricia Pugh

BERNARD SHAW, IMPERIALIST

Toward the end of the Naughty Nineties, when Britain was passing through its most acquisitive, pugnacious, and exhibitionist stage, Bernard Shaw, sickened by jingoism, began analyzing imperialism and concomitant militarism. This article will place his study in the context of contemporary thought, identify the incidents that moved him to develop his analysis, and describe the different means he used to elucidate his conclusions and make people think about them.

The Fabian Society, Shaw's most amenable political platform, was founded in 1884, the same year as the opening of the Conference of Berlin that agreed to divide Africa among the Great Powers. Although public interest in imperial affairs had been awakened by controversy over the Jameson Raid, Queen Victoria's diamond jubilee glorification of empire, the Colonial Conference's discussion of closer collaboration among the colonies of white settlement, and the deterioration in relations with Germany and France over Africa, the Society paid little attention. It regarded the ideal commonwealth as a fable by William Morris until almost the end of the century. This was rather strange, since two of its earliest recruits and outstanding personalities, Sydney Olivier and Sidney Webb, were resident clerks at the Colonial Office. The three friends—Shaw, Webb, and Olivier—instead emphasized the Fabians' prime purpose of helping to regenerate society by defining the principles of socialism, collecting statistics for use in lectures and tracts, putting their socialist theories into practice in local and national government and in industry, and converting middle-class London and the industrial provinces to their own version of socialism.[1] In *Fabian Essays in Socialism*, William Clarke alone dealt with the classic socialist thesis that recent industrial development had increased greed, which had contributed to imperial expansion and exploitation of Africa and Asia, which in turn had led to wars between the Great Powers, the scramble for Africa, and the dispute with China over trading rights.[2]

When war with the Boers became inevitable, Olivier and Shaw realized that if Fabians confined themselves to studies and statements on Webb's beloved "gas and water" socialism, the Society would cease to be regarded as a political think tank.[3] Foreign affairs affected everyone when they curbed domestic development and trade. Acccordingly, the two convinced Webb that the Fabian autumn lecture courses for 1898 and 1899 should be on the relevance of socialism to racial problems, militarism, foreign trade and protection, and all aspects of "Imperial England."[4] Such confusion about empire arose within the Society from the outbreak of the Boer War in October 1899 that a larger number of members than ever before met in Clifford's Inn the following February to hear Shaw speak for the first time on the ethics of empire.[5]

Lord Rosebery had called imperialism a "greater pride in Empire . . . a larger patriotism." For years some philosophers and academics had tried to define it as a political theory embodying a moral code. Jeremy Bentham preached that, although colonies bestowed international influence upon a European power, they were an economic burden best relinquished.[6] Professor J. R. Seeley, the Imperial Federationist, taught his Cambridge undergraduates that, contrary to politicians' rhetoric, empty sectors of the globe were not necessarily worthless impedimenta but could become an actual extension of the occupying state, providing land for the landless and wealth for the impecunious. Finding no inherent reason for colonies to seek independence, he declared that either England would be ruined if it lost its overseas territories or, within fifty years, it would be destroyed by the United States and Russia if it failed to balance their increasing power by a strong federation of colonies.[7] Bentham and Seeley agreed, however, that in India Her Majesty's Government had incurred a moral responsibility to continue British rule. The philosopher Herbert Spencer, friend and mentor of Beatrice Webb, defined this as the indissoluble interdependence of the guardian and the captive.

J. A. Hobson, who gave courses at the London School of Economics (founded by the Webbs to teach political science), first propagated his theory of underconsumption as the root cause of unemployment in one of the Fabian lectures. It forced him to investigate imperial relations, but he did not become the Independent Labour party's guru until after the editor of the *Manchester Guardian* sent him to South Africa to report on the dispute that led to the Boer War. His best-known work, *Imperialism,* was not published until after Shaw brought forth *Fabianism and the Empire* as the Society's manifesto for the 1900 general election.[8] Although they agreed on some points, their attitudes toward empire differed. To this divergence in attitude can be traced the division within the Labour movement between those in the I.L.P. who wished to cleanse themselves abruptly of all taint of imperialism and those Labour party members who accepted the moral responsibility of empire and supported controlled devolution of power as colonies attained certain stages of development.

Rank-and-file socialists were also troubled by the dichotomy between free trade and protection. Their profession of the brotherhood of mankind implied that all people everywhere were entitled to sell their products in a free market, while their belief in workers' solidarity entailed collective action to protect their own jobs and rates of pay by preventing foreign imports produced by sweated labor from undercutting British goods. When the press began inciting public indignation against General Hertzog and the Boers for daring to defy the British mandate in South Africa, socialists readily shelved this problem (complicated by favored-nation and colonial-preference agreements) and made the simpler choice between resisting or succumbing to the emotional stimulus of war fever. This was the point at which Bernard Shaw entered the debate.

As an Irishman he had been born into an awareness of imperial rule. This began to find expression in his early plays, but it took an ideological eruption within the Fabian Society to concentrate his mind on the subject. In October 1899, disagreement arose within its Executive Committee about whether to comply with a member's urgent request to submit this motion to a meeting:

> That this meeting expresses its deep indignation at the success of the infamous conspiracy against the independence of the Transvaal, which has resulted in the present wanton and unjustifiable war, tenders its heartiest sympathies to the gallant people whose sole crime is that they love too well their liberty and independence, and trusts that it may yet be possible to secure a cessation of the hostilities while leaving the Boers in possession of liberties guaranteed them by the 1884 convention.[9]

Shaw's group, the "Old Gang," was reluctant to do this because if the motion were approved the Society would have to publish a policy statement, and that would contravene the tradition that it comprised a broad church able to accommodate a wide range of views about any particular subject.[10] After long, heated discussion, they prevailed upon the Executive Committee, by a narrow margin, to advise members to reject the plea of urgency for the motion and thereby provide a month's cooling-off period before it was submitted in the normal manner. The members disregarded this advice and insisted on debating the motion at great length. After the majority had withdrawn from the battle, exhausted by the heat and emotion in the hall, the remnant voted 26 to 19 against the motion.

No one was content to let the matter rest there. While the Executive dithered, the rank and file became more agitated. A rift developed between those who deplored war in any circumstances (and especially between different sections of the empire) and those who thought that if the ambitions of the Boers were not nipped in the bud worse would ensue, and the British Empire would disintegrate as some journalists predicted. Even the "Old Gang" held divergent views. Sydney Olivier, who supported Ramsay MacDonald's antiwar stance in the Executive, was appalled that it refused to give members a lead in making up their minds and dashed off a leaflet about the bearing of the Transvaal war on socialism. Sidney Webb would have liked to sit on the fence but was forced by his own logic to accept that the Transvaal and the Orange Free State ought to remain part of the empire. Shaw and Graham Wallas inclined to condone this second war with the Boers as the only means left of solving the problem of South Africa.[11]

Shaw led the Executive Committee in rejecting as not even of academic interest Olivier's proferred tract on the justifiability of empire; since Britain *had* an empire, it had to bear the consequences and fulfill the responsibilities. Aware that reading Greats at Oxford had made Olivier's thought processes extremely convoluted, the publishing committee divided the rest of his vast synopsis into tract-size sections for other authors and discreetly buried the project. Clarity and simplicity were essential for any Fabian pronouncement on the current situation.

The more Shaw and the rest of the Executive thought about the war and imperialism and agreed that it was the Society's duty to produce suggestions for the equitable settlement of South African problems, the larger the task became. To comply with Fabian tradition, they decided that the Society should take time to examine the feasibility of local autonomy in the Transvaal and Orange Free State over purely domestic matters, home rule for the gold district, a federal system in southern Africa, and some means of combating capitalist domination there and making the gold mines defray the cost of the war.[12] Had Britain not been at war, the Society might have been able to pursue the investigation in the accepted, gradualist manner, and a first volume of *Fabian Colonial Essays* might have appeared in 1901 instead of 1945. The Executive eventually announced that although the Society really ought to issue a tract on imperialism, all consideration of content and authorship would be dropped for the time being. Procrastination and acts of attrition could not, however, drive the problem away or make the dissension within the Society disappear.

At this point Shaw and his wife went on a cruise on the *Lusitania*, relying on letters from Edward Pease, the general secretary, to keep him *au fait* with what was happening in the Society.[13] Although he made his usual initial profession of reluctance to be involved, on his return to London Shaw emerged as one of the principals in the debate. He placed his popularity with the members and his considerable ability to convince by entertaining at the disposal of those who believed that holding the Society together was the most important issue. As a form of unifying action he suggested that it "work out a practical scheme for securing the mines when we 'resume' the Transvaal."[14]

Olivier, about to sail for Jamaica as its colonial secretary and thus eased out of this Fabian dissension, cast his mantle on S. G. Hobson, another *enfant terrible* who blamed Sidney Webb for the Society's refusal to tackle any problem other than specific social phenomena.[15] Instead of lecturing on the Far East on 8 December, Hobson submitted a resolution calling for the Fabian Society to dissociate itself from capitalist imperialism and vainglorious nationalism and to "pledge itself to support the expansion of the Empire only in so far as that may be compatible with the expansion of that higher social organization which the Society was founded to promote."[16] He maintained that the Outlanders' demand for the vote had not caused the war but that modern economic and political theories had created the conflict between Britain's desire for dominance from the Cape of Good Hope to the Zambezi and the Boers' determination to remain independent. Hobson blamed imperialist fervor for distracting attention from development at home, debasing the conscience and democratic spirit of the English, and enabling a conspiracy between financiers and armaments manufacturers to advance militarism and thwart the spread of socialism by forcing new imperial responsibilities upon the British people. Accordingly he asked that the Fabian Society should clearly declare its attitude toward the war and enlarge its attack upon commercialism.

Hobson's abstract terms gave Shaw an opportunity for greater pragmatism when, at the Executive's behest, he examined and reported on the resolution and presented the alternative case the same evening.[17] Shaw's amendment, while tallying with the motion in some respects, introduced a number of novel concepts which the Society found difficult to accept at first. He, too, debunked the official line that the war was being fought to protect the Outlanders' democratic institutions, declaring the mere acquisition of the parliamentary vote not worth fighting over; if it were, one-third of the men and all of the women in the United Kingdom would at that very moment be in armed revolt. For him, democratic institutions had a much wider connotation, one which embraced both government protection against speculators in the people's inherent rights in their country's natural resources and state protection of workers' health and safety. If Britain won the war, he believed that the people had a right to expect the British government either to nationalize the Rand mines or to exact royalties to their "full economic rent," first in order to recoup "a reasonable share of the expenses of the war," then to spend on public works (whether in Africa or Britain is not specified). If the state failed to do so, it would be blamed for outraging humanity and spending the nation's lifeblood and wealth merely to serve the sordid interests of speculators. In addition, he demanded that the British government enforce a stringent Mines Regulation Act to protect the miners. Colonial industrial and welfare legislation was indeed a startling proposition at this time, but it had become accepted policy by the time the third Labour government took office in 1945. The Fabian Society's duty was, in his view, to educate the public in the realities of the situation as he presented them and to agitate for complete agreement about them among conscientious Englishmen of all political persuasions. Both resolution and amendment were printed in *Fabian News* so that the whole membership (and, incidentally, the press and politicians) could see what was disrupting the Fabians.

At that meeting on 8 December, the audience was intrigued by Shaw's fifteen-minute presentation of his newly constructed colonial policy but needed more time to think about its implications.[18] The amendment was therefore rejected by 58 votes to 27—an unprecedented defeat for Shaw. The Executive Committee managed to evade a precipitate vote for Hobson, which could have threatened the future of the Society, by moving the previous motion shortly before the closure at five minutes before ten. That left the subject open for further discussion with an extremely interesting problem to resolve. As Shaw remarked, the fun was only just beginning.

At the first Executive Committee meeting of the new century, Ramsay MacDonald, as Olivier had done earlier, demanded a referendum to find out what Fabians really wanted.[19] After some wrangling, he had his way and departed for a lecture tour in America, leaving his colleagues to ask all members a simple question: "Are you in favour of an official pronouncement by the Fabian Society on imperialism in relation to war being made now?"[20] He returned home just in time for the meeting, at which the result of 259 votes to 217 against publishing any statement was announced immediately before Shaw began his lecture "Imperialism."[21]

When lecturing, Shaw habitually threw out an axiom designed to shock and annoy; next, by offering a series of paradoxes, he goaded the audience to discard hidebound theories and prejudices in order to examine the proposition from the opposite point of view; finally, he would demonstrate that what his original statement had implied to them was not what it really meant to him. After a certain amount of discussion, the audience would depart, refreshed by having been forced into some lateral thinking and at least three-quarters convinced that what the great man had said was right. On this occasion he declared, "For good or evil, it is we [Fabians] who have made England imperialistic." Many were riled, even though they knew he was up to his usual tricks, because they considered imperialism to be synonymous with the jingoism of many Conservatives and Liberal imperialists.

He refrained from analyzing in detail the various changes in attitude toward empire during the previous twenty years which had created the current confusion over imperial policy; he merely reminded his listeners that in the 1870s both Whigs and Tories would have been delighted to relieve the United Kingdom from the burden of empire. Developing his theme that Fabians had invented imperialism in the "best sense," he explained that they believed that "the most governed state over the largest area is preferable to a number of warring units with undisciplined ideals." Imperial expansion was impossible to halt because the world necessarily evolved toward big and powerful states which, in the interest of good government, had to suppress unruly enclaves set up on their borders by misfits who had fled from good government at home. In this way the borders of each strongly governed state spread outward until they met similarly expanding borders of another state desirous of strong home rule. Small states inexorably had to come within the borders of large ones or be "crushed out of existence."

Shaw then proceeded to prove to his audience that administering an empire was not an act that would damn the immortal Fabian soul, that in fact it was a duty thrust upon the British people. He took for granted the audience's awareness of the reversal of policy on dependencies from disposal to development, imposed on the Government over the previous five years by Joseph Chamberlain as Secretary of State for the Colonies and elucidated in his speeches to businessmen as well as to M.P.s. With his customary effrontery, Shaw attributed this reversal to the Fabian Society's transformation of socialism by removing militarism, class war, and revolution, thereby making it acceptable to the ordinary, peace-loving citizen. Since capitalism prevailed in South Africa, he declared that it was far better for it to do so under the control of the British Empire than under that of Dutch farmers. This view clashed with Olivier's percipient observation that Britain's ability to govern South Africa was an illusion and that South Africa would develop along its own line without British interference.

Shaw argued that Fabian socialism had replaced belief in individualism with a sense of the supreme importance of the duties of the community. This, in turn, had created a climate of opinion in which imperial federation and imperial expansion were "inevitable deductions" because they averted the capitalist evil of the Chartered Companies. Finally, he introduced the concept of a league of Great Powers, saying that even a federal imperial system achieved by aggression could end war within its own borders and bring general peace by alliance with similar federations.

Although Fabians were necessarily theoretical imperialists (having created imperialism in the "modern sense"), they were not obliged to approve of every act of the imperial government; their role was to remain critics. By startling and sparkling, Shaw drove his message home; by overstatement, he provoked listeners into thinking for themselves. No one knew better than he that Fabian socialism was not the sole begetter of the revival of interest in the empire and acceptance of its responsibilities, but it was an indisputable emanation of the recent revision in moral values and therefore a contributory element. Shaw sat down to enthusiastic applause before catching and hurling back with augmented force the shafts aimed at him in the subsequent discussion.

Only eighteen members, 2 percent of the whole, left the Fabian Society as a result of the referendum. Inevitably, Ramsay MacDonald was one, but he was out of line with Webb and the others over many internal issues in a way described by Shaw as psychological. Another was a Colonial Office clerk, Frederick Green, who years later became a stalwart of the Labour Party Advisory Committee on Imperial Questions. The disturbance, therefore, was far less than anticipated, and the "Old Gang" congratulated itself that the Society had lost only those who could not tolerate ideas in socialism that differed from their own.[22]

Nevertheless, the rift in the Society did not close. The strong faction favoring the statement circulated a policy paper and canvassed for votes at the next election of officers, the first time that had happened. Webb, Bernard and Charlotte Shaw, and five other candidates of their persuasion felt obliged to send out their own "letter" to all those Fabians who had voted no in the referendum or had abstained, telling them (without paying any attention to the other side) to vote for whomsoever they wished.[23] Webb personally addressed two hundred envelopes, and Shaw undertook to make sure that his chief opponent, Hobson, was nominated.[24] The members elected a fairly equal balance of the two factions, and the Society settled down to prepare, as was its custom, a manifesto for the next general election.

As Bernard Shaw wrote later to Beatrice Webb, imperialism was the political boom of 1895–1905 just as socialism had been in the previous decade.[25] Since the new manifesto would have to declare the Fabian position on imperial policy, Webb hurriedly delegated the drafting to Shaw in August 1900, the closed season for Fabian meetings, because he foresaw an autumn election. Within a month, *Fabianism and the Empire* had been circulated in draft and approved by every member of the Executive Committee, including Hobson.[26] Shaw, however, claimed merely to be its editor.[27] According to Fabian practice, eight hundred

galley proofs were prepared so that each member might comment before it was finally passed by the publications committee for printing.[28]
One hundred thirty-four were returned with penciled comments in their
specially wide margins and covering letters, all of which were read and
considered by Shaw before he revised the draft. Unfortunately, none of
the annotated galleys still exist, but a surviving letter from Graham
Wallas points out that Shaw had ignored the rights of nonwhites. A
passage was accordingly inserted defending Britain's bureaucratic rule
in Africa as preferable to white-trader rule, which would reintroduce
black slavery and extermination.[29] A proposal by Hobson that an imperial institute be set up in every port or important trading town to advise
and assist reputable British merchants, and to exclude undesirable speculators and the trade rings which involved the Great Powers in wars, was
also added.[30] There are probably other insertions, but Shaw's verbal
mastery concealed all grafts.

Possibly the most important point made in *Fabianism and the Empire*,
one that had to be restated periodically by the Labour party's policymakers in order to convince the rank and file, was that whether the people
wished it or not, Britain possessed an empire, and socialists had to face
up to this and do the best they could with it. Because the Empire had to
be administered, a constitutional policy was needed, for mismanagement
was a far greater danger to the colonial territories than attack from
without. Moreover, Shaw warned that if South Africa were treated in the
same way as Ireland and the United States, the Empire would begin to
fall apart, and if Britain treated the people of India like children, they
would rebel.[31] Indeed, Britain would not be able to hold the white colonies permanently by force against the will of the white inhabitants, even
though it might be "governing in the interests of civilization as a whole."
Shaw suggested that the part of the Empire run but not populated by
Englishmen would require bureaucratic administration rather than the
controlled democratic form of government that should be granted to the
white colonies as soon as possible, while some form of compromise would
be necessary in both India and South Africa. For South Africa, Shaw
recommended formal incorporation of the Boer republics in the Empire, with control of all measures concerning native interests remaining
in the hands of British officials. There he foresaw the possibility of
secession from the Empire if the bargain to be made with Britain in the
peace settlement proved unsatisfactory. Palestine did not become a mandated territory for another twenty years, and so there were no comparable predictions about British trusteeship in the Middle East.

Shaw proposed world federation as the ideal way to govern dependent
territories, with the Great Powers deploying their own military forces as
an international police force. Until that was accomplished, responsible

imperial federations should act as surrogates. Meanwhile, the British government would have to grant colonies constitutions more liberal than either the British or the American, providing for freedom of speech, the press, and combination, and instituting responsible ministerial governments answerable to a representative imperial council in permanent session, sitting at first in London but eventually moving about the Empire. His imperial policy had been noticeably elaborated since his lecture in February.

With a certain degree of modification, much of what Shaw presaged has indeed come to pass. Not all the reforms can be attributed to Labour governments, but Fabians have always insidiously permeated the policies of other parties with their ideas when they had something reasonable and practical to offer. Since colonial and commonwealth policy *sua natura* has been bipartisan for long stretches during the last hundred years, Fabian ideas have tended to bear fruit, whoever was in power.

Shaw adopted much of Seeley's earlier federal ideal when he argued in *Fabianism and the Empire* that there was need for "a well-considered policy to be pursued by a Commonwealth of the communities flying the British flag." Fabians, he said, were concerned that this policy should be a socialist one designed to bring about "the effective social organization of the whole Empire" and to rescue it from "the strife of classes and private interests." Fabians subscribed to organization and efficiency; they abhorred a laissez-faire policy. So did Seeley. He saw Greater Britain as carrying "not merely the English race, but the authority of English government" to overseas territories where legislative assemblies grew up naturally "because it was the nature of Englishmen to assemble."[32] Shaw also envisaged development of international communications, revitalizing and extending the Greater Britain concept in such a manner as to transform the Empire into a strong federation of countries populated and run by Englishmen. He further argued that, if such countries saw that they would benefit from federation as much as Britain, they would gladly adhere to the mother country. Consequently, since Britain could not hold the Empire by force, membership should be made a privilege to be earned, and expulsion from it the ultimate sanction.

He also took for granted that a nation had no right to do what it liked with its own territory without consulting the interests of the rest of the world, and that international rights of travel and trade existed. Eventually the Great Powers would impose "commercial civilization" on all refractory countries. The morality of this policy depended partly on ensuring that "no flag that does not carry a reasonable standard of life with it shall be the flag of a Great Power" and partly on accepting the principles of free trade and reciprocal rights.[33]

Shaw maintained that morally Britain led the world as a proponent of free trade and that, rather than resort to protective tariffs, it should be prepared to change either its products or its methods of manufacture if comparable goods could be produced more cheaply overseas, provided the industry involved did not compose "a necessary part of a complete communal life." The proviso was of paramount importance in order to avoid the economic imbalance described in the first act of *The Apple Cart*, in which Birmingham had become the workshop of the world in the Christmas-cracker trade, while Gateshead and Middlesborough were turning out twenty thousand tons of chocolate creams a day after poverty in Britain had been averted by the big businessmen who had sent "our capital abroad to places where poverty and hardship still exist: in other words, where labor is cheap. We live in comfort on the imported profits of that capital. We are all ladies and gentlemen now."[34] The play was written just before the second Labour government took office and Sidney Webb, as Lord Passfield, was made Secretary of State for the Colonies, more than a quarter century after Shaw had declared the practical moral of the Fabian manifesto to be that "Empire will ruin us, as it ruined earlier civilizations, unless we recognize that unearned income, whether for British individuals living unproductively on British labor or British islands living unproductively on foreign labor, is a cancerous growth in the body politic."[35] It cannot be said that Shaw successfully resolved the parallel problems of the economic interdependence of territories at different stages of industrial development within an imperial federation or that federation's economic relationship with the rest of the world.

He was on much firmer ground when writing on how to educate imperial administrators. Soon after arriving in London in 1876 he had embarked on a crammer's course to prepare for the civil-service examination. This he abandoned after a couple of months. Since then he had absorbed the criticisms of Webb, Olivier, and Green on the structure of the Colonial Office and the Treasury. Now he asserted that "the competitive examinations by which we obtain our upper division civil servants would be as likely as not to exclude the sort of man who would be successful in organizing British trade in a foreign market."[36] To produce the new kind of men needed to implement his imperial policy required technical training and political science for the administrators and education in citizenship for the administered. The press also needed similar training in politics so that it might in turn educate "the man in the street sufficiently to compel editors to respect his intelligence" because the combined force of an ignorant press and an ignorant public was "strong enough to dissolve an Empire."[37] In fact, brains and political science were what the Empire most needed, together with a strong initiative from the Cabinet to offset the civil servants' control over policy. The idea sown here that the Colonial Service needed various kinds of experts took nearly half a century to germinate, but it bore fruit in 1946 when Creech Jones became colonial secretary.

Fabianism and the Empire, only half of which was concerned with imperialism (the rest being a straightforward domestic election manifesto), was published by Grant Richards on 2 October as a shilling book "to catch the carriage trade." Twelve hundred copies were sold within ten days, and 250 were distributed to newspapers, politicians, and men of influence. Reviewers treated it kindly, one judging it the best statement on policy produced at that election. But it had no noticeable effect on the voters, most of whom seemed to have no thought beyond beating the Boers. The publications committee floated the idea of producing a penny version, but in 1901, with the Conservatives firmly in the saddle, sales stuck at 2,000, and eventually the rest of the stock was remaindered at threepence a copy. However, Shaw's words had by that time permeated the minds of those few who would from 1918 serve on the Labour party Advisory Committee on Imperial Questions, created and chaired by Webb to supply a colonial group in the Parliamentary Labour party. Copies of the book found their way into university and public libraries, where they are still studied side by side with J. A. Hobson's *Imperialism*. Fabians in 1902 so much preferred Shaw's hypotheses on the economy of empire to Hobson's underconsumption theory, claiming that he had confused imperialism with both jingoism and capitalism, that Pease felt the need to warn them against considering *Fabianism and the Empire* as binding.[38]

The theater obviously provided Shaw with a much wider platform than the Fabian Society. Edward Pease always maintained that he taught more socialism by means of his plays than he ever did by writing political tracts. The intellectual inconsistencies and dramatic conflict Shaw uncovered while investigating militarist and imperialist attitudes were translated into part of the substance of several plays. The event that seems to have triggered the analysis, that made him first respond emotionally and then think about the nature of imperialism, was the popular reaction to the death of General Gordon at Khartoum. Shaw prided himself that "every subject struck [his] mind at an angle that produced reflections new to [his] audience."[39] *Arms and the Man* provides an outstanding example of his refractory talent.[40] There, against the tide of demand for revenge, and indignation that the army had lost control of the Sudan, he satirized military heroics in the person of Sergius.[41] In the plays Shaw tried to make the audience face up to its own moral and political preconceptions and prejudices, hoping eventually to persuade it "to take its conscience and its brains" to the theater.[42] In prefaces to the plays, in tracts, and in articles he presented relatively straightforward argument about the same issues and offered positive solutions and policies. Several distinct dialectical progressions run through the plays. Shavian imperialism as it developed independently of Fabian imperialism thus infiltrated the dialogue of plays on nominally quite unrelated themes.[43]

Having exposed the ridiculous aspect of small-scale nationalism in *Arms and the Man,* Shaw analyzed the moral justification of empire in the "bravura piece," *The Man of Destiny.*[44] In a flight of mellifluous rhetoric, Napoleon describes how the Englishman can overcome the tyranny of his scruples when inspired by a "burning conviction that it is his moral and religious duty to conquer those who possess the thing he wants." Sustained, and deluded, by the belief that he champions freedom and national independence, he unblushingly conquers and annexes half the world. Shaw encapsulated the popular view of empire building in two sentences: "When [the Englishman] wants a new market for his adulterated Manchester goods, he sends a missionary to teach the natives the Gospel of Peace. The natives kill the missionary; he flies to arms in defence of Christianity; fights for it; conquers for it; and takes the market as his reward from Heaven."[45]

Captain Brassbound's Conversion further dissected common attitudes toward empire.[46] When persuading Ellen Terry, against her own inclination, to play the part of Lady Cicely Wayneflete, Shaw exhorted her, "Think of all that has been rising up under your eyes in Europe for years past, Bismarck worship, Stanley worship, Dr Jim [Jameson] worship, and now at last Kitchener worship with dead enemies dug up and mutilated."[47] Kitchener's revenge for Gordon's death, when he allowed his men to destroy the Mahdi's tomb and desecrate his body after the Battle of Omdurman the previous year, had so outraged Shaw's sensibilities that he referred to it with fastidious distaste in letters, a preface, the·Fabian manifesto, and even in the article "Civilization and the Soldier," written three years later.[48] He now told the actress that in the role she would stand

> in the very place where Imperialism is most believed to be necessary, on the border line where the European meets the fanatical African, with judge on the one hand, and indomitable adventurer-filibuster on the other, said ind-adv-fil pushing forward "civilization" in the shape of rifles & pistols in the hands of Hooligans, aristocratic *mauvais sujets* and stupid drifters.[49]

Moral superiority was the essence of Lady Cicely, who had walked across Africa and written about it in the *Daily Mail.* Shaw acknowledged that the material of the play owed much to the writings of African explorers Mary Kingsley and Henry Stanley.[50] But Lady Cicely, in her exploits, genteelly determined manner, and English-country-garden clothes, bears a stronger resemblance to Flora Shaw, journalist and friend of Rhodes and Goldie, who traveled for the *Times* through South Africa and the Yukon before marrying another empire builder, Lugard. In addition, when telling Brassbound "I know your men will get on perfectly well if they are properly treated," she is the epitome of the Fabian Women's Group.[51] This middle-class, socialist-humanitarian theme is developed when, by commenting on the "niceness" of the brigands' faces and confidently assuming that her requests will be fulfilled, she extracts from them civil behavior and docility. Humanitarians' views on native administration emerge in her insistence that to escape being killed by savages, one should not aim pistols at them but be polite and say "Howdyedo."

On the other hand, the mate Drinkwater voices the views of the average, newspaper-ridden Englishman on the scramble for Africa, on Britain's natural right to imperial possessions and to trade wherever it pleased, and on its civilizing mission. Justifying his master's dubious activities, he says,

> Ahrs is a Free Tride nition. It gows agin us as Hinglishmen to see these bloomin furriners settin ap their Castoms Ahses and spheres o hinfluence and sich lawk hall owver Arfricar. Daownt Harfricar belong as much to huz as to them? thets wot we sy. Ennywys, there ynt naow awm in ahr business. All we daz is hescort, tourist h o r commercial. Cook's hexcursions to the Hatlas Mahntns: thets hall it is. Waw, its spreadin civlawzytion, it is. Ynt it nah?[52]

When the unsuccessful missionary, Rankin, asks whether Brassbound's crew was equipped for such a mission, Drinkwater gives him an account of their rifles and is most indignant that anyone should sell arms to "eathen black niggers" when told that the local sheikh possessed an American machine pistol vastly superior to any of those. Yet, observing the venality of the Moorish porter who led Sir Howard Hallam and Lady Cicely to the missionary's house, he could remark, "Hooman nitre is the sime everywheres. Them eathens is jast lawk you an' me, gavner."[53] Brassbound's assessment of the sheikh as a judge responsible for maintaining law and order in the Atlas Mountains, and thus Sir Howard's peer, agrees. His cynical observation that the Battle of Omdurman was fought less to avenge Gordon's death than to promote Rhodes's dream of a railway from the Cape to Cairo further illustrates the Napoleonic motif of English imperial duplicity. Brassbound disparages both Britain's rule in Africa and its imperial power, attributing the rescue of the British party to American gunboat diplomacy.

Seeley's theory that America would take over the role of a great imperial power from Britain was exploited by Shaw in "Civilization and the

Soldier," written for the *Humane Review* when the effects of the general election of 1900 were beginning to be felt. While enjoying a Mediterranean cruise, Shaw had time to cogitate on the militarism rife in London and to observe the kind of patriotism evinced by his fellow passengers, who believed that Britain would "endure to the end, our Empire growing ever greater, until the Last Judgment shall be enacted—probably in Westminster Abbey—and the millennium inaugurated by the extension of British Rule to the entire universe."[54] Transience of empire was now his theme, for he had come to the conclusion that no form of civilization had ever survived the "imperialist stage of democratic capitalism." He argued that throughout the nineteenth century, empire had been "stealing upon us as steadily as the hand of a clock," but now that England possessed an empire, it did not really have the nerve to rule it by force of arms. Writing while the Fabian manifesto was still on sale in the bookshops, he claimed that he had been vigorously reviled for his conviction that there was no humanitarian side to the Boer War and that the inevitable political reconstruction of South Africa by absorbing the Transvaal Republic could only have been brought about by external force. Putting a military leader in charge of imperial policy was a governmental mistake because soldiers always chose armed force as the easy way to solve political problems. To rule an empire required "the courage to look realities in the face and the energy to adapt social organization to the needs of the modern conscience, and so substitute a fruitful life for a fool's paradise."[55] The fool's paradise was the blind belief that England was still the all-powerful center of the British Empire and would remain so even after imperial federation was achieved. In his view, American tourism was already devitalizing England, and when the federation had taken the serious business of empire from her "fat and nerveless fingers" she would decline into "the white-cliffed island where a once famous nation will live by letting lodgings."[56]

For the time being, Britain could still raise battalions to enforce her will, for no other Great Power had yet built up sufficient arms to challenge her by land or by sea. Therefore internal disintegration, decolonization, became Shaw's next theme. One cause defined in "Maxims for Revolutionists," appended to *Man and Superman,* was direct confrontation of the British imperialist by the colonial imperialist (nationalist) who raises his own troops, sloughs off Colonial Office control, acknowledges only allegiance to the Crown, and thereby "cuts the painter."[57] The most intellectually disintegrative political force was, and still is, Ireland, but that, as the title *John Bull's Other Island* emphasizes, was part of the British Isles, not a true colony. As a putative part of the Empire after the grant of home rule, however, Ireland was used by Shaw to illustrate the way in which independent members of the British Commonwealth would still expect the British navy and other fighting forces to come to their aid in the event of conflict with any other countries.[58] He also used Irish home rule as a hook upon which to hang his argument that self-government "is a necessity . . . for all constituents of the Federations of Commonwealths which are now the only permanently practicable form of Empire"[59] because nations invariably demand political independence even when that entails jettisoning good, impartial government and democratic institutions.

Major Barbara, with a plot based on the conflict between those whose spheres of influence, at first contiguous, begin to encroach upon each other, dramatizes many points made in *Fabianism and the Empire,* and it is possible to see the play as an allegory of competing empires.[60] In the Preface to *Major Barbara,* Shaw discusses the subjugation of the minds of inferior (black) races by Christian missionaries to exploitation by European capitalism, and echoes of this theme can be heard in the discussions of the problems of poverty in the play itself.

The role of religion, the conflict between imperial powers, the inevitability of federation despite all its hazards, and the decline and fall of the British Empire are the dominant issues in the rest of Shaw's pronouncements on imperialism. In the lecture "The Religion of the British Empire," given in 1906, he asserted, "You cant have an empire without a religion," by which he meant that all the people must believe the same truth, namely, that each one is the instrument of a higher Power, even though the ways in which that truth is expressed may vary from person to person.[61] Such toleration would bring unity to the British Empire, most sections of which had highly civilized religions of their own.[62] However, according to Lord Summerhays, former governor of Jinghiskhan, who in *Misalliance* represents the education of dependent peoples by the imperial power, the Empire had no religion, for in his province, as indeed in any Muslim part of the empire, "it was a punishable offence to expose a Bible for sale." He believed in maintaining order by law, persuasion, force, or fraud rather than making the native into half an Englishman, "improving the other chaps," which the wealthy linendraper Tarleton considered the good, unselfish side of imperialism.[63]

External threats invariably unify the state. By August 1909, when *Press Cuttings* was first read at a Fabian summer school, Germany was expanding her navy, and jingoism, out of favor at the 1906 general election, was again rampant.[64] Shaw, therefore, created the imperial expansionist Mitchener, not only to declaim that "the Germans have never recognized, and until they get a stern warning they never will recognize, the plain fact that the interests of the British Empire are paramount, and that the command of the sea belongs by nature to England," but also to prophesy in Wellsian fashion to Balsquith that in these days of aeroplanes and Zeppelin airships the question of the moon is becoming one of the greatest importance. It will be reached at no very great distant date. Can you, as an Englishman, tamely contemplate the possibility of having to live under a German moon? The British flag must be planted there at all hazards.[65]

Yet, when war actually came, its immediate effect on the activities, minds, and characters of people at home took precedence over its imperial implications.

No one can doubt that, even in a minor play, there was serious political intent behind the creation of such characters and the words they spoke. Shaw intended his audience to recognize later the "moral" of a play, which it had absorbed unconsciously while being entertained. That in recognition they would probably believe they had created for themselves an inner meaning to the play bothered him not at all. That was, indeed, his intent, for people are far more likely to be convinced by a theory they think they have constructed for themselves than by any didactic argument, however well presented.

Recruited and guided by the Webbs, Leonard Woolf produced for the Fabian Research Department a report on the ideal terms for a peace settlement which proposed an international body to supervise the several Great Powers' administration of their respective colonies and protectorates.[66] Other groups were considering the idea. If it were to become part of the postwar settlement, British imperial relationships would have to be redefined. The Fabians wanted to be first in the field, and so, in January 1917, the Executive asked Shaw to obtain the members' approval for a new committee to construct a radical new constitution for the Empire in which the hereditary monarchy might be replaced by a president.[67] After the Empire Reconstruction Committee had sat for eight months under his chairmanship, one of the younger members, Duncan Hall, was asked to draft the report. Sidney Webb, however, diverted Hall's attention to an investigation of the Spry *Report on Military Training*, and so the report did not emerge until 1920, by which time it had become a more personal expression entitled *The British Commonwealth of Nations*.[68] However, in *How to Settle the Irish Question*, Shaw, calling himself "the spokesman of Common Sense," in 1917 aired some of the ideas floated by his committee. These included replacement of "the now hopelessly obsolete institution at Westminster that calls itself an imperial Parliament, and is neither imperial nor national nor English nor Scottish nor Irish, neither fish nor fowl nor good red herring,"[69] by an imperial conference far more acceptable to the Dominions, which preferred a weak monarchy to a strong presidency. As a representative, advisory, nonexecutive body, it would consider the empire's affairs as a whole and, through a permanent secretariat, recommend ways of collaboration to federal Parliaments in all parts of the empire, including Britain. With moral, not executive, influence, the conference Shaw advocated was very like the modern Commonwealth Secretariat.

Germany's defeat in the 1914–18 war made Britain, in Shaw's view, "the most dangerous and widely dreaded Imperial Power left in the world," just as the jingoists and Liberal Imperialists had intended.[70] A vigorous league of nations would have to be set up, rather like a police force, to exert the moral and physical coercive force of idealism in international affairs and to maintain the balance of power in favor of peace.[71]

During the First World War, and indeed the Second, many British politicians expected the United States government to collaborate actively in postwar economic development of colonies. Shaw's assessment of it as a competing imperial power was far more discriminating. *The Apple Cart,* his play about the delusion of ministerial power, which was performed for the first time in England soon after the second Labour government took office in 1929, presents a subtle analysis of the relationship between America and Europe, with a strong warning that if Britain wanted to preserve her national identity, the politicians should resist any offer of rapprochement by the United States couched in the form of debt amnesty.[72] Fortunately, as he pointed out, the British Commonwealth's strongest constitutional defense against being submerged by America was the deceptively powerless monarchy, which would "swim to the last." Cultural merger with the New World was, admittedly, irreversible.

The inevitable dissolution of empire was a common motif in the later plays, most fully developed in *Geneva*. Writing after the invasion of Abyssinia by Mussolini, Shaw revealed his profound disappointment in the League of Nations on the grounds that

> the moment the League of Nations does anything on its own initiative and on principle, it produces, not peace, but threats of war or secession or both, which oblige it to stop hastily and do nothing until the Great Powers have decided among themselves to make use of it as an instrument of their old-fashioned diplomacy.[73]

Although the Great Powers ignored the League's Covenant and made secret treaties, the organization could still restrain them to some extent: it could sidetrack them, shame them, sabotage their actions, or "make things difficult or impossible that used to be easy." But it was not able to prevent empire seeking or the resultant wars. Therefore, in a Preface to

Geneva written after World War II, Shaw laid down his three final imperial maxims:

> If [conquerors of empires] substitute civilization for savagery they make good, and establish a legitimate title to the territories they invade.
> Ethical victories endure. . . . Civilizations have never finally survived: they have perished over and over again because they have failed to make themselves worth their cost to the masses whom they have enslaved.
> The rule of vast commonwealths is beyond the political ability of mankind at its ablest.[74]

Nothing was seen of Shaw's influence on political thought about colonialism during the first brief Labour government of 1924. J. H. Thomas, not a Fabian and thus not subject to Shaw's domination, was well out of his depth as Secretary of State for the Colonies. The mistakes he made then, and in both the Dominions Office and the Colonial Office between 1929 and 1935, had far-reaching effects on imperial relationships. Sidney Webb, whom MacDonald raised to the peerage and appointed colonial secretary in 1929, was imbued with Fabian imperialism. In the interest of running the British Empire efficiently, he attempted to introduce such socialist measures as the encouragement of trade unionism in the colonies. But he was hamstrung by the financial crisis caused by the world trade recession. Most colonial reforms were carried out on a shoestring, but reforms become impossible when even the shoestring reaches the breaking point.

When Malcolm MacDonald was placed by his father in charge of imperial affairs in the 1930s, the more liberal attitude he encouraged in the Colonial Office vernalized some of Shaw's ideas. The seedlings had to be carefully nurtured during the forcing period of World War II, not only by colonial civil servants but also by the Labour party Advisory Committee on Imperial Questions and the Fabian Colonial Bureau. By the time Arthur Creech Jones entered the Colonial Office after the war, they were ready to be planted out by that dedicated Fabian imperialist. A colonial mining policy was ready for implementation; the new Colonial Service was designed to have experts on many scientific, technical, economic, and industrial matters; both practical businessmen and academic economists were serving as ministerial advisers; and local-government plans were being introduced. The old British Empire was undoubtedly crumbling, but everyone confidently expected it to be superseded by a commonwealth of nations, of which it was a privilege to be a member and where the greatest sanction was to be denied membership. Bernard

Shaw was by no means the sole begetter of any of these changes, but he foresaw and prophesied, and his ideas, offered in many forms and allowed to permeate the climate of opinion in true Fabian fashion, contributed to their creation.

Notes

1. Edward Pease, *The History of the Fabian Society* (London: A. C. Fifield, 1916), pp. 120–39; Margaret Cole, *The Story of Fabian Socialism* (London: Heinemann, 1961), pp. 98–101; A. M. McBriar, *Fabian Socialism and English Politics, 1884–1918* (Cambridge: Cambridge University Press, 1962), pp. 119–30; P. M. Pugh, *Educate, Agitate, Organize: 100 Years of Fabian Socialism* (London: Methuen, 1984), pp. 16–40.
2. *Fabian Essays in Socialism* (London, 1889).
3. Fabian Society Papers, Nuffield College, Oxford, C 53/2 ff 23–35, F 130/2 Item 1.
4. Ibid., C 7, C 8, C 37, C 63/2.
5. *Fabian News* 10, no. 1 (March 1900).
6. L. J. Hume, *Bentham and Bureaucracy* (Cambridge: Cambridge University Press, 1981), pp. 126, 191–92.
7. J. R. Seeley, *The Expansion of England* (London: Macmillan, 1881), pp. 54, 69, 88, 177.
8. J. A. Hobson, *Imperialism: A Study* (London: James Nisbet, 1902). See also his earlier publications *The War in South Africa: Its Causes and Effects* (London: James Nisbet, 1900) and *The Psychology of Jingoism* (London: Grant Richards, 1901).
9. Fabian Society Papers, C 7.
10. Ibid., C 37.
11. Margaret Cole and Barbara Drake, eds., *Our Partnership* (London: Longmans, 1975), pp. 188–89.
12. Fabian Society Papers, C 7
13. Ibid., A 1/1.
14. Ibid., A 1/1 ff 13–14.
15. Ibid., A 7/3 ff 44–47.
16. *Fabian News* 9, no. 10 (December 1899).
17. Ibid.
18. Fabian Society Papers, C 37.
19. Ibid., C 8.
20. Ibid., C 7.
21. *Fabian News* 10, no. 1 (March 1900).
22. Fabian Society Papers, C 54/1 ff 1–2.
23. Ibid., C 8.
24. Ibid., A 3/6 ff 27–30.
25. Dan H. Laurence, ed., *Bernard Shaw: Collected Letters, 1898–1910* (London: Max Reinhardt, 1972), pp. 232–35.
26. Fabian Society Papers, E 3.
27. *Fabianism and the Empire: A Manifesto by the Fabian Society* (London: Grant Richards, 1900), Editor's Preface.
28. Laurence, pp. 159–63.

29. Fabian Society Papers, A 9/2 ff 32–33.

30. *Fabian News* 10, no. 1 (March 1900).

31. *Fabianism and the Empire*, p. 15.

32. Seeley, pp. 49, 59.

33. *Fabianism and the Empire*, p. 55.

34. *The Apple Cart, Collected Plays with Their Prefaces,* ed. Dan H. Laurence (London: Max Reinhardt, 1970–74), 6: 308.

35. *Fabianism and the Empire*, p. 54.

36. Ibid., p. 89.

37. Ibid., pp. 92–93.

38. *Fabian News* 12, no. 2 (February 1902).

39. Stanley Weintraub, ed., *Shaw: An Autobiography, 1856–1898* (New York: Weybright and Talley, 1969), p. 112.

40. *Arms and the Man, Collected Plays with Their Prefaces* 1: 389–472.

41. Seven years later, this lesson was driven home in the Preface to *Three Plays for Puritans,* where he warned that "men will be slain needlessly on the field of battle because officers conceive it to be their first duty to make romantic exhibitions of conspicuous gallantry." *Collected Plays with Their Prefaces* 2: 26.

42. Preface to *Mrs Warren's Profession, Collected Plays with Their Prefaces* 1: 236.

43. For example, *Misalliance, Collected Plays with Their Prefaces* 4: 11–253, where the theme is education of the young.

44. *The Man of Destiny, Collected Plays with Their Prefaces* 1: 607–61.

45. Ibid., p. 658.

46. *Captain Brassbound's Conversion, Collected Plays with Their Prefaces,* 2: 317–417.

47. Laurence, 8 August 1899, p. 98.

48. Ibid.; *Fabianism and the Empire*, p. 33. "Civilization and the Soldier," *Humane Review* 1 (January 1901), 305; reprinted in *SHAW* 9 (University Park: Penn State University Press, 1989), 99–112.

49. Laurence, p. 98.

50. *Captain Brassbound's Conversion,* Leaflet distributed with the Programme, 1912, *Collected Plays with Their Prefaces,* 2: 428.

51. *Captain Brassbound's Conversion,* p. 345.

52. Ibid., p. 329.

53. Ibid., p. 330.

54. "Civilization and the Soldier," p. 299.

55. Ibid., p. 311.

56. Ibid., p. 313.

57. *Man and Superman, Collected Plays with Their Prefaces* 2: 782.

58. Preface to *John Bull's Other Island, Collected Plays with Their Prefaces* 2: 830.

59. Ibid., p. 871.

60. *Major Barbara, Collected Plays with Their Prefaces* 3: 9–185.

61. *Christian Commonwealth* (29 November 1906).

62. Preface to *Androcles and the Lion, Collected Plays with Their Prefaces* 4: 577.

63. *Misalliance,* pp. 187–88; also, 236–37.

64. Fabian Society Papers, G 13; *Press Cuttings, Collected Plays with Their Prefaces* 3: 840–83.

65. Ibid., pp. 854–55.

66. Before publication in the *New Statesman,* the paper was discussed at a Barrow House conference by Fabians and others with similar aims, such as the Bryce Committee. Pugh, pp. 129–31; *New Statesman Supplement* (July 1915).

67. Fabian Society Papers, D 3.

68. H. Duncan Hall, *The British Commonwealth of Nations* (London: Methuen, 1920).

69. G. B. Shaw, *How to Settle the Irish Question* (Dublin: The Talbot Press; London: Constable, 1917), pp. 23–24; reprinted in Dan H. Laurence and David H. Greene, eds., *The Matter with Ireland* (New York: Hill and Wang; London: Rupert Hart-Davis, 1962).

70. G. B. Shaw, *Peace Conference Hints* (London: Constable, 1919), pp. 19, 35.

71. Ibid. pp. 56, 59.

72. Ibid., p. 39.

73. *Geneva, Collected Plays with Their Prefaces* 7: 99.

74. Ibid., pp. 25, 36, 39.

Peter Archer, Q.C., M.P.

SHAW AND THE IRISH QUESTION

Whatever the respective merits of Shaw and Shakespeare, the wisdom of the Englishman was manifested by his decision not to write prefaces to his plays, explaining what he meant and enlarging on the implications. If we are looking for a timeless quality, we are more likely to find it in a play than in a preface. *Richard III* may be set firmly in its own period, but it is about ambition and self-delusion, about hubris and nemesis, abstractions which we have with us always.

John Bull's Other Island is Shaw's only systematic treatise on the relations between the respective patrimonies of St. George and St. Patrick, and while the incidents belong to 1904, the themes are timeless. That is not to say that the characters still typify contemporary attitudes. The insensitive arrogance of the upper-middle-class Englishman is now replaced by a bewildered renunciation of any claim to economic or technical preeminence. The assumption of an imperial destiny, held in 1904 even by those who, like Broadbent, ostentatiously renounced it, has been overtaken by a less ambitious resolve to be internationally competitive. The condescension toward foreigners is now simply a characteristic of the Alf Garnetts of this world, the Cockney counterparts of Archie Bunker.

But the self-centered and opinionated complacency of Broadbent is as apparent in the contemporary English yuppie as in the Edwardian man of affairs. The mutually uncomprehending encounter of cultures, the erecting into universal importance of what is merely local and transient, and the seeing in part and prophesying in part are all aspects of the human condition which transcend period.

It is when Shaw composed his 1906 "Preface for Politicians," and wrote expressly of political matters, that he was most obviously a child of his time. It is not that his diagnosis no longer applies. Ireland's condition is depressingly persistent. What has been falsified is his expectation that there could be a simple solution.

He is right in denouncing England's deliberate and repeated sabotage of the Irish economy in order to benefit its own, although more usually the English attitude was one of indifference to distress which was far enough away to be forgotten. The example most frequently cited, the blight of the Irish potato crop in the years from 1845 to 1848, was not brought about by the English government. Indeed, Peel sent a scientific mission to ascertain the causes of the infection, and (of more immediate use) he imported Indian corn. The Whig administration which succeeded him initiated a program of relief work, and even many of the despised landlords contributed to the assistance. But the wheat grown on the best land continued to be exported to England.

Of course, governments in London showed scarcely greater compassion for the sufferings of the poor in England. The outburst of the valet, Hodson, against English landlordism and Irish immigrant labor (evils which for him are inseparably intertwined) is a restrained expression of the bitterness among the underprivileged in the larger island. The difference is that while the English victims had to find a conceptual framework of class politics into which to channel their indignation, the Irish found a ready-made vehicle in the national resentment against the exploiters from over the water.

But the roots of that resentment were not economic. Nor did Shaw pretend that the departure of the last Englishman from Irish soil would ring the death knell of exploitation. Patsy Farrell will be no better off when his Irish neighbors have the ordering of affairs.

Shaw did not identify nationalism with an economic or social program. Indeed, it acted as an antidote to any such program. Nationalism for Shaw is not a crusade for social justice. It is a stage through which a people which perceives itself as enslaved must pass. And all other issues will remain in abeyance until the nationalist aspiration is satisfied.

"A conquered nation," he wrote, " is like a man with cancer: he can think of nothing else, and is forced to place himself, to the exclusion of all better company, in the hands of quacks who profess to treat or cure cancer."[1]

It may be replied that the concept of the conquered nation is flexible. The Welsh do not perceive themselves as a conquered nation. They prefer to see their future as part of Britain and have used their considerable energies to procure for themselves a predominant voice in British politics. They are well represented in the House of Commons, in the Civil Service, and on the High Court Bench. And they have secured what most of them regard as the appropriate measure of regional autonomy, conscious that if they wish to vary the degree, they are in a strong position to do so, provided they themselves are broadly in agreement.

The Scots are largely content to maintain their identity within the United Kingdom, and their periods of doubt are inspired by the severely practical circumstance that they differ politically from the governments repeatedly chosen by the electors of southeast England. The people of Cornwall do not perceive themselves as a nation at all, despite a strong local pride in their ancestry and in their traditions.

Irish nationalism is different. It is reenforced by a number of factors. First is the physical separation of the island from what the English regard as the mainland. Second is the trick of history which, in the sixteenth century, caused the Irish to cling to the old faith while England was led by the sexual proclivities of Henry VIII to the Protestant side of the dispute. It is possible to argue that this was no accident. Most European peoples (or at least their rulers) were choosing between a Mass recited in Latin and one declaimed in their own tongue. For the Irish, the choice was between Latin and English.

It does not follow that, 250 years later, every Irish patriot (even excluding Protestant freethinkers like Shaw) was a submissive child of the Church. Anticlericalism was as widespread as in most other Catholic countries. Financially exploited, intellectually straitjacketed, and socially enthralled, many Irish recognized the Church of Father Dempsey as the Church of Pius IX and Cardinal Cullen. But that is a quarrel within the family. It does not diminish the gulf which separates even mystics, romantics, and rebels like Keegan from the Protestant ethic.

Of all this Shaw is fully aware, and it is portrayed with an ample measure of Shavian wit. But he saw Irish nationalism as an ephemeral obstacle which, once satisfied, would make way for real political debate in Ireland. When the nationalist aspirations were fulfilled, the Irish would turn their attention to the questions which, for other peoples, constitute the stuff of politics. And Shaw assumed that fulfillment would come with the achievement of home rule.

In his 1906 "Preface for Politicians," he accepted that home rule was the ultimate aspiration of Irish nationalism. He did not envisage that this demand would be overtaken by an insistence on total separation. Sinn Fein did not take the stage until the following year. And there is little doubt that an unconditional offer of home rule would have settled the issue for at least a generation. True, the Irish Republican Brotherhood had other ideas, but such vitality as it possessed was located in America, and its relationship with events or opinions in Ireland was similar to that of Trotsky in exile with everyday life and politics in the Soviet Union. It was the failure to achieve home rule in 1913 that finally discredited the constitutional nationalists, persuaded the new generation of Irish nationalists that the issue must be resolved outside Westminster, and increased the stake to total severance. Even in 1917, Shaw was seeking to warn the Irish that independence was a dangerous snare: "If the English had a pennyworth of political sagacity," he wrote, "instead of being, as they are, incorrigible Sinn Feiners almost to the last man, they would long ago have brought the Irish to their senses by threatening them with independence."[2]

Even more significantly, Shaw was no more percipient than any of his contemporaries in foreseeing a divided Ireland. Consequently, he failed to appreciate that when Irish electors gained control of four-fifths of the island, they would not then proceed to debate the issues of social justice, but would simply continue to dispute who was the most implacable enemy of English colonialism. Still less was it predictable that this situation would continue long after the great majority of Irish people ceased to visit, to understand, or to care about the Six Counties.

Shaw was right in insisting that nationalism is not a prescription for paradise. It may or may not be associated with any other aspirations. Irish nationalism has shared few visions with its counterparts in other areas of Europe. Cavour condemned it on the ground that Ireland would be economically better off as part of the United Kingdom. Mazzini rejected it because it expressed no sense of mission or moral purpose for the Irish nation.[3]

Rosa Luxemburg referred to nation-states and nationalism as "empty vessels into which each epoch and the class relations in each particular country pour their particular material content."[4] The tragedy of Ireland is that no one poured in anything. The vessel remains empty. Of course, there are those in Ireland who are anxious to debate real politics. But as the class politics of Connolly and Larkin were never more than minor themes in a symphony about home rule, so the advocates of social justice still remain electorally on the fringe. And in Northern Ireland the energy and passion of political debate are channeled into sterile arguments about constitutional solutions, and those who seek to raise other issues are eventually pressed to declare themselves on the side of Pope or Queen. Conversely, there are those who are primarily nationalist but who sometimes speak the language of class politics. There are elements within Sinn Fein that claim to be Marxist, but the Marxism amounts to little beyond the hijacking of useful economic issues and the insertion as an afterthought of a few buzzwords.

The running sore is of course the existence of the border. And in 1904 it did not occur to anyone that the result of the conflict between an irresistible campaign for home rule and an immovable attachment to the Union Jack would be a divided Ireland which would sterilize the politics of the new freedom and destroy the attachment of the English to the Union.

At the time, the advocates of home rule, encouraged by the active commitment of the Liberal party, saw no reason to compromise. English Unionists were concerned for the integrity of the empire, and they spoke of playing the Orange card not to share the kitty, but to win the game. Ulster Unionists were determined to resist separation not merely for themselves, but for any part of Ireland. When introducing the first Home Rule Bill in 1886, Gladstone had offered to consider whether "Ulster itself, or, perhaps with more appearance of reason, a portion of Ulster, should be excluded from the operation of the Bill,"[5] but the offer was not pursued by any of the principal groups concerned.

After 1921, expectations had changed, with the paradoxical consequence that attitudes remained frozen. It was inevitable that when Ireland (or even four-fifths of it) was free, the dreamlike quality of the new age would pass. Throughout the long years of the struggle, the Irish people had been upheld by the belief that with independence would come the solution to all their problems. Whether a free Ireland would return to the romantic world of the past, as the writers of Young Ireland appeared to assume, or whether it would apply an unencumbered mind to resolving economic and social questions, as Shaw hoped, there had appeared little need to consider in advance the solution of practical problems in the golden age. A measure of disillusionment was bound to follow when daily life under the new dispensation was found to be scarcely less pedestrian than before. But while there remained fuel to support the nationalist dream, while it was possible to relegate utopia yet further into the future, the facing of reality could wait.

Of course, Shaw was conscious of the ingredients which were to interact with such fateful consequences. As a part of the Protestant Ascendancy with nationalist sympathies, he delighted in the paradox which associated Catholicism, the creed of authority, of tradition and submission, with revolt, while the Protestants, whose spiritual ancestors had emphasized individualism and the right of protest, supported the establishment.

He was well aware, too, of the importance of mutual caricature in perpetuating a quarrel. He may even have appreciated, though he did not emphasize, that an effective caricature must contain a germ of truth. The Irish Protestant's picture of himself as honest, hardworking, realistic, practical, and successful becomes his rival's caricature of a dour, humorless, unimaginative grafter with no time for the better things of life. The Irish Catholic's self-portrait as an artistic, community-loving, unselfish, and lovably untidy dreamer becomes in the eye of the Prod the exposure of a lazy, feckless, unsuccessful, and untrustworthy good-for-nothing.

This mutual distortion is facilitated by segregation within the educational process. The Catholic church prefers to educate its future generations in Catholic schools. Protestants have no complaint, since this leaves them with a virtual monopoly of the state system. And many young people in Northern Ireland have reached adulthood without once in their lives actually meeting anyone from the other tradition. Shaw spoke of education in Ireland as a hellish training which prolongs "the separation of the Irish people into two hostile camps."[6] At once a consequence and a cause of segregation is the drawing of the "battle lines" which followed the renewal of violence in 1969, when Belfast families living in areas dominated by the other tradition moved away to the safety of homogeneous housing areas.

The natural distortion within Northern Ireland is true to a lesser degree between Irish and English. The misapprehensions between Doyle and Broadbent in *John Bull's Other Island* are amusing and instructive not, as Shaw would persuade us in the Preface, because they represent total self-delusion, but because enshrined within them is a germ, though only a germ, of truth.

Sometimes it is necessary to invent a caricature in order to explain away what would otherwise spoil the argument. Those who seek to understand why Irish Protestants have been so reluctant to accept rule from a Catholic-dominated south are fobbed off with accounts of Catholic social teaching. What Protestant, it is asked, shares the Catholic view of divorce, or contraception, or a national health service? The answer is "most Irish Protestants." The Presbyterians of Ulster have been in total agreement with Catholic teaching on all these subjects, at least throughout most of the period when they have resisted incorporation. Recently, indeed, there has emerged a generation which has questioned such teaching. But equally there have been nationalists who reject it. The issue in Northern Ireland is not individual liberation.

And Shaw was aware of the importance of history in Irish discourse, and specifically of the history which is taught in the respective traditions. The English, who, with an effort, can recall from schooldays the year of the Battle of Hastings, fail totally to understand the number of events of which the least scholarly Irishman can recall the precise dates, and which accordingly are celebrated each year, reviving afresh the passions which were evoked by the original deed.

Of course, the history is sometimes edited, as it is in most educational systems, to exemplify what is required of it. The Battle of the Boyne (1690), celebrated annually by Ulster Protestants, may have been won by predominantly Protestant mercenaries over Catholic ones, but it occasioned great joy to the Pope, who gave thanks for the discomfiture of James's patron, Louis XIV. The tragic Battle of the Somme in 1916 may have cost the lives of virtually an entire Protestant division, but there were as many bereaved Catholic families in Ireland.

Shaw must have known that the events thus remembered are not thought of as history. For the participants, the massacres of Drogheda or of Scullabogue are eternally reenacted. And it is hard for the English, whose island has been relatively free from bloodshed for three centuries, to appreciate how, for the Irish, political violence has rarely been far away, and how martyrdom is a perpetual recognition of the tragedy in the very substance of the Godhead.

But Shaw had little to say about all this because when he wrote *John Bull's Other Island* in 1904, the dispute appeared to be between Irish and English, not between Taig and Prod. And he believed, rightly, that English Unionism was a temporary phenomenon. Even in 1929, when he wrote a sequel to the 1906 Preface, he failed to appreciate the paralyzing pervasiveness of the sectarian division within Ireland. He argued that by cutting off the industrial economy of the northeast from the conservative influence of the agricultural areas, the employers in Ulster had deprived themselves of their allies against the growing power of the working class. And he concluded that they would be driven to seek a federal government embracing the two parts of Ireland.

This is a thesis which he first set out in *How to Settle the Irish Question* in 1917, and he was still arguing it in 1950 when, six months before his death, he wrote to Sean O'Casey,

> Now we are an insignificant cabbage garden in a little islet quite out of the headlines; and our Fianna Fail Party is now The Unionist Party and doesnt know it. I have nothing to tell them except that the Ulster capitalists will themselves abolish the Partition when the Labor [*sic*] Party is strong enough to threaten them with an Irish 1945 at the polls, and they must have the support of the Catholic agricultural south to avert it.[7]

What still eluded him was the persistent stranglehold of the rival nationalisms upon the industrial workers to whom he looked for a political initiative. The employers of Ulster still sleep easy in their beds, or at least their anxieties are not evoked by any demand among their workforce for a more substantial share of the profits. The trade unions are too busy coping with potentially divisive cultural conflict, and the electorate continues to listen to sectarian rallying cries.

Perhaps Shaw's greatest contribution to the discussion is his exposure of the uncomprehending, flat-footed, hazily indignant reaction of the English to Irish affairs. In 1904 he was devastatingly derisive of the clumsy devices adopted by the English to maintain their colonial rule. And even before Protestant nationalism became a coherent political force, he had stripped away the claim of the English to serve as an honest broker.

In other parts of the world, they had rejoiced in the role of arbitrator between bickering factions. But the English were dealing with peoples who, at that time, had few aspirations to democracy. In a country which aspired not only to self-government but to representative government, the uninvited umpire was a nonstarter.

Shaw dismissed the suggestion on two distinct grounds. First, the roles of judge and governor are inconsistent: "For there is only one condition on which a man can do justice between two litigants, and that is that he shall have no interest in common with either of them, whereas it is only by having every interest in common with both of them that he can govern them tolerably."[8] The very lack of sympathetic understanding of, or interest in, Irish affairs which might have qualified the English to help negotiate a final settlement of the dispute was their gravest disqualification from governing any part of Ireland in a continuing situation.

But, second, England had hardly presented itself as just and principled in its dealings with Ireland. And the more complicated the situation has become since 1904, the more tragic its consequences, the less consistent have become the turns and twists of the English as they grab at any solution. The one theme on which the people of both traditions in Northern Ireland are in complete agreement is that it is pointless to address to the English a principled argument relating to the merits. Ultimately, they insist, the English will opt for the line of least resistance. They will succumb to the most troublesome and most immediate threat.

In the 1929 Postscript Shaw returned to the theme of English ineptitude with the additional ammunition provided by the Government's response to the Easter Rising. But he failed to foresee where it would lead. With only one other party to the dialogue, there remained hope that more rational voices in England would prevail, and that a little goodwill and tolerance might resolve the problem. But confronted by two deeply entrenched and internecine forces, each dedicated to resisting any concession to the other, the English were out of their depth.

The purpose of English policy in Ireland has changed since 1904. The hope then was that, by being granted home rule, Ireland would be satisfied to remain politically a part of the British Isles and content to be shown as red on the map. Today, England's most fervent hope is to find a way of abdicating further involvement with the quarrels of Ireland. It is a policy of disengagement. The debate about the border is perceived as a dialogue of the deaf, and the search for a peaceful solution as a quest for an illusion. Northern Ireland is seen largely as a security problem, and England's policy has become an exercise in crisis management.

The difficulty is how to leave without unleashing a bloodbath and how to disengage without being seen to back away in the face of violence, and so encourage terrorism. It would be unfair not to add that the English pride themselves still on their sense of justice and their real compassion for the Irish people, and that they would be reluctant to admit that they had departed with no heed for the consequences for all the people of

Northern Ireland. The Irish perception of England's unprincipled convolutions, like every other aspect of the relationship, is a mixture of truth and caricature.

But what Shaw could not be expected to foresee are the consequences of the subsequent troubles for the three generations in Ireland who have known little else. Their experiences have changed the very nature of Ireland. No one purporting to write about the country in the last decade of the twentieth century would have written *John Bull's Other Island,* nor yet a treatise like the 1906 "Preface for Politicians," even together with its Postscripts.

Shaw recorded in the 1906 Preface that the play was produced in London rather than at the Irish Literary Theatre, for which it was written, because "It was uncongenial to the whole spirit of the neo-Gaelic movement, which is bent on creating a new Ireland after its own ideal, whereas my play is a very uncompromising presentment of the real old Ireland."[9]

Yeats and O'Leary, Davis and Hyde undoubtedly altered the course of Irish history. The old Ireland was destined to change. But they were not to foresee the Ireland which they helped to conjure. Ideas change reality, but the changes are not necessarily reflections of the ideas, for the ideas need to activate the men of deeds, and they are by definition different from the scholars.

Even of them it can be said that they knew not what they did. Those who seek political aims by violence fail all too often to realize that bloodshed easily becomes an end in itself. It is a way of life which gradually loses its relationship with the original objective. And even where it is successful, it changes and distorts its own purpose. The analogy is not of a destination with violence as only one option among the various routes. The destination itself is destroyed.

A peaceful, free, and united Ireland cannot be achieved by violence, repression, and division. Violence leads only to further violence. An outrage is requited with a further outrage, and that in turn with the next. For the patriot, the original vision is lost. For the community, life becomes a nightmare of perpetual anxiety and fear.

The violence discourages economic investment, and the distortion of political debate perpetuates the deprivation. The result is to provide paramilitaries with a source of resentful, frustrated, and frequently unemployed potential recruits. And there has evolved a class of godfathers whose power, prestige, and prosperity depend upon perpetuating the rival paramilitary systems, and therefore the divisions, the myths, and the hatred which nourish them.

Only those who see bloodshed from a safe distance can long entertain illusions about its romance or its purifying qualities. Shaw in a cynical mood had replied to those who warned of bloodshed if the English withdrew from Ireland that "civil war is one of the privileges of a nation." He added, "if hatred, calumny and terror have so possessed men that they cannot live in peace as other nations do, they had better fight it out and get rid of their bad blood that way."[10]

It is doubtful whether this was ever more than an exercise in shocking the English. As early as 1903, when he wrote his Preface to "The Revolutionist's Handbook" (added as an appendix to the text of *Man and Superman*), he dismissed political violence as futile. Having conceded that improvement was unlikely to come about through persuasion, he continued:

> I make a present of all these admissions to the Fenian who collects money from thoughtless Irishmen in America to blow up Dublin Castle; to the detective who persuades foolish young workmen to order bombs from the nearest ironmonger and then delivers them up to penal servitude. . . . But of what use is it to substitute the way of the reckless and bloodyminded for the way of the cautious and humane? . . .
>
> No: what Caesar, Cromwell and Napoleon could not do with all the physical force and moral prestige of the State in their mighty hands, cannot be done by enthusiastic criminals and lunatics.[11]

It has to be admitted that this denunciation of political violence stemmed (ostensibly at least) from a developing conviction that eugenics was more helpful than politics as a method of improving the world. Already in 1903 Shaw was beginning to despair of the human material with which politicians have of necessity to work. His contribution to the debate might have been more effective had he used his dramatic genius to expose the tragedy and ugliness of political violence.

In *Saint Joan,* he tore away the euphemisms from physical suffering. After de Stogumber, who had called throughout for the burning of Joan and had been driven mad by the reality when he saw it, indicates in the Epilogue that he has become a different man as a result, Cauchon asks, "Must then a Christ perish in torment in every age to save those that have no imagination?"[12] It is a question which he might well have asked of Ireland in the twentieth century.

But perhaps it would have been demanding too much to expect that Shaw should have appreciated the reality of the continuing, apparently endless conflict in Northern Ireland. If he could have done so, would he have resigned himself to the belief that nothing can improve the world except the gradual evolution of a superior race? Fortunately, there are those who believe that hope still lies in the real human beings whose actions will determine the foreseeable future. Shortsighted, prejudiced, arrogant, and aggressive as we are, we may yet not be past redeeming. And if there is a suffering remnant to whom there may be vouchsafed a redeeming insight into the human condition, it may well be the Irish.

Notes

1. "Preface for Politicians (to the First Edition in 1906)," *Collected Plays with Their Prefaces,* ed. Dan H. Laurence (London: Max Reinhardt, 1970–74), 2: 841.

2. *How to Settle the Irish Question* (London: Constable, 1917).

3. See, for example, Nicholas Mansergh, *The Irish Question* (London: George Allen & Unwin, 1965), chapter 2.

4. Paul Frolich, *Rosa Luxemburg* (London: Victor Gollancz, 1940), p. 45.

5. *Hansard's Parliamentary Debates* 304 (3rd series), col. 1053.

6. Michael Holroyd, *Bernard Shaw: The Pursuit of Power, 1898–1918* (London: Chatto & Windus, 1989), p. 385.

7. *Bernard Shaw, Collected Letters, 1926–1950,* ed. Dan H. Laurence (New York: Viking, 1988), pp. 864–65.

8. "Preface for Politicians," pp. 832–33.

9. Ibid., p. 808.

10. Holroyd, p. 390.

11. "Preface to The Revolutionist's Handbook," *Collected Plays with Their Prefaces* 2: 761–63. There is an echo of this in *The Intelligent Woman's Guide to Socialism and Capitalism* (1928), chapter 75, and in *Everybody's Political What's What?* (1944), chapter 30.

12. *Saint Joan, Collected Plays with Their Prefaces* 6: 202.

C. E. Hill

SHAW AND LOCAL GOVERNMENT

A democratic State cannot become a Social-Democratic State unless it has in every centre of population a local governing body as thoroughly democratic in its constitution as the central Parliament.
Bernard Shaw, *"The Transition to Social Democracy"[1]*

The work of Bernard Shaw contains frequent descriptions of British local government in his own day as linked to a vision of the future, a "municipal socialist future" where the land and industry of whole towns would pass into municipal hands and the House of Commons would become a mere "organ for federating the municipalities, and nationalizing inter-municipal rents by an adjustment of the municipal contributions to . . . taxation."[2]

Local government in Britain has a long and complicated history, going back to Anglo-Saxon and Celtic times. A multiplicity of different bodies and authorities emerged during the years, including, in some areas, vestries. As late as the 1890s the vestries remained, and Shaw's first venture into local government was as a vestryman, rather than as a councillor. In the late nineteenth century, a number of important enactments, prepared by governments of both the Conservative and Liberal parties, resulted in England and Wales enjoying a two-tiered structure of local government, with a limited third tier for some of the smallest communities. The main bodies in 1899 were county councils, county borough councils (for the larger towns and cities), and, in parallel as it were, the London County Council. Figure 1 illustrates their positions.

Shaw had become a noted political speaker and pamphleteer in London during the 1880s and early 1890s and had made a small reputation in the national arena, yet he never ran for public office during this period. However, following the famous Fabian policy of "permeation," Shaw sought election to the School Board of St. Pancras Vestry in 1894 and was roundly defeated.

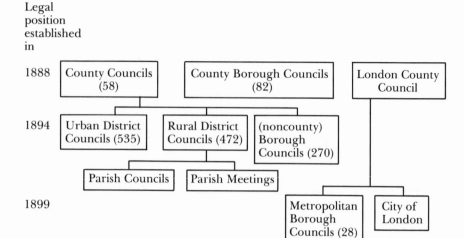

Legal
position
established
in

Fig. 1. Local Government in England and Wales in 1899[3]

Not discouraged, Shaw was nominated again for municipal office in May 1897. Since there were only five candidates for five positions, he found himself appointed to the Vestry Committee of Ward Seven of St. Pancras after an uncontested election. In fact, the main business of the vestry was not conducted by the committees of the constituent wards, but by the vestry as a whole in regular fortnightly meetings or by its ten subcommittees, which met more frequently. The 167 vestrymen of St. Pancras and their chairman represented two hundred thousand inhabitants of urban north London, including those of Shaw's home in Fitzroy Square, not far from Tottenham Court Road north of Soho.

With his fellow vestrymen, Shaw brought local knowledge to bear upon local problems, and he was twice appointed to the Subcommittee on Health, once to the Officers' Subcommittee (which, in modern terminology, performed a personnel-management function), and once to the Subcommittee for Electricity and Public Lighting. Many years later, Shaw explained to readers of *Everybody's Political What's What?* that under this municipal committee system such subcommittees "consider all questions appropriate to their departments and report their conclusions to the whole body. The reports can be discussed and accepted or amended or sent back for further consideration on their merits."[4] In theory this method of organization ensured democratic control by the whole authority over municipal policy, but also encouraged individual members to develop detailed knowledge in particular areas of responsibility. Shaw's experience of working in detail on questions of public health, personnel management, and electricity supply had notable effects on some of his published writings, from *The Common Sense of Municipal Trading* to *The Doctor's Dilemma*.

The effect of the London Government Act of 1899 was to replace the St. Pancras Vestry with the Metropolitan Borough of St. Pancras. While many of the old personnel and problems remained, there were several new administrative rules and formulas. For example, on the one hand the main civic dignitary of St. Pancras became a mayor rather than the vestry chairman; on the other, the council had new internal electoral boundaries. Shaw's ward was amalgamated with a neighboring one, and he was obliged to fight a contested election for one of six seats on 1 November 1900. In fact, Shaw's council work had clearly been appreciated by his constituents, despite a long absence from vestry meetings in 1899 while convalescing after a foot injury. He was second in the poll of ten candidates, with 704 votes, and was thus elected.

Although the "progressive" party on the London County Council was very successful and led that body from 1892 to 1907 (at the same time that Shaw was serving as a St. Pancras vestryman and borough councillor), within St. Pancras there was little support for the idea of "municipal socialism." Shaw found a few allies for his various local campaigns (notably the Methodist clergyman Ensor Williams), but he was frequently frustrated by colleagues he believed to be "absurdly unequal" to their tasks. He was also personally hindered both by ill health and by his literary work. This in turn led to frequent absences from the council chamber. He missed 129 meetings out of 321 between November 1900 and September 1903.

Michael Holroyd has suggested that the success of the Vienna production of *The Devil's Disciple* in February 1903 was one factor that induced Shaw to retire from local politics at the 1903 elections, but this ignores that in March 1904 he stood unsuccessfully as a "progressive" candidate for the London County Council in South St. Pancras. Shaw may have been disillusioned with the political caliber of his colleagues on the borough council, but he was still willing to join forces with like-minded people, including several Fabian socialists, on another body, thus seeking to continue to serve the people of London and St. Pancras. Shaw's interventions in the local politics of St. Pancras were intermittent during his six years of formal office, but there have nevertheless been a few attempts to chronicle them in detail.[5]

Among noteworthy features of Shaw's work in local government were his unsuccessful attempts to persuade the municipality to use its local planning powers to acquire a municipal monopoly on building. He argued that if the council vetoed lucrative private developments and then undertook the work itself, it would be able to "balance the books" on the loss-making provision of dwellings for the poor, a public duty since Disraeli's Artisans' and Labourers' Dwellings Improvement Act of 1874.

Another unsuccessful Shavian campaign related to the provision within the borough of free public lavatories for women. Shaw campaigned vigorously but unsuccessfully on this matter in the borough's local press and through the Fabian Tract *Women as Councillors*,[6] but he was defeated by the weight of conventional prejudice. Other Shavian failures (again related to his work on the health subcommittee) were abortive plans to build a crematorium in St. Pancras (in 1902 and 1903) and his proposals to appoint additional sanitary inspectors (urgently necessary because of the slum-ridden character of the borough, and particularly so after the smallpox outbreak of 1901).

Following Shaw's advocacy, St. Pancras joined a newly formed municipal-insurance organization in 1904. By pooling their risks, the member local authorities greatly reduced their premiums. Strangely, this was only agreed to reluctantly, and the delays were such that St. Pancras joined the plan only some time after Shaw ceased his activities as a councillor. Nevertheless, his proposal clearly was consonant with the primary goal of the majority of St. Pancras councillors, the reduction of the authority's short-term expenditure, and furthered Shaw's own broader aims as well.

His opposition to the spending of the St. Pancras ratepayers' financial contributions on the official regalia of council office is relatively well known. Perhaps it is an aspect of the antiaristocratic bias of Shaw's politics that he found it particularly objectionable that middle-class councillors should ape the pomp of nobility. He also viewed the use of council office to promote a personal interest as a form of corruption and seldom took part "in debates on local theatres, libraries and music halls" lest he be accused of promoting his own interests.[7] There are penetrating and amusing comments on municipal corruption, or something very like it, in two plays written before Shaw had any direct personal experience of local government and certainly before he served on any local government body. In *Widowers' Houses* (1892), the humble and downtrodden rent collector, Lickcheese, brings about a dramatic and drastically effective transformation in his personal fortunes by judicious working of compensation legislation. In *Candida* (1895), the less than wholly scrupulous Burgess, Candida's father, described as a man "made coarse and sordid by the compulsory selfishness of petty commerce," has a very sharp eye for the possibility of seizing local-authority contracts by backstairs methods.

In fact, the practice of manipulating a municipal office for private gain was notorious—not just in St. Pancras—and is no doubt still with us. As Shaw wrote in *Everybody's Political What's What?* forty years after his own experiences, "when some big growing business wants to gain more space to have a street closed . . ." it does not distribute ten-pound notes among the municipal councillors. Its manager gets elected to the municipality, and makes himself popular by entertaining his colleagues at banquets where champagne flows like water, besides being always ready with a subscription to this or that good cause in which the councillors are interested. A conviction soon spreads that the street in question is useless, dangerous and ought to be abolished. It is closed; and the manager thereupon disappears from public life, and is seen no more in his aldermanic gown. (*EPWW*, p. 272)

Yet Shaw did not enter the council chamber with only a strong moral sense to inform his activities there. His "political mind" was by no means a *tabula rasa*. He was already a committed Fabian socialist, and his Fabianism clearly influenced his approach to local government.

There is abundant evidence that, during the 1880s, Bernard Shaw "flirted" with a variety of unorthodox political opinions. From the late 1880s onward, however, he was in broad agreement with the general politics of the Fabian Society. Indeed, he became one of the major public advocates of "Fabian socialism" in England and edited the *Fabian Essays* of 1889. Nevertheless, long before he wrote *The Intelligent Woman's Guide*, Shaw was a most unorthodox Fabian. His famous proposal for equal incomes first appeared in 1910.

Indeed, Shaw's Fabian socialism was largely predicated on one view that he had retained from some of the more extreme political adventures of his youth: that a true community could only exist following the abolition of those inequalities of income that arose from private property in the means of production. Until 1910 he was willing to accept that it might be necessary to replace such inequalities with other (democratically agreed) forms of income disparity, in order to attract persons of the correct abilities into the appropriate forms of work, but he always favored measures that tended toward equality of income and public ownership of the means of production.

While Shaw supported universal male and female suffrage, he did not generally favor fully participative democracy. His *political* egalitarianism was tempered by an assumption that an altruistic elite (either self-selecting or part of a preselected panel of rulers) must be entrusted with the task of resisting sinister interests (the *bête noire* of his polemic against "municipal corruption").[8] The essential function of universal suffrage was to provide security against misrule by the elite, who could always be dismissed from office at election time. Given a "career open to all the talents"—that is, an open elite—there was no special reason why the opinion of "everyman" and "everywoman" should be given *special* consideration. However, the decentralization of government (as implied by the concept of "municipal socialism") would allow politicians to keep in closer contact with their electorate and give *appropriate* consideration to the views of the ordinary citizen. The ruling elite should be aware that failure to "deliver" a certain quality of services could be best detected by public opinion, but the technical measures necessary to achieve that quality generally should be left in their expert hands. Given such basically liberal-democratic assumptions, Shaw was able to accept the constitutional and reformist strategy of the Fabian Society for many years.

Fabian "constitutionalism" and "reformism" were generally synonyms for a strategy of propaganda designed to influence the existing national electorate (about 60 percent of the adult male population, or 30 percent of the whole adult population) and the elected (and unelected) members of a variety of governmental institutions in favor of various collectivist reforms of the law. Even Annie Besant's Fabian Parliamentary League of 1886–88 was never intended as a "Fabian political party," and the Society as a whole sought "influence" rather than "office." It was intended that the influence should affect members of all other parties, including Conservatives. But as we have seen, the pursuit of influence did not exclude Fabians from actually seeking election to office themselves when there was a realistic chance of success and it was an economical exercise of members' time.

Typically the Fabians favored "rational," nonconfrontational debate, and, as Shaw wrote in 1896,

> when the House of Commons is freed from the veto of the House of Lords and thrown open to candidates from all classes by an effective system of Payment of Representatives and a more rational method of election, the British Parliamentary system will be in the opinion of the Fabian Society, a first-rate practical instrument of democratic government.[9]

In correspondence with Belfort Bax in the *Saturday Review* of 1900, Shaw defended the constitutional monarchy, and so, even if we were ignorant of his activities in St. Pancras, there would be no grounds for surprise that the mature Shaw was willing to participate in the workings of another (and much less ancient) branch of the British constitution, namely, its system of local government. For many years, such bodies were in some respects more democratic than national government, elected as they were by a ratepayer franchise, which included female property owners. However, the transition to a universal adult franchise in local government elections was delayed until 1945, while it was more or less achieved for Westminster elections by 1928.

Despite his concern for local democracy, Shaw argued in a series of other writings from 1896 onward that capitalism systematically deceived the electorate and prevented democracy from performing its true function of restraining special interests. Many socialists would agree with him on this point, but Shaw took the argument much further and contended that the "common man" was intrinsically incapable of seeing through this deception, which implied that a more closed form of government than the parliamentary one was needed to ensure expert legislation and administration.

Certainly the failure to secure the election of "progressive" councillors and M.P.s had been anticipated by Bernard Shaw and that other Fabian luminary, Sidney Webb, for a number of years. They expected it on the grounds that "practical remedies" for social ills had to be "demonstrated" before they could attract widespread support. Hence, there was good reason for attempts to "capture" individual councils or poor-relief authorities ("Boards of Guardians") as "laboratories" for collectivist "experiments." Yet, at the same time, Fabian socialist writings in the 1880s and 1890s were vigorously arguing against both privately organized socialist colonies (such as Robert Owen's New Harmony) and nationally funded "labour colonies" for the unemployed.[10] If the first type of enterprise could not succeed in a predominantly capitalist environment, the second could not realistically expect to be funded by taxes raised by a "capitalist" parliament. Thus, even leaving aside explicitly antisocialist arguments, the validity of a third enterprise of "municipal socialism" was not necessarily obvious by inspection. For instance, unlike a socialist "colony," a socialist municipality was not self-selecting in the sense that a small or large minority of its members might well vote for nonsocialist councillors, nor was it self-contained, since its collectivist regulations might well affect the electorate of other municipalities. Given these considerations, "municipal socialism" could only succeed if its "socialism" was not an ideological "blueprint" overtly hostile to private property, but a limited set of pragmatically agreed collectivist reforms that enjoyed a measure of consensual support. The Fabians had no difficulty with this (indeed, for Webb it was a great virtue), but they never satisfactorily answered another major counterargument. In any nonfederal or nonconfederal system, local taxation is only national taxation "at a distance" (in effect, it could be said to be collected locally for convenience only), and central government, which in the Western world will normally be overtly "capitalist" in orientation, will be bound to take measures to prevent the open-ended development of municipal collectivism, hence restricting the "inevitability of gradualness."

Whatever the merits of the idea that British municipalities could form "islands of socialism," Shaw certainly used it as the basis of a major strand in the political strategy which he advocated over a number of decades.

Shaw argued that the socialist Left should seek electoral support on the basis of administrative expertise and efficiency in administering the existing system of local government, while at the same time seeking national legislative reforms that would greatly extend the role of local government as both a regulator and as a corporation able to act to some extent on its own account in the local and national economy. This was virtually the same general strategy advocated by Sidney Webb.

In the late 1880s, both Webb and Shaw were impressed by what they termed the "efficiency" of English local government in such model cities as Birmingham and, nationally, in the wake of the creation of county councils by act of Parliament in 1888. For Webb the term "efficiency" usually meant the ability of a national society to provide adequately for the physical health and social competence (that is, the technical skills and moral awareness necessary for social living) of the individuals who collectively made up the nation. Webb believed that the ability of Victorian local government to provide technical and secondary education, sanitation, health and factory regulation, subsidized housing, free school meals, and public bathhouses all contributed to "efficiency" as he understood it, and this was the focus of much of his propaganda for "municipal socialism."

Although Shaw was impresssed by these arguments, his own views were slightly different in that he tended to emphasize abstract grounds for believing in the injustice of the existing distribution of wealth in Victorian Britain. His arguments suggested that "municipal socialism" would redistribute the "unearned" rents of land and capital to the community which had created them, and thus avoid the waste of physical resources that resulted when the capitalist and aristocratic classes spent their money on luxuries that could not be used by the population at large.

From a Fabian point of view there was much to be done, and, as Shaw commented in the *Fabian Essays*, "the Local Government Board of the future will be a tremendous affair."[11] There seems to have been a measure of continuity between the ideas behind Shaw's "libertarian" socialist views of the early 1880s, when he advocated widespread competition between private and public bodies (drawing upon his knowledge of the thought of Proudhon), and his views in the late 1880s, when he argued that local rather than central government should provide the basis for a more limited range of competitive public bodies. By introducing competition where there had previously been monopoly, Shaw expected a reduction of "unearned" rents and a superior service to the consumer/citizen. In the long run, he believed that local public enterprise would drive competitors out of business— first the small-scale "sweating" employer and subsequently the larger monopolies—thereby leaving only a small residual role for private enterprise.[12]

This theme was continued in Shaw's 1896 *Report on Fabian Policy* with the central argument that "the State should not monopolize industry as against private enterprise or individual initiative further than may be necessary to make the livelihood of the people and their access to the sources of production completely independent of both."[13] Furthermore, the assumption clearly was that this state control of industry would be administered from subnational levels. Three such forms are listed before the central government is even mentioned. The reader is frequently reminded that Fabian socialism is *state* socialism—in the 1890s (if not before), Shaw and the other leading Fabians had little time for either communist anarchism or producer cooperatives:

> Socialism, as understood by the Fabian Society, means the organisation and conduct of the necessary industries of the country, and the appropriation of all forms of economic rent of land and capital, by the nation as a whole, through the most suitable public authorities, parochial, municipal, provincial, or central. . . . The Socialism advocated by the Fabian Society is State Socialism exclusively.[14]

The *Report on Fabian Policy* provides short and cogent summaries of the Shavian/Fabian view on many issues in the mid 1890s. There is much less than one might like, but Shaw defended (by implication) the role of that infant institution the municipal civil service (at any level above that of the parish council) when he explained,

> The Fabian Society energetically repudiates all conceptions of Democracy as a system by which the technical work of government administration, and the appointment of public officials, shall be carried on by referendum or any other form of direct popular decision. Such arrangements may be practical in a village community, but not in the complicated industrial civilizations which are ripening for Social-Democracy.[15]

While the *Report on Fabian Policy* was drafted before Shaw's practical experience of local government began, his most extensive discussion of the subject was written at the end of his council career.

In the Preface to the first edition of *The Common Sense of Municipal Trading* (1904), Shaw observed that

> the question whether municipal trading is sound in principle cannot be settled by the figures of this or that adventure in it, any more than the soundness of banking or insurance can be settled by the figures of this or that big dividend or disastrous liquida-

tion. Counters of a much more spiritual kind are needed, and some imagination and conscience to add them up, as well.[16]

The arguments in the text are at a certain level of generality, and Shaw deliberately omitted statistical data in an attempt to popularize the work. His central argument for municipal trading was that it produced commodities at "the current cost of production plus a rate of interest which includes no insurance against risk of loss," since investors in municipal debt received a fixed return and did not have to risk a share of any possible losses on the terms associated with equity capital. Furthermore, profits were not distributed as dividends but returned "to the ratepayer in relief of rates or in public service of some kind." On these terms it was Shaw's opinion that "it will always be possible for a municipality of average capacity to underbid a commercial company" (*CSMT*, p. 4).

Shaw recognized that such success was not always achieved in practice, sometimes as a result of financial incompetence on the part of the municipality and sometimes because of the exceptional managerial talent of private competitors (*CSMT*, pp. 5, 16). In contradiction to his earlier (more youthful) views, Shaw argued that municipalities were unsuited to organizing industrial production unless they could ensure that their own demand for the product was "sufficiently extensive and constant to keep the necessary plant fully employed" (*CSMT*, p. 13). Drawing upon his own experiences and the arguments of H. G. Wells (in a paper to the Fabian Society given in 1903),[17] Shaw acknowledged that the existing British municipalities were insufficiently large to trade adequately in something as capital intensive as electricity production and that it was also the case that the price of urban land was sufficiently high to make municipal housing for the poor extraordinarily expensive (*CSMT*, chapters 7 and 8).

However, these difficulties were not intrinsically unsolvable. A redrawing of municipal boundaries in order to take into account "distribution of population" and "natural" (meaning geographical) "configuration" (*CSMT*, p. 61) would allow local government to trade effectively in electricity and other industries with significant economies of scale. Hence, following Wells, Shaw was one of the first advocates of (in effect) a regional tier of government for the United Kingdom. His solution to the municipal housing problem, however, espoused a different type of radicalism. He argued that the municipality should *own* the whole of "the land within its jurisdiction," charging rents according to "the commercial or residential desirability" of its holdings, but modifying market forces by pooling its total rent income and thereby establishing and subsidizing a "moral minimum" of house accommodation at a "fair rent" (*CSMT*, p. 72). Hence, by implication, the elimination of the lowest strata of housing (the Dickensian slums) would be paid for by those living in the most desirable properties, rather than by the ratepayers as a whole, while local authorities would become giant freeholders.

Thus Shaw's original view of the importance of local democracy and municipal socialism seems to have changed between the late 1880s and the early 1900s. While the optimum role for the local state was still very significant, by implication it was no longer to be all-embracing. Shaw's practical experiences of the failings of local government provided data for this modification, but the character of national political debate in Britain had also changed in the wake of the Boer War. The Fabian Society had become embroiled in national controversies regarding imperialism and the idea of tariff reform (the famous challenge by Joseph Chamberlain to Victorian orthodoxy on free trade). One explanation might be that the greater role for *national* government advocated in *Fabianism and the Empire* and *Fabianism and the Fiscal Question* implied a subtle shift in Shaw's political thought toward the general proposition that central government should enjoy greater powers. This did not necessarily imply a diminution of local authority, but there certainly does seem to have been a change in the "center of gravity" of Shaw's Fabian politics during the period. At about this time, there may be detected an ironic paradox in Shaw's view, of which he seems to have been unaware. At the same time, he was asserting that the larger entity, the British Empire, was justified in imposing its will and power on the Boers, simply because, apparently, largeness and efficiency were the same thing in international affairs, whereas, in the field of local government, he insisted on the need to strengthen borough authorities.

The older Shaw seems to have deemed his contribution to political economy in the 1880s of greater intellectual value than his early forays into literature. However, the Fabian theory of rent was always elaborated at a level of general abstraction, and not until the early 1900s did specific questions about taxation and government revenues become central to Fabian debates. Hence, it is not entirely surprising that Shaw's most elaborate comments on the subject of municipal finance also date from this period.

Shaw considered various reforms of local taxation that would recognize the socialist judgment "that personal industry is often in inverse ratio to income" (*CSMT*, p. 94). He concluded that, in fact, the mode of taxation was less important than the urgent need for a system of exemptions and abatements from payment to benefit low-income holders of small property, such as owners of shops, workshops, and normal residential homes.

A secondary but nevertheless important priority was that rate charges should reflect the potential value of properties as development sites, rather than the potential rental incomes from the existing buildings on the sites. While Shaw recognized that this mode of taxation would deter the improving landlord from investing in property (and would not really touch those whose income was derived from industrial dividends or government stock), he believed that it would also reduce the level of those rental incomes that increased as a result of changes in the character of a neighborhood, involving no personal effort by the owner (*CSMT*, pp. 92–95). He accepted that there was a good case for central government "grants-in-aid" to municipalities, in order to assist the provision of specific public services, and saw no good theoretical arguments against a local income tax (or local tariffs) as alternative means of raising municipal revenue (*CSMT*, pp. 99–100). However, Shaw predicted that these alternatives would not be adopted unless there was an "absolute refusal of the electorate to sanction sufficient . . . taxation to meet the growing necessities of the municipal exchequer" (*CSMT*, p. 100), and in fact British local government has "muddled through" with a system of finance by rates and "grants-in-aid" (the latter under a variety of names) until the late 1980s. In 1989 a new system of local government finance was introduced in Scotland, and in 1990 the same system was adopted in England and Wales. The new system (based on a Community Charge, or 'poll tax," levied on all adults living within each local authority area) has proved very unpopular. The U.K. Government has recently announced its intention to reestablish a form of local property tax by 1993.

Shaw's two major sustained works on political questions, *The Intelligent Woman's Guide to Socialism and Capitalism* and *Everybody's Political What's What?*, were both composed in the latter part of his life. In *The Intelligent Woman's Guide* (first published in 1928, and written in a style to appeal to the general reader, that is, to the intelligent woman, rather than to a man accustomed to discussing politics and economics in meaningless jargon), the reader will find that typical municipal services such as "the lighting of the streets . . . paving them . . . bridges across the rivers . . . and . . . the removal and destruction of dustbin refuse" are described as examples of "Communism"![18] Shaw used the word to shock some readers. A more sober usage would be "collectivism," but regardless of the verbiage, Shaw defended resolutely the principle that municipal services should be "paid for out of the common stock made up by our rates and taxes . . . for the benefit of everybody indiscriminately" (*IWG*, p. 13), although he recognized that, in practice, unequal incomes meant that the rich were the greater beneficiaries.

In *The Intelligent Woman's Guide*, Shaw's general defense of municipal enterprise was little different in character from that which he had put forward a quarter of a century before, but it was qualified by the observation that "local authorities, in order to carry on their public services, have to buy vast quantities of goods from private profiteers who charge them more than cost price, and . . . this overcharge is passed on to . . . [the] ratepayer" (*IWG*, p. 112). Yet this was in itself no justification for the centralization of public services, since exactly the same phenomenon took place with regard to central government and its taxation. On the other hand, there were powerful arguments for "nationalisation" (that is, the establishment of centralized public corporations that administered all of the nation's productive activity in specific industries) on other grounds. But all socialized production had to be at cost price. Shaw vehemently opposed those who argued that profits from municipal or nationalized trading were an index of business efficiency. Furthermore, he seems to have concluded that competition between public and private enterprise was both wasteful and unjust, in that private capital concentrated its resources on the "easy markets," leaving public enterprise to bear losses elsewhere. Hence, in the late 1920s, Shaw assumed that expropriation with compensation must become an increasingly important weapon in the socialist armory.

One further argument that Shaw put in *The Intelligent Woman's Guide* concerned the proposition that the committee system of decision making as practiced in English local government was vastly superior to the Westminster or "British Party System," where every issue became (in effect) a vote of confidence in the government and deterred members from judging issues "on their merits." He pursued this argument with much greater vigor sixteen years later, and the passage from the "Political Summary" of *Everybody's Political What's What?* that begins "The British Party System should be ruthlessly scrapped" and ends "All others are independent of party considerations in their votes on the reports" is certainly a fine piece of political rhetoric, whatever its merits as constitutional history or rigorous argument (*EPWW*, p. 353).

Two further points arise from *Everybody's Political What's What?* In chapter 4, Shaw concluded that "the rates" were not merely an imperfect instrument of local government finance, but positively harmful to municipal enterprise. That they were not directly related to ability to pay encouraged undercapitalization. The old "progressive" slogan "High Rates and a Healthy City" was not practically sufficient. Shaw denounced local authorities as "Parliaments of the Poor" and in chapter 31 suggested that the relative poverty of councillors was a major reason why they frequently felt unable to resist inducements to give favorable treatment to vested interests. The idea that the whole political elite (not just local councillors) should be preselected by criteria of education and character was a major theme in Shaw's later political writings, and he proposed it as the solution for this particular municipal problem (together with the equalization of incomes). An element of benevolent elitism was always present in Shaw's thought—but later in life he had grave doubts that such a benevolent elite would emerge "spontaneously."

The institutions of local government in the United Kingdom today are served by a far more sophisticated and complex bureaucracy than anything known to Shaw. Since 1945 (and to some extent before that), observers have often asked whether unpaid, part-time councillors can adequately control and supervise professional, full-time officers in the conduct of local government business. In other words, "How does one professionalize the councillors?"

Although financial reward does not guarantee expertise, it can be the first step to its achievement. For example, by strongly advocating that the mayor of St. Pancras should receive a salary, Shaw was providing a justification for the modern attendance allowances available to all councillors, and (given the workload of a modern council committee chairman) the more recent innovation of "special responsibility payments." In 1900, Shaw had pointed out that it was not merely that St. Pancras needed a full-time advocate in national government circles, but that the absence of payment "might prevent a poor man accepting the office."[19] The payment of councillors has ensured that at least some citizens from less-privileged backgrounds have been able to enter a form of public service that might previously have been closed to them.

It is now eighty years since the pioneering work of H. G. Wells (encouraged by Shaw and other Fabians) which pointed out that the United Kingdom has no structure of regional government. Today this is still the case despite the advocacy of Shaw in *The Common Sense of Municipal Trading*, W. A. Robson, and many others. That the two main Opposition parties in Parliament (Labour and Liberal Democrats) all have had manifesto commitments to such a structure might suggest that another Shavian idea has come of age.

However, all the opposition parties have other policy priorities, which may only be tempered by the need to meet nationalist aspirations in Scotland. Thus, it may be many years before legislation reaches the statute books. The present Conservative government may of course be reelected in the early 1990s, and it is well known for lacking sympathy with the idea of regional government, although previous Conservative governments have experimented with a larger scale of subnational authority. In 1963 a supercounty authority was created for London (the Greater London Council), and in 1972 six large-scale metropolitan county councils were created to administer the broad environmental services of planning, transport, and highways in the conurbations of the Midlands and the North. Nevertheless, clashes of responsibility with borough councils were frequent, and the Local Government Act of 1985

abolished these metropolitan authorities. Their functions were transferred back to the smaller councils or to ad hoc joint boards. The immediate (but publicly denied) cause of the 1985 act was political disagreement
between the Labour leaders of the authorities and Conservative ministers, but it may be the case that such authorities (a hybrid between
traditional local and regional government) would have been shortly superseded anyway.

For example, neither the London County Council nor the Greater
London Council (both now abolished) nor the Kent County Council (still
existent) could have adequately dealt with the problems arising from the
rail link to the new tunnel under the English Channel now being constructed by Eurotunnel. The solution imposed by Westminster has been
seen by many as ignoring local sensitivities, but a regional authority for
southeast England *might* have been able to combine local knowledge with
the breadth of competence necessary both to oversee such a large-scale
project and to design a more satisfactory solution. Certainly such environmental questions will add a new dimension to the debate about regional
government in the foreseeable future. It is hard to imagine that the
administration of important services, with transport the outstanding example, for the vast Greater London area will be possible without a central integrating authority.

Any attempt to assess the influence of a practical politician or a writer
is notoriously difficult. If a proposal for a legislative or administrative
measure is passed by one vote, every legislator who voted for the measure can claim to have had a decisive influence on its success. Shaw was a
practical politician whose proposed measures were nearly always defeated, and his claim to "influence" is even more precarious.

Shaw's main claims to fame lie elsewhere, but when measuring the
influence of a writer, the task is even more difficult. Clearly all authors
continually draw from a fund of past experiences, including the experience of reading, in order to find words to express their thoughts, but it is
dangerous to take parallel trains of argument or snippets of autobiography at face value. The reader of a text may claim to have been inspired
by a reading, but the use to which that reading is then put may be purely
to illustrate concepts that were already formed (and hence merely con-
firmed by agreement). Alternatively, a favorable reading (whether acknowledged or unacknowledged) may merely provide a shortcut to a
conclusion that was implicit in an already existing proposition and therefore *might* have been reached anyway. Meanwhile, an unfavorable reading ("negative influence"?) may also provoke interesting arguments, but
the previous qualification will again apply. Hence, in a sense, Shaw is a
figure in the development of Anglo-Saxon conservative thought thanks

to his debates with Mallock. Furthermore, *The Common Sense of Municipal Trading* prompted R. P. Porter to publish *The Dangers of Municipal Trading* in London in 1907.[20]

Fortunately, with Bernard Shaw's writings on local government, the task of assessing influence is somewhat easier than it might have been. It is hard to find evidence that subsequent writers on the subject claimed inspiration from Shaw, despite the wide circulation of the *Fabian Tracts* and his other more general works. A search for the more problematic phenomena of unacknowledged or unconscious influence is also likely to prove disappointing since no specifically Shavian ideas on local government have been outstandingly popular in British political circles. The most favorable interpretation is that Shaw probably reinforced the limited popularity of ideas of land-value taxation (already closely associated with Henry George), of municipal socialism (already closely associated with Sidney Webb), and of the application of the municipal committee system to national politics (already closely associated with the Labour M.P. Frederick Jowett), given that Shaw wrote about such matters in an accessible and witty style and that his books were widely distributed.[21] As to land taxation and municipal socialism, Shaw made great use of the concepts already formulated by George and Webb; Shaw and Jowett appear to have developed their ideas on committee government separately. On committee methods, it has to be said that, in both national and local government, the party system and voting on party lines are now even more firmly entrenched than in Shaw's day.

Shaw's writings on local government contributed to the development of a significant (but minority) left-of-center opinion in British political life, but he was by no means a trailblazer. Shaw's earliest socialist writings are notable for their references to Proudhon and Lassalle as well as to Marx, and it seems that for a time "the municipality" replaced the "self-sufficient association of producers" in his political affections. The older Shaw recognized that the early Fabians overestimated the strength of the social trends favoring political decentralization before World War I, and in later life he espoused a variety of political tactics aimed at realizing some of the goals of his socialism, some of which were remarkably illiberal. It could be, therefore, that the main value of a consideration of Shaw's writings on local government is that it reminds us that "Fabian" socialism was not always identical with the pragmatic, centralizing "welfarism" of the postwar, pre-Thatcherite era in Britain and invites us at least to consider alternative possibilities of economic and political organization. Against this, and to bring the matter up to date, it is possible that the Thatcher years, which have seen on the whole a great diminution in the importance and powers of local government, may give way, with the inevitable swing of the pendulum, to another look at the possibilities of wider development of powers at a local level. If that proves to be so, the work and thinking of Shaw may make a contribution.

Notes

1. Bernard Shaw, "The Transition to Social Democracy," *Fabian Essays in Socialism* (London: Allen & Unwin, 1948), p. 174.

2. Ibid., p. 185.

3. Tony Byrne, *Local Government in Britain*, 4th ed. (Harmondsworth: Penguin, 1986), p. 15. For further details see pp. 10–17.

4. Bernard Shaw, *Everybody's Political What's What?* (London: Constable, 1944), p. 353. Subsequent references to *EPWW* appear in the text.

5. The most successful of these attempts seem to be Michael Holroyd, *Bernard Shaw: The Search for Love, 1856–1898* (London: Chatto & Windus, 1988), pp. 412–25, and H. M. Geduld, "Bernard Shaw, Vestryman and Borough Councillor," *Californian Shavian* 3, no. 3 (May–June 1962). Also, the *Shavian* 2, no. 9 (June 1964), 7–13, has a shortened version.

6. Bernard Shaw, *Women as Councillors*, Fabian Tract no. 93 (London: Fabian Society, 1900).

7. Holroyd, p. 419.

8. See A. M. McBriar, *Fabian Socialism and English Politics, 1884–1918* (Cambridge: Cambridge University Press, 1962; reprinted 1966), pp. 89–90.

9. Bernard Shaw, *Report on Fabian Policy and Resolutions Presented by the Fabian Society to the International Socialist Workers and Trade Union Congress*, Fabian Tract no. 70 (London: Fabian Society, 1896), p. 5.

10. See Sidney Webb, *Socialism: True and False*, Fabian Tract no. 51 (London: Fabian Society, 1894).

11. Shaw, "The Transition to Social Democracy," p. 185.

12. Ibid., passim.

13. Shaw, *Report on Fabian Policy*, p. 6.

14. Ibid., p. 5.

15. Ibid.

16. Bernard Shaw, *The Common Sense of Municipal Trading* (London: Constable, 1904), p. v. Subsequent references to *CSMT* appear in the text.

17. See H. G. Wells, "The Question of Scientific Administrative Areas in Relation to Municipal Undertakings," *Mankind in the Making* (Leipzig: B. Tauchnitz, 1903), pp. 213–38.

18. Bernard Shaw, *The Intelligent Woman's Guide to Socialism and Capitalism,* Popular Edition (London: Constable, 1929), p. 12. Subsequent references to *IWG* appear in the text.

19. *Saint Pancras Gazette* (1 December 1900), p. 5.

20. For the precise details of its publication, see Robert P. Porter, *The Dangers of Municipal Trading* (London: G. Routledge & Sons, 1907), pp. v–vi.

21. See McBriar, pp. 324–25.

John V. Antinori

ANDROCLES AND THE LION HUNTER: G.B.S., GEORGE SYLVESTER VIERECK, AND THE POLITICS OF PERSONALITY

One of the more curious aspects of Bernard Shaw's life is his attraction and loyalty to controversial literary associates, even ones whose values and ideas were inimical to his own, such as Gabriel Pascal, Frank Harris, and Hubert Bland. Shaw had a similar relationship with George Sylvester Viereck, whose notoriety among his contemporaries rivaled that of Harris. A German-American poet and journalist, Viereck gained infamy as a propagandist for the Kaiser during and after World War I, and as an apologist for Germany between the World Wars. He eventually served time in prison as a result of his activities in defense of Adolf Hitler in the 1930s. Although the two men shared some similar experiences—both worked as propagandists, and both were suspected of being pro-German during World War I—they were markedly different. Shaw performed most of his political work without fee; Viereck profited from his work for the Germans. Shaw was Puritan in his personal habits; Viereck was a self-proclaimed moral and sexual relativist. Shaw was deeply suspicious of jingoistic patriotism; Viereck was an ardent German nationalist.

H. G. Wells introduced Viereck to Shaw sometime before World War I, and over the next several decades Viereck made regular pilgrimages to London to visit and interview the famous playwright. The interviews were published in William Randolph Hearst's *New York American*, *Liberty* magazine, and in Viereck's own periodical, the *American Monthly*. However, the accurate recording and disseminating of Shaw's thoughts and wisdom were not always Viereck's primary purposes. Viereck and Shaw's personal and professional association lends important insights into the politics and personalities of both men. What did each hope to gain from the relationship? What motives did Viereck have in pursuing Shaw's favor over the course of decades? Did Viereck hope to enlist the great man's name in support of his political priorities? If so, to what degree did he succeed? Why did Shaw continue to associate with Viereck, given the latter's shady professional ethics and unsavory reputation? Why did Viereck so charm Shaw that even after the German-American's support of Hitler became evident, the playwright could refer to Viereck, upon his release from prison, as a martyr?

Viereck's interviews with Shaw provide some answers. He took great liberty with Shaw's opinions, at times passing his own views off as his subject's, but Shaw tolerated Viereck's less-than-scrupulous reporting. Despite obvious differences in personality and individual values, each man found in the other qualities which complemented his own ego. Also, similar views on World War I and other political issues, and their common experience of isolation during the war, made it natural for them to be attracted to one another.

Viereck claims to have visited Shaw once each year, but he mentions in an interview that apparently took place in 1926 that three or four years had passed since his previous visit to Adelphi Terrace.[1] Except for the dates on the publications in which they appeared, there are few indications to show when the actual meetings with Shaw took place. Viereck had to be vague because one visit to Shaw could spawn several separate interviews, although they would not be identified as emanating from the same meeting. For example, Viereck visited Shaw on 8 June 1926 and from this meeting was able to cobble more than a year's worth of interviews. Like so many things concerning Viereck, the frequency of the visits is difficult to ascertain. What is certain is that after World War I, Viereck paid yearly visits to Europe and would attempt to meet Shaw on each occasion. In 1929, protesting at Viereck's inaccurate reporting, Shaw withdrew his permission for Viereck to publish further interviews. But by the mid 1930s Viereck had resumed interviewing Shaw. Whether the two still met between 1929 and 1934 is not clear, but if they did, it appears that Shaw did not allow their conversations to be published. Their association exists almost entirely on paper—in the interviews and in infrequent correspondence.

Replying to a questionnaire from Viereck biographer Elmer Gertz, Shaw noted that their acquaintance consisted of "Talk, Talk, Talk. No incidents." Answering Gertz's question about what it was in Viereck's personality and character that irritated him, Shaw wrote, "He doesn't irritate me. I like the German touch in him." He also noted that Viereck was "echt Deutsch," a true German, and that his general reaction to the propagandist was, "On the whole, pleasant." Shaw also recognized the aesthetic strain in Viereck, chiding him for being "too romantic."[2]

Shaw was not alone in finding Viereck pleasant. In the introduction to his book *Glimpses of the Great*, Viereck refers to himself as a lion hunter, his game being the intellectual and political lions of his day. In the course of his career, he enjoyed the acquaintance of Theodore Roosevelt, Sigmund Freud, Albert Einstein, Leon Trotsky, and Eugene Debs, among others, many of whom he interviewed as he did Shaw. Throughout his life, he maintained a singular attachment to the former German Kaiser Wilhelm II, for whom he served as a personal publicist during the deposed monarch's exile at Doorn in the Netherlands.

The controversy surrounding Viereck during the 1930s and 1940s cost him many friends, but obviously he was a man of some appeal. Woodrow Wilson's confidant Edward M. House found him "a romantic figure, always the poet, although he has a full grasp of the practical. He has a charm that is almost impossible to resist, once one knows him. He is one of the most charming, likeable men I know."[3] Publisher and writer Alexander Harvey observed of Viereck's paradoxical nature, "He feared no revelation of himself on any plane. He shocked. He charmed. He shocked again. The antagonism at times seemed almost violent. But still the charm was there . . . after a first repulsion."[4]

Inseparable from his agreeability was an overwhelming egoism and an obsessive interest in himself and in his self-proclaimed genius, a preoccupation which publisher E. Haldeman-Julius, a former collaborator and one-time admirer of Viereck's, noted in a letter: "You are like myself in one respect—ever ready to turn the limelight on a deserving soul, provided you can find a way to get into the picture. I thought that was exclusively my own characteristic, but I must confess that you do it with a facility that equals my own." Viereck's reply to Haldeman-Julius is at once honest and egotistical: "Defying single-handed the lords of letters and of news, we are compelled to create our own backgrounds. We must keep up our faith and that of our followers. In addition to that, we are both amazingly interested in ourselves."[5] This willingness to acknowledge his status as a player of public roles turns up throughout Viereck's public and private writings.

Viereck could captivate, but he also possessed a genius for alienating his friends. Haldeman-Julius was among those who could not forgive Viereck his work for the Nazis, and his final verdict on his former crony is typical of the nearly hysterical denunciations almost routinely leveled at Viereck during the 1930s. Haldeman-Julius said that history would remember Viereck as

a lickspittle of swinish exploiters who are able to pay him well. . . .
He is dangerous, because he is subtle and vicious. In all, I find
him loathsome. Always plausible, always oily, always sweetly reasonable, he serves the most outrageous cause since the end of the
Inquisition . . . or, to put it another way, if someone were to offer
him $1751 today, he would quit Hitler and lead a new crusade
against that murderer. Anybody can buy him—the only trouble
(from his viewpoint) is that there are so few swine ready to bid for
his services.[6]

In less flamboyant terms, Freud broke with Viereck over the journalist's inability to understand why Freud desired to identify himself as a
Jew rather than as an Austrian. In an earlier time, Viereck's politics
prior to World War I had cost him the goodwill of Theodore Roosevelt.
Shaw, unlike many of his contemporaries, was unwilling to denounce
Viereck publicly, and his private rebukes were often tinged with
amused affection.

For his part, Viereck's characterization of his relationship with Shaw is
typically ambiguous. In one letter to Elmer Gertz he refers to "my revered friend Bernard Shaw," but, in other correspondence with Gertz,
he admits that Shaw had not read his work and did not really know him.
On another occasion he observed, with some accuracy, that he was certain that Shaw disapproved of him, but that the playwright liked him.[7]
Viereck also asserted that Shaw was one of the few people whose intellect
he admired. This claim seems sincere since Viereck emulated Shaw's
ability to make the world take notice of him. When Shaw once asked him
whether he earned his money honestly or "merely by writing," he responded, "Like you, Mr. Shaw, I live by my wits."[8] The published interviews provide ample evidence of genuine admiration.

The interviews were of obvious financial worth to Viereck and, equally
important, served his ego by permitting him to share the limelight with
the great Bernard Shaw. For students of both men's lives the content and
the compositional process of the articles are of keen interest, revealing
what Viereck hoped to gain from the relationship and raising the question of why Shaw perpetuated it. The subject matter of the interviews is
almost wholly political, with discussion of literary issues occurring only as
a by-product of talk about the politics of Shaw's plays and prefaces. The
topics were varied, often within the same interview: Shaw on the General
Strike of 1926, on the prospects for disarmament, on the efficacy of the
Soviet system, on love in literature, and, most significant for Viereck, on
Germany after the war and on Hitler and Germany during the 1930s.
When disseminating these opinions, Viereck was not always concerned
with preserving the essence of Shaw's thinking. The former Austro-

Hungarian diplomat Constantin Dumba's opinion of Viereck as a journalist was that he "writes in a brilliant way, but looks for sensation. He wishes to dazzle and to amuse. As to accurate information, use of authentic sources, I believe he is not very anxious to secure them."[9] Viereck admitted as much in detailing his philosophy and method as an interviewer. He did not choose his "lions" by any attraction to political ideology, although that could be important, or through journalistic pursuit of a story needing reportage. Rather, he chose his subjects based on his continual interest in strong, male personalities (an interest Shaw held also), particularly those he could appropriate for his own use. He interviewed them because of their involvement with world events or because they could serve as mouthpieces for his own views.[10]

Viereck's method guaranteed inaccuracies. He described himself as an artistic photographer, "selecting some characteristic views or some view that appeals to my own idiosyncrasy." He took extensive notes during each interview, but, often unable to read them, relied on his memory to reconstruct a conversation. When memory failed, he consulted his imagination to fill in the gaps. He then submitted the manuscript to his subject for revision.[11] With Shaw, the revision could be quite extensive since he was accustomed to writing self-interviews, but such revision did not ensure accuracy. This process of writing produced articles which were pastiches of different discourses, interviews in which it is impossible to tell what belongs to Shaw and what to Viereck.

The interviews generally lack any center, the headlined topic often no more prevalent in the article than any other subject. Although Viereck provided Shaw the space in which to expound his views, the dialectical nature of the articles is always noticeable: the author is careful to include himself in the spotlight with his literary lion.

"Shaw Looks at Life at Seventy," published in the 13 August 1927 issue of *Liberty* and reprinted in *Glimpses of the Great,* illustrates Viereck's unorthodox method of composition, or what he called artistic photography.[12] This article is a product of his 1926 visit to Shaw, showing that, more than a year after their meeting, Viereck could still assemble an interview from snatches of remembered conversation, a few visual impressions, and quotations from previously published interviews or private letters. The interview is unfocused, covering a surprising number of topics, but each has little development. The first topic of discussion is religion, but this discourse consists of a few Shavian epigrams about Creative Evolution, padded with Viereck's dramatic intrusions describing Shaw's wit, kindness, and spirit in flattering terms.

In the first substantive section of the interview, Shaw calls attention to his prefaces, asserting, over Viereck's objections, that they were the chief tasks of his life. The language of these passages closely resembles that of a letter Shaw wrote to Viereck in June 1926. The passage from the letter reads:

> The preface to Androcles—the preface, mind, not the play—is my testament on Christianity; but my magnum opus in that line is my preface on the religion of Creative Evolution to Back to Methuselah. All my prefaces are important, especially that to Major Barbara on Poverty. These prefaces have practically nothing to do with the plays, and are treatises of considerable length. Prefaces are in the English classical tradition.[13]

The passage from "Shaw Looks at Life at Seventy" is as follows:

> The preface to Androcles and the Lion—the preface, mind, not the play—is my testament on Christianity. But my *magnum opus* in that line is my preface on the religion of Creative Evolution to Back to Methuselah. All my prefaces are important, especially the preface to Major Barbara. The preface to Major Barbara is my testament on Poverty. The preface to Getting Married is my testament on marriage. . . .

This list is extended to include a number of important prefaces, and then, two paragraphs later, Shaw states, "It is a classical tradition in English literature to publish plays with prefaces that have nothing to do with them." The similarity of the two passages indicates that Viereck drew from the letter in writing his article a year after his meeting with Shaw in June 1926. It is more likely that Viereck paraphrased from memory than that G.B.S. actually said these words. The entire passage appears to be fabricated by Viereck. The paragraph in the article that follows Shaw's discussion of his prefaces is lifted verbatim from the June letter and is characteristic of Shaw's attitude toward Viereck. "But you really must read my works if you wish to write about them without making a hopeless mess of it. You will never get any real quality into articles written in the dark."[14]

In a dramatic transition from Shaw's remarks about Joan of Arc to comments on *The Inca of Perusalem,* Viereck wrote that Shaw, who had been pacing the room as he spoke, paused beside the mantelpiece of the Adelphi Terrace flat, which bore the motto "Thay haif said! / Quhat say thay? / Lat thame say!" Viereck does not ask Shaw whether it is his motto because, he reports, "Shaw is compelled to expend half of his time explaining to visitors that the inscription was there when he took the apartment."[15] Viereck knew the truth about the motto because Shaw had explained it to him in a letter of 24 February 1926: "That motto is not mine: I spend a large part of my life explaining that it was in the house before I came into it."[16] Viereck frequently incorporated quotations from letters or recycled descriptive passages from old articles. Without access to the entire Shaw-Viereck correspondence, it is impossible to determine how much of the interview is constructed from previous discourse.

Shaw was exceedingly unhappy with the original draft of the interview, having spent some time during his Easter holiday revising the letter. He was annoyed enough to complain about the interview in two letters, one in April 1927 and the other in May. In the first, Shaw wrote, "I really must protest against these faked interviews which I am forced to rewrite to avoid a fresh addition to the mass of legends and misunderstandings under which my reputation groans."[17] In the May letter, after alluding to his lengthy revision of the article, Shaw told Viereck not to come to London if his only business was to visit him, since "I have not changed since we met; and no new records have been added to my conversational repertory."[18] Shaw's experience of editing "Shaw Looks at Life at Seventy" made him wary of the prospect of being quoted by Viereck.

When the interview was published in *Liberty*, it was accompanied by a disclaimer from Shaw. He stated in the first paragraph, "Don't say I authorize the publication of this interview. I don't. If you get me into hot water, I can always say: 'You know Viereck—he is a poet, endowed to a marvelous degree with the creative imagination.' "[19] The publicist in Viereck must have been overjoyed when he read this comment about creative imagination. It was to assume a life of its own, for Viereck had it reprinted on the dust jacket of his novel, *My First Two Thousand Years*, and on flyers advertising *My Flesh and Blood* and *The Kaiser on Trial*. Viereck used the remark as a professional endorsement so frequently that Nat Ferbes cited it in a review article in the *New York American* and Samuel Lembeck referred to it when completing one of Gertz's questionnaires.

Even though Viereck allowed Shaw to revise the interviews before publication, Shaw was not always happy with the results. By the end of the 1920s, Shaw was sufficiently incensed to halt, temporarily as it turned out, their professional relationship. Viereck published an interview in the *New York American* on 20 October 1929 and reprinted it on 10 November in the London *Sunday Express*. Shaw disavowed the interview in a letter published in the 17 November edition of the *Sunday Express* although the reprint included a facsimile of Shaw's revision of a portion of the interview. Shaw wrote to Viereck in December, rebuking the journalist for inaccurate reporting. The letter indicates the degree to which Shaw believed his views to have been distorted and the consternation this caused him:

4 Whitehall Court SW1
6th December 1929

My dear Viereck

There is only one authentic sentence in the interview; and that is "I wont be interviewed." How would you like to find in the papers G.S.V.'s views on love, literature, politics, art etc. etc., by G.B.S.? Would you not protest that you made your living by expressing your views for yourself and not by imparting them to me for grotesque misrepresentation? You think you understand what I say; but you never do: you simply report some notion of your own which is suggested by the subjects I mention. You know nothing about music; and when I tell you something that Einstein said about Mozart you turn it into utter nonsense by substituting Beethoven for Mozart. In the case of Einstein you have the excuse that as he is not a professional journalist like myself you are doing for him something that he cannot do for himself. In my case, or in that of any writer, you have no excuse at all for giving anything more than simply news which it may be convenient to have published at my own express request. But the sort of thing you are doing now, in violation of my repeated injunctions to the contrary, and in spite of the trouble you made before by the remarks you attributed to me about the British Navy, is quite out of order. I am forced to disclaim it. I have done so in terms far more considerate than you deserve; but I have had to do it decisively.

So, no more interviews.

faithfully

G. Bernard Shaw[20]

Despite this angry lecture on ethics and despite the problems Viereck's interviews caused him, Shaw did not hold to his pledge of no more interviews, and by the mid 1930s Viereck was publishing on Shaw again. Given the annoyance of extensive revisions which still failed to protect him from being misrepresented, it seems odd that Shaw continued to associate with Viereck. His motives for seeking Shaw's acquaintance and Shaw's willingness to perpetuate the relationship offer important insights into both men's characters.

It was natural and almost inevitable that Viereck sought Shaw's acquaintance. No less eminent an observer than Sigmund Freud identified in Viereck a father complex that prompted him to seek out the company and goodwill of successful older men. This interest in strong individuals frequently transcended politics and ideologies, enabling Viereck to admire personalities as distinct from one another as the socialist hero Eugene V. Debs and Albert Einstein on the one hand, and Adolf Hitler and Benito Mussolini on the other. So varied were his allegiances that he once mentioned letters he had received from Wilhelm II and Debs in a letter to Leon Trotsky.[21] He campaigned for Senator Robert La Follette and wrote glowingly of Debs, but he also composed a poem lauding J. P. Morgan. Shaw's status as the premier dramatist and international sage would, on its own merits, have been sufficient reason for Viereck to want to ingratiate himself with G.B.S., but Shaw was particularly attractive game for the lion hunter because of his publicized pro-Germanism and his controversial stands during the war. Shaw's high opinion of German culture and his criticism of the Treaty of Versailles made him that much more attractive to the propagandist.

Viereck's pro-German sympathies vastly influenced his behavior. In a career marked by shifting values, self-proclaimed moral relativism, and uncertainty about professional interests and moral ends, his loyalty to Germany remained a solitary constant. By 1935 his support for the fatherland had become so automatic that he could not bring himself to break with the Nazis.

Shaw's respect for Germany may be traced, in part, to his initial success in that country. As early as the season of 1909–10, there were fifty-four productions of his plays in forty cities. By the outbreak of World War I, eleven of Shaw's plays had been produced in Germany.[22] In the furor that followed the publication of *Common Sense About the War*, Shaw was widely accused of being pro-German. Hoping to nurture that idea, German propagandists frequently appropriated portions of *Common Sense* and passages from letters to his translator, Siegfried Trebitsch, for publication in German newspapers.[23] In a sense, then, Viereck fits into a tradition of attempts to misuse or enlist Shaw's statements to further German causes.

For all Shaw's real or imagined pro-Germanism, Viereck was keenly aware that Shaw was a loyal, if sometimes difficult, English citizen.

> In spite of his philosophy, in spite of his Irish blood, in spite of his gospel of proletarian brotherhood, Shaw remains a British citizen, if you scratch deep enough. While he assailed the British Government during the war with the utmost courage, he refrained from any criticism that would have weakened the cause of the Empire. In fact, Shaw's insistence upon free discussion immeasurably strengthened the English cause among the idealists of all lands.[24]

Viereck voiced a similar opinion in a letter to Shaw in January 1929.[25] But while Viereck realized that Shaw was more British than he was German, he also knew that he could harness Shaw's iconoclastic views in support of his own aims.

Shaw and Viereck frequently trod similar political ground, but they arrived there by different paths and had different ideas about where they should go. Shaw's opinions on international politics were formed by his intense desire for peace, a desire which led him to criticize wartime propaganda, defend the Kaiser, and, later, advocate appeasement of Hitler. Viereck, on the other hand, subjected most issues to the litmus test of how a policy would affect Germany. Thus, the two men often shared the same goal, but for cross purposes. During World War I, both energetically refuted the Allied propaganda which portrayed Belgium as a helpless victim of a demonic Kaiser, most notably by Shaw in *Common Sense* and by Viereck in the pages of the *Fatherland*, a magazine he founded in 1914 to support fair play for Germany. Shaw felt that if the war had to be waged, and any profit were to accrue from it, it had to be seen for what it was—a balance-of-power conflict brought on by the machinations of scheming diplomats—and not as a patriotic crusade. Anxious over Allied propaganda successes, and realizing that most of the war news reaching the United States came from British sources, Viereck published his magazine, books, and pamphlets to offset this bias.

On the surface, the two men's politics were similar. Both advocated shared war guilt and modest war reparations. Both were critical of the Treaty of Versailles, and both vilified British Foreign Secretary Sir Edward Grey. Shaw included Grey in the same species as militarist Prussian landowners, and he observed that, since the foreign secretary deserved an equal share of the war guilt, "If we send the Kaiser to St. Helena, we must send Sir Edward Grey there too."[26] After the war, Viereck published a series of articles in the *New York Evening Graphic* which, among other things, implicated Grey in the scheming that precipitated the war.

Aware that their opinions overlapped, Viereck was undoubtedly pleased to publish Shaw's thoughts on the war and international politics. The 10 June 1927 *New York American* carried another Shaw interview, "Bernard Shaw: Real Disarmament Is Impossible," which ranged freely over a variety of political topics. The article illustrates how Shaw could be of value to Viereck in promoting policies favorable to Germany. As the title indicates, Shaw predicted the failure of future disarmament talks because "everytime you decide to disarm, your armament is already antiquated. Nations can never really disarm even if they want." Armies, he observed, were always improvised, citing Germany, England, and France as unprepared to fight the type of war in which they had become involved in 1914.[27] Viereck shared Shaw's lack of faith in disarmament

conferences, but for different reasons. Shaw believed the idea impractical; Viereck opposed such conferences on purely partisan grounds. Before and during World War I, Viereck frequently expressed a longing
for union between the "great Germanic Peoples" of England, Germany,
and the United States. After Versailles, he lost whatever faith he had in
the efficacy of an international order to achieve fair play for Germany.
After the armistice, his nationalism became more dominant in shaping
his worldview, and he believed that German rearmament was essential to
undoing the injustice of Versailles. Thus he had vigorously opposed the
disarmament conference in 1921 because he believed that it would
weaken American naval forces and cede unquestioned maritime superiority to England.[28]

For similar reasons, Viereck disapproved of the League of Nations,
and, in the interview, he quietly enlisted Shaw in this opposition: "Because
he is a real idealist, Shaw objects to the sham of the League of Nations and
of disarmament conferences contrived to deceive the world."[29] This sentence places Shaw's comments on disarmament in a deceptive context. In
the interview, Shaw doubted the efficacy of disarmament conferences, but
not the sincerity of the people organizing them. The claim that Shaw
thought the League of Nations a sham is simply untrue. Shaw and his
fellow Fabians were instrumental in conceiving the idea of the league, and
although Shaw was critical of the organization that eventually evolved, he
never believed it a sham. In fact, when Shaw was critical of the league, it
was because of the intense nationalism of a number of delegations, a
nationalism Viereck epitomized.[30] Ironically, Viereck and Shaw held a
number of opinions in common, Viereck because of his adherence to
nationalism, Shaw because of his abhorrence of it.

During the early part of the century, Shaw was in reality what Viereck
only claimed to be: a man who was compelled by his perception of a
government's deceit to criticize his country, but whose loyalty remained
firm. During World War I, Viereck printed on the masthead of the
American Monthly the motto "My country right or wrong. If right to be
kept right, if wrong to be set right." This motto applies more to Shaw
than to Viereck. Shaw made no secret of his desire for an English victory.
He once asserted that even if the Germans withdrew, the Allies would
have to fight on because the war was "a romantic dream from which
Germany had to be awakened."[31] After the war, he noted, "I felt as if I
were witnessing an engagement between two pirate fleets. . . . [A]s I and
my family and friends were on board British ships I did not intend the
British section to be defeated if I could help it."[32] Viereck was never
traitorous, and he even made a great effort to demonstrate the opposite,
but his first loyalties were always to Germany. He claimed that Germany
was his mother by birth and the United States his wife by choice and that,

forced to decide between the two, he would painfully choose the latter. But for some men the apron strings are difficult to break. During the 1930s, Viereck's loyalty to Germany cost him a number of friends and earned him lasting notoriety and public enmity.

Viereck himself observed that it was inevitable that he would be charmed by Hitler. He first interviewed him in 1923, and by the early 1930s Viereck had found the answer to his own desire for Barbarossa rising. Viereck responded to attacks on National Socialism in much the same way that he had defended Germany in 1914. Niel Johnson believes that his defense of the Nazis was in part a function of ego. Having established himself in 1914 as Germany's most prominent defender in America, he felt compelled to live up to his reputation in 1935.[33]

Viereck was writing for *Liberty* magazine during the mid 1930s. His articles were both sympathetic to the Reich and reminiscent of 1914, attempting to capitalize on American disillusionment over the previous war to promote neutrality in the coming one. An article entitled "It Can Happen Again" warned that "the same intrigues that went on before 1914 are going on today; the same surreptitious whispers make the rounds; the same obscure plots are being spun from continent to continent, from ocean to ocean. The same old atrocity stories will soon bob up in new disguises."[34] Other articles during the decade adhered to the official German line: Czechoslovakia denied complete equality to its German citizens, Hitler had no designs on Alsace-Lorraine, and the Reich's assumption of guardianship of all Germans in bordering countries was the German equivalent of the Monroe Doctrine. Propelled by ego and a compulsive pro-Germanism, Viereck responded to the events before World War II almost exactly as he had to the events before World War I. He was never able to perceive with what different emotions the world responded to the Kaiser and to Hitler, and it is doubtful whether he fully recognized the moral difference.

Friends and professional acquaintances constantly pressed Viereck to condemn Hitler's campaign against the Jews. Viereck lost the goodwill of many because of the distinction he made between National Socialism and anti-Semitism, believing that they existed independently of one another and that one could condemn the bigotry without condemning the system that expressed it. Viereck was not an anti-Semite, vigorously denouncing anti-Semitism as "legally a monstrosity, economically a catastrophe, ethically an error, politically a blunder, intellectually an imbecility, humanly a barbarism, esthetically bad taste."[35] Yet too often such denunciations were quickly qualified by his listing atrocities committed against German citizens and his criticizing Hitler's anti-Semitism for its negative effects on *Germany* rather than on Jews. He could not bring himself to criticize Germany publicly.

To Peter Pollack he wrote that he did not wish to make a choice between Jews and Germans, but that if the Jews forced him to do so, he would side with his "own people." He also believed that because he was not a German citizen he did not have to make a choice.[36]

When Viereck resumed interviewing Shaw in the 1930s, he once again sought to enlist Shaw's reputation in service of his own politics, publishing "Bernard Shaw Says Jews Should Marry Gentiles" in 1935. Aware of the controversy and bias associated with his name, Viereck published the article under an infrequently used pseudonym, Donald Furthman Wickets. Like the interviews in the 1920s, this article covers a number of topics, ranging from Soviet Russia to love, but most important to Viereck was what Shaw said about Germany and Hitler.

Again Shaw's politics appeared conveniently similar to Viereck's. Almost unique among Western cultural figures, Shaw expressed some positive opinions of Hitler. He believed that the führer's rise was an inevitable result of Versailles. It was also consistent with Shaw's theories on great men and dictators, which he explained in the preface to *The Millionairess*. Shaw's association with Lady Astor and the so-called Cliveden Set, as well as his continual advocacy of a form of appeasement, furthered the impression that he was pro-German. However, Shaw's position owed more to his desire for peace than to any approval of Hitler. For Viereck, however, why Shaw said something was less important than his having said it.

In "Jews Should Marry Gentiles," Shaw declared that "there is much to be said for Hitler, but his anti-Semitism is nonsense." Wickets-Viereck, playing the devil's advocate, then offered the view that "anti-semitism seems to be a concomitant of Fascism," an opinion Viereck demonstrably did not hold. This prompted Shaw to answer that "the *Judenhetze* is an absurd irrelevance of National Socialism. Anti-Semitism is not natural to Fascism. Anti-Semitism is Hitler's greatest mistake."[37] Clearly this is closer to Viereck's position, but while Viereck could overlook the mistake, Shaw could not.

Three years later, Shaw stated in the *New York Times* that Hitler "has not solved it [the Jewish problem] at all. He has created it. It has damaged his intellectual credit to an extraordinary extent." He continued, "The amazing thing about it is that the anti-semites do not see how intensely Jewish it is. The fault of the Jew is his enormous arrogance, based on his claim to belong to God's chosen race."[38] Although Shaw rejected the validity of the Jewish stereotype, he did believe that the Jews were responsible for maintaining their sense of separateness. There is a difference between observing the racial solidarity of Jews and holding them culpable for the bigotry directed against them. However, in the racially charged atmosphere of the 1930s, this distinction was easily blurred. Shaw had to be aware of possible misinterpretations of such sentiments. Certainly he should have known that Viereck might misuse similar statements.

Shaw says in the *Liberty* interview, "The Jews are not entirely free from blame if they are misunderstood. They have reared ghettos around themselves. . . . Germany made a great mistake when she set the Jews against herself. They are a clever people and it is not wise to court their hostility." It is uncertain whether Shaw revised this article, or to what extent this language is Viereck's and not his. Either way, such a statement comes dangerously close to invoking the Jewish stereotype and partly exonerating Germany. When asked by Viereck whether he considered the Jewish boycott of Germany a clever policy, Shaw replied that it tended to prove Hitler's point "that there is a world-wide conspiracy against Germany fostered by the Jews. And yet, I don't know what else they should do."[39] Here, interviewer and subject may have intended the reader to draw different conclusions. Shaw was commenting that Hitler could point to the boycott as a rationale for the very policy it protests, but Viereck might have hoped to obscure the issue of Hitler's anti-Semitism.

This interview further demonstrated Viereck's capacity for sensationalism and distortion. The article has a headline reading "George Bernard Shaw Says Jews Should Marry Gentiles," accompanied by the subheading "And if he were Hitler, He'd make it Compulsory! . . . The Amazing G.B.S. explodes a new Bomb." Carrying a pseudonymous byline, and illustrated by page-length facing photos of Shaw and Hitler in semi-profile, it was tasteless journalism, but effective publicity. These choices were editorial, but they were dictated in no small degree by the subject matter and indicate Shaw's value to Viereck.

By 1935, Shaw was familiar with Viereck's journalistic method and partisan interest in the issues discussed in the interview. He must have realized the danger of Viereck's distortions of sensitive subjects. Despite these dangers, he irresponsibly let the piece be published. Shaw's provocative suggestion that provided the article's title occupies a mere two lines of a five-page interview. Shaw was, no doubt, being satirical when he remarked, "If I were Hitler, I would make it a crime, punishable like incest, for a Jew or a Jewess to marry anyone except a Christian."[40] Shaw appears guilty of trivializing the issue with such jokes (an accusation Rabbi Stephen S. Wise leveled at him in an invited response to the interview). Shaw's patronage of Viereck in this instance is analogous to Viereck's rising to the defense of the Reich. Having established his reputation as a defender of the unpopular in general, and of Viereck in particular, Shaw may have felt compelled to reassociate himself with the propagandist, who was about to make himself extremely unpopular once again. Just as Viereck's consistent support for Germany caused him to skirt the morality of certain issues, Shaw's consistent compulsion to support the German-American outsider led him, in this instance, to trivialize the moral dilemma of Hitler's Jewish policies. The desire to arouse controversy was a trait the two men shared throughout their lives.

However, Shaw did recognize the difference between 1914 and 1939 and warned Viereck not to take sides in the war. Viereck had written to Shaw after attending a performance of the New York production of *Geneva* early in 1940. In the letter, Viereck continued to defend German war motives and faulted Shaw for being unsympathetic to Hitler and portraying the führer as a maniacal braggart without providing any indication of his greatness as a statesman. He admitted that much of the problem lay with the actor who was deliberately caricaturing the führer, but Viereck did not pardon the playwright for failing to explain Hitler's power over the German masses.[41]

Shaw answered, "I think I made Hitler give a better account of himself than he has ever done in real life" and that he "will have all his work cut out for him to keep out of St. Helena or Chislehurst or Doorn."[42] He then cautioned Viereck against becoming too involved: "You are safe in America. Do not take sides. You can do nothing to help or hinder Chamberlain, though you can damage yourself if you try; so sit tight as a 100% American."[43]

Shaw's decision to continue to allow Viereck to represent his views, after having severed their professional relationship in 1929, reveals much about Shaw. On one level, he was flattered by Viereck's regular pilgrimages to Adelphi Terrace, Whitehall Court, and Ayot St. Lawrence, as well as by the younger man's lavish praise of him in print. Each interview contains several paragraphs of panegyric, providing flattering descriptions of G.B.S.'s physical appearance and glowing estimations of his status as a cultural figure. "There was a ruddy tint in his cheeks for which I was not prepared . . . as if his youth were a glorious sun shining through the mists of the years gilding those mists dazzlingly, poetically, perfectly."[44] "It was some time after Shaw's seventieth birthday. Snow was in his hair, in his beard, and in those bushy eyebrows. But his eyes did not lack fire." "His presence pervaded the chamber like a dynamo. The noises of London died in the distance. Nothing seemed real except the voice of George Bernard Shaw."[45] If these almost reverential descriptions are indicative of Viereck's behavior in Shaw's presence, it is easy to believe that Shaw enjoyed the hero worship.

Shaw must also have been amused by Viereck's frequently ending the interviews with melodramatic attempts to evoke a sense of profundity. The final paragraph of "Jews Should Marry Gentiles" ends, "As it [the door] closed, he hurried back to his desk to write out in his small and unmistakeable script, maybe some letter to the London Times. Or maybe some new dialogue in a play that will make the world spin faster in its ceaseless progress toward some unknown goal."[46] The conclusion to "Shaw Looks at Life at Seventy" reads, "Dark had fallen. Outside the lights of the city shone through the mist like a thousand will-o'-the-wisps. In the darkening room gleamed the eye of B.S. the evangelist, the whiteness of his beard and of his hair fashioning a fantastic aureole for his head."[47]

During the week of Shaw's eightieth birthday, Viereck published in *Liberty* "A Final Statement of Faith" by George Bernard Shaw "in a Colloquy with George Sylvester Viereck." The contrast between Shaw's perfunctory answers to Viereck's questions and Viereck's exaggerations of their importance is striking and humorous. The article is also notable because it is essentially apolitical. Viereck had sent Shaw a questionnaire asking him philosophic questions about Creative Evolution, thermodynamics, reincarnation, and immortality. Shaw's written reply was billed by Viereck as a summary of Shavian philosophy. In his introduction to the interview Viereck noted, "I have at various times discussed philosophy with him; but never have my questions been so searching nor his answers so profoundly stirring as in this my long-distance interview with Shaw on the threshold of eighty." Shaw's signature, dated 23 March 1936, is reproduced with the article and indicates that G.B.S. was on a ship sailing eastward through the Gulf of Venezuela. Viereck interpreted the signature sensationally: "He [Shaw] must recognize the significance of his message, because in signing it he carefully states not only the date on which it was written, but the location, giving to a great utterance its exact plane of reference in space and time."[48]

For all its supposed profundity, the actual colloquy is less than two pages long, including illustrations. Viereck's questions are indeed searching: "To what extent has your philosophy of life, time, infinity, death been influenced or modified by the discoveries of Einstein, Planck, or the theories of Jeans, etc.?" "Do you believe in the eternal recurrence of things and personalities, a theory advanced by Nietzsche?" Shaw's answers to such questions were polite, but hardly revealing or incisive, some of his replies being no longer than the question.[49]

Viereck's roguish behavior and towering ego amused Shaw even where they antagonized others. He had a keen delight for the scandalous and appreciated Viereck's puckish qualities despite being annoyed by his ethical lapses. This amused exasperation permeates Shaw's answers to the Gertz questionnaire, the tone almost that of an adult speaking of a child. When asked how long he had known Viereck, he replied, "Ever since he was an adult. But my personal contacts with him hardly total up to three whole days." Had he ever engaged in any controversy with him? "Ask him. I forget." What aspects of his career and work most interested him? "I never know what he is up to." What is his place in international affairs and history? "Don't know. Neither does he." Notably abrupt and dismissive, these perfunctory answers indicate that Shaw did not spend a great deal of time thinking about George Sylvester Viereck. Still, when he did consider him, his sentiments were generally positive. What was his general reaction to Viereck? "On the whole, pleasant."[50]

Although Shaw enjoyed the propagandist's infrequent company and was amused by his excesses, it is still difficult to understand why Shaw tolerated Viereck, given his moral ambiguities and the gravity most public men and women attached to them. While Shaw frequently rebuked Viereck for his unethical journalism, he apparently never reproached him on moral grounds.

Shaw quite probably concluded that Viereck had been so thoroughly judged and condemned by others that he himself hardly needed to join the effort. That Viereck was often reviled in public made him an attractive figure in the always iconoclastic eye of Bernard Shaw. Whatever his motives, Viereck had the courage to face the scorn of public opinion at the high cost of political and social isolation, an experience familiar to Shaw. He could appreciate the loneliness Viereck experienced during his years of defending Germany. Both men had faced professional ostracism. In the fall of 1915, the Dramatists' Club, in a meeting to which Shaw was not invited, voted to expel him from their ranks in response to the scandal over *Common Sense About the War*. Shaw refused to recognize the expulsion on the grounds that it was undemocratic and without legality, but he resigned his membership all the same because of the politicizing of a literary organization. In that same year a vocal minority of the Society of Authors protested his continued membership in that fraternity, but Shaw did not resign.[51] Four years later, in similar circumstances, Viereck was expelled from the Authors' League and from the Poetry Society of America, an organization he had helped found. Undoubtedly remembering his own brushes with intolerant fellow writers, Shaw wrote to Viereck in support.

> If the Authors' League or the Poetry Society or any other organization expels a member because of his political opinions, it thereby constitutes itself a political body and violates whatever literary charter it may have. Literature, art, and science are free of frontiers; and those who exploit them politically are traitors to the greatest republic in the world: the Republic of Art and Science.[52]

Shaw was in part shielded from professional antipathy by his international prestige; Viereck was not. Writers, critics, and scholars in the United States conspired to expunge him from the literary record by not mentioning Viereck in public, even abusively. Nearly twenty years later, in 1935, when Elmer Gertz solicited information for *Odyssey of a Barbarian,* a number of respondents complained that even mentioning Viereck negatively would serve his ego by perpetuating his public existence. This near-boycott of the propagandist partly accounts for Viereck's obscurity today. Shaw, ever aiding the underdog, had not observed the boycott.

Viereck was conscious of Shaw's generosity: "Often in the long course of years, when I wrote him flattering letters he did not answer at all, but whenever I was in any trouble, he responded at once." He cites Shaw's aid to Frank Harris and to "innumerable others; newspapermen out of a job, who came to him for a loan and received an interview worth many times the amount they had asked in money."[53] If Shaw could assist the often-vilified journalist by allowing him to appropriate his name and reputation, he would do so, trusting that his standing was secure enough to weather any embarrassments Viereck could bring upon him.

Until near the end of his life, Shaw would remain loyal to his notorious associate. In 1942, Viereck was tried and convicted on a charge of failure to comply with the procedure for registering in the United States as a foreign agent. His conviction was eventually overturned by the U.S. Supreme Court, but he was convicted again in a second trial in 1943 and sentenced to from one to five years in a federal penitentiary. In September 1947, Shaw noted Viereck's release from prison in complimentary terms: "You seem to have stood it with extraordinary spirit. Most martyrs are duds."[54] Apparently Viereck had no dearth of material comforts while in prison: a local paper reported the size of his library and the number of luxury items found in his cell.

Although their individual egos and creative energies expressed themselves in vastly different ways, it seems natural that Shaw and Viereck were fascinated by one another. Like Viereck, Shaw was a hunter, his game being the ideas found in rigorous and free intellectual exchange. In Viereck, he recognized someone who, for admittedly questionable motives, promulgated unpopular ideas, many designed to shock established opinion. Their contrasting politics delineate one another's motives and goals. Viereck revealed his inveterate hero worship, his egotistical need to enlist great men in service of his own preoccupations, and his predilection for the sensational and the romantic. Shaw demonstrated his penchant for championing unpopular causes and his loyalty to friends and associates.

Both men were keenly aware that they were playing to an audience. Shaw once observed that "the celebrated G.B.S. is about as real as a pantomime Ostrich. . . . I have played my game with a conscience. I have never pretended that G.B.S. was real: I have over and over taken him to pieces before the audience to shew the trick of him."[55]

In a letter to the journalist Fulton Oursler, Viereck recognized the artifice of his own persona. "As far as impertinence is concerned, I carefully cultivated it in my youth, walking in the steps of O.W. [Oscar Wilde] and G.B.S. That of course is not really impertinence. It is either a literary pose or a defense mechanism. I am not aware that I have been impertinent in the good old style for many years."[56] Thriving on impertinence "in the good old style" himself, Shaw had let Viereck play his political games to the end. After all, no one had listened to the lion; why should anyone pay more attention to the lion hunter than to buy his copy?

Notes

1. George Sylvester Viereck, "Reason Alone Can Cure Ills of Social Organism: Shaw," *New York American* (13 June 1927), p. 1.

2. Bernard Shaw, letter to Elmer Gertz, 15 February 1935, and Bernard Shaw, letter to George Sylvester Viereck, 9 May 1927, Elmer Gertz Papers, Library of Congress, Washington, D.C.

3. Elmer Gertz, *Odyssey of a Barbarian* (Buffalo: Prometheus Books, 1978), p. 206.

4. Ibid., p. 58.

5. Ibid., pp. 182–83.

6. Haldeman-Julius, answer to questionnaire from Elmer Gertz, Elmer Gertz Papers, Library of Congress, Washington D.C.

7. George Sylvester Viereck, answer to questionnaire from Elmer Gertz, 7 March 1935; Viereck, letter to Elmer Gertz, 26 August 1935; Viereck, answer to questionnaire from Elmer Gertz, no date; Elmer Gertz Papers, Library of Congress, Washington, D.C.

8. Donald Furthman Wickets [George Sylvester Viereck], "George Bernard Shaw Says Jews Should Marry Gentiles," *Liberty* (27 June 1935), p. 28.

9. Gertz, p. 143.

10. Viereck, 7 March 1935.

11. Ibid.

12. George Sylvester Viereck, "Shaw Looks at Life at Seventy," *Liberty* (13 August 1927), pp. 7–10, reprinted in George Sylvester Viereck, "The Gospel According to Bernard Shaw," *Glimpses of the Great* (New York: Macaulay, 1930), pp. 8–22.

13. Bernard Shaw, letter to George Sylvester Viereck, 2 June 1926 (copy), Institute for the Arts and Humanistic Studies, The Pennsylvania State University, University Park.

14. Viereck, "Shaw at Seventy," p. 8.

15. Ibid., p. 9.

16. *Bernard Shaw: Collected Letters, 1926–1950,* ed. Dan H. Laurence (London: Max Reinhardt, 1988), p. 13.

17. Ibid., p. 53.

18. Shaw, 9 May 1927.

19. Viereck, "Shaw at Seventy," p. 7.

20. Shaw, *Collected Letters,* pp. 546–47.

21. Gertz, p. 166.

22. Bernard Shaw, *Bernard Shaw's Letters to Siegfried Trebitsch,* ed. Samuel A. Weiss (Stanford: Stanford University Press, 1986), p. 16.

23. Stanley Weintraub, *Journey to Heartbreak* (New York: Weybright and Talley, 1971), pp. 92, 95.

24. George Sylvester Viereck, "Bernard Shaw: Real Disarmament Is Impossible," *New York American* (10 July 1927), p. E-1.

25. Weintraub, p. 138.

26. Ibid., p. 57.

27. Viereck, "Disarmament," p. E-1.

28. Niel M. Johnson, *George Sylvester Viereck: German-American Propagandist* (Urbana: University of Illinois Press, 1972), p. 113.

29. Viereck, "Disarmament," p. E-1.

30. Gerard Anthony Pilecki, *Shaw's "Geneva"* (London: Mouton, 1965), p. 136.

31. Weintraub, p. 137.

32. Bernard Shaw, *What I Really Wrote About the War* (London: Constable, 1931), p. 2.

33. Niel M. Johnson, "Pro-Freud and Pro-Nazi: The Paradox of George S. Viereck," *Psychoanalytic Review* 58 (Winter 1971–72): 561.

34. George Sylvester Viereck, "It Can Happen Again," *Liberty* (13 April 1937), pp. 31–32.

35. Gertz, p. 261.

36. George Sylvester Viereck, letter to Peter J. Pollack, 29 October 1936, Elmer Gertz Papers, Library of Congress, Washington, D.C.

37. Viereck, "Jews," p. 28.

38. "Nazi Racial Ideas Assaulted by Shaw," *New York Times* (10 July 1938), p. 18.

39. Viereck, "Jews," p. 29.

40. Ibid.

41. George Sylvester Viereck, letter to Bernard Shaw, 13 February 1940, Elmer Gertz Papers, Library of Congress, Washington, D.C.

42. The residences in exile for Napoleon, Napoleon III, and the Kaiser, respectively.

43. Shaw, *Collected Letters,* pp. 490–91.

44. George Sylvester Viereck, "Diary of G.S.V.," *American Monthly* (October 1926), p. 247.

45. Viereck, "Shaw at Seventy," pp. 7–8.

46. Viereck, "Jews," p. 31.

47. Viereck, "Shaw at Seventy," p. 10.

48. Bernard Shaw, "A Final Statement of Faith," *Liberty* (1 August 1936), p. 18.

49. Shaw, "Faith," p. 19.

50. Shaw, 15 February 1935.

51. Weintraub, pp. 119–21.

52. Johnson, *Propagandist,* p. 74.

53. Viereck, "Jews," p. 31.

54. Bernard Shaw, letter to George Sylvester Viereck, 25 September 1947, Elmer Gertz Papers, Library of Congress, Washington, D.C.

55. Bernard Shaw, "The Chesterbelloc," *New Age* (15 February 1908), reprinted in *Pen Portraits and Reviews* (London: Constable, 1931), p. 73.

56. George Sylvester Viereck, letter to Fulton Oursler, 18 April 1935, Library of Congress, Washington, D.C.

Michel W. Pharand

ABOVE THE BATTLE?
BERNARD SHAW,
ROMAIN ROLLAND, AND
THE POLITICS OF PACIFISM

Few of Shaw's contemporaries so rival his prolific literary output as does Romain Rolland (1866–1944): five novels, ten biographies, fifteen plays, about twenty-four volumes of musical essays and sociopolitical criticism, more than thirty volumes of correspondence, and an important volume of drama theory.[1] Furthermore, Rolland was one of the rare French intellectuals to have followed Shaw's career from across the Channel. Both men were consumed with a passion for social improvement, a crusade they carried out most energetically in wartime in very different ways. Although they were both music critics, art lovers, and avid pacifists, Rolland's romantic panhumanism and idealistic internationalism did not coincide with Shaw's pragmatic turn of mind.

In the beginning, Rolland's critical appraisal of Shaw's work was somewhat negative. In 1912, he found *Mrs Warren's Profession* "amusant, mais conventionnel—même quand cela veut être au rebours des conventions" [entertaining, but conventional—even when it flies in the face of conventions].[2] But in a letter of 6 December 1913 to Jean-Richard Bloch, Rolland admitted that he was not very familiar with Shaw, and that any judgment on the playwright's work must be considered provisional:

> Il a vu des choses neuves et profondes, surtout dans l'âme féminine. Il a troué les voiles de la moderne hypocrisie, sociale, morale et littéraire. Pour mon goût, son oeuvre est viciée par le bluff et le dandysme—comme celle de plus d'un Anglais, en lutte avec les mensonges de sa race (voir Byron). Je trouve plus de probité dans

l'effort de Wells, qui a moins de génie, et qui pourtant va loin, à force de sérieux.

[He has seen new and profound things, especially in the feminine soul. He has pierced the veils of modern hypocrisy, social, moral, and literary. For my taste, his work is tainted by bluff and dandyism—like that of more than one Englishman, struggling with the lies of his race (see Byron). I find more integrity in the effort of Wells, who has less genius, and who nevertheless goes far, by dint of seriousness].[3]

Although he admired Shaw's insights into the feminine psyche and his debunking of social hypocrisy, the Frenchman felt that the Irishman's flippant, cynical persona got in the way. Rolland was no ironist, and it was probably quite difficult for him to appreciate Shaw's witty polemics.

This basic difference in temperament was also present in his appreciation of Shaw's "courageuse défense"—in the *Manchester Guardian* of 22 July 1916—of Sir Roger Casement, soon to be executed for high treason for planning to incite the Sinn Fein rebellion. In the speech Shaw wrote for him to deliver at his trial, Casement was portrayed not as an English traitor but as an Irish patriot. Although Shaw's speech was read to the jury, this was after Casement was found guilty and sentenced to be hanged. Unfortunately, wrote Rolland, "le ton habituel de plaisanterie paradoxale qui est sa marque est, pour la majorité de ses lecteurs, un prétexte à ne pas le prendre au sérieux" [the usual tone of paradoxical joking which is his hallmark is, for the majority of his readers, a pretext for not taking him seriously].[4] Once again, what Rolland interpreted as a lack of earnestness went counter to his own uncompromising stance, a stance that would alienate his friends when he needed them most.

Nonetheless, Rolland continued to explore Shaw's work. At the end of 1916, he listed as his "lectures de ces derniers temps" [latest reading] six plays by Shaw: *Candida, Le héros et le soldat, L'homme du destin, L'homme aimé des femmes, Non Olet,* and *On ne peut jamais dire* [*Candida, Arms and the Man, The Man of Destiny, The Philanderer, Widowers' Houses,* and *You Never Can Tell*], far more works by a single author than his other readings (*Journal,* p. 859). But he was disappointed, and he wrote to his mother that he was reading Shaw "sans enthousiasme, et même avec quelque étonnement de la médiocrité du talent, parfois" [without enthusiasm, and even with some amazement at the mediocrity of the talent, sometimes].[5] As we shall see, however, Rolland's reservations about Shaw's talent as a dramatist would not stop him from enlisting the Irishman's help as a fellow humanitarian and pacifist.

Although he was as spiritually engagé as Shaw during the Great War, Rolland preferred to take a neutral position, writing articles—from self-imposed exile in Switzerland—in which he urged intellectuals to act on the dictates of conscience rather than on the false idealization of militaristic patriotism. Rolland felt that they had been swept up by the war effort and had forsaken their duty as guardians of culture. These sixteen open letters, essays, appeals, and manifestos were published in 1915 under the title *Au-dessus de la mêlée,* an unfortunate expression that Shaw would invariably disparage as elitist and escapist. Rolland's manifesto is usually translated as *Above the Battle* or *Above the Conflict,* but the words are ambiguous. A "mêlée" is a scuffle, fray, or free-for-all; to be "au-dessus de la mêlée" or "à l'écart de la mêlée" means to stay on the sidelines or to remain aloof.[6]

Although he admired Rolland's political commitment, Shaw could not subscribe to what he interpreted as the Frenchman's philosophical aloofness. "For I entirely refused Romain Rolland's invitation to *planer au dessus de la mêlée,*" he wrote, "and survey the war from the empyrean of a morality which none of the combatants could possibly practise even if, like myself, they recognized that morality as their natural own, and regarded war with implacable horror and disgust."[7] Rolland's highly rhetorical style may have suited his abstract idealism, but it is not surprising that Shaw would balk at the Frenchman's utopianism: "L'esprit est la lumière. Le devoir est de l'élever au-dessus des tempêtes et d'écarter les nuages qui cherchent à l'obscurcir. Le devoir est de construire, et plus large et plus haute, dominant l'injustice et les haines des nations, l'enceinte de la ville où doivent s'assembler les âmes fraternelles et libres du monde entier" [The spirit is light. It is our duty to raise it above the storms of life and to dispel clouds which seek to obscure it. It is our duty to build, broader and higher, far above the injustice and hatred of nations, the fortress of the city where the fraternal and free souls of the entire world must gather together].[8]

Shaw was not alone in misconstruing Rolland's manifesto. In the eyes of the French, Rolland's neutral stance and his pleas for Franco-German cooperation and reconciliation made him an intellectual traitor, even a collaborator. Many parents even forbade their children to read his texts. "In months, the darling of the French literary left and the cultivated public became a pariah. . . . After 1914 his works were misrepresented and slandered. . . . For the remainder of his life, opponents would attack Romain Rolland ad hominem by invoking the slogan 'above the battle' " (Fisher, p. 43). In his letters discussing both world wars, Shaw himself was to do so at least half a dozen times.

One of the articles in *Au-dessus de la mêlée,* "Pro Aris," was a protest against the German bombing of Rheims Cathedral, a devastating event which Auguste Rodin, in a letter to Rolland, compared with the fall of Constantinople, the burning of the library of Alexandria, and the destruction of the Temple of Jerusalem.[9] In "Pro Aris," Rolland describes the cathedral in lyrical terms as the stone organ in which France's centuries shudder like a symphony and as the light of the spirit more necessary to the soul than the sun itself.[10] Rolland sent a draft of "Pro Aris" to his English publisher, Heinemann, who not only published it without Rolland's permission in a deluxe edition on glossy paper, but in a badly edited version as well. The new document had, in Rolland's words, a "violence déclamatoire excessive," an especially misleading tone in view of the fact that Rolland considered his protest "un brouillon de lettre hâtivement envoyé dans un moment de passion" [a mere draft of a letter sent hastily in a moment of passion].[11] Nonetheless, almost all the thousand or so thinkers to whom the protest was sent signed the appeal. Of the 279 English intellectuals—including 110 authors, among whom were Bennett, Galsworthy, Gosse, Kipling, Moore, Murray, Pinero, Wells, and Yeats—Shaw was one of the few who refused to sign. He wrote to Heinemann that Rolland ought to know better than to repeat "halfpenny newspaper rubbish," declaring,

> I am one of the two or three people in Europe who really care about Rheims; but if I were a military officer defending Rheims I should have to put an observation post on the cathedral roof; and if I were his opponent I should have to fire on it, in both cases on pain of being court-martialled and perhaps shot. If this war goes long enough there will not be a cathedral left in Europe; and serve Europe right too! The way to save the cathedrals is to stop fighting, and not to use them as stones to throw at the Germans. I won't sign. (*Journal*, p. 126)

Rolland replied to the disgruntled Shaw on 18 November 1916, reassuring him that he was perfectly justified in abstaining, something Rolland himself would have done had he seen his protest printed in such large type and grandiose format. He said that although he admired Shaw the writer, "je crains que vous n'eussiez été bien mauvais général. Les batailles ne se mesurent pas au nombre de morts qu'on fait et de pouces de terrain qu'on gagne" [I am afraid you would have made a very bad general. Battles are not measured by the number of men we kill and the inches of ground we gain] (*Journal*, p. 126).

Shaw responded to Rolland indirectly in a letter to Mrs. Mary Bedford on 8 December 1916, explaining that fear of censorship had prevented him from speaking out freely and urging her to tell Rolland that "not only are his [Rolland's] views sympathetic to me; but he is, like myself, an old musical critic, apparently nursed on music as I was; so that I have a key to his writings that our unmusical literary men lack." He went on to explain some of his own struggles with controversial documents: he would not let his *Common Sense About the War* be translated into French; in any case, Augustin Hamon refused to translate it. Neither did Hamon translate a long interview made by Shaw for France, but instead made a précis which failed to get published at the right moment. "I have been violently attacked in the French papers, but without any knowledge of what I think." He ended by stating that he was "perhaps the only writer in England who has looked at the war from the point of view of the French Revolution. If I could only get a hearing in any French paper, I should astonish M. Davray and the rest of my French critics very considerably" (*Journal*, p. 1007). Like Rolland, Shaw had been misunderstood and maligned by the press, and although he could sympathize with Rolland's plight, he steadfastly refused to sign the manifesto.

The refusal did not deter Rolland from requesting Shaw's support again a few years later. In the hope of restoring tolerance among the intellectual elite, and as an antidote to the destructive militarism around him, Rolland proposed in 1918 the formation of an "Internationale de l'esprit," an International of the Mind,[12] whose apolitical, pacifist members would help curb the cultural nationalism, ethnocentrism, and xenophobia then at their height. His elitism was tempered by the suggestion that all endeavors should be immediately accessible to the masses via reports, a newspaper, and a multilingual journal. On 26 June 1919, two days before the signing of the Treaty of Versailles, "Fière déclaration d'intellectuels" [A Proud Declaration of Intellectuals] appeared in Paris in the socialist newspaper *L'Humanité*. This was signed by some of the world's leading thinkers, among them Einstein, Hesse, Croce, Russell, Zangwill, Zweig, Gorky, Stieglitz, Upton Sinclair, Tagore, Alain, Barbusse, Duhamel, and Augustin Hamon.[13]

The Declaration was an ambiguous document: it began with a call to the "Workers of the Mind" to regroup into a fraternal union, but soon turned into a harsh indictment of intellectuals for their betrayal of noble ideals in the service of warfare. Rolland urged them to follow the Mind, to sweep aside nationalism in the name of "le Peuple—unique, universel, . . . le Peuple de tous les hommes, tous également nos frères" [the Nation—unique, universal, . . . the Nation of all men, all equally our brothers]. But the unrelenting accusations only served to weaken the closing plea for "l'Esprit libre, un et multiple, éternel" [the free Mind, one and manifold, eternal], and some intellectuals were very critical of this *Déclaration d'Indépendance de l'esprit* [Declaration of Independence of the Mind], as it became known in final draft.

As Rolland himself soon recognized, there were two principal objections to his manifesto: first, some thinkers were afraid to make an openly international profession of faith, and second, they were reluctant to condemn the misbehavior of fellow intellectuals during the war (*Journal*, p. 1819). Others had personal reasons, such as Anatole France—who did not respond at all—and Marie Curie, who refused to sign. According to Rolland, the elderly skeptic "se calfeutrait . . . dans un prudent silence capitonné" [shut himself up smugly . . . in a discreet, padded silence], while Curie could not forget the sinking of the *Lusitania* (*Quinze ans*, p. lxiv).

Some of those who signed did so hesitatingly: Benedetto Croce and Heinrich Mann had reservations; Max Eastman published Rolland's manifesto in the New York City periodical the *Liberator*, but appended his own Marxist critique; Bertrand Russell's support included lengthy reservations as to the penultimate paragraph, which he found accusatorial. He wrote to Rolland in French that many intellectuals regretted what they had done during the war, that he had "no wish to impose upon them the task of saying publicly: Peccavi" (*Journal*, p. 1791). Rather than a critique of past failings, Russell suggested an overview of the great tasks which lay ahead. On 4 May, he sent Rolland a long alternate paragraph which stated that "les intellectuels devraient contribuer à la réédification du monde en ruines" [intellectuals should contribute to the rebuilding of a world in ruins], and urged moral and intellectual unity (*Journal*, p. 1818). Rolland disagreed: he felt that one should "ne pas se hâter de passer l'éponge sur les trahisons d'hier, car on livre ainsi la place aux trahisons de demain" [not rush to wipe the slate clean of the treasons of yesterday, for if we do so we are simply giving way to the treasons of tomorrow] (*Journal*, p. 1814). He expressed his disillusionment to Russell on 4 June, lamenting that it was impossible to unite a few free intellectuals around even a harmless, watered-down text. "Ma Déclaration a reçu de différents côtés tant de demandes de modifications ou d'atténuations, qu'en les réalisant, il n'en resterait plus rien que le titre" [My Declaration has received so many demands for modifications or toning down from different sides that if they were accepted, nothing would be left but the title] (*Journal*, p. 1819). When one considers the sheer number of different changes suggested to the Declaration, this is no exaggeration.

Not surprisingly, perhaps the most critical reaction of all—and certainly the most fully documented by Rolland—came from Shaw. Rolland wrote to him on 25 April 1919, urging him to support "ce défi . . . à l'asservissement volontaire de presque toute l'élite européenne" [this challenge . . . to the voluntary enslavement of nearly the whole European elite]. His was a plea on behalf of "une jeunesse intellectuelle qui attend, désorientée, angoissée, que les aînés la rallient et lui rendent confiance dans le pouvoir de l'Esprit libérateur" [an intellectual youth which waits, disoriented, anguished, for its elders to rally to it and restore its confidence in the power of the liberating Mind]. Idealist intellectuals employed their pens instead of swords, he wrote (*Journal*, p. 1796).

Shaw went one better than Russell: with his reply to Rolland in French dated 7 May 1919, he returned the Declaration, extensively revised in his own hand, with the cautionary note that "il faut une confession plutôt qu'un reproche: sans cela, nous aurons l'air d'être Pharisien, même snob. Pour l'éviter, j'ai osé raccommoder un peu votre brouillon. Qu'en pensez-vous? Naturellement, vous saurez rédiger mon baragouin: je suis vil linguiste" [we must have a confession rather than a reproach: without that, we will appear to be Pharisees, even snobs. To avoid this, I have dared to mend your draft a little. What do you think of it? Naturally, you will know how to emend my gibberish: I am a vile linguist] (*Journal*, p. 1815). The self-deprecation was perhaps intended to assuage Rolland's reaction to Shaw's considerable "mending": he had in fact rewritten about one-third of the document.

The tone of the Declaration was at times vituperative indeed: "Les penseurs, les artistes, ont . . . travaillé à détruire la compréhension mutuelle entre les hommes. Et, ce faisant, ils ont enlaidi, avili, abaissé la Pensée, dont ils étaient les représentants" [Thinkers and artists have . . . worked to destroy mutual understanding among mankind. And, in so doing, they have disfigured, demeaned, debased, and degraded Thought, of which they were the representatives] (*Journal*, p. 1770). Although he left this passage untouched, Shaw manipulated the preceding paragraph in such a way as to make it seem that the conditions of war had obliged the intellectuals to act as they did, as opposed to Rolland's placing the blame entirely on the intellectuals themselves. "La guerre a jeté le désarroi dans nos rangs" [The war has cast confusion in our ranks], wrote Rolland. "La plupart des intellectuels ont mis leur science, leur art, leur raison, au service des gouvernements" [Most intellectuals have put their science, their art, their reason, at the disposal of governments]. In Shaw's version, this became "Elle [war] nous a obligés à mettre notre science, notre art, notre raison, au service de nos gouvernements" [It has forced us to put our science, our art, our reason, at the disposal of our governments]. Shaw went on to replace Rolland's realization of "la faiblesse des âmes individuelles et la force élémentaire des grands courants collectifs" [the weakness of individual souls and the elemental force of great collective currents] with the somewhat brutal advice that in time of war,

> . . . il faut sacrifier et même prostituer à la défense nationale non seulement la vie, mais l'âme, l'esprit, la conscience, et manier le mensonge aussi peu scrupuleusement que la baïonnette et la

bombe. Nous avons beau chercher à planer au-dessus de la mêlée. Inutile: à la guerre, le premier devoir est au foyer, au voisin, la tâche suprême d'en détourner la mort.

[. . . one must sacrifice and even prostitute not only life, but soul, spirit, and conscience for the sake of national defense, as well as handle lies with as few scruples as one would a bayonet and a bomb. It is no use trying to soar above the battle: in wartime, one's first duty is to home, neighbors, and the supreme task is to keep death away from them].

It is little wonder that the gentle pacifist Rolland considered this passage shocking and deeply offensive, antithetical as it was to his goal of quashing what he would later refer to as "nationalismes sanglants" and "religions de patriotisme jaloux" [bloody nationalisms and religions of jealous patriotism] (*Quinze ans*, p. 9), as well as to his persistently reiterated insistence on pan-nationalism: "Non, l'amour de ma patrie ne veut pas que je haïsse et que je tue les âmes pieuses et fidèles qui aiment les autres patries. Il veut que je les honore et que je cherche à m'unir à elles pour notre bien commun" [No, love of my country does not require me to hate and kill those pious and faithful souls who love other countries. It demands that I honor them and seek to unite myself with them for our common good] (*Au-dessus de la mêlée*, p. 30).

After placing the blame on war itself and, in typical Shavian rhetoric, propounding survival at whatever intellectual or moral costs, Shaw apologized for the actions of the intellectuals. He replaced "Debout! Dégageons l'Esprit de ces compromissions, de ces alliances humiliantes, de ces servitudes cachées!" [Rise up! Release the Intellect from its compromises, from its humiliating alliances, from its secret slavery!] with an even more forceful passage:

Tout cela n'est peut-être pas plus horrible pour nous, penseurs et artistes, que ne l'est le meurtre, l'incendie, surtout la famine voulue, pour nos frères poilus. Mais c'est infiniment plus difficile d'en arrêter l'opération. A l'armée, on donne l'ordre: "Bas le feu partout!" et le feu cesse. Qui sait donner pareil ordre à la pensée fausse, à l'empoisonnement de l'esprit? Pourtant, il faut faire l'essai. La menace qui nous a forcés de piller les trésors et profaner les temples de l'esprit n'existe plus. La paix nous rend la liberté. Hâtons-nous donc de nous dégager de ces alliances, de ces servitudes dénaturées, imposées par la guerre.

[All that is perhaps no more horrible for us, thinkers and artists, than murder, fire, and deliberate famine are for our fellow soldiers. But is infinitely more difficult to stop its operation. One gives the army the order to "Cease fire!" and it does. Who can give such an order to false thought, to the poisoning of the mind? And yet, one must try it. The menace which has forced us to plunder the treasures and desecrate the temples of the mind no longer exists. Peace restores our freedom. Let us therefore hasten to extricate ourselves from these alliances, from these unnatural constraints, imposed by war].

"Tout cela," of course, refers in part to Rolland's scathing accusation that intellectuals had "enlaidi, avili, abaissé, dégradé la Pensée." In comparing intellectuals to soldiers, Shaw reiterated his thesis that war calls for drastic measures by thinkers as well as fighters—with the essential difference that soldiers can be ordered and controlled, whereas thought has a volition all its own.

Despite Shaw's more gentle concluding remarks urging immediate extrication from the shackles of war, Rolland was nonetheless offended by what must have seemed to him a very callous attitude. In his reply of 28 May, Rolland admitted that Shaw was correct in warning against self-righteousness. But he objected vehemently to Shaw's propounding of sacrifice and self-prostitution in the service of the state: "Jamais je n'admettrai que le premier devoir de l'homme de pensée soit la défense nationale; il est, pour moi, la défense de la pensée. Je ne mets pas la nation, la patrie, le foyer, avant tout. Avant tout, je mets la conscience libre. . . . Que l'esprit reste sauf!" [Never will I concede that the thinking man's first duty is to defend his country; it is, in my opinion, to defend the intellect. I do not place country, homeland, hearth, before everything. Before everything, I place the free conscience. . . . May the mind remain unharmed!]. He ended with a plea for "une Internationale de la pensée, une Conscience mondiale!" [an International of the mind, a worldwide Conscience!] (*Journal,* p. 1917).

Shaw answered on 27 June, criticizing Rolland's notion of the omnipotence of Thought or Intellect, reminding him that the man of intellect did not exist. "Moi, je ne suis pas la Pensée. Je suis Bernard Shaw. Vous êtes Romain Rolland. Nous mangeons, et huit heures après, nous oublions notre philosophie, et sentons seulement la faim. . . . Nul homme n'a été au-dessus de la mêlée. Une telle prétention répugnerait le monde et briserait notre influence. Pardonnez-moi ma brusquerie; en écrivant l'anglais, j'ai assez de tact; mais dans une langue étrangère, on écrit comme on peut" [I am not Thought. I am Bernard Shaw, and you are Romain Rolland. We eat, and eight hours later, we forget our philosophy, and feel only hunger. . . . No man was ever above the battle. Such a claim would disgust people and ruin our influence. Pardon my bluntness: in writing English, I have some tact; but in a foreign language, one writes as one can].[14]

Rolland replied immediately, on the 29th, that it was not necessary to forget one's ideas when one is hungry; even then men were dying for their ideas. "Je ne suis pas au-dessus des mêlées,—de toutes les mêlées. J'ai été, je suis, je serai toujours 'au-dessus de la mêlée' des nations et des patries. Mais je suis dans le combat contre les nations, contre les patries, contre les castes, contre toutes les barrières qui séparent les hommes" [I am not above battles,—all battles. I have been, I am, I will always be 'above the battle' of nations and homelands. But I am in combat against nations, against homelands, against castes, against all barriers separating human beings] (*Par la révolution*, p. 14).

This important distinction helps clarify Rolland's adherence to an international "mêlée" of intellects struggling for world harmony, as well as his denunciation of one nationalistic "mêlée" fighting another in a struggle for military glory. The difference is one of theory and practice: while striving to create a world community of pacifist nations, Rolland had to confront the more pragmatic—and human—notions of patriotism and individualism. It was inevitable that he should have been disappointed by human nature. In the end, and in spite of the recommendations and objections of Shaw and others, the published Declaration was virtually identical to Rolland's first draft of 16 March 1919. Only one sentence was altered: the original read "Nous prenons l'engagement de ne servir jamais que la Vérité" [We are engaged to serve only Truth]; the final version deleted the word "engagement" to become "Nous honorons la seule Vérité" [We honor Truth alone].

Looking back upon his debate with Shaw almost two decades later—in his 1935 introduction to *Par la révolution, la paix*—the controversy then seemed to Rolland to have been one of form rather than of content. He came to the conclusion that the form was not only more suited to Shaw's nature, but also probably "la plus efficace à flétrir le servile égarement de la pensée enrégimentée pendant la guerre" [the most effective for condemning the servile aberration of enlisted thinking during the war] (*Par la révolution*, p. 14). More importantly, the passionate debate with Shaw over the Declaration had provided Rolland with the impetus to define the ideology behind the unfortunate expression "au-dessus de la mêlée." Echoing his letter to Shaw, Rolland wrote that he was above the bloody battles of a nationalism "se baignant dans des torrents de sang,—sang infécond, sang maudit, qui ne fait qu'appeler le sang vengeur" [bathed in torrents of blood,—barren blood, accursed blood, which summons up only vengeful blood]; but he was very much "*dans la mêlée*, délibérément, ou, d'un terme plus digne, dans le combat organisé contre toutes les forces oppressives du passé . . ." [*in the fray*, deliberately, or, to use a more dignified term, in the struggle organized against all the oppressive forces of the past . . .] (*Par la révolution*, p. 15). But in the end, and despite Shaw's pragmatic advice, Rolland's credo had been repeated, contradicted, and ultimately ignored.

Perhaps Shaw's only genuine endorsement of Rolland's work was reserved for *Liluli*, a satiric antiwar play which Rolland sent him soon after its completion in November 1918. Shaw read the play in French and responded on 7 October 1919 with somewhat overabundant enthusiasm: "*Liluli* est kolossal, grossartig, wunderschön, magnificent. Je l'ai goûté énormément; sans bornes, avec extase. Ma femme partage mon admiration" [*Liluli* is colossal, grand, very beautiful, magnificent. I enjoyed it enormously; boundlessly, with ecstasy. My wife shares my admiration]. Shaw went on to say that he had suggested to H. W. Massingham, editor of the *Nation*, that he obtain the rights to publish *Liluli* in serial form and have it translated by Laurence Housman, "plume délicate, esprit sympathique" [delicate touch, likeable mind] (Starr, p. 5). Thanks to Shaw, Rolland's play was performed in England by Massingham.

Liluli is one of Rolland's rare forays into the ironic mode, and—despite Shaw's praise—not an altogether successful one. In keeping with the frenzy of war which it mocks, it is fraught with fast-paced confusion. We meet the conniving, blond enchantress Liluli, or Illusion; Truth, the dark, lively gypsy; the barbarous Llôp'ih, mute Opinion; majestic, ineffectual, white-bearded Master-God; Polonius, the pompous, bemedaled Academician; armed Peace; indifferent Love; three termagant sisters, Equality, Liberty, Fraternity; and so on. Polichinello, the play's Everyman, rejects Liluli's enticements, for she has already lulled the innocent eighteen-year-old Altaïr into the arms of army recruiters. He also refuses the headstrong seductions of Truth, admitting "un mignon petit mensonge est bien plus doux à peloter" [a pretty little lie is nicer to fondle].[15] Master-God sells little idols and fetishes and always sides with the powerful. The two crowds—one French, the other Germanic—join in a cacophonous, gluttonous orgy, while the Diplomats maintain that diplomacy is a chess game: "Pour gagner, la règle veut que l'on perde des pions. Les pions sont là (*Ils montrent les peuples*)" [To win, the rule says that one must lose pawns. The pawns are there (*Pointing to the people*)] (*Liluli*, pp. 115–16). When half-naked Truth is bound and gagged on a throne, the leering crowd cheers, "Long live Truth!" Bloodthirsty Liluli encourages best friends Altaïr and Antarès to kill one another, exclaiming "À qui perd gagne! Qui me veut gagner, qu'il se perde! [Whoever loses wins! Whoever would win me, let him lose himself!] (*Liluli*, p. 186). Naked, cadaverous Opinion presides over the final conflagration, during which the Intellectuals, having spoken eloquently, look on, rest, and mop their foreheads: "Souffrez, mourez, manants! C'est pour mon chant" [Suffer, die, yokels! It's for the sake of my song] (*Liluli*, p. 214). The play culminates in everything collapsing on Polichinello's head.

The foregoing synthesis does not account for the dozens of other groups that weave their way through the allegory: children, fat men, thin men, pageants, "fettered brains," workers, peasants, merchants, and others. Like a dissonant fugue, the harried, topsy-turvy madness builds upon puns, rhymes, and an endless conglomeration of characters until the entire hullabaloo explodes onto the head of Polichinello.

What is puzzling is that the outright didacticism of *Liluli* runs counter to Rolland's own theory of drama published five years earlier, *Le théâtre du peuple: essai d'esthétique d'un théâtre nouveau*, in which he vehemently condemns moralizing and didacticism: "Le théâtre populaire doit éviter deux excès opposés, qui lui sont coutumiers: la pédagogie morale, qui, des oeuvres vivantes, extrait de froides leçons, . . . et le dilettantisme indifférent, qui veut se faire uniquement, à tout prix, l'amuseur du peuple" [The popular theater must avoid two customary opposing excesses: moral pedagogy, which extracts cold lessons from living works, . . . and indifferent dilettantism, which only wants to be, at all costs, the people's entertainer].[16] *Liluli*, a savage attack on militarism and a highly entertaining spoof, does not conform at all to Rolland's theoretical precepts. Nonetheless, like his Declaration, the play is a diatribe against the vanities of war. However, a satiric attack on human foibles in theatrical form would understandably be more appealing to Shaw's sense of the dramatic than the sterner chiding of a manifesto.

Very different from Shaw's praise of *Liluli* is Rolland's scathing attack on *Saint Joan*, hidden away in the epilogue to the second volume of his *Péguy*, completed in 1944, the year of his death. Although he admits that *Saint Joan* is "une assez bonne pièce, qui a de l'esprit et de l'émotion, qui est intelligente, vive et humaine" [a fairly good play, which has wit and emotion, is intelligent, lively, and human], when compared to Péguy's staunchly Catholic interpretation of the same theme in his four Jeanne d'Arc plays, it fails dismally, "superficielle, dénuée de toute vraie spiritualité, surtout absolument étrangère à l'esprit du catholicisme" [superficial, devoid of all real spirituality, most of all absolutely foreign to the spirit of Catholicism]. Even the trial scene, bolstered as it is by historical documents, is "déplorablement sommaire, futile, un paresseux dessin d'élève brillant et léger, qui a feuilleté à peine les textes, y a piqué ça et là quelques répliques authentiques de Jeanne, sur un fond de dialogue de théâtre, fait pour des spectateurs frivoles et pressés" [deplorably brief, futile, a lazy drawing by a brilliant and thoughtless student who has barely skimmed through the texts, picking here and there a few of

Jeanne's authentic lines, on a background of stage dialogue made for shallow and hurried spectators].[17]

But the more serious problem, according to Rolland, is that Shaw is not a "believer" in the strict religious sense, and thus any attempt at portraying a passionately religious being can be only artificial and ineffective. *Saint Joan* is therefore based on "le vide esthétique et moral d'un cosmopolitisme d'art 'intellectuel', qui ne croit pas à la réalité intérieure de ce qu'il raconte. . . . Il [Shaw] n'a aucune idée du monde intérieur qui remplit l'âme de Jeanne" [the aesthetic and moral void of a cosmopolitanism of "intellectual" art which does not believe in the interior reality of what it is about. . . . He has no idea of the interior world which fills Jeanne's soul] (*Péguy*, p. 251).

Rolland's efforts at gathering the European community under a single ideological banner were noble but, in the end, ineffectual. In late 1919 and early 1920, along with Duhamel and Barbusse, he attempted to prepare for the first in a series of International Congresses of Intellectuals, but nothing came of it.[18] In the words of one critic, "Despite disclaimers, Romain Rolland tended to attribute to the intellectual priestly qualities and divine functions." He wrote to "inspire his readers to goals he deemed transcendent and eternal" (Fisher, p. 76). Although the very same thing could be said about Shaw, the Irishman's approach was often more pragmatic, even at the risk of offending and alienating his peers. However, the fact remains that despite his admiration for Shaw's independent and idiosyncratic temperament, Rolland the solitary, indignant moralist was ultimately disappointed that Shaw did not take a more militant stand in troubled times. What he was aiming for can best be summarized as "un organisme intellectuel mondial, qui fût en quelque sorte le cerveau de la société à venir" [a world intellectual organism, which would be as it were the brain of the society to come] (letter to E. D. Morel, 30 March 1919, quoted in *Quinze ans*, p. xiv). This is a very Shavian idea, with the important difference that Rolland's organism is communal, whereas Shaw's is individual.

Requests for Shaw to participate in the war effort with other intellectuals would continue into World War II. Henri Barbusse, campaigning with Rolland, invited Shaw to be a member of the organizing committee of an antiwar coalition called the Congress against War, under the aegis of the Committee of International Co-operation (C.I.C), created in 1921 by the League of Nations to foster internationalism in art, science, and literature. The Congress against War included some twenty members, among them Rolland, Barbusse, Einstein, Dreiser, Dos Passos, Upton Sinclair, Gorki, Wells, Russell, and Gilbert Murray, who served as chairman from 1928 onward.[19]

Shaw wrote to Barbusse on 4 May 1932 that he would allow his name to be used only with great reluctance—"All that happens is that our names lose all their value by futile repetition"—and stipulated that the C.I.C. should organize the Congress, especially since it had long been "impotent and almost useless because nobody takes any notice of it." He chided Barbusse for convening his Congresses as if the C.I.C. did not exist, and lamented the futility of "reading moral lectures at Geneva" (*Collected Letters* 4, p. 292). But "Barbusse, Romain Rolland & Co . . . repudiated my suggestion as 'bourgeois' " (*Collected Letters* 4, p. 505). It is no wonder, as he wrote Hamon, that people took "no more notice of a Barbusse–Romain Rolland manifesto than of the clock of Notre Dame striking twelve" (*Collected Letters* 4, p. 295). Indeed, the C.I.C. itself fell upon hard times: the franc's devaluation reduced its effectiveness and, according to Shaw, "intellectually it sank into profound catalepsy."[20] Its only merit for Shaw seems to have been as the impetus for his play *Geneva* (1936), which satirizes the Committee's efforts to achieve world peace, but, as he wrote to Murray, "in such a way as to make this the first step to its publicity and popularity" (*Collected Letters* 4, p. 585).

It is a measure of Romain Rolland's complexity as both pacifist and activist that Shaw's estimate of him, despite differences in ideology, remained high. Shaw wrote in May 1930 that his opinion of the Frenchman would require "a book as long as Romain Rolland's opinion of Beethoven" (Starr, p. 6). Not until 1940, when Shaw was in his eighty-fifth year, could he allow himself to make light of Rolland's much maligned and misunderstood slogan: "I can only *planer au dessus de la mêlée* like Romain Rolland when the siren does not remind me that I am crawling *au dessous des bombiers*" (*Collected Letters* 4, p. 578). Shaw knew that in time of war, bombs fall on the sidelines as well as on the battlefields—something of which Rolland, the untiring apologist for non-violence, needed to be reminded.

Notes

1. See David James Fisher's thorough study, *Romain Rolland and the Politics of Intellectual Engagement* (Berkeley: University of California Press, 1988), pp. 355–58. Subsequent references appear parenthetically in the text.

2. William T. Starr, "Romain Rolland and George Bernard Shaw," *Shaw Bulletin* 2, no. 3 (September 1957), 1. Subsequent references appear parenthetically in the text. Starr quotes from previously unpublished material, but his translations from the French are highly corrupt.

3. Romain Rolland, *Deux Hommes se recontrent. Correspondance entre Jean-Richard Bloch et Romain Rolland (1910–1918)* (Paris: Albin Michel, 1964), p. 211–12.

4. Romain Rolland, *Journal des années de guerre, 1914–1919* (Paris: Albin Michel, 1952), p. 875. Subsequent references appear parenthetically in the text.

5. Quoted in R. A. Francis, "Romain Rolland and Some British Intellectuals During the First World War," *Journal of European Studies* 10 (1980), 197.

6. For Rolland's pacifist ideology, see Fisher, pp. 38–48.

7. *What I Really Wrote About the War* (1930), p. 1. This is volume 21 of *The Collected Works of Bernard Shaw*, 30 vols. (New York: Wise, 1930–32), and includes his controversial *Common Sense About the War* (14 November 1914).

8. Romain Rolland, "Pro Aris," *Au-dessus de la mêlée* (Paris: Ollendorff, 1915), p. 10. Subsequent references appear parenthetically in the text.

9. Frederic V. Grunfeld, *Rodin: A Biography* (New York: Holt, 1987), pp. 624–25.

10. "Pro Aris," *Au-dessus de la mêlée*, p. 37.

11. *Journal*, pp. 160 and 125. For a partial list of signatories, see pp. 1842–43.

12. "Pour l'Internationale de l'esprit" in *L'Esprit libre* (Geneva, 1971), pp. 322–31. For Rolland's approbation of the Bolshevik Revolution, as well as his reservations about Marxist-Leninist ideology, see Fisher, pp. 53–58.

13. Of the 952 signatories, 251 represented the intellectual elite. Spain had 100, France 58, Germany 21, the United States 14, Italy 10, Belgium 10, Switzerland 6, England 5, Sweden 4, and Russia 4. For a partial list, see Fisher, pp. 314–15; for dissenting opinions on the Declaration, see pp. 68–76. The full text of the Declaration is reprinted in the *Journal*, pp. 1769–71, and in Rolland's collection of wartime writings, *Quinze ans de combat (1919–1934)* (Paris: Rieder, 1935), pp. 1–3, including on pp. 7–10 Rolland's introduction—"sur le malentendu mortel qui risque de séparer les intellectuels et le peuple ouvrier" [on the deadly misunderstanding which risks separating intellectuals and working-class people]—appended to the English translation of the Declaration published in E. D. Morel's *Foreign Affairs* (August 1919), where he concludes that the intellectuals must illuminate the road that the workers have to build. Subsequent references to *Journal* and *Quinze ans* appear parenthetically in the text.

14. Quoted in Romain Rolland, *Par la révolution, la paix* (Paris: Éditions Sociales Internationales, 1935), pp. 13–14.

15. Romain Rolland, *Liluli* (Paris: Albin Michel, 1919), p. 125.

16. Romain Rolland, *Le théâtre du peuple: essai d'esthétique d'un théâtre nouveau* (Paris: Hachette, 1913), pp. 116–17. Appended is Rolland's manifesto for an International Congress on Popular Theater (pp. 209–11), propounding the breakdown of religious, political, moral, and social barriers, with Art as the savior of humanity.

17. Roman Rolland, *Péguy* (Buenos Aires: Viau-Feugere, 1946), p. 250. Subsequent references appear parenthetically in the text.

18. See Fisher, p. 313, n. 40.

19. See Fisher, p. 160. After World War II, the scope and purpose of the C.I.C. were encompassed by the program projected at the United Nations for UNESCO (see Dan H. Laurence, ed., *Bernard Shaw: Collected Letters, 1926–1950* (New York: Viking, 1988), p. 291.

20. Dan H. Laurence, ed., *Bernard Shaw: Collected Plays with Their Prefaces*, 7: 166.

Eric Wallis

THE INTELLIGENT WOMAN'S GUIDE: SOME CONTEMPORARY OPINIONS

The Intelligent Woman's Guide to Socialism and Capitalism was published in 1928. It was acclaimed by Ramsay MacDonald, who had served briefly as a Labour prime minister and was to do so again, as the world's most important book since the Bible. With perhaps becoming modesty, the author himself described it as "a tremendous job of real literary work; not like play writing." It is said that the origin of the book was a request by Shaw's sister-in-law that he should write an explanatory pamphlet on socialism for the members of her local branch of the Women's Institute, and the amusing legend is that the lady was immensely surprised when she was finally presented with a substantial volume of more than four hundred pages.

In fact, it is extremely unlikely that the lady could have been as surprised as all that for, as is clear from his correspondence, Shaw made frequent reference to the heavy demands being made upon him by "my confounded book for women on Socialism." However, there can be no doubt about the serious sense of purpose which drove him to write it. Despite the great success of *Saint Joan* (which had made him the most famous living playwright) and the "hideous calamity" of the award of the Nobel Prize (he used this term because of the spate of begging letters to which the award had given rise), he felt it his duty to society to write a textbook. As he said in a letter to H. G. Wells dated 4 August 1927,

> Baldwin's position is not ascertainable: he is in the air between Capitalism become impossible and Socialism not yet become comprehensible. MacDonald's position *is* ascertainable; but we have to ascertain it for him: the men of action and the parliament men have no time to think. That is why I have left 12½ plays unwritten to produce this book on Socialism with which the printer is now in travail.[1]

When Shaw wrote the book, the war of 1914–1918 was still very much in mind and political difficulties, stemming in part at least from the turmoil of the war, were still very great. In Britain, the so-called General Strike of 1926 had left the political scene in confusion. Despite the solidarity of the trade unions, the strike could only be regarded as a failure. Baldwin led a Conservative government which showed no more likelihood of bringing about the "land fit for heroes to live in," promised in the wartime slogan, than had the short-lived minority Labour government of 1924 that had been brought down by a combination of its own ineptitude and the skill of the Opposition in raising a false cry of political interference with the course of justice. Incidentally, and, in view of the title of Shaw's book, in a striking coincidence, the year 1928 saw the granting of the vote to women at the age of twenty-one, after a probationary period since 1918 when the male legislators had graciously extended the franchise to include women over thirty.

It cannot be said that, despite the extravagant praise of Ramsay MacDonald, the first appearance of *The Intelligent Woman's Guide* was given an overwhelmingly favorable critical reception. Some reviewers appeared to have forgotten Shaw's long years of service in the Labour and socialist movement and seemed to think it something of an impertinence for a mere playwright to interfere in the sacred realms of politics and economics. There were even facetious references to the effect that the young woman on the dustjacket, lightly but quite decorously clad, was not intelligent enough to earn money with which to clothe herself adequately.

Yet, among those who gave the book more careful consideration than was possible in the first quick reviews written for the press, there were several who perceived that Shaw was right, at least in attempting to provide a restatement of the fundamentals of socialism. Shaw tried to combine an approach to the more or less common reader—that is, to the intelligent reader—with a submission, or even a direction, to the party leaders. It is the former purpose which is most apparent in his opening words:

> It would be easy, dear madam, to refer you to the many books on modern Socialism which have been published since it became a respectable constitutional question . . . in the eighteen-eighties. But I strongly advise you not to read a line of them until you and your friends have discussed for yourselves how wealth should be distributed in a respectable civilized country, and arrived at the best conclusion you can.
>
> For Socialism is nothing but an opinion held by some people on that point.[2]

This tone of jaunty but, at the same time, substantial and confident authority, is maintained throughout the four hundred or so pages. He covers, among many other topics, such subjects as "How Much for Each," "Oligarchy," "Eugenics," "The Courts of Law," "The Idle Rich," and "Merit and Money," as well as nationalization and different aspects of marriage and the care of children. Everything was grist to Shaw's socialist mill.

Among the publications in which the book was treated most seriously was the *Criterion*. This was a literary magazine, at times monthly, at others quarterly, which never had a large circulation but which had an influence, in literary and cultural circles generally, totally out of proportion to the small number of copies that were printed. This influence was largely the consequence of the great and growing reputation of the editor, T. S. Eliot. Eliot combined a concern with literature in the limited sense, to be expected of a leading poet, with an interest in religion and its effect on politics and society generally. In 1928 he formulated his position in the celebrated trilogy of assertions which appeared in *For Lancelot Andrewes*. At that time, he defined his attitudes as "classicist in literature, royalist in politics, and Anglo-Catholic in religion." It would be unlikely that anyone with such an outlook would feel in sympathy with Shaw on many, or even any, subjects. Indeed, Eliot could rarely bring himself to recognize much in Shaw, except the ability to write good prose. Later in life, Eliot said that one of Shaw's greatest claims to distinction was his ability to make his readers and his audiences think that they were more intelligent than they were in fact.[3] Such a comment may rebound against the person who makes it, for if, as Shaw did in *The Intelligent Woman's Guide,* he was able to help his readers to understand some of the abstruse workings of the financial and banking systems, he was performing a useful service. In any event, it may be thought a sign of grace on the part of Eliot that he recognized *The Intelligent Woman's Guide* as being of sufficient importance to be given generous space in the *Criterion* issue of December 1928. Accordingly, comments were printed by four writers of differing points of view, and the collection made up a valuable indication of the contemporary response.

The first of the four was Harold J. Laski. In 1920, he had become a lecturer in political science at the London School of Economics, a constituent college of the federal University of London since 1920. In 1926, he had been appointed professor. He was a prolific writer, an eloquent speaker, and a very successful and popular teacher. In general, he was on the left of the Labour party and did not limit his political interests and activities to the academic field alone. In 1945, he became chairman of the Labour party. He was never a slavish follower of the party line and, indeed, he is more often remembered in some quarters for his readiness to tell the politicians what to do rather than to accept their lead.

In his comments on Shaw's book, he began with kind words about its importance but then proceeded to attack the main thrust of the argument, the need for equality of income. He thought that Shaw was logically successful but empirically unsuccessful. It may be doubted, however, whether Laski himself was any more successful, either logically or empirically. Doubtless, there is a moral case against great disparities of wealth and income in a civilized society, but short of legal confiscation it is hard to think of what can be done. No law could have prevented such successful popular entertainers as the Beatles, for example, from gaining (the word "earning" might be questioned) the large sums they did, and even income taxation at rates over 90 percent would have left them far better off than the rest of the population. Laski's own two principles, an upper limit to income and a rough (but it is never stated how rough) "proportionality" between income and function, would be no easier to operate in practice than would Shaw's proposed equality. Shaw later changed his mind on the basic idea, and in *Everybody's Political What's What?*, published in 1944, he conceded that mathematical equality was not an end in itself, and that there would be a level at which this would cease to matter even under unrestricted capitalism. However, Laski was not to know that in 1928.

Laski attacked Shaw on other grounds. He was far from convinced by Sidney Webb's theory of the inevitability of gradualness, and he was not inclined to agree that socialism was the inevitable outcome of advanced capitalism. Thus he considered Shaw to be weak in what he had to say about the transition phase. In Laski's view, Shaw lacked a sense of the way in which institutions worked and did not realize the limitations of government action. In addition, he failed to comprehend the extent of the voluntary effort that would be required if socialism (and Laski put socialism and democracy together) were to succeed.

As might be expected, the second contributor, the Reverend M. C. D'Arcy, S.J., took a somewhat different view from that of Laski. First, he found Shaw defective in his general approach. The eminent Jesuit thought that sentiment was suppressed in Shaw's mind and that all that was left was cold as ice. Moreover he felt that, reading Shaw, he was in the presence of a monomaniac without understanding or reverence. He then went on to criticize Shaw as a product of the late Victorian era, by which he meant a period of materialism and Fabianism. Shaw had therefore "nothing of the breadth of an Aristotle or the height of a Plato." To say, however, that a writer or thinker fails to reach these standards is not, of itself, enough to find him devoid of merit. In fact, Father D'Arcy, alone of the contributors, emphasized the lucidity of Shaw's writing, finding his prose "worthy of a Platonic dialogue."

D'Arcy was not at all convinced by Shaw's arguments on equality of income. His chief objection, not surprisingly, coming from a religious propagandist, was that Shaw did not show that his socialist state would be either capable of achievement or desirable if it could ever be created. Shaw points "the way to the promised land, but like Moses he knows that he will not live to see it and tells us little about it." Father D'Arcy found that he was left to divine for himself what Shaw's socialism would be like. He did not approve of what he could see. He found the emphasis not on virtue but on freedom from material cares and on leisure. D'Arcy was at one with Laski in finding that Shaw disregarded the individual. Yet it is easy to imagine Shaw replying that the Jesuit father had ended his argument where the real questions about Shaw's proposals ought to be asked. D'Arcy maintained that "the ideal is the free exercise of virtue and the common good." There are several passages in *Major Barbara* in which Undershaft, either the devil's advocate or, in some senses, perhaps the devil himself, beats down the Christian Barbara by the force of his argument that Christian doctrine cannot be preached to empty stomachs. It is not necessary to agree with all of Undershaft's contentions, and it is dangerous to assume that a character in a play can be taken as expressing the views of the author as one would find them in a directly polemical work. There is, however, something to Shaw's argument, running through the whole of *The Intelligent Woman's Guide*, that all members of the community, as all members of a family, are entitled to be looked after. This is not far distant from some essential tenets of the Christian faith, with which Father D'Arcy, rather than Shaw, might expect to sympathize.

Dr. A. L. Rowse is the only one of the four contributors who is still alive, and it is only fair and courteous to make it clear that the views he expressed in 1928 are not being attributed to him today. Dr. Rowse, as he now is, was then a young and enthusiastic socialist and was twice a Labour party parliamentary candidate. Since then, he has written with distinction on a wide range of subjects, chiefly literary and historical, and it seems clear that his political views have changed through the years. However, his spirited comments in the *Criterion* may be taken as representative of the views of some young socialists of the time. In brief, Rowse was overwhelmed by the book and thought it essentially important because it represented schools of thought and opinion that viewed Shaw's work as an inspiration to the whole of society. So highly did Rowse value what he called "a masterpiece of political pamphleteering" that he thought Shaw's gifts as a social critic constituted his greatest claim to lasting fame, whereas he would be outclassed by a good half-dozen of his contemporaries as a literary artist.

The fourth contributor to this particular symposium was Kenneth Pickthorn (later Sir Kenneth). He was a distinguished historian (his specialty was Tudor history, as was that of A. L. Rowse). He was, in succession, Fellow, Dean, Tutor, and President of Corpus Christi College, Cambridge, and later became a member of Parliament on the Conservative side. From 1951 to 1954, he was parliamentary secretary at the Ministry of Education. He was not thought to have been a great success in that position, but he made many friends among teachers. He was of an independent frame of mind and was never afraid to criticize the Government of which he was a supporter. In his analysis of *The Intelligent Woman's Guide,* he showed a relentless attention to detail and, at the same time, condemned much in Shaw's general approach that led him to sweep over flaws in his argument and to surge on to conclusions which, Pickthorn suggests, were frequently not supported by logical process. He admired Shaw's "intellectual breadth and rectitude" where he found it, but in a disturbingly high number of instances he convicted Shaw of something very near to deliberate intellectual sleight of hand. The comment by Pickthorn was certainly a good counter to the enthusiasm of Rowse, but for all his cool analysis of the technical faults in Shaw's reasoning he may have failed to give sufficient weight to the fact that Shaw was trying to work out something like a blueprint for a better order of society. It might be too much to say that the Pickthorn article exudes a serene complacency, but it is hard to avoid the impression that in the author's opinion Shaw was being rather silly and taking an unnecessary amount of trouble in bothering himself about such matters.

One incidental, but important, feature of the Pickthorn criticism is that he found the book ill written in the sense that there is a "want of order in the argumentation." This criticism gives less than due credit for the clarity which Shaw brings to his explanation in relatively simple terms of matters and functions that are all too often presented in the jargon of the politician or the economist. It may be that Pickthorn was able to detect some of the effort which the writing of the book entailed for Shaw and that he was therefore aware that the prose lacked some of the author's normal felicity.

It is surprising that none of the four commentators paid attention to the title of the book. As already mentioned, the idea of something written specifically for the woman readers was, to an extent, in Shaw's mind at some early stage in the inception of the work, but he certainly did not expect it to have an exclusively female readership. The way in which the pronoun "she" is used throughout (where "he" would always be employed in the orthodox textbook) has its amusing side, but the eloquent and indeed noble closing passages must make an appeal to interested readers of either sex. While Shaw always deplored the one-sidedness of political life, wanted more women in Parliament, and later (in the Preface to *"In Good King Charles's Golden Days"*, for example) advocated a double, or coupled, vote, the book does not read as an exercise in feminist propaganda or proselytizing.

No doubt, it has had enthusiastic women readers, but it has had many male admirers as well. It was brought out in the paperback Pelican edition in 1937, with additional chapters on Sovietism and fascism, and has remained in print, which may be taken to indicate continuing interest and probably readership. There are no statistics to identify the readers of the book, but it is reasonable to suppose that it has made a special appeal to Labour party members and trade unionists, as well as Left-inclined intellectuals generally. Yet it is doubtful whether it has ever become widely popular. Hugh Dalton, the Labour chancellor of the exchequer in the postwar government led by Clement Attlee, spoke of the book with approval, although not uncritically, in a Fabian Memorial Lecture in 1951, but Shaw has not been regularly quoted or referred to since then as much as might have been expected.[4] In the last few years, however, the rigor of the Thatcher "experiment" in making the rich richer and the poor poorer has led a few writers to look again at Shaw's ideas on equality (notably Professor Raymond Plant and the novelist Margaret Drabble, in Fabian Society lectures), but Shaw cannot be said to have been adopted as a prophet.[5]

From the perspective of more than sixty years after the publication of *The Intelligent Woman's Guide,* there seems to be a curiously old-fashioned air about the whole argument. Equality of income, if mentioned at all in political programs, is to be found in the appeals only of small sects that have little influence. Scientific socialism, out of Marx and developed and expounded by Lenin, Trotsky, and Stalin, appears to have destroyed itself in the Soviet Union and Eastern Europe. It is so easy to treat all socialism as tainted with the color of a failed experiment that even the least totalitarian of its adherents are cautious about using the word for fear of misrepresentation in the press and elsewhere. Social democracy may be due for a revival, although Eduard Bernstein has few readers outside academic circles. Moreover, John Maynard Keynes, while certainly no socialist himself, felt it necessary to warn nonconservatives to be careful not to underestimate the recuperative power of conservatism, although he did not estimate the price in human suffering of that recuperation. It remains to be seen whether international capitalism has the recuperative power of earlier national forms of capitalism to recover from present ills.

Shaw could not have foreseen in 1928 a world where manufacturing industry was a minority employer (although King Magnus and some of the ministers came near to it in *The Apple Cart,* only a year later), where tourism has become a major industry, where the environment and the quality of life appear to have become all-important concerns in the Western world (which now includes Japan, Australia, and New Zealand). A new political agenda is in the making, where it could be that socialism of the traditional kind has little place. No longer does such a party as Labour rely primarily on the working class (whatever that might have been) as the foundation of its voting strength. Class itself seems to have been replaced by racism, sexism, and other "-isms" as motivating forces in politics.

Rereading *The Intelligent Woman's Guide* serves as a reminder that the kind of polemical writing undertaken by Shaw is now out of fashion. As a critique of capitalist society, *The Intelligent Woman's Guide* stands alongside the writings of Marx, Proudhon, and Trotsky, and, as those are, it is penetrating and destructive rather than imaginative and constructive. As a prescription for curing the ailments of capitalist society, it is no better and no worse than they. As did the earlier writers, Shaw sought the truth. That, like them, he failed to find it is no discredit to him. The great feature of capitalism is that it still exploits human labor. It leads to vast inequalities in the standard of life of people, and these inequalities are rarely determined to any great extent by virtue or the extent of effort. It leads to a system of justice that values property above human beings. It leads to ringing declarations that people must stand on their own two feet while ensuring that those who try to do so are, except for a fortunate few, knocked down again and again. It extols the virtues of competition and creates monopolies to ensure that capitalism itself is untouched by those virtues. Some of these things Shaw perceived as clearly as anyone has done in the present century. If his vision was flawed in places, the eyes of few others were sharper, and the diagnosis of few others was put with more intelligence and wit.

Notes

1. *Bernard Shaw, Collected Letters, 1926–1950,* ed. Dan H. Laurence (New York: Viking, 1988), p. 58.
2. *The Intelligent Woman's Guide to Socialism and Capitalism* (New York: Brentano's, 1928), p. 1.
3. T. S. Eliot, *To Criticize the Critic* (London: Faber, 1965), p. 143. It may be only fair to Eliot to explain that the references to Shaw appear in the text of a lecture, "The Literature

of Politics." It had been delivered to a specially political audience, the London Conservative Union, and this may explain, in part, the polemical tone of Eliot's remarks.

4. C. E. M. Joad, ed., *Shaw and Society* (London: Odhams Press, 1953), p. 250.

5. Raymond Plant, *Equality, Markets and the State* (London: Fabian Society, 1984), Fabian Tract no. 494, and Margaret Drabble, *The Case for Equality* (London: Fabian Society, 1988), Fabian Tract no. 527. The Drabble lecture, but not the Plant, considers Shaw's views.

BERNARD SHAW'S
"INTELLIGENT WOMAN'S GUIDE."
SOME OPINIONS

I

By HAROLD J. LASKI

Mr. Shaw's book has the merit which belongs to all works of serious importance—it drives back its reader to the foundations of his own beliefs. It compels him not only to face Mr. Shaw's own convictions, but to try and produce a reasoned case for his own. Few books on social science since the war can claim this quality; Tawney's *Acquisitive Society,* the Webbs' *Socialist Commonwealth,* Cole's *Social Theory,* Salter's *Inter-allied Shipping Control;* it is with some half-dozen books of this real eminence that Mr. Shaw's belongs.

It seems to me that he does one thing supremely well, one thing with great skill, and one thing not at all. His case against the existing order is made with an incisive pungency as effective as anything in modern times. No one who reads his indictment of capitalist civilization can say afterwards that it is, as a civilization, in any coherent and ordered way reconcilable with moral principle. And, in the long run, civilizations only survive by being capable of effective reconciliation with moral principle. This, the easiest part of his task, Mr. Shaw performs with the dexterity one would expect. It is not an easy thing to do, especially when, as Mr. Shaw nowadays mostly does, you address an audience which resides, for the most part, in Mayfair and the Lido, Park avenue and Newport, Rhode Island. But Mr. Shaw makes even denunciation artistic, much as Dean Swift used to do, by his genius for deliberate understatement. He makes his case convincing by always knowing where to stop and what to omit. In this aspect, I do not know how his book could have been better done.

But this is also the easiest part of his task. If capitalist civilization is to go, what is to take its place? Mr. Shaw votes for equality of income; and he proceeds to demonstrate its adequacy by the annihilation of all alternatives. Here, as I think, he is logically successful, and empirically unsuccessful. It is not, I believe, logically possible to show that any differences in income are referable, in their exact proportions, to principle. You cannot prove that the average Lord Chancellor is justly or wisely remunerated at twice the salary of a judge of the High Court and nearly seven times the salary of a County Court judge. You cannot, either, prove that there is the slightest relationship between sound principle and the relative incomes, say, of Sir Ronald Ross and a fashionable women's doctor in Harley Street. Nor is it, I think, on the evidence deniable that a society in which, for whatever cause, there are wide disparities of income will be a society in which personality is largely evaluated in terms of the income to which it is annexed; men will be judged important not for what they do or think, but for what they can spend. This, again, produces a society in which the realization of moral principle is irrelevant.

But this seems to me a case not for a rigorous equality of income, but rather for the simultaneous application of two principles: (a) the establishment of an upper limit of income, and (b) the attempt at a rough proportionality between income and function. Pace Mr. Shaw, I do not see why society is really better off if a professional boxer has the same income as Mr. Shaw; and I think that if we tried to pay the same income to a Prime Minister as to a milkman, we should be driven to juggling with systems of allowances which would make equality without any meaning. There is, moreover, the problem of establishing the equality; and to get it would, I believe, necessitate a bloody civil war in which the army supporting the government would be given a special rate of pay to persuade it not to desert to the other side.

This brings me to the third aspect of Mr. Shaw's book—his method of dealing with the problems of the transition. Here, with great respect, I suggest that he has nothing at all to say of any constructive value. He begins by demonstrating the probable impotence of revolution; and he continues by a simple faith in Mr. Webb's "inevitability of gradualness" with a remarkable affirmation that conservative parties will probably do as much for socialism (in Mr. Shaw's sense) as socialist parties. All this, of course, is a gross over-simplification of the issues involved. It is obvious that no revolution is ever consolidated by the mere seizure of power; and it is obvious, also, that an attempt at such seizure which fails, leaves the last case worse than the first. But it is also true that no ruling class has ever in history voluntarily abdicated; and it is therefore not in the least clear that the problem of transition to a new social order is capable of being effected, without the use of violence. Nor is there any reason to suppose, as Mr. Shaw does, that socialism is the inevitable and inescapable result of industrial evolution. I do not observe in history any inherent logic of that kind. And his discussion totally omits the factor of time which I believe to be vital to the discussion. The rate of change in our epoch is so rapid that it is to me, at least, exceedingly improbable whether "gradualness" will satisfy the demands we confront.

The view, moreover, that the operation of party-politics will persuade the Tory party to outbid its rival for the sake of office seems to me, at the best, dubious. In the nineteenth century, the governing class was prepared to make great concessions because the margin of security which surrounded it was ample. That is no longer the case in this country. Mr. Shaw does not convince me that party leaders will persuade their followers easily to sacrifices of which the price is the loss of their social and economic authority. "Men," said Machiavelli, "will sooner forgive the death of their relatives than the confiscation of those relatives' property." 1789 in France and 1917 in Russia seem to me ample proof of that axiom. Mr. Shaw would have us believe that they are actually prepared to sacrifice their own property in order that a handful of their party may sit round a table in Downing Street. I take leave to doubt it.

In a word, I think Mr. Shaw is largely lacking in a sense of institutions. He can see desirable principle with unsurpassed clarity; he does not understand the processes by which principles are translated into the event. Here, perhaps, I may add two other observations. Mr. Shaw has, as I believe, an amazing faith both in the power and the desirability of government action; he has rarely stopped to consider either the limits of effective legal action or the degree to which the quality of a social order depends upon the release of voluntary effort as opposed to compulsory regulation. The first is of great importance because we tend, especially in Western civilization, to overestimate the value of expertise and to allow it, accordingly (e.g. in foreign affairs, disarmament, education), an authority of decision it does not always deserve; and the second is important because most of what is best in a society is the product of spontaneity and not of compulsion. When Mr. Shaw studied economic and political theory, centralization and the expert were just emerging into fashion. He writes as though they had not, in more senses than one, been discovered to have grave limitations. At the bottom of all worth while in society is the need to leave room for the individual to experiment with his life on a reasonable scale. My ultimate doubt of Mr. Shaw's social philosophy lies in my fear that he is really not very interested in the problem of leaving such room. In other words I doubt whether he really cares very much about individual freedom.

II

By The Rev. M. C. D'ARCY, S.J.

Mr. Bernard Shaw has written this book on Socialism as an Intelligent Woman's Guide. The reader should mark the word "intelligent," because Mr. Shaw has a clear mind, and, as always, prefers reason to emotion or sentiment in argument. For this cause amongst others I do not think that his views will commend themselves to the majority of Socialists, and needless to say, he never tries to win the sympathy of Liberals or Tories. He belongs to a generation which some will say is dying, thank Heaven, and best forgotten; that is to say, if titles must be given, he is of the rationalist school of thought and not of the more recent and modernist. He hates to be stampeded by the emotions; he deprecates force; he forbids the expropriation of the Capitalist; he will have nothing to do with the alarums and excursions of a Wells, a Maxton or a Lenin. Time for him is a factor in all change, and he is content to show what precisely the economic condition is, what measures are available to bring about a far-off end, and for the rest to gather in a well-merited income. He might almost be an Aristotle at the court of King Alexander of Macedon. I say "almost" because there are two failings which place him below the Greek and go far to spoil all his constructive thinking. The first is found notably in certain Irishmen, and is the opposite of sentimentalism. In the complete thinker sentiment and reason coincide happily. Here, however, sentiment is suppressed and leaves the mind hard and cold as ice. But it seems to find its revenge and outlet through satire and derision. Throughout the Intelligent Woman's Guide Mr. Shaw shows a kind of feline humour which is amusing enough; but when he begins to chuckle in real earnest I feel as if in the presence of a monomaniac without understanding or reverence.

The second defect is closely connected with the first. Mr. Shaw is an intellectual, but the sources of his intellectual creed are the tenets of the late Victorian era. He is a Fabian who has been taught by the materialism of his first schooling to keep his eyes steadily looking down to earth. He has therefore nothing of the breadth of an Aristotle or the height of a Plato. And as evidence of this we have only to turn to the remedy he would provide for all the ills of humanity, namely equality of income. So persuasively and skilfully does he prepare the mind to agree with him that the reader may be bewitched and forget to question the cure. But if he does, then it must appear well-nigh incredible that a philosopher could have hoped to beautify human nature by such a prescription.

Of the merits of Mr. Shaw as an economist I must leave others better qualified than myself to judge. But I do not think that his most bitter critic can fail to acknowledge his genius as a guide. Economics is supposed to be an involved and abstruse subject, yet here we have the secrets of it set forth in a prose worthy of a Platonic dialogue. There is the same lucidity, the concrete and illuminating example, the effortless thinking in the simplest terms. Experts have told me that the explanations are so simple as to be sometimes misleading, that the map of the social world is pre-Copernican and useless to the Socialist of to-day. This may be true, but I suspect that the book will remain a classic when many of the critics have been forgotten.

There are, no doubt, inconsistencies and errors. To the average reader it would seem, for instance, that Mr. Shaw is attempting the impossible when he advocates both equality of income and the abolition of unearned income. If all are to share alike, then the strong and the weak, the skilled and the unskilled, the intellectual and the manual worker must get more or less than they earn. The two principles must clash unless there is equality also in nature, human nature and in their products. Quite apart from the fact that men's wants and preferences differ so widely as to defy an arithmetical equality, there are, as we know, good and bad fields and material, climates and foods; there are best slices from the joint and best seats in a theatre, and there are jobs no one wants and jobs snug enough to attract everybody. Mr. Shaw admits that persons with a lucrative talent should be allowed to benefit by it, and he hides the gravity of this admission by joking about prima donnas and surgeons; but the truth is that once we admit this exception there is an end to his sacred principle. He avoids the difficulty of unpleasant and easy work by suggesting that workers in the hardest occupations should be compensated by shorter hours. This measure would have as effect that greater numbers would have to be employed at the uncongenial labour, and if the work were injurious to the health or dangerous to life, we should have a state more like a Purgatorio than a Paradiso.

My chief complaint however is that Mr. Shaw never shows that his Socialist state when realized is either practical or desirable. Like many other Socialist writers he follows the practice of calling Socialistic every measure which helps to remove what is evil, and everything evil Capitalistic. Furthermore he shows the way to the Promised Land, but like Moses he knows that he will not live to see it and tells us little about it. We have therefore to guess what it would be like from the nature of the proposals he makes to reach it. And here there is a difficulty, for it is possible to agree with many of the proposals to remove present conditions without agreeing with Mr. Shaw's theories. Mr. Shaw's fundamental law is equality of income, but behind this law there are certain convictions and a philosophy of life. To the Catholic critic that philosophy appears an extreme which is unworkable because it is false. Its aim is to produce happiness, and by happiness, is meant, so far as I can gather, freedom from material cares and leisure. The emphasis is not on virtue but equal income, not on self-determination but leisure, not on unselfishness and duty but comfort and employment. What conception of human nature is behind this I do not know and the remarks bearing on morality are too inconsistent to help. He is a strict moralist as incorruptible as Robespierre, and yet a philosopher of change. "Good conduct," he tells us, "is a respect which you owe to yourself in some mystical way; and people are manageable in proportion to their possession of this self-respect." This appeal to mysticism is very feeble and the word "manageable" is significant of Mr. Shaw's mind. If morality is treated as a mere means to a successful Socialist state it is bound to suffer, and the reverence which is essential for a continued observance of law must gradually disappear. The Catholic holds that family is a sacred institution and that civic virtue cannot endure unless it be preceded and supported by the virtues of the home. Again, if the pleasures of married life be used without their corresponding duties, human nature is sapped of its strength and inevitably declines to hedonism. Mr. Shaw is oblivious of this. He manipulates marriage laws, continence and child-bearing according to the needs of his prospective State. The same policy is noticeable in his treatment of God and religion. He believes in God, but it is a woe-begone Deity who has no say in human affairs, and is the servant of man and not his Lord. This conception of God I believe to be utterly false, but it is the consequences of the view which we must consider. The first is the end of all true religion. Mr. Shaw deprecates the talk of Socialism as a religion, but his attitude towards it is not so very different from the Bolshevist anticlericalism which he deplores. "A live religion alone can nerve women to overcome their dread of any great social change, and to face that extraction of dead religions and dead parts of religions which is as necessary as the extraction of dead or decaying teeth. All courage is religious; without religion we are cowards." Unfortunately the courage of the religious will be shown in fighting to the death his religious and social legislation, and as Christianity has in appearance no likelihood of becoming extinct, the perfect Shavian State will be more like a Mexico or Rome under Nero than a Utopia of peace.

Internecine war then and not peace is the first consequence of this new Sermon on the Mount. Another will be the loss of all those virtues which cluster round holiness. The quotation given above shows the heights which religious people are expected to reach—and many of us think such heights not very elevated and look elsewhere to a Joan of Arc or Anselm or Sir Thomas More for loftiness of spirit worthy of imitation. And I am sure that a State in which the virtues of such saints lose their savour or are forgotten can have neither permanence nor beauty. This last sentence suggests a final criticism. Mr. Shaw does not accept the truth of the text: "Render to Caesar the things that are Caesar's and to God the things that are God's." That is, he does not believe in the distinction of the two kingdoms. At one place his own good sense forces him to admit that morality must have its sanction. "Faced with this matter-of-fact scepticism (of the child) you are driven into pure metaphysics, and must teach your child that conduct is a matter, not of fact, but of religious duty." But instead of arguing logically from this admission he begins to chuckle about the Big Papa God in his Sunday clothes. Yet as he ought to see, God or the supernatural or religion—call it what you will—cannot be just a convenient stopgap. Once admitted it affects the whole outlook, and it is the claim of Christianity that human nature without religion is more than half blind. Morality suffers because it has no ultimate sanction, and the State becomes an organism without a soul. Mr. Shaw looks at human beings but he never appreciates them. Their soul is subject to the State; their freedom time to amuse themselves. And so whereas both Mr. Shaw and the Christian moralist look at the same world and are often willing to pass the same measures, even at times to call themselves Socialists of a kind, their end is quite different. The Christian may curtail liberty; he may demand the nationalisation of certain industries; prohibit alcohol and tax the rich. But such legislation need not be ideal either in theory or in practise; it may well be a measure of safety when the foundations of society are threatened. The ideal is the free exercise of virtue and the common good. Religion with its warnings of an afterlife, its promise of final justice and its incitement to love for the highest motives is essential for the continued welfare of the State. It co-operates by appealing to the soul, whereas the State charges itself with man's duties as a member of society. Each in its own way desires that the individual should, as the phrase goes, be able to call his soul his own. The State strives to enlist the good will of the citizen, guarantees his fundamental rights and in return calls for due service which may entail a partial sacrifice of powers and privileges. But freedom and conscience cannot be totally surrendered. Every human being has a personal life which transcends his activities as a social or political being. Religion here takes up the task of morals and establishes the true relation between the self and God.

It follows therefore that Mr. Shaw's Social State is an extreme and not an ideal. The problem of all societies is to fix the right proportion between the common good and the rights of free persons. In the perfect State free persons give of their own accord and by virtue co-operate in the general welfare. Too much reliance on human nature has led, in the past—most notably when Christian principles have been set aside deliberately—to the Capitalist State. Too little reliance on human nature would, if we harkened to Mr. Shaw, lead to a State in which all opportunities for abuse would have been taken away. But with their removal the State would be a corpse, because most of the opportunities for personal life and virtue would have gone. The true social policy is therefore necessarily a compromise. Were the citizens virtuous legislation and the limitation of liberty would be considerably reduced. History shows the need of adapting legislation and the exercise of authority to the various stages of development among nations, and the same adaptation is visible before our eyes in education. But the principle governing all educational and State activity is the same; that is, to develop and not to take away self-determination and the power to use rightly what falls within one's sphere of action or opportunity. In the nineteenth century economists left out the word "rightly" and extolled competition as "in political economy what gravitation is in physics,"[1] and as a "grand and noble moral therein."[2] What they really meant by Competition was Avarice, and this, as Mr. Lilly[3] pointed out, "the ethical teachers, from whom the western world learnt for a thousand years, numbered among the seven deadly sins."

1. Bastiot.
2. Francis Newman.
3. W. S. Lilly, Idola Fori.

III

By A. L. ROWSE

This book sums up one side of Shaw's life in thought, as *Back to Methuselah* was the summing up of another, and *St.* [*sic*] *Joan* of a third, and perhaps rarer, creative activity. But I am not sure for all that, whether the "Guide" does not represent the most important side of his work. After all, Shaw as an artist is likely enough to be outpassed by a good half-dozen writers of our time, in the memory of the future. But as a social critic he has had no equal in his own lifetime, nor will have probably for a long time to come.

One has heard various criticisms of his book, more or less justified: that it is dull (and in places it is—that is, for Shaw); that there is a good deal of repetition (there is, and one can only too well understand why); that the history is in parts elementary and a little ludicrous (this he shares with all the other contemporary prophets of a certain standing); that there is nothing very new in the book (it is not important that there should be: it is a summary of a lifetime's thought); that its economics are all wrong (and this is a question of opinion).

For very curiously, many of the criticisms of which the above are a sample, do not go to the heart of the matter: the book was certainly not intended as a *jeu d'esprit,* nor even as a treatise on economics. It is a masterpiece of the art of political pamphleteering, on a somewhat biblical scale.

To take the criticism on the score of its economics, for a good deal of attention has been concentrated on this point; and perhaps in examining it another side to the character of the work will emerge.

Shaw has himself contributed largely to this concentration, for constantly he overemphasizes the importance of equality of income as the essential aim of Socialism. It may well be in the long run an essential aim; but it is not an immediate pre-condition of Socialism. As against his opponents: any argument therefore that the equality of income which the book preaches, is impracticable in the present state of affairs, may be quite right, but is in fact entirely irrelevant. It is made clear in the course of the book, and especially in the section "Change must be Parliamentary," that however desirable equality may be, it is regarded as the *end* of social effort and not as an immediate step. Practical Socialism is much more closely defined (p. 384) as "an active interference in the production and distribution of the nation's income," and the rest of the book supplies with what purpose, namely to the end of equality. With that view of the argument all who call themselves Socialists would agree; and almost all would follow Shaw in his view of the gradualness of the process, and on the point (p. 389) that "the business of Socialist rulers is not to suppress private enterprise as such, but to attain and maintain equality of income."

But even the practicability of Socialist measures in the direction of greater equality has been regarded too complacently by certain economists as a closed question. In a sense Shaw has the angels on his side; the whole tendency of modern taxation is towards a redistribution of wealth so as to level up incomes to the line of subsistence at least. And apparently so great a master of capitalism as Walther Rathenau (v. *Life* by Graf Kessler) thought it not improbable that the solution of the chronic conflicts of capitalism would be found in the direction of equality. One would rather trust this combination of opinion than that of any academic economist, however distinguished.

To my mind, the real clue to the book is to be found not so much in the sections on equality, as in sections 67 and 68, on "Capitalism in Perpetual Motion" and "The Runaway Car of Capitalism"; for these contain the diagnosis of the disease for which equality is only part of the remedy. The essence of Socialism, and here there is universal agreement, is that there must be unified, directive and representative control of the economic system for the benefit of society as a whole. Instead of which, the antithesis of [S]ocialism presents us with a state of affairs whose very *raison d'etre* is lack of control. There are some departures from this in recent capitalist theory, for example, Mond's *Industry and Politics* on the one hand and the *Liberal Industrial Report* on the other. The absence of social control is what is characteristic of capitalism; and even if self-control by means of combines and rationalization comes into being, it is still irresponsible as far as the community is concerned, i.e. it is not Socialist. And the lack of control constitutes the danger to society which is a motive power of all Socialist thought. The idea of the present industrial and political system as a great engine crashing on we don't know where, is only too fully justified by the wars and conflicts and rivalries of the present century. And here Shaw speaks for all of us.

There is no stability about the thing as it is. What Socialists want is a series of gradual, but radical changes, which will end in a state of equilibrium. That is, after transition, stability, and there is no likelihood of stability before the necessary Socialist changes, for it is unthinkable that our social and political structure can attain equilibrium in standing on its head. It must be turned the right side up, and based like a pyramid, upon its broadest foundation; that is, upon the working people of the country. It is curious that people never see that that having being attained, the workers are potentially the most conservative interest in the whole community. For they stand to lose much more than anybody else by the mismanagement of the country's affairs. In case of disaster to our social welfare, a capitalist can transport himself abroad—already a large part of his holdings are held abroad; even our duchesses may take their jewels with them and live on the proceeds ever afterwards; and our bishops would all find employment for their unction in America. But though a workman here and there might emigrate, the whole working class of the country couldn't leave it in case of damage to its prosperity and a lowering of its standards. They are much more closely bound up with the country's safety and well-being than any other class in it.

It is because of that that Socialism means essentially the achievement of social responsibility by and for the working class. And in expressing this (it is obvious from every page of the book that Shaw has no more patience with non-workers than St. Paul had), Shaw is at one with the fundamental principle of Socialism. Further, he has the flowing tide of intelligent opinion with him.

My opinion is then, that the real importance of the book is its representative character. One doesn't look for anything particularly new in it, for it is of more value as a summary, highly individual, yet typical in its modes of thought of a strain of social criticism, which beginning in the heyday of late Victorian imperialism (*Lord of our far-flung battle-line*, indeed!), has swollen to include nearly the whole province of the social and political thought of our time. Old men tell one there is nothing constructive in Shaw or in Socialism: What rubbish! There is no denying, whether one agrees or not with either, that they have contributed more largely and more vitally to our intellectual life than any other system or creed. In one place Shaw refers to his possessing all the fruit at their ripest and their best: and no wonder. It has been given to no one else of his generation (except perhaps, on a lower plane, to Wells) to see his speculations more exactly borne out, or to find himself at the head of a body of intelligent opinion which no one did more than himself to create. It is a fine commentary on the work of an old man and on the character of a young generation that opinion is setting in the way he pointed out. For when the age of the "Recessional" is left, with its author, definitively behind and out of memory, and the various attempts to resuscitate outworn religious beliefs have perished of their own inherent perversity, still the magnificent sanity, the reasonableness and the hope of Shaw's life-work will go on in the spirit and the effort of a younger generation.

IV

By KENNETH PICKTHORN

Mr. Shaw has the great merit that if he makes too much fuss about the fallacies of the conventional and finds too many fallacies there, at least he is not altogether blind to the fallacies of the forward-looking. He sees that eugenics will not do, because apart from all other reasons you don't know in the case of human beings what you want to breed for. He observes that if Trade Unions, and Married Women with property, were once a little ill-treated by the law, now they are too well treated. He knows that most workmen do not want to think about their work. He expounds clearly the great virtue of the two-party system: "That the government should be unsparingly criticized by a rival set." He does not hide the limitation of parliamentarism: "The point at which the people who are out-voted in Parliament will accept their defeat." He laughs at "our . . . toleration of conscription" during the last war as "quaint and illogical."

So much intellectual breadth and rectitude demand admiring recognition. But there is also scattered about the book a good deal which seems to an unconverted reader intellectually rather less than straight even if not quite crooked morally. Not the worst sort of intellectual dishonesty, but one of the least pleasant, is trying to get laughs from what you know not to be funny: here Mr. Shaw is still permitting himself a forced and facetious boasting which he must know to be no longer either useful or amusing. He is also very careless about statements of fact: sometimes, of course, especially in connection with a more or less remote past, there may be fair room for disagreement: yet his account, for instance, of the beginnings of the cabinet system is beyond defence and almost beyond criticism; his statement that Germany was starved out in spite of her military successes is outrageous; a much more material instance is his treatment of the question how the condition of the people has been affected by recent history. Poor women, he says, never attribute dearness of food to governments but always to "bad harvests or hard times or strikes or anything else that must be put up with": the gentry force the common people to work still harder and accept still less, "so that the modernization of industry has actually left the poor much worse off than they used to be when there was no machinery at all": at the same time, or almost the same time, Mr. Shaw can remember when poverty in the East-End was even more dreadful than it is now, and when "the Registrar-General's returns of the causes of the deaths during the year always included starvation as a matter of course"; he is aware of the difference made to poor women by the changed conditions of conception and travail, and by widows' pensions; he explains that infants used to be exploited to bring down adult wages, that it "is no longer quite true" that the wage workers have "not benefitted by the introduction of machinery," that "modern taxes have transferred purchasing power from the rich to the poor," and that public loan charges are "a redistribution of income among the capitalists, leaving the proletariat rather better off than worse."

Nor is Mr. Shaw always above dispute on matters of fact which he might easily have verified first hand. Mr. Ramsey Macdonald [sic] may be surprised to learn that the socialist front bench are "to an extraordinary degree better educated and more experienced than their opponents," in the ranks of Labour careers being not only open to the talents but "absolutely closed to nonentities": and the Federation of British Industry may be not less surprised to be told that "Diehard Capitalism is now sorely tempted to try a British-Fascist *coup d'état* followed by a dictatorship." Mr. Shaw thinks that during the war we each had to take our turn and do our bit, in spite of the "exemption of the money of the rich from the conscription that was applied ruthlessly to the lives and livelihoods and limbs of the poor." Modern war is "much more dangerous than it has ever been before." "What we call the dole" feeds the unemployed for nothing. The general strike ("which need not have alarmed a mouse") "frightened and infuriated the Government." "You would certainly think anyone mad if he claimed to own the air or the sunlight or the sea." Covetousness is "only a part" of human nature, "and one that vanishes after it is satisfied." Parsons teach "deference to the merely rich, and call that loyalty and religion"; if they do not, "They are ill-spoken of themselves in the most influential quarters." Billionaires have "very ordinary portraits"; this is true only if they go to very ordinary artists; I have seen a bust of Mr. Rockefeller which says much more efficiently than Mr. Shaw can everything there is to be said against modern capitalism.

Mr. Shaw's argumentative methods are not always more convincing than his assertions: the obligation among the early Christians to throw all property into the common stock "was so sacred," he says, "that when Ananias and Sapphira kept something back for themselves St. Paul struck them dead for 'lying to the Holy Ghost.' " St. Paul did indeed strike them dead (or at least the early church believed so) precisely for lying to the Holy Ghost, and not at all for infringing any sacred obligation to communism: "Whiles it remained was it not thine own? and after it was sold was it not in thine own power?" A somewhat similar argumentative trick is to attribute to one what is true of all or of many: as, for instance, to the Church of England a belief in the impassibility of God, a temptation to sycophancy, or a liberty without contradiction to tell little children lies about the Bible. Another is to use as evidential arguments what are only fashionable sentimentalities: "the clearest case in the world of a person producing something herself by her own painful, prolonged and risky labour is that of a woman who produces a baby"; "the most important work in the world is that of breeding and rearing children: for without that the human race would presently be extinct." It is just as "important" to grow from infancy to puberty, and Mr. Shaw should not giggle at St. Paul for saying in forgetfulness of babies, "He that will not work neither shall he eat" (especially as a few pages later he himself complains that "the law that all must work, which should come before every other law, is a law that the rich never make"): and it is just as "important" (though it is not so arduous) to beget children as to bear them.

The simplicity of political economy is proved by the argument that "the nation has a certain income to manage on just as a housekeeper has"; though the income is not certain, and it is not certain that it should all be treated as belonging to the "nation," nor that the nation had not better busy itself with increasing than with distributing it. The propositions that "horses and human beings are alike in that they very seldom object to be directed," and that authority and subordination are never in themselves unpopular are proved (so that "you may take it as certain") partly from the admiration won by Nelson, Lenin and Mussolini, partly from the docility of Mr. Shaw (although "by profession an original thinker") in accepting the directions of porters, "because I want to be directed and want to get into the right train." But of course he doesn't really want to be directed by authority but only to be enabled by information to check his own direction: he would not like it a bit if tyrannical railway porters prevented his going anywhere but from Dublin to Moscow and from Moscow to Dublin.

This is an instance of the well-known argumentative trick of laying down a premiss which is something like the truth and then, with ostentatious gestures of self-congratulation to deceive the slow-eyed, drawing forth a deduction which is anything but the truth. Here is another, more serious, instance. It is asserted that "all the soldiers get the same, all the judges . . . and all the members of parliament . . ." and that a doctor can give no better reason for his scale of fees "than that he is asking what all the other doctors ask." In real life all soldiers do not get the same, nor all judges, nor all doctors, and no two Members of Parliament have equal incomes: still, these slight extravagances of premiss are nothing to the wild bound of the next step, which is to conclude that "you may, with the utmost confidence take it as settled by practical experience that if we could succeed in distributing incomes equally to all the inhabitants of the country, there would be no more tendency on their part to divide into rich and poor than there is at present for postmen to divide into beggars and millionaires." As if judges, soldiers and postmen were not abnormally likely to stay equal when put equal, each class being composed of men similar in temperament and breeding; and as if they did in fact stay equal; not to mention the consideration that the entrants to those professions are attracted to them, in an unequal world, because the sort of rewards they offer about suit their sort of ambitions and capacities.

Then there is the other trick, conscious or unconscious, which consists in using the same word in different senses. Capitalism is spare money: sometimes this means money a man has beyond what he needs to support himself, sometimes beyond what he likes spending. "Capitalism has no conscience and no country." Capitalism is the Manchester School. It is not very old established. The capitalist principally trusts to unaided private enterprise. "Capitalists *as such* (my italics) have provided neither brains, genius, courage, nor resolution." Capital "has always ended in the past by taking its passengers over the brink of the precipice at the foot of which are strewn the wrecks of empires."

But all such minor weaknesses of logic are trifling compared with the farcical over-use of the favourite progressive false argument that you cannot have too much of a good thing. For Mr. Shaw, to show that a thing is good is proof enough that you'd much better not have anything else. It does not seem to have occurred to him that because braces are best adjusted by individuals, industrial relations had better be, but he does suggest that because the posts are nationalized or communized therefore it is ridiculous for any one to oppose the nationalization or communization of anything. It is true that in another place he restricts his advocacy of communization to "whatever is used by everybody or benefits everybody," but he never makes clear any distinction between communization (of which one example is the Church of England) and nationalization, or what if anything is to be exempted from either or both, or how Socialism (or anything else) differs from the Communism "which preaches that all the necessary business of the country shall be done by public bodies and regulated by public law." Public lighting, paving, police, rubbish destruction, army and navy are not only Communistic, they are Communism. A similarly false argument is applied to religion: "it is probably that we think about Mrs. Eddy exactly as a Roman lady in the third century A.D. thought about the mother of Christ. . . . You may be right or you may be wrong: but for all you know Mrs. Eddy a thousand years hence may be worshipped as the Divine Woman by millions of civilized people. You never can tell. People begin by saying, 'Is not this the carpenter's son?' and end by saying, 'Behold the Lamb of God!' "

But that is not the invariable procedure; in fact the odds against it are almost infinite. And it's no use saying you never can tell. You must tell. Perhaps it is enough to tell with all your head and with all your heart and you may be forgiven for telling wrong. Perhaps, even, no one ever has told or ever will tell quite right, but what surely can not be forgiven is to think that it does not matter. Mr. Shaw indeed says himself that the main difficulty about the business of establishing Socialism is the metaphysical one, and that if there were no God it would be necessary to invent him, and yet here he is, for all his bragging, so defeatist as to suggest that it does not matter how many gods we invent, or of what sort. Similarly his chief negative argument for equal incomes (the chief positive one being the alleged existing equality between doctors and between postmen) is the defeatist argument that all other methods of distribution are too difficult. "You never can tell" whether rewards and merits are fitting one another, therefore you may as well call it six of one and half a dozen of every other. Besides begging the important question whether "you" (i.e. the community or that part of it which controls government) have the right or the power to control all distribution, this argument too has the fatal disadvantage of being defeatist. To give up trying because you don't expect success can hardly be a moral principle.

And this brings me to what I think the general and immense and unpardonable fault of Mr. Shaw's book: it is not ordered: "I could go on like this for ever" he says somewhere, and indeed it may be believed that he could: only it isn't going on, it's going round, and, incidentally, with a deleterious effect on his prose style, which in this book hardly ever attains rhythm; it does not rise and fall, but seems perpetually to be slipping down a series of declines up which it has been periodically hauled. Much more important still is the want of order in the argumentation. The book might have started from a moral principle and demonstrated step by step that that principle must be realized by socialism and by no other method. Or it might have begun with an exposition of a completed socialism and then proved that out of such a system, and only out of such a system, moral perfection might flower. Any argument for a great remodelling of human society must follow one of these two methods, or else it cannot put moral values highest. Mr. Shaw evidently means to keep morality sovereign, but he does not explain what his morality is nor make clear its connection with that equalization of incomes which according to him is Socialism. "If poor and pretty young women find, as they do, that they can make more money by vice than by housework, they will poison the blood of rich young men": exactly how enormous a libel on the poor and pretty this is it is difficult to estimate; impossible to deny that it is an enormous libel, and anyway the relevance is rather to prophylaxis than to virtue. Mr. Shaw thinks Magee very foolish for saying that he would rather see England free than England sober, "as if a drunken man can be free in any sense": but it is not so certain that a drunken man cannot be free in any sense, and if Mr. Shaw had written more soberly he would have noted that England is not a man: it is, in this connection, a great many men and women, and it is not foolish to think it worth while having a few of them drunk or even drunken, if that is a condition of having all of them free. Nor is it by any means certainly foolish to think that the minimum restriction on action leaves the maximum liberty of behaviour, and that freedom, not freedom from the necessary conditions of physical existence nor even from the exigencies of competitive economic arrangements, but at least some measure of freedom from direct penally sanctioned personal imperatives, is a prerequisite for moral values.

This is a view which Mr. Shaw merely neglects: but it cannot be neglected. Great numbers of men, or women, cannot be converted to an immense change of all social arrangements except by a change of their moral presumptions, implicit or explicit. They can be induced to communize light-houses, or even mines, or to rub at enormous inequalities of income, by considerations of convenience: not so can they be induced to work for a complete recasting of society, not though they be assured that it is to be gradual or inevitable or both. What moral argumentation Mr. Shaw does provide is horribly like a vicious circle. Socialism and nothing but Socialism is to set virtue free, and Socialism is to come because "Capitalism tends always to develop industries until they are on the scale of public affairs and ripe for transfer to public hands"; a little also because "all reforms are lucrative to somebody"; more because those who get the best of capitalist arrangements are only one in ten of the population (the rest being in a condition of complete slavery), most of all because "the advantages to be gained by Socialism for the proletariat and the fact that proletarian parents are a huge majority of the electorate, may be depended on to bias moral education more and more in favour of the movement towards Socialism." The Socialist State, when it arrives, must not only forbid the Christian Catechism but also "inculcate whatever doctrine will make the people good Socialists."

"Reason only discerns the shortest way: it does not discern the destination." Mr. Shaw's reasoning about the means seems to me sometimes vicious and sometimes vitiated by false history: I may be wrong: but I can hardly believe that he is right in hopefully advocating as an end a state of socialism in which we shall have no chance of changing masters, in which there shall be no freedom of instruction or discussion, in which there shall be no room for exceptions (unless they be public entertainers, who may be rewarded with luxuries), in which parentage may be imposed or forbidden as easily as military service, and all this on the ground that proletarians are in the majority and won't see any personal loss in any one of the necessary steps.

Walter Elliot and Bernard Shaw

EVERYBODY'S POLITICAL WHAT'S WHAT?: A REVIEW AND A REPLY

Walter Elliot was a Conservative member of Parliament for many years and was highly respected on all sides. At different times, he served as minister of agriculture and fisheries, secretary of state for Scotland, and minister of health. His ministerial career ended with the fall of the Chamberlain government in 1940. He was generally considered to be on the liberal wing of the Conservative party and had wide-ranging interests which included a special concern for education. He was elected to the honorary position of Rector in several Scottish universities. As is clear from the exchange, he was on good terms with Shaw personally, but perhaps not up to the task of taking him on in political debate. Elliot died in 1958.

Herbert Morrison was a powerful (ruthless, some would say) leader of the Labour-controlled London County Council during the 1930s, and his success as the "boss" of the greatest local government authority in the country explains Walter Elliot's reference to him. He became a minister in the Churchill coalition government during the war and held several high offices with the Labour government when Attlee succeeded Churchill in 1945.

The SPECTATOR,
22 September 1944

BOOKS OF THE DAY

The Sage of Eyot [*sic*] St. Lawrence
Everybody's Political What's What? By Bernard Shaw. (Constable. 10s.)

James Bridie has recently pointed out that a post which the British public has created and keeps constantly filled is that of a Sage. By some tacit agreement there is never more than one Sage at a time; at most, there is a Sage and an Aspirant-Sage. Physically, a Sage of Great Britain must be easily recognisable, both in person and in picture—if possible, he should be identified by a beard. His literary output must be voluminous. His political opinions must be of the Left—with flashes of extreme Rightness. Above all, his utterances must be oracular, which is to say authoritative, but capable of more than one interpretation. Given these qualities he will, eventually, be accepted as an authority about anything he likes— for as long as he likes. It is not necessary that anyone should listen or do what he says. But the British nation, which is deeply reverential, feels the better for having such a figure around. Just as India feels the better for the possession of Mr. Gandhi. Apart from India and Britain, no nation goes in for Sages.

The present holder of the office, Mr. Shaw, is one of the most successful Sages ever produced. To fulfil the terms of his appointment, which are communicated to each Sage, no one knows how, he has written a new book. Not a play, alas. These he turns out for a living. This is the Sage, and he is doing his stuff. As one who has read, for his own sake, every line that Mr. Shaw has ever written, including *The Common Sense of Municipal Trading* (I am not in favour of municipal trading) and *The Quintessence of Wagnerism* [*sic*] (I am profoundly anti-Wagnerian), I solemnly testify that this book is unreadable. I have worked through it because I have been paid to do so. It is a good thing that some should be so paid. But I am willing to bet a handsome sum that many of them will shirk their work. In fact, Mr. Shaw admits as much, and inserts a small chapter (leaving out all the plums) called "For the Reviewers."

The book is entitled *Everybody's Political What's What?* It is not meant for everybody. Nor are any of the best bits about politics, even in the widest sense; and it gives much inaccurate information about What's What. Its real interest is in the autobiographical details which are embedded deep in the intricacies of its 364 pages. They are interesting because they are the first-hand observations of a highly intelligent man. The political observations are blurred recollections of what someone else once told him, unchecked by any personal investigation or practice, save for that brief period, about the time of the Crimean War, when Mr. Shaw was a member of a London local government body. Mr. Shaw states—and it can only be because someone told him, for he is an intelligent man and would not have thought of it for himself—that Parliament, to be all right, must amongst other things be elected for fixed and unalterable periods. If he looks across the Channel he will see the ruins of a State which was governed by a Constitution which had this as one of its cardinal principles. He believes that "in the Four Years War most of the Allies borrowed its cost from England, and England borrowed it from the United States," although any American, smartingly conscious of the many billions of dollars which other countries borrowed direct, could have told him otherwise. He believes that municipalities, because of their virtuous systems of election and methods of working, are free from party politics. Heavens above! I wish he saw Glasgow. Or, if that is too much to hope for, he might take a mild look at Mr. Herbert Morrison. When facts jolt themselves for a moment into his consciousness, he escapes from them by saying, for instance, that the remedy for party politics in municipal affairs is the exclusion of "ovines" from the municipal panel. I do not know how it is in other cities. But anybody meeting a majority of Glasgow Town Councillors and proceeding on the assumption that what he was encountering was "ovines" would do better to take a refuge in a cage of Bengal tigers.

Which brings me to the parts of the book devoted to Mr. Shaw's opinions; and these parts are[,] if anything, worse than the parts devoted to his political facts. "The choice (of leaders and rulers)," says he, "should therefore be limited to panels of persons who can pass such tests as we can devise of their wisdom, comprehension, knowledge and energy." But who are "we"? This question is not answered. It is the kernel of the book. No one has the right to propound such a solution seriously and bolt from the techniques involved. Give me the drawing-up of a questionnaire and I will guarantee its answers. Give me the right to lay down "tests" and I can nominate any "panel" you can think of. (Otherwise, says Mr. Shaw, we shall have stampedes led by liars like Titus Oates— believing apparently that Titus Oates obtained power at some hotly-contested by-election.)

I said there were good bits in this book; and there are, excellent bits, wonderful bits. The whole of Mr. Shaw's philosophy is revealed, with the greatest honesty, by his casual remark that on a piece of perfectly stationary dry land in Chelsea he visited the facsimile of the first-class passengers' quarters in a modern P. & O. liner, and that in the passage between the P. & O. cabins he suddenly felt seasick and had to beat a hasty retreat into the gardens. The power of Mr. Shaw's imagination, its utter disregard of anything that conflicts with his mental conceptions, could not be more vividly demonstrated.

Oh dear, oh dear; I would swop [*sic*] the whole darn book for the two words "maternal massarzh" in which Mr. Shaw, crashing into a recent controversy, summed up his own ideals as to child welfare and sketched, instantaneously, the kindly American judge who had informed him. Why a man who could do that, or who could write *In Good King Charles' Glorious Days* [*sic*], should blanket the light of his mind in 364 pages of abracadabra is beyond human comprehension. This nation works its Sages too hard. Carlyle thought it necessary to write forty volumes on the merits of Silence. But even he stopped at last. Mr. Shaw might well be content to let his eighty-eight years testify to his views on biology; and let his conduct reveal, to those who would study it, the secrets of his doctrines.

Walter Elliot

The *SPECTATOR*
29 September 1944

LETTERS

The Sage of Ayot St. Lawrence (29 September 1944)

SIR,—My friendly reviewer Colonel Elliot is mistaken in supposing that I have said or written that "municipalities, because of their virtuous systems of election and methods of working, are free from party politics." I have carefully stated the exact contrary. What I have devoted a specially emphasised chapter of my book to is that our parliamentary party system does not exist in our municipalities. The two propositions are different and independent. Colonel Elliot refers me to the Glasgow municipality as a glaring example of the existence of parties in city corporations. I know all about Glasgow, as every Socialist of my generations does. It pioneered municipal Socialism bravely in my day. It could not have done so had it been paralysed by the Party System as the House of Commons is paralysed. Of course it was made up of parties: Socialists, Unsocialists, Progressives, Conservatives, Associated Ratepayers, with their ovines and bellwethers and whips and chairmen all complete. But when by happy chance there arrived among them a serious student of politics, capable of thinking for himself and voting on the merits of a question without any prompting—such a man as Colonel Elliot in short—he could vote for the public welfare every time without the slightest danger of changing the Government, losing his seat, and having to face a General Election to regain it. I was in that position myself on the St. Pancras Borough Council, and when I write about such matters I know what I am writing about. I repeat, I have known men who had sat in Parliament for thirty years, and had never voted on the merits of a Bill at its second reading, but always on the single question of whether their party should remain in office or not, and they personally should lose their seats and have to spend £1,000 or more in an uncertain effort to regain them. In Opposition they had to defeat and throw out the Government on, for instance, Bills for the extension of the Franchise and for Irish Land Purchase, and, on their party succeeding to power, voting for the very measures they had just voted against. Such a situation is unknown and impossible in our municipalities, with the result they have made advances in social organisation in a fortnight over which Parliament struggles vainly for forty years.

How is it that so keen and trained a political critic as Colonel Elliot has missed the point of an argument elaborated so fully in my book? The explanation is obvious enough to me. He found my book unreadable. He frankly says so. I do not doubt his word that he "worked through it" because he was paid to do so. But he was in the same predicament as I am. As an old Socialist I cannot read books on Socialism. If I have to "work through" them I fall asleep or daydream about something else all the time; for I know what the writers have to say, and could say it better myself. That is what has happened to Colonel Elliot. I am an old Fabian, and he is an old Knight of the Round Table which took up the work of the founders of the Fabian Society. He did not work through my chapter on the Party System: he slept through it. I should have done the same myself. We are both in the same boat. We can and do think for ourselves, and are accordingly ruled out of Government practice by the Party System as dangerous men. But I believe I could read a book by Colonel Elliot. If he will write one on the System I shall certainly try—Faithfully,

G. Bernard Shaw

David Nathan

FAILURE OF AN ELDERLY GENTLEMAN: SHAW AND THE JEWS

Bernard Shaw's belief in the possibility of a better world, in which every citizen had the right to justice and good drainage, did not conflict with his well-attested tenderness of heart which extended to all creation and was one of the reasons why he ate vegetables instead of pork chops. But a huge gap developed in the 1930s and 1940s between his claims to be the great realist and the fact, increasingly obvious to lesser minds and possibly harder hearts, that the dictators he championed were not supermen who would lead the world to a bright socialist future, but super-murderers who would lead millions to their deaths.

Even after the war, when the Nazi killing camps had been exposed, Shaw maintained that the heaps of corpses were more the consequences of incompetent guards and food shortages than the inevitable product of Hitler's policies, most of which he had approved. He did deplore Hitler's regrettable tendency to persecute Jews as a vulgar diversion from the main task of destroying the democratic sham and building a new order. In addition, he dismissed as newspaper lies the charges that Stalin was responsible for the deaths of millions of peasants, but cheerfully accepted a notion that some deaths were the inevitable price of progress, just as the show trials were a necessary step on the road to the perfect justice which would result at some unspecified date in the future.

Shaw's abhorrence of anti-Semitism arose more from impatience with its stupid distraction from more important matters than from sympathy with its victims, except those he knew and liked personally. He could not abide cruelty, but he never had much time for victims in their multitudes, whether they were European Jews or Ethiopians bombed with mustard gas by Mussolini's airmen. Prejudice was common to all groups, as he indicated in his 1936 Preface to *The Millionairess:*

> Now no doubt Jews are most obnoxious creatures. Any competent historian or psycho-analyst can bring a mass of incontrovertible evidence to prove that it would have been better for the world if the Jews had never existed. But I, as an Irishman, can, with patriotic relish, demonstrate the same of the English. Also of the Irish. If Herr Hitler would only consult the French and British newspapers and magazines of the latter half of 1914, he would learn that the Germans are a race of savage idolaters, murderers, liars, and fiends whose assumption of the human form is thinner than that of the wolf in Little Red Riding Hood.
>
> We all live in glass houses. Is it wise to throw stones at the Jews? Is it wise to throw stones at all?[1]

He had expressed the same attitude thirty-seven years earlier in a letter to A.J. Marriott (1 May 1899):

> *All* sects, secular and supernaturalist, exist to do all the wicked things you impute to the Church. Take the case of the anti-Dreyfus people. What is it they do? Why, pick out all the general vices of humanity—all its greed and ambition and sensuality—and denounce the Jews for them, as if Christians were any less greedy, ambitious and sensual.[2]

In March 1906 the Countess Feodora Gleichen appealed to Shaw to support her friend Sir Alfred Gilbert, the sculptor. He had accepted a large sum of money from the Jewish novelist Julia Frankau—who wrote under the name of Frank Danby—for a monument to her late husband. Gilbert neither delivered the memorial nor returned the money. Shaw told the countess (22 March 1906).

> If I were you I would make a statue of Mrs Frankau for nothing, to commemorate her very proper and public spirited action. It is the best virtue of the Jew that when he (or she) makes an agreement {he/she} means it. She paid her money honestly. That was not mean. Gilbert took it and denied her the agreed consideration. What do you call that? *I* call it Christian roguery. There![3]

In August Shaw began working on *The Doctor's Dilemma* (first performed in November 1906) in which Schutzmacher, the Jewish doctor, refuses to lend Dubedat any money: "he made a very uncalled-for remark about a Jew not understanding the feelings of a gentleman," Schutzmacher tells his colleagues. "I must say you Gentiles are very hard to please. You say we are no gentlemen when we lend money; and when we refuse to lend it you say just the same. I didn't mean to behave badly. As I told him, I might have lent it to him if he had been a Jew himself." Told that "you chosen people" certainly stand by one another, Schutzmacher explains his reasons:

> Not at all. Personally, I like Englishmen better than Jews, and always associate with them. Thats only natural, because, as I am a Jew, theres nothing interesting in a Jew to me, whereas there is always something interesting and foreign in an Englishman. But in money matters it's quite different. You see, when an Englishman borrows, all he knows or cares is that he wants money; and he'll sign anything to get it, without in the least understanding it, or intending to carry out the agreement if it turns out badly for him. In fact, he thinks you a cad if you ask him to carry it out under such circumstances. Just like the Merchant of Venice, you know. But if a Jew makes an agreement, he means to keep it and expects you to keep it. If he wants money for a time, he borrows it and knows he must pay it at the end of the time. If he knows he cant pay, he begs it as a gift.

Ridgeon asks, "Come, Loony! do you mean to say that Jews are never rogues and thieves?" Schutzmacher explains, "Oh, not at all. But I was not talking of criminals. I was comparing honest Englishmen with honest Jews."[4]

In the early years of World War I, Maxim Gorki asked Shaw for an article, forecasting the future, for publication in Russia. Shaw sent him a letter for publication (29 December 1915). He said that although the Western nations could hardly be perceived as champions of liberty and democracy by such important neutrals as America and Sweden, the czarist government "engages in an unexampled persecution of the Jews, enabling eminent Jewish authors and orators to rouse Western audiences to intense indignation by a recital of its horrors, whilst the Germans lose no opportunity of circulating the news in all the neutral countries."[5] Not surprisingly the czarist censor refused to permit publication in Russia, and Shaw's words appeared instead in the *Metropolitan Magazine* of New York in May 1916 (C2057).

By April 1921 he was becoming more troubled about anti-Semitism and wrote to J. E. Spingarn, the American critic and literary adviser to the publishers Harcourt, Brace and Howe:

> Somebody ought to write a powerful counterblast to the Anti-Semites; and the somebody had better be an intelligent Gentile: [Max] Nordau and [Israel] Zangwill will not be listened to on this subject as Wells or I would be. But it would be a very big job, and a difficult one, as a criticism of the Zionist experiment in Palestine (which is very open to criticism) would have to come into it—also a criticism of Nationalism generally, which might appeal to Wells.
>
> I daren't even think of it at present: I am old [he was almost sixty-five]; and all my bolts are shot. Perhaps if I wrote a play about a Jew, it might be published with a preface; but I have no intention of doing so.[6]

But in the very act of denouncing anti-Semitism he was capable of expressing an anti-Semitic idea, thus raising two questions: if a characteristic which is usually considered contemptible is attributed to a Jew, but with praise instead of condemnation, is it any the less anti-Semitic? And if not anti-Semitic, is it nevertheless as harmful—or even more harmful—because it lends support to a prejudicial stereotype?

In the course of a letter to Augustin Hamon, his French translator, dated 3 December 1925, Shaw discusses the vulgarity of anti-Semitism and says that in Britain the Jews already treated him as conspicuously pro-Jew, that his best-known translators, Trebitsch (German) and Hugo Vallentin (Swedish), were Jews, and that he heartily wished he (Hamon) and Agresti (Italian) were Jews, "as I should have made much more money."[7] He frequently referred to a Jewish capacity for making money and an overall interest in it ("my ducats, my daughter"!) although he himself was hardly inefficient in making, and looking after, his own fortune.

Shaw connects Jews and money in his short play on the Balfour Declaration, the 1917 statement issued by the British government through Arthur Balfour, the foreign secretary, which promised a Jewish homeland in Palestine. Fenner Brockway, the left-wing politician, who prompted Shaw to write a playlet about the Balfour Declaration, but claimed that the play's copyright was his, says it was first published in the *New Leader* on 29 November 1936, under the title *Arthur and the Acetone* (C3166), and it appears in the Dodd, Mead edition of Shaw's plays and prefaces (1962). It seems to have had only one production when, translated into Hebrew, it was transmitted by the BBC's Hebrew-language section of the World Service sometime in the 1960s.

Brockway, in a newspaper interview, says that the play was written in 1936 as a comment on the establishment of Jewish nationalism in Palestine and that Shaw had sent it to him to express his disagreement with an

Independent Labour party policy statement on Palestine. Brockway said that the ILP

> took the view that the British, in promising Palestine as a home-land for the Jews, were really hoping, not only to get a mandate over it, but to use it as an imperialist base in the Middle East.
>   Shaw said this was all nonsense. He sent me a three-act play [an exaggeration] in which he says that Balfour gave Dr Weizmann Palestine in return for a chemical microbe to be used in the war for killing Germans.[8]

In the playlet, Arthur (clearly Arthur Balfour) discovers that because of the expense of acetone it costs more than £5,000 "to kill a single German." When he learns that "a chemist in Manchester . . . has a mi-crobe that makes acetone for next to nothing," he orders his attaché to "send him here instantly," but there is a problem:

> ATTACHE. He is a Jew, sir.
> ARTHUR.   Is his microbe a Jew?
> ATTACHE. I suppose not, sir.
> ARTHUR.   Is Sir Herbert Samuel a Jew or is he not? Is he in the Cabinet or is he not?
> ATTACHE. But it is a coalition Government, sir. All sorts of people are let in.

Threatened with being transferred to the trenches, the Attaché relents but comments, "We shall lose tone."
     When Weizmann appears, he surprises Arthur by stating "I do not ask for money," to which Arthur responds, "There must be some misunder-standing. I was informed that you are a Jew." When Arthur's offer of a title also fails him and he asks "what the devil do you want?" Weizmann replies simply, "I want Jerusalem," and Arthur immediately responds, "It's yours." The play ends with the response of Bernard Shaw: "An-other Ulster! As if one were not enough."[9] Shaw based his playlet on an entry in the second volume of Lloyd George's *War Memoirs*. Lloyd George, who was minister for munitions in the early stages of World War I, recorded that he told C. P. Scott, editor of the *Manchester Guardian*, about the acetone problem and that Scott told him that Chaim Weiz-mann, a "remarkable" professor of chemistry at Manchester University, might be able to help. Lloyd George invited Weizmann to London and told him of the problem; Weizmann said he would try to solve it. By March 1916 a factory was making acetone from maize by the Weizmann

process and, before long, it was also being obtained from horse chest-
nuts.

Lloyd George writes,

> When our difficulties were solved through Dr. Weizmann's ge-
> nius I said to him: "You have rendered great service to the State,
> and I should like to ask the Prime Minister to recommend you to
> His Majesty for some honour." He said: "There is nothing I want
> for myself." "But is there nothing we can do as a recognition of
> your valuable assistance to the country?" I asked. He replied:
> "Yes, I would like you to do something for my people." He then
> explained his aspirations as to the repatriation of the Jews to the
> sacred land they had made famous. That was the fount and origin
> of the famous declaration about the National Home for Jews in
> Palestine.[10]

Weizmann told a very different story in his autobiography. In response to a general circular issued by the War Office in 1914 which
asked scientists for any useful knowledge they might possess, he had
reported his acetone discovery and had heard nothing further. It was
not until he learned of the problem though a casual conversation with
the research chemist of a large explosives factory that he realized its
potential. Weizmann's opinion was that

> his [Lord George's] narrative makes it appear that the Balfour
> Declaration was a reward given me by the Government when Mr.
> Lloyd George became Prime Minister, for my services to England.
> I almost wish that it had been as simple as that, and that I had
> never known the heart-breaks, the drudgery and the uncertain-
> ties which preceded the Declaration. But history does not deal in
> Aladdin's lamps.[11]

A British Government committee gave Weizmann a token award of 10s
(50p) for every ton of acetone produced. The total came to £10,000.

As early as 1901, Shaw had spoken in support of a Jewish homeland at
a pro-Zionist rally sponsored by Israel Zangwill, but he had reservations
about the later course that Zionism might take as an instrument of British foreign policy. He signed the Palestine policy statement, prepared by
Brockway. This was produced in collaboration with Yitzhak Yitzhaki, a
Palestinian Marxist, and called for the establishment of a Jewish-Arab
Committee to Combat British Imperialism and appealed to both Jewish
and Arab workers to "unite in one socialist party for the sake of the anti-
Imperialist struggle."[12]

Although he regularly condemned Nazi anti-Semitism even before Hitler achieved power in Germany in 1933, Shaw still supported the dictators and, as others were to maintain, although with an entirely different motive, identified similarities between Hitler and Mussolini on the one hand and Stalin on the other. On 30 May 1934 he wrote to the Communist Christina Walshe that the British parliamentary system "with its mask of democracy, liberty, and all the rest of it" must be smashed before any serious changes could be made, and replaced by a constitution which would have a good deal in common not only with the Russian constitution but also "with the Corporate State of Mussolini and the National Socialist State of Hitler."[13]

Yet in May 1933, Shaw had written to his German translator, Siegfried Trebitsch, whose father was a Jew, to tell him of the appeals for help he had received from Germany. Trebitsch is very vague about his Jewish connections in his autobiography[14] and had declared himself a Protestant after his colonel had insisted that an officer of the Austro-Hungarian army was expected to acknowledge some religious affiliation. Shaw told Trebitsch, "I receive piteous letters from Jews, notably Alfred Kerr and Julius Bab, asking me to help them. But how can any private purse help in a wholesale catastrophe like this one?"[15] On 27 June 1935 he wrote to Trebitsch: "Tell Colonel Goering . . . that I have backed his regime in England to the point of making myself unpopular, and shall continue to do so on all matters in which he and Hitler stand for permanent truths and genuine Realpolitik. But this racial stuff is damned English nonsense."[16]

Shaw's championship of the dictators has always created problems for his admirers. But Dan H. Laurence, editor of the Shaw letters, makes a rare error when, in introducing the 1937–1943 section of the *Collected Letters, 1926–1950*, he maintains that in this period Shaw's sympathy with the fascists waned and that he finally drew the line on the issue of anti-Semitism, calling the Nazis' Judophobia "a very malignant disease" which "destroyed any credit the Nazis might have had." As evidence of Shaw's suggested change of heart in the late 1930s, Laurence calls on a statement made by Shaw: "A party, he averred, 'which condescends to the phobias [of its most rabid citizens] must be desperately hard up for a program. "No program: try a pogrom" must be,' he told the *Jewish Chronicle*, 'the very last resource of a mentally bankrupt party.' "[17] The letter from Shaw which contained these statements cannot be witness to a change of mind between 1937 and 1943, for it was published in the *Jewish Chronicle* on 2 December 1932 (C2978), before Hitler became chancellor. [However, "Bernard Shaw Answers Eight Questions" in the *Daily Express* (26 March 1938), also published as "Shaw Compares Hitler Acts to Witch Burning" in the *New York Journal American* (26 March

1938), listed by Laurence as entry C3245, does suggest a change of heart.]

Shaw supported the dictators for many years afterward and made no bones about it. If the resultant contradictions cannot be attributed to humbug or to a mind irremediably muddled—neither of which would be sustainable in any other area of his life—it must be said that they baffled his friends then as much as they perturb his admirers now.

In May 1933, after a cruise around the world, he wrote to Trebitsch to say he had been questioned about Hitler in every port and that he had

> said that a statesman who began by a persecution of the Jews was compromised as hopelessly as an officer who began by cheating at cards. . . . I admitted that the Germans had as much right to exclude non-Germans from governmental posts as the Americans to reserve the presidency for Americans, but insisted that displaced Jews should be compensated and not driven out penniless by hounding the mob to attack them.[18]

Trebitsch, a Viennese who idolized Shaw, passed gentle judgment on him in *Chronicle of a Life:*

> . . . Bernard Shaw, who always found it much more difficult than the world in general imagines to judge a non-English person, especially if that person was in a high position, took me no little aback with his view of the terrible upheaval in Germany. However much he had been upset by Rathenau's assassination because he had met him personally on the occasion of a visit, he was very far from taking a sufficiently serious view of the events that had occurred since the Nazi seizure of power in Germany and even refused to see that the murder of Dollfuss was a sure sign that Austria's independence was now very gravely threatened.[19]

Shaw was nevertheless sensitive about the situation of the Jews in England, where they faced nothing comparable to what was happening in Germany. On 3 November 1936, he wrote to Matthew Forsyth, the director of the first English production of *The Millionairess:* "The sweater [sweatshop owner] and his wife speak Whitechapel cockney. . . . The pair would ordinarily be Jews; but you must carefully avoid any suggestion of this at present, as it would drag in current politics."[20] More than a year later (6 February 1938) he wrote to Beatrice Webb:

> I think we ought to tackle the Jewish question by admitting the right of States to make eugenic experiments by weeding out any

strains that they think undesirable, but insisting that they should do it as humanely as they can afford to, and not shock civilization by such misdemeanors as the expulsion and robbery of Einstein.

And the great antivivisectionist added, "The prevailing thoughtlessness is damnable. . . ."[21]

He was particularly incensed about the Nazis' treatment of Albert Einstein. In 1940 he drafted a radio speech which was not transmitted, but was later published in *Journal of the War Years* by Anthony Weymouth (B332), in which he declared how much he admired Hitler, who had adopted not only his diet but also many policies that he had been advocating for years. "I was a National Socialist before Mr Hitler was born," he had intended to say over the BBC:

> My quarrel with him is a very plain one. . . . I have a friend who happens to be a Jew. His name is Albert Einstein: and he is a far greater human prodigy than Mr Hitler and myself rolled into one. . . . Well, Adolf Hitler would compel me, the Nordic Shaw, to insult Albert Einstein; to claim moral superiority to him and unlimited power over him; to rob him, drive him out of his house, exile him, be punished for miscegenation if I allow a relative of mine to marry a relative of his, and finally to kill him as part of a general duty to exterminate his race. . . . We ought to have declared war on Germany the moment his police stole Einstein's violin.[22]

It is not surprising that Duff Cooper, the minister of information, shouted, "I won't have that man on the air." The year 1940 was not an appropriate time to justify the war as a reaction to the treatment of one man, no matter how eminent.

Two years earlier (18 March 1938), by which time Einsein had long been deprived of his violin, Shaw wrote an article for the London *Evening Standard* (C3244) approving Hitler's annexation of Austria and told Trebitsch, temporarily safe in Prague, that he had sent a postcard to his Vienna address congratulating him on the glorious achievement of the *Anschluss* "by your fellowcountryman, the Führer. And now," Shaw continued,

> you reproach me because I did not write letters pointing out that you are a Jew marked out for Nazi persecution.
> You say that I am the only one of your friends who has not done this. In that case I am the only one of your friends who is not a mischievous fool. As for you, you have many merits and talents;

but in politics you are the most thoughtless idiot in Europe. You
are furious with me because I did not betray you to the police,
who are pretty sure to read all your correspondence.

I hope my unfeeling conduct helped you to get a passport.[23]

He sent Trebitsch £50. Trebitsch records it as "a rather large sum of
money" and adds,

> Shaw had written me several postcards when I was still in Vienna
> with "Heil Hitler" and expressions of admiration for National
> Socialism which had irritated me very much, as indeed they still
> did in retrospect. I made no bones about it but complained bit-
> terly. At this he assured me very seriously: "Whether you believe
> it or not, if you were quite unmolested for four whole days and
> could fly to your lecture in Prague without anyone's stopping you,
> it's owing to nothing but these postcards—it's all my doing! Are
> you really stupid enough to believe that I'm pro-Hitler?"
>
> I did not want to contradict him, and also refrained from saying
> too much about all I had lost, because Shaw would have thought it
> "sentimental"—the expression he had ready to hand for practi-
> cally all the feelings that he himself refused to have anything to do
> with, if only out of complacency.[24]

The Nazis had not been fooled by Shaw's postcards. Trebitsch and his
wife, Tina, fled Vienna with one suitcase each and, by January 1939,
they were in Nice. Among other refugees there was a Viennese journalist, Leopold Lipschütz, a relative of Trebitsch. Lipschütz and his wife
killed themselves in a suicide pact and the Trebitsches found the bodies.
Shaw wrote,

> What a frightful experience! Next time you have to break a door
> open do not take Tina with you. Nowadays we are accustomed to
> read about such things and hear about them; but to *see* them upsets
> one for days. The effect will pass away, as such effects always merci-
> fully do; but in the meantime dont talk to her about it: there is
> nothing to be done but rock her in your arms and kiss her.

Unbelievably, he goes on: "You see, I was right about Hitler. His speech
was a wonderful performance: nobody else in Europe could have made
it. Of course the part about the Jews was stark raving nonsense: . . . but
the rest was masterly."[25] In his autobiography Trebitsch does not say a
word about the finding of the bodies, or Shaw's response to the event,
and his love for Shaw was undiminished. Blanche Patch, Shaw's secre-

tary, describes how after the war Trebitsch came to England several times and "the venerable pair (Trebitsch was now almost 80) would sit discussing their vanished royalties, for Trebitsch was no longer rich and his health was going too."[26]

With *Geneva*, which he began in 1936, Shaw tried to reconcile his admiration for the dictators and his detestation of their unfortunate tendency to kill Jews. Naturally, he chose a dramatic form. *Geneva*, if anything, only made things worse. The basic notion of the play is that certain aggrieved persons, including a Jew, use a little-regarded agency of the League of Nations to haul the dictators Battler (Hitler), Bombardone (Mussolini), and Flanco (Franco) before the International Court of Justice in The Hague. The play was presented in Warsaw in July 1938, at the Malvern Festival in August of that year, and then in London in November, some six weeks after Neville Chamberlain had returned with the Munich Agreement. In New York, the Theatre Guild, founded by Lawrence Langner and others in 1919, turned *Geneva* down. The Guild was Shaw's principal theatrical ally in America, having presented fifteen of his plays, among them *Heartbreak House*, an uncut *Back to Methuselah*, *Saint Joan*, *The Apple Cart*, *Too True to Be Good*, *The Simpleton of the Unexpected Isles*, and *The Millionairess*.

Langner, born in Swansea, South Wales, in 1890, was devoted to Shaw and thought him "one of the most stimulating, witty, wise and argumentative voices in the modern world." But he was "deeply hurt" when he was sent a privately printed copy of the first version of the play, even though it was personally inscribed to him by the author. On 26 August 1938 he wrote to Shaw:

> I do not believe that you will want future generations of Jewbaiters to quote you as part authority for a program of torturing, starving and driving to suicide of Jews all over the world. Yet ... you give Battler (obviously Hitler) a speech in which he justifies everything that has been done recently in Germany and Austria, on the ground that in every country "the foreigner is the trespasser." As the thought is presented so convincingly by him, it seems that you do not take into account that Jews have lived in Germany for over 1700 years; that they have contributed largely to the cultural and scientific life of Germany; that during the last war alone over 30,000 Jews died in the German armies, and that but for a Jewish scientist, Haber, who invented the method of abstracting nitrogen from the air (which scientist later committed suicide) the Germans would have been defeated in 1916 instead of 1919 [*sic*]. You give the Jew merely the *weak answer:* "For my race, there are no frontiers," as though the German Jew of today

had anything to do with the historic reasons, beginning with the Roman armies and ending with Torquemada and others, as a result of which some of the Jews found themselves in Germany.

Langner's lengthy diatribe against *Geneva* raises other disturbing charges: Shaw tends to "justify Hitler," while having the Jew "*present the weaker side* of his case;" he offers an "absurd libel" by implying that "all that the Jews have contributed to German civilization can be expressed as 'trade and finance;' " he glosses over the injustices of persecution, concentration camps, and murder perpetrated against Jews. After noting that Shakespeare's Shylock and Dickens's Fagin "have added greatly to the cross of hatred which future generations of Jews must bear," Langner suggests that "you, who have always been so understanding through your entire life, will surely not want to add another figure to a collection which breeds intolerance and racial hatred." In Langner's opinion, Shaw made his Jew "a pitifully inferior mouthpiece to express his case, thus playing into the hands of the breeders of racial hatred by ranging yourself unconsciously on their side." The rest of the letter complains that although Shaw appears to come down on democrats and fascists equally, he gives a magnificent speech to Bombardone and conveys the impression that he is ranged on the side of the dictators.[27]

Shaw answered hardly any of Langner's criticisms. On 20 September 1938, he replied,

> Can you wonder at Hitler (and now Mussolini) driving out the Jews? Here am I who have written a play in which I make ruthless fun of British Cabinet Ministers, of German and Italian dictators, and Cockney young women, of the Buchmanite Oxford movement, of Church of England bishops, and of the League of Nations. Everyone laughs. Not a voice is raised in their defence.
>
> But I have dared to introduce a Jew without holding him up to the admiring worship of the audience as the inheritor of all the virtues and none of the vices of Abraham and Moses, David and Isaiah. And instantly you, Lawrence, raise a wail of lamentation and complaint and accuse me of being a modern Torquemada.

Shaw states that he has "been far less kind to the Irish characters [in *John Bull's Other Island*] than I have been to the Jew in Geneva, who is introduced solely to convict the Nazis of persecution" and complains that Langner "will not allow him to do exactly what an able Jew of his type would do when Gentiles were swallowing a terrifying Press canard: that is, go into the money market as a bear speculator and make his fortune." After telling Langner that he is "the most thoughtless of Sheenies," Shaw says that "to please you, I have written up the part a bit. Musso let me down completely by going anti-Semite on me; and I have had to revise the third act."[28]

Langner, hardly appeased, replied on 7 October: "If I am really one of the most thoughtless of 'Sheenies,' then you are one of the most inconsistent of 'Micks.' " He expresses his hope that Shaw's revision will show that Mussolini's "anti-Semitism does not spring from any nobler source than the fact that he believes it is a good way to stir up the Arabs against the British." After changing the subject to the racial mixtures of "practically all the great nations of the world," referring to the mixture of Celt and Spaniard that produced the "black Irish," and adding that "a number of the Spaniards were Maranos—or converted Jews," Langner focuses on "a certain admixture of Jewish and Irish people" to turn the tables on Shaw:

> Undoubtedly, you are one of the striking examples of this mixture, since you possess all the virtues of Moses, Spinoza, Heine and all the other Jewish prophets. Then, take your moneymaking ability. Nine-tenths of the radical playwrights starve to death; you make a fortune at it. Then look at your Socialism. Don't you know that, according to Hitler, all Socialists are Jewish? Yes, G.B.S., the truth will out. You too are a Sheenie: and as to that red beard of yours, did you not know that the medieval Jew always had a red beard? A friend of mine recently visited what remains of the Pharisees. He found that they had red beards and blue eyes. You are undoubtedly a Pharisee throw-back. . . .[29]

The New York Theatre Guild never did produce *Geneva*, mainly on the grounds that Shaw's recent plays had resulted in financial loss. According to Langner, the 1932 production of *Too True to Be Good* had "had a mediocre reception and must be counted a failure," while the 1935 production of *The Simpleton of the Unexpected Isles* had resulted in "further financial losses." The Theatre Guild concluded, as it had earlier with *The Millionairess* and *On the Rocks*, that it "could not risk the financial sacrifices involved," and subsequent events seemed to prove the Guild right. When Colbourne and Gilbert Miller opened *Geneva* in New York on 30 January 1940, the play soon failed.[30]

Some of the passages to which Langner had objected had been deleted in revision, but enough remained for it to be still considered a wholly inadequate response to the events of the 1930s. There were four versions altogether. The deletions marked by Shaw on the copy he sent to Langner were, in fact, made. The first rehearsal copy bears the title "Geneva; A Fancied Page of History by a Fellow of the Royal Society of

Literature." The second rehearsal copy, "revised after Bombardone's conversion to anti-Semitism," is now entitled "Geneva: A Fancied Page of History in Three Acts by Bernard Shaw." A third draft was published in 1939, revised for a third printing in 1940, and revised again for a French translation in 1946. An additional act was included for the standard edition in 1947. The preface was written in 1945. In (1) the Jew says, "Anti-Semitism is an outrage on the intellect of Europe. Its attack on the persons and property of the Jews are a violation of European justice." These words are omitted from all subsequent editions.

When Battler asks of what he is accused, the Jew says (1) "Of murder. Of an attempt to exterminate the upper layer of the human race." In subsequent versions he says ". . . exterminate the flower of the human race." Battler replies, "Then what right have you in my country? You do not belong to my people [in (1) Battler says: "A marriage between you and them is miscegenation." This is subsequently omitted]. I exclude you as the British exclude the Chinese in Australia, as the Americans exclude the Japanese in California." Instead of pointing out that neither the British nor the Americans deport people from the country they were born in, the Jew merely replies that the British exclude the Chinese because the Chinaman is so industrious that nobody would employ a white British workman or caretaker if there was a yellow one within reach, and that the German reason for excluding the Jew is that the Germans cannot compete with his intelligence, his persistence, his foresight, his grasp of finance. "It is our talents, our virtues, that you fear, not our vices." Neither (1) nor (2) contains this passage. Battler continues after ". . . Japanese in California" with "I may not set foot in England until I declare that I will do no work there and that I will return to my own country in a few weeks. In every country the foreigner is a trespasser." There is much more in this vein, all to the effect that the Jew is as much a foreigner in the land of his birth as any alien.

This is precisely what the Nazis proclaimed and, in that sense, Shaw was perfectly right in putting it into Battler/Hitler's mouth. But all the Jew is given to say in reply—and this runs through all versions—is "A Jew is a human being. Has he not a right of way and settlement everywhere upon the earth?" To which Battler quite properly replies, "No-where without a passport. That is the law of nations." The Jew declares, "I leave myself in the hands of the court. For my race there are no frontiers. Let those who set them justify themselves." This most arrogant claim runs through all versions.

Shaw's prescience took a knock with his treatment of Bombardone/ Mussolini. The first version has Bombardone tell the Judge, "if you allow Ernest [Battler] to start on the Jewish question we shall get no further before bed-time. He has compromised the cause of Fascism throughout

Europe by confusing it with Anti-Semitism. I do not persecute the Jews."
Mussolini introduced his race laws in 1938, and Shaw had to amend
Bombardone's speech to ". . . bed-time. He should have waited for a lead
from me before meddling with it and forcing me to banish the Jews lest
my people should be swamped by the multitude he has driven out." This
is clearly not in accordance with historical fact, and Shaw seems to have
gone beyond the limits of dramatic license. Mussolini's race laws were
directly solely against Italian Jews. German refugees, in general, did not
see fascist Italy as a haven from persecution by the Nazis.

In the copy of the first version sent to Langner, there is a note on page
80 in Shaw's handwriting, saying, "these are the cuts made at Malvern.
The producer said they were more than the exhausted audience could
stand." One of the cut passages is the Jew's response to the Judge's
reminder to Battler that he is there to answer "an accusation by a Jewish
gentleman of unlawful arrest and imprisonment, assault, robbery and
denial of his right to live in the country of his birth." This is the first
mention of the essential fact of birthright after a good deal of the court's
time has been concerned with the quite different and separate issue of
countries' refusing entry to, or extraditing, people born outside their
borders. Battler says that he does not condescend to defend himself,
adding, "I have already remarked that the Jews are a noxious species
which we refuse to tolerate, just as we refuse to tolerate venomous
snakes."

The Jew's response in (1), later deleted by the author, is to remind the
court that Jews are not, as a matter of scientific fact, venomous snakes
and that the vulgar prejudice against them is not nearly as strong as the
prejudice against dictators and persecutors.

> We Jews have been driven into trade and finance until we have
> become more skilful at them than our lazy persecutors. This has
> made us their bankers and employers and to that extent their
> masters. The remedy is very simple. They have only to cultivate
> their brains as they cultivate their muscles. Then they will no
> longer be our slaves; and we shall be able to endure their society
> on equal terms. We may even intermarry with them and help
> their development in that way.

In (2) and (3) the Jew says instead,

> You mean that you have no defence. You cannot even find a
> Jewish lawyer to defend you, because you have driven them all
> from your country and left it with no better brains than your own.

> You have employed physical force to suppress intellect. That is
> the sin against the Holy Ghost. I accuse you of it.

Possibly the first remark made by a Jew in such circumstances would
not be a reference to the Holy Ghost, but the main objection to the play
remains the scene toward the end. The case is interrupted when the
Judge receives a telephone call (if it is a "terrifying Press canard," as
Shaw described it in his reply to Langner's protests, it is not obvious to
those in court or in the audience). The Judge writes down what he is
being told, which is that "astronomers report that the orbit of the earth is
jumping to its next quantum. Message received at Greenwich from three
American observatories. Humanity is doomed."

There follow explanations that the world will turn to ice, whereupon
the Jew excuses himself by saying that he has to telephone. The British
Foreign Secretary says that the report must be officially contradicted, lest
otherwise people throw off all decency and all prudence.

> Only the Jews, with the business faculty peculiar to their race, will
> profit by our despair. Why has our Jewish friend just left us? To
> telephone, he said. Yes; but to whom is he telephoning? To his
> stockbroker to sell gilt-edged in any quantity, at any price, know-
> ing that if this story gets about before settling day he will be able to
> buy it for the price of waste paper and be a millionaire until the
> icecap overtakes him.

It is nonsense, and insulting nonsense, today; in 1938 it was insulting and
dangerous nonsense. Jews were being killed because people believed
things about them which made this farrago look as sober and as factual
as a government paper on agricultural policy.

The additional act, introduced after the war, is set in the lounge of a
fashionable restaurant overlooking the Lake of Geneva. It takes place
before the trial scene and involves most of the characters except Bombardone and Battler. The play is still set in 1938. The Jew rhetorically
asks, "Have you been robbed? Have you been battered with clubs?
Gassed? Massacred? [The last two questions would have been unthinkable in 1938.] Have you been imprisoned in concentration camps com-
manded by hooligans? Have you been driven out of your country to
starve in exile?" In reply, a character called the Newcomer tells him that
he should not have been born in Germany but in Jerusalem, to which the
supposedly witty and urbane Jew replies, "And you shouldn't have been
born at all." The Spanish widow tries to shoot him because he killed
Christ but finishes up by accepting an invitation to dinner. She still
charges that the Jews kill Christian babies, to which the Commissar says

that they do not in Russia, though he has no doubt that they are capable of anything when corrupted by capitalism.

This was written in 1947, while the survivors of the camps were still dying. When the play's Preface had been written in 1945, the corpses were still being counted. In the Preface, Shaw maintains that most of the concentration-camp deaths resulted from overcrowding and lack of food. The guards were not fiends but only incompetents, who "could do nothing with their unwalled prisoners but kill them and burn the corpses they could not bury." Atrocities stemmed from the "natural percentage of callous toughs among them." He himself had written in *Time and Tide* in 1938 that although Hitler was in many respects an able man, he had a bee in his bonnet about Jews.

> We all know private persons who have these hobbies. We laugh at them. But on the part of an autocrat they are no laughing matter. When they take the form of an attempt to exterminate a section of the human race something may have to be done about it by other States. . . . We talk about a Jewish problem. There is no problem: there is only the crude fact that Herr Hitler is plundering the Jews as Henry VIII plundered the Church, and that we are expected to support them. I have almost damned myself politically by defending the German and Italian leaders against the silly abuse heaped on them by the spokesmen and journalists of our pseudo-democracy; but now that they have let me down by condescending to anti-Semitism, I must really disown all sympathy with that anachronism, and point out the way to stop it.[31]

Shaw's method of stopping it was for the League of Nations to appoint a committee, assisted by an international staff of expert psychiatrists, to look at the Nazi anti-Jew legislation. If their report was that Hitler and Mussolini were in the grip of pathological phobia, they would be certified as lunatics unless they canceled their anti-Jew legislation and stopped the persecution. Shaw confidently expected that the dictators would be so put out by such a threat that they would do as he said. This is the notion of a rational lunatic, of someone who can totally disregard his own experience and the world's history to hold the sublimely ridiculous belief that, in order to get irrational people to behave sensibly, all that is necessary is to tell them that they are behaving irrationally. In the same article in which Shaw propounded his scheme, he accepted that Hitler was "trying to exterminate a section of the human race." Ten years later, when it was clear that the attempt had been translated into action, all he could find to say about it was that it grew out of incompetence among the lower orders of Nazism.

Shaw's friend and admirer St. John Ervine knew him as "an exceptionally kind man" but thought that

> *Geneva* was not only untimely but seemingly callous. It was distressing to his friends at this period of his life to find G.B.S. making excuses for barbaric deeds, which, had Americans or Britons committed them, would have made him furious. Gentiles were as angry as the Jews about these aberrations; and no ingenuity of argument could convince them that he was right in defending and applauding the dictators. . . .
>
> He was sufficiently impressed by Langner's protest to make some excisions and modifications in *Geneva*; but his partisan spirit had given his mind some of the consistency of ferro-concrete, and it is still saddening stuff to read. As a play, it dissatisfied him; for the version which appears in the Standard Collection has four acts instead of three as in the original version. The additional act improves it, but it is almost certain to be thrown into the discard, so far as performances are concerned.[32]

Perhaps, as Churchill said of him earlier, Shaw had blinded himself to reality, but there were many who had tried to open his eyes. In 1938, Desmond MacCarthy, theater critic of the *New Statesman*, reviewing *Geneva*, wrote, "What do you think of introducing such an incident, *and at this moment in European history* [his italics] as symbolic of the Jewish soul when revealed under the stress of disaster? Speaking for myself, it made me ask if it were possible that I had been a fool about Bernard Shaw all my writing life."[33] He did not think that he had, but thought that Shaw's age had brought about a serious decline in his judgment.

Forty years later, Benedict Nightingale, formerly professor of drama at the University of Michigan, a leading critic in Britain and the United States, and now theater critic of the London *Times*, was still capable of being shocked by the *Geneva* episode. He commented, "Shaw had a chance to display more humanity in the play's preface . . . five years before his death, at a time when the full monstrosity of the 'final solution' was becoming clear. He did not take it."[34]

Shaw's brilliance illuminated and changed the lives of millions. It may well be, however, that, despite his piercing perceptions of the nature of man, his belief in society's eventual perfectability made him incapable of seeing the depth of the evil to which he gave his weighty support. All the same, that fundamental failure sees the great campaigner against oppression, the apostle of liberty, the vigorous champion of social justice, the brilliant polemicist, totter into history in the ignoble company of the seedy revisionists who say the Nazis did not do it, or that if they did do it, it was unplanned and unintentional. Uniquely, he links the fascist right with the fascist left, for he also ignored the Stalin terror. The deaths he excused and the deaths he denied number millions.

Notes

1. Bernard Shaw, Preface to *The Millionairess, Complete Plays With Prefaces* (New York: Dodd, Mead, 1962), 6: 190–91.

2. Bernard Shaw, *Collected Letters, 1898–1910*, ed. Dan H. Laurence (London: Max Reinhardt, 1972), p. 88.

3. Ibid., p. 611.

4. Bernard Shaw, *The Doctor's Dilemma, Complete Plays With Prefaces,* 1: 127–28.

5. Bernard Shaw, *Collected Letters, 1911–1925*, ed. Dan H. Laurence (London: Max Reinhardt, 1985), p. 343.

6. Ibid., p. 714.

7. Ibid., p. 923.

8. "Three-Act Play in 1,000 Words: Shaw's Reply to M.P.," The *Times* (16 January 1961), p. 41.

9. Bernard Shaw, *Arthur and the Acetone, Complete Plays With Prefaces*, 3: 751–53.

10. *War Memoirs of David Lloyd George* (Boston: Little, Brown, 1933), 2: 50.

11. *Trial and Error: The Autobiography of Chaim Weizmann* (New York: Harper & Brothers, 1949), p. 150.

12. Joseph Gorny, *The British Labour Movement and Zionism: 1917–1948* (London: Frank Cass, 1983), p. 159.

13. Bernard Shaw, *Collected Letters, 1926–1950*, ed. Dan H. Laurence (London: Max Reinhardt, 1988), p. 374.

14. Siegfried Trebitsch, *Chronicle of a Life* (London: Heinemann, 1953), pp. 242–43.

15. *Collected Letters, 1926–1950*, p. 338. Kerr (1867–1948) was an influential Berlin critic. Bab (1880–1955), another critic, published a study of Shaw in 1910, revised and rewritten in 1928. Kerr escaped to England and Bab emigrated to France, subsequently moving to the United States.

16. Ibid., p. 413.

17. Ibid., p. 457; brackets Laurence's.

18. Ibid., p. 336.

19. Trebitsch, p. 346. Walter Rathenau (1867–1922), German Jew, foreign minister of the Weimar republic, was murdered by Austrian anti-Semites. Englebert Dollfuss (1892–1934), Austrian chancellor, was murdered by Austrian Nazis.

20. *Collected Letters, 1926–1950*, p. 444.

21. Ibid., p. 493; ellipsis Shaw's.

22. Allan Chappelow, *Shaw—"The Chucker-Out"* (London: George Allen & Unwin, 1969), pp. 199–200.

23. *Collected Letters, 1926–1950*, p. 496.

24. Trebitsch, p. 371.

25. *Collected Letters, 1926–1950,* p. 525.

26. Blanche Patch, *Thirty Years with G.B.S.* (London: Victor Gollancz, 1951), p. 58.

27. Lawrence Langner, *The Magic Curtain: The Story of a Life in Two Fields* (New York: E. P. Dutton, 1951), pp. 454–56.

28. *Collected Letters, 1926–1950,* p. 511.

29. Langner, p. 458.

30. Langner, pp. 290, 293–94.

31. Bernard Shaw, *Time and Tide* (26 November 1938), quoted in Chappelow, pp. 197–98.

32. St. John Ervine, *Bernard Shaw: His Life, Work and Friends* (London: Constable, 1956), pp. 564–65.

33. Desmond MacCarthy, *Shaw* (London: MacGibbon and Kee, 1951), p. 195.

34. Benedict Nightingale, *A Reader's Guide to Fifty Modern British Plays* (London: Heinemann, 1982), p. 45.

H. J. Fyrth

IN THE DEVIL'S DECADE: *GENEVA* AND INTERNATIONAL POLITICS

"The Devil's Decade" was the name given to the 1930s by the British journalist Claude Cockburn, an acute observer and himself a small-part player in the drama of those years. Stanley Baldwin, the Conservative prime minister, had already asserted that the forces of evil were manifestly abroad, and indeed, if one believed that the Prince of Darkness goes about like a roaring lion seeking whom he may devour, he was certainly having a rich feast.

The decade may be said to have begun in October 1929, when the bottom fell out of the New York stock market, and to have ended in world war. By the winter of 1932–33, Britain had three million as an official counting of unemployed (the real number was nearer four million), Germany had six million out of work, and the United States had twelve million workless. In Britain the "National" Government found new ways of torturing the poor, with a means test under which a man out of work for six months could get no relief while his son or daughter could assist him, or while he had a gramophone or a piano unsold. Many, not merely those on the political Left, concluded that capitalist civilization had collapsed. For Britons there was an extra turn of the screw when the Indian portion of the empire, reinforced by Gandhi's civil-disobedience campaigns, clamored for independence.

The political picture was no brighter than the economic. Hitler, coming to power in 1933, proceeded to destroy the Weimar republic, incarcerate or murder his political opponents, disband workers' organizations, and persecute the Jews. Mussolini had already established his fascist state in Italy, and by the mid 1930s a number of European states were under the control of right-wing dictatorships. In 1934 France tottered on the brink of fascism, and by 1939 Spain had been pushed over that brink. In the Soviet Union, Lenin's mantle had fallen on the shoulders of Stalin, whose determination for rapid industrialization of Russia and collectivization of peasant farms resulted in a policy of terror that turned the revolutionary party into an authoritarian instrument for the management of society.

Thirteen years after the war that was supposed to end all wars, the first shots of a new world conflict were fired when Japan invaded Manchuria. Hitler prepared for war and joined Mussolini in sending arms and men to help General Franco overthrow the Spanish government. In 1938 and 1939, Austria, Czechoslovakia, and Albania went down before the fascist dictators. Throughout these eight years of accelerating aggression, the British and French governments acted as accessories before, during, and after the fact.

Fortunately for the human race, and for Britons in particular, the forces of light, gradually increasing in strength, opposed the forces of darkness. In Britain, the unemployed, refusing to starve in silence, organized themselves for hunger marches and courtroom battles. Hundreds of thousands of men and women joined organizations, rallies, and conferences to try to find ways of preserving peace. Democrats of all shades stood against Sir Oswald Mosley's Jew-baiting blackshirts at home and called for collective action to save Abyssinia and Czechoslovakia abroad. The military revolt in Spain brought immediate support from myriad groups which collected to send medical teams and food ships to the aid of the Republic, to care for refugees, and to receive four thousand Basque children into Britain. Some four thousand Britons went to fight against Franco. All these efforts failed, but the common purpose of democrats, socialists, communists, humanitarians, and patriotic conservatives alike was important for Britain in World War II.

How did Shaw respond to these momentous years of horror and of hope? The world in which he had produced his greatest work and in which his ideas had been formed had passed away. When Wall Street crashed he was already in his seventy-fourth year, but he was as lively as ever in his speech and writing and in his other activities. The most revered figure in world theater, a respected and puckish sage, he continued to offer provocative statements which still delighted the press and the public.

His political approach to the decade was directed by long-held principles which had been reinforced by the experiences of his middle years— the Great War bringing the collapse of so much of what had been regarded as European civilization, and having been followed by an era of great incompetence on the part of European, and especially of British, governments and the willingness of electorates to put up with what, to any intelligent and sensitive person, should have been seen as follies and outrages, or to follow demagogues who promised them work and national glory.

On his return from the Soviet Union in 1931, Shaw told the *Observer,* "After you have seen Bolshevism on the spot there can be no doubt but that capitalism is doomed."[1] The second part of the sentence was not, in fact, a conclusion drawn from the first part. He had been convinced that captialism was doomed nearly half a century earlier, when he knew William Morris, H. M. Hyndman, and the Fabians and read Marx, as he liked to boast, before Lenin did so. The events of the 1920s and 1930s merely reinforced his views.

Shaw had long called himself a socialist and a communist, and he continued to claim these titles until his death. In the Preface to *The Millionairess,* he declared,

> it is always the greatest spirits, from Jesus to Lenin, from St Thomas More to William Morris, who are communists and democrats, and always the common-place people who weary us with their blitherings about the impossibility of equality when they are at a loss for any better excuse for keeping other people in the kitchen and themselves in the drawing room.[2]

"Democrats" should here be considered in a rather more profound sense than that of the parliamentary party system which it means in much common parlance, and for which Shaw had less than no time at all. Democracy was to him the hot-air balloon which diverts the attention of the public while its pockets are being picked.[3] This belief led him to choose some strange bedfellows between the wars, but it is difficult not to sympathize when he writes in *The Intelligent Woman's Guide,*

> The belief in the magic of the vote was so fervent that I could not be forgiven for warning the suffragettes that votes for women would probably mean their self-exclusion from Parliament, and that what they needed was a constitutional law that all public authorities should have a representative proportion of women on them, votes or no votes. The next general election shattered the illusions of the enthusiasts, and delighted the Conservatives and reactionists who had consented to the enfranchisement of women because they saw that it would reinforce their party. . . . Parliament after the election presented the extraordinary spectacle of an assembly of 614 men and one women representing a community of nineteen millions of men and twenty-one millions of women.[4]

There was plenty in the history of Britain in Shaw's lifetime to under-line his contempt for the parliamentary system, but at the root of his doubts lay something darker—a lack of confidence, bordering on con-tempt, for what were then called "the Common People." Unlike those socialists who put their faith in "the workers" or "the masses," Shaw understood that—except in those exceptional circumstances which are the great turning points of history—the majority of people are politically and socially conservative, whatever party labels they may wear. But in the 1930s he saw them as something more—potential followers of fascist dictators. They were

> the huge majority which never dreams of conspiring against estab-lished order, and thinks those low societies [which do] ought to be put down by the police; . . . that crowds to coronations, royal wed-dings, or the trooping of the color on the Horse Guards Parade; that stands in a queue five miles long to see a dead monarch lying in state; that thinks it has a creed and a code, but really does what everybody does and is shocked by anyone who doesnt. . . .
>
> They are patriotic, these people, by which they mean that God created them superior to the natives of other countries. . . . His-tory is known to them, when it is known at all, as a string of battles in which their side has been victorious. (*IWG*, p. 483)

Since so little could be expected of such people, hope must lie with the strong man who would lead the people to socialism. The superman com-plex had created Julius Caesar, Andrew Undershaft, and King Magnus, among others. Transferred from the stage to the 1930s' world of dictator-ships, this doctrine produced statements which shocked many of Shaw's admirers, as when in 1927 he said that Mussolini had gone further in the direction of socialism than the English Labour party could venture if they were in power. It must, of course, be remembered that Mussolini had been a revolutionary socialist in his youth, that he was widely admired in Brit-ain, in both the Conservative and Labour parties, and that when, two years later, Labour did form a government, it did not take one step "in the direction of socialism." It is easier to criticize many of Shaw's statements with the benefit of hindsight than it was when they were made.

After explaining in *The Intelligent Woman's Guide* just how the fascist dictators had opiated and manipulated the public, he wrote, "So far, Fascism is better than Liberalism . . ." (*IWG*, p. 492), but he had already said that fascism would not do. It would fail because "Fascist geniuses are not immortal, and . . . may wear out before they die" (*IWG*, p. 486). (He used "fascism" rather inexactly to include the rule of Napoleon, Julius Caesar, and Peter the Great.)

And then there is the romantic appetite for military glory and warrior virtue which Leaders must gratify or promise to gratify. . . .

But all these weaknesses in Fascism are trifles compared to the vice in it which makes it useless for the checking of that ride to the abyss which has hitherto been the end of all Capitalist civilisations. . . .

Thus when the Leader has played skittles with the poor with ridiculous ease, and, having plundered them of their savings, finds that to carry out really big schemes of social reconstruction he must proceed to plunder the rich, he suddenly finds himself powerless. . . .

If he goes further than this in the direction of Socialism he becomes a revolutionary, a Bolshevik. Now the modern Leader's trump card is that he has come to save society from Bolshevism, *alias* Communism, which has come to mean any proletarian movement whatever. . . . (*IWG,* pp. 486–88)

Shaw denied that he was a fascist in sympathy. Meditating in 1939 on his play *Geneva,* he wrote,

When I point out the obvious fact that adult suffrage . . . is a guarantee of petty snobbery and parochial ignorance in the choice of rulers, and that the party system in Parliament has made the House of Commons quite useless as a check on plutocratic oligarchy and completely effective in paralyzing the government industrially and reducing all democratic leaders to helpless impotence, it is immediately assumed that I have renounced democracy and socialism and am now a Fascist and adore Messrs Mussolini and Hitler, who, not being reduced to impotence by membership of our House of Commons, have both done a lot of things that badly want doing here, but cannot be done because to do them would infringe British liberty to be governed by Begonia [a foolish character in the play].[5]

What Shaw perceived, and what many antifascists refused to see, was that fascism, however evil its aims and however brutal its methods, had a populist side, and could take and hold power only because it did provide an immediate solution to many wrongs from which people were suffering, such as unemployment, which liberal-democratic governments were failing to tackle.

Sovietism, for Shaw, was a different matter. During his visit to the Soviet Union in 1931, together with the wealthy Tory Lady Astor and the Liberal peer Lord Lothian, Shaw was delighted with what he saw.

Writing to the *Times* in August 1931, he argued that "Russia's solution of the democratic problem so far" was superior to Britain's: "liberty does not mean liberty to idle and sponge. The political machinery is built for immediate positive use; and it is powerful enough to break people who stick ramrods into it. In short, it is much more democratic than Parliament and party."[6]

In 1934, arguing with H. G. Wells in the pages of the *New Statesman and Nation*, which had printed verbatim Wells's interview with Stalin, he wrote,

> Here is Russia solving all the problems which we are helplessly trying to buy off with doles, to frighten off with armaments, and to charm away by prayers for a revival of trade. In the course of solving them political discoveries in applied political science of the most thrilling interest and vital importance have been made.[7]

He likened the members of the Soviet Communist party to Wells's "Samurai," the dedicated elite who would save society, for Wells shared Shaw's belief that salvation could come only from superior leaders. In a previous contribution to the discussion, he had made his famous statement about the support which he and Sidney Webb gave to the Soviet Union:

> I have long been laughed at in Russia as "a good man fallen among Fabians" [Lenin's remark]; but the two old hyperfabian Fabians, Webb and Shaw, have stuck to their guns like Fox whilst the sentimental Socialists have been bolting in all directions from Stalin, screaming, like St. Peter, "I know not the man." Stalin is almost *persona grata* at the Foreign Office as our only bulwark against Japanese Imperialism, whilst our professedly Socialist Societies and Parties are blindly helping the rabble of capitalists who are trying to export our too scanty money to secure a share in the exploitation of Manchukuo and China. . . .[8]

Shaw's devoted, although not uncritical, belief in Stalin's Russia, its democracy and economy, may seem, to say the least, misplaced. But he was far from alone. The industrialization of the five-year plans, the growth of education and culture among a largely illiterate people, the establishment of social services which were, in principle if not in achievement, in advance of those of many Western countries, and the speed with which the legacies of czarism and civil war were being tackled aroused interest and sympathy far beyond the ranks of those who called themselves socialists or communists, and many saw what Sidney and Beatrice Webb called "A New Civilisation" as the alternative to a collapsing capitalist system. The wheel has turned, but in judging Shaw, one should not forget where it stood then. Comparatively little was known of Stalin's terror when Shaw wrote in the *New Statesman*. What was known, and believed, was too easily excused in the context of the aftermath of war, revolution, invasion, and civil war. When Lady Astor asked Stalin why he had killed so many Russians, he argued the exigencies of revolution and added that "the need for dealing with political prisoners drastically would soon cease."[9] The "need" may have done, but in 1931 Stalin's worst excesses lay ahead.

A mixture of common, often comic, sense and a very Olympian and dogmatic disregard for the realities of the time can be seen in much that Shaw wrote and said during the "Devil's Decade." Early in 1934 the British Broadcasting Corporation invited a number of distinguished people (eleven men and a viscountess) to broadcast their views on the theme of *Whither Britain?* Shaw began his contribution in fine style, and with echoes of Captain Shotover:

> Whither Britain? What a question! Even if I knew, and you all know very well that I do not know, could I tell you in half an hour? Now put a reasonable question, say a little part of the big question: is Britain heading straight for war? That's what you want to know, isn't it? Well, at present Britain is not heading straight for anywhere. She is a ship without a pilot, driving before the winds of circumstance; and as such she is as likely to drift into a war as into anything else, provided somebody else starts the war.[10]

Prophetic words! He proceeded, with justification, to lambast the Disarmament Conference, set up by the League of Nations, as

> really an Armament Conference, vainly trying to regulate armaments; . . . because not one of the Powers has, or ever had, the very slightest intention of disarming or of refraining from pursuing researches into the newest and most frightful methods of slaughter with all the diligence that terror can inspire.

He argued that "disarmament will not prevent war." On the contrary, the more frightful weapons became, the more they would enforce peace:

> What will London do when it finds itself approached by a crowd of aeroplanes, capable of destroying it in half an hour? London will surrender. . . . But our own air squadrons will have already started to make the enemies' capitals surrender. From Paris to

Moscow, from Stockholm to Rome, the white flags will go up in every city . . . and the most inglorious war in history will peter out in general ridicule.

The same argument had long been used, and it still lives on in the belief that nuclear weapons are the ultimate deterrent. When, in 1945, Shaw came to write his Preface for *Geneva*, he had changed his mind:

Some of them [the Allies] are now consoling themselves with the hope that the atomic bomb has made war impossible. The hope has often been entertained before. . . . At every development it is complained that war is no longer justifiable as a test of heroic personal qualities, and demonstrated that it has become too ruinous to be tolerated as an institution. War and imperialist diplomacy persist none the less.[11]

Much of his 1934 broadcast was taken up with an attack on the post-1918 policies of the victorious governments and their financial pundits. They had crippled Germany with reparations which had, in turn, ruined the countries which received them. Money had then been lent to Germany to pay its debts and to restore its industry, so tariffs had to be put up against German goods. British debts to the United States had led to financial collapse. The only solution was to wipe the slate clean of all international debts.

And now comes the question—when we have wiped the slate, what then? Are we to continue to live under a dictatorship of bankers and ship-owners, with cabinet ministers as their puppets and scapegoats? If so, what will happen? . . . As the waste of life under Boss Syndicalism is much worse than the slaughter in old-fashioned war, civilization may be in greater danger from peace than from war.

Finally he turned his guns on the British Empire:

As between the present arrangement of forty-five million pink men sitting on the heads of three hundred million brown and yellow men, and the international co-operation insisted on by Mr Wells, I am on the side of Mr Wells; and Wells and I are both much cleverer and more disinterested than the Boss Syndicalists.

I do not know what effect these words had upon those despised persons "whose routine of dullness" had "only quite lately begun to be enlivened by the wireless," but I do know one schoolboy who chortled with delight as he listened to the old sage. What, however, is apparent to that same listener now is that the broadcast might have been made some years earlier. Its wit obscured the fact that the world of 1934 was different from that of the 1920s. Men in brown shirts were wrecking Jewish shops in Berlin, and their imitators in London were doing the same while, in the month of Shaw's broadcast, their counterparts in Paris attempted to seize power in three days of street fighting, and in Vienna Shaw's socialist friends were being crushed by the artillery of a little dictator backed by Mussolini. Of all this, there was not one word in Shaw's view of Britain's possible future.

In *Geneva* one of the characters says, "You know very well that after a certain age a man has only one speech." Would it be too unkind to suggest that sometimes the cap seemed to fit the author himself? When, two and half years after the broadcast, a center-left government in Madrid was faced with a right-wing military revolt, supported by Italian and German arms and fighting men, Shaw's usual speech about parliamentary democracy seemed peculiarly out of touch with new circumstances. Today, many historians, whether of Left or Right, see the Spanish Civil War as determining much of what has followed, as one of the catalytic moments in modern history. At the time large numbers of Britons, as of other nationalities, saw the Republic as the last barrier against the spread of fascism in Europe, and its survival as the last opportunity of preventing a European war. The earliest opinion polls in Britain, taken in 1938 and 1939, showed that fewer than 10 percent supported General Franco, while a growing majority supported the Republic. These feelings produced the sustained and widespread campaign of Aid for Spain.

Early in 1937, the writer Nancy Cunard asked all available British writers which side they supported and published their replies in a pamphlet. Five supported Franco, sixteen were neutral, and some one hundred supported the Republic. Shaw's reply fitted none of the categories. It came too late for inclusion and had to be printed on the back cover of the pamphlet. He wrote,

> In Spain the Right and the Left so thoroughly disgraced themselves in the turns they took in trying to govern their country before the Right revolted, that it is impossible to say which of them is the more incompetent. Spain must choose for itself; it is not really our business, though of course the Capitalist government have done everything they possibly could to help General Franco. I, as a Communist, am generally on the Left; but that does not commit me to support the British Party Parliamentary

system, and its continental imitators, of which I have the lowest opinion.

At present the Capitalist powers seem to have secured a victory over the General by what they call non-interference, meaning their very active interference on his side; but it is unlikely that the last word will be with him. Meanwhile, I shall not shout about it.[12]

To many of Shaw's admirers, it seemed as if his preoccupation with the follies of parliamentary government, his belief that fascism was better than liberalism, and his rather lofty socialism blinded him to the real problem of the time.

On the eve of the Spanish war, Shaw was writing his political play of the era, *Geneva*. In April 1939 the third act was one of the first dramatic pieces to be televised in Britain. All that can be said of the first two acts is that it is hard to believe that they came from the same pen as *Major Barbara* and *Saint Joan*. For the benefit of televiewers they were summarized by Shaw in the *Times*. Presumably it was assumed in 1939 that anyone owning a television set also read the *Times*. His telescoping of the two acts explained how there came to the office of the Committee for International Co-operation in Geneva one morning five people, each with a grievance for the Committee to remedy. Begonia Brown, the typist who runs the office,

> has not the faintest idea of how to set about it until the first visitor, a persecuted Jew, suggests that she apply to the International Court at The Hague for a warrant against his persecutors. The second visitor is a British democrat who has been locked out of a colonial legislature to which he has been elected. The third is the widow of a Central American President who has been shot. . . .
> The fourth is an English Bishop whose grievance is that the Bolshevists have converted his footman to Communism. The fifth is a Russian Commissar who has to complain on behalf of his Government that the Church of England, by number 18 of the 39 Articles, declares that all Russians are accursed. The Bishop drops dead on discovering that he has dined with the Commissar under the impression that he was a Conservative; . . .[13]

The third act takes place before the International Court, with the Judge, the Secretary of the League of Nations, and Sir Orpheus Midlander, the British Foreign Secretary, present. The accused are Signor "Bardo" Bombardone, Herr Ernest Battler, and General Flanco de Fortinbras. Commissar Posky, one of the plaintiffs, is based on Maxim

Litvinov, Soviet commissar for foreign affairs in the 1930s, who was distinguished for his support of collective security and his attempts to build an alliance of Britain, France, the Soviet Union, and Czechoslovakia. Litvinov was a cultured Jew who had lived in England and had married an Englishwoman. Hence the Bishop's error.

The hearing before the International Court allows Shaw to air some of his favorite themes and to ridicule the pretensions both of the dictators and of the British establishment. When Herr Battler asks the British Foreign Secretary if he does not agree that the world should be ruled by the most advanced race, he replies,

> With certain reservations, yes. I do not like the term "advanced race." I greatly mistrust advanced people. In my experience they are very difficult to work with, and often most disreputable in their private lives. They seldom attend divine service.[14]

There are the usual shots at liberal democracy. Accused of the "murder and destruction of democracy in Europe," Bombardone replies,

> One cannot destroy what never existed. Besides, these things are not my business. My business is government. I give my people good government, as far as their folly and ignorance permit. What more do they need? (7:133)

When a Deaconess bursts into the Court and calls on the dictators to turn to God's work, Bombardone replies,

> We are here to do it for Him. If we neglect it the world falls into the chaos called Liberty and Democracy, in which nothing is done except talk while the people perish. . . . His political work cannot be done by everybody; they have neither the time nor the brains nor the divine call for it. (7:142)

Is this Shaw, or is this merely a representation of Mussolini? A similar question comes to mind when Commissar Posky speaks:

> These gentlemen talk of their countries. But they do not own their countries. Their people do not own the land they starve in. Their countries are owned by a handful of landlords and capitalists who allow them to live in it on condition that they work like bees and keep barely enough of the honey to keep themselves miserably alive. Russia belongs to the Russians. (7:152)

However, Shaw can put no favorable speech into the mouth of Battler. His views are brutally Hitlerian:

> . . . I have stretched out my hand and lifted my country from the gutter into which you and your allies were trampling it, and made it once more the terror of Europe, though the danger is in your own guilty souls and not in any malice of mine. And mark you, the vision does not stop at my frontiers, nor at any frontier. (7:143)

The best defense that Flanco can put up to the accusation that he had devastated his own country and indiscriminately massacred its inhabitants is to say,

> That is my profession. I am a soldier; and my business is to devastate the strongholds of the enemies of my country, and slaughter their inhabitants.

And he adds as his excuse,

> I stand simply for government by gentlemen as against government by cads. (7:148)

When all have finished arguing, the Judge sums up:

> Your objective is domination: your weapons fire and poison, starvation and ruin, extermination by every means known to science. You have reduced one another to such a condition of terror that no atrocity makes you recoil and say that you will die rather than commit it. You call this patriotism, courage, glory. There are a thousand good things to be done in your countries. They remain undone for hundreds of years; but the fire and the poison are always up to date. If this be not scoundrelism what is scoundrelism? I give you up as hopeless. Man is a failure as a political animal. The creative forces which produce him must produce something better. (7:154–55)

There are some shrewd knocks at British policy. Bombardone tells the court,

> I must explain to the court that England is no longer of any consequence apart from me. I have dictated her policy for years. (7:121)

Between the first writing of the play and its performance, the British foreign secretary, Sir Anthony Eden, was forced to resign, very largely as the result of Italian pressure on the British prime minister, Neville Chamberlain. A moment after Bombardone's claim to have dictated English policy, Battler tells Sir Orpheus Midlander,

> I tore up your peace treaty and threw the pieces in your face. You did nothing. I took your last Locarno pact and marched 18,000 soldiers through it. I threw down a frontier and doubled the size and power of my realm in spite of your teeth. What did you do? Nothing.

Sir Orpheus replies,

> Of course we did nothing. It did not suit us to do anything. . . .

At this point Bombardone tells him,

> You are quite right Excellency. It was your folly and France's that blew Ernest [Hitler] up the greasy pole of political ambition. (7:122)

As always, there are shafts of wisdom.

At one point Bombardone reminds Battler that he must have Jewish blood since everyone alive today must be descended from Abraham. When the Deaconess asserts that the solution to the world's problems is that we should love one another, the Secretary of the League of Nations tells her,

> It turns out that we do not and cannot love oneanother—that the problem before us is how to establish peace among people who heartily dislike oneanother, and have very good reasons for doing so: in short, that the human race does not at present consist exclusively or even largely of likeable persons. (7:144)

There are two passages in the play which seem to look forward to the future. At one point the Judge suggests that what were later called war criminals should be brought to trial. And the play ends with a scene that appears to foreshadow the consequences of ecological disaster. What Shaw was indeed doing was producing a deus ex machina to bring his play to a climax, but it does perhaps speak to us. As the Judge gives his verdict the telephone rings, and he announces that scientists have discovered that the Earth is about to make a quantum leap into a new orbit. Ice

will cover the whole globe and even the polar bears will freeze to death.
He rises and tells the assembled company,

> Fellow citizens: this is the end. The end of war, of law, of leaders
> and foreign secretaries, of judges and generals. A moment ago we
> were important persons: the fate of Europe seemed to depend on
> us. What are we now? Democracy, Fascism, Communism: how
> much do they matter? Your totalitarian Catholic Church: does it
> still seem so very totalitarian? (7:158)

The scene breaks up in confusion. Of course, the news is a fabrication,
and Shaw gets in a dig at the credulity of a public, ignorant of science,
when scientists speak. Clement Attlee, the British prime minister when
the atom bombs were dropped on Japan, later confessed that not one
member of his cabinet understood the bomb or what was involved in its
explosion. Shaw's quips often held more wisdom than appeared at first
hearing.

There is an epilogue to Shaw's pronouncements on the events of the
decade. A little more than four months after *Geneva* was televised, Germany invaded Poland. Three days later Britain and France were at war
with Germany. Within a few days Poland collapsed, and the Soviet
Union, in accordance with a secret clause in its nonaggression pact with
Germany, seized the eastern territory of Poland which the victorious
powers at Versailles had intended to allocate to czarist Russia. The first
phase of the war had ended without Britain being involved on land.
There followed the months of the "phoney war" when there was no
fighting in Europe.

At this point, Shaw's was one of many voices calling for peace. His
views were delivered, with all his pugnacity and wit, in a long letter to the
New Statesman and Nation. The editor, Kingsley Martin, felt it necessary to
declare, "Manifestly, we are not to be taken as endorsing the views expressed by our contributors. . . ." Shaw was his usual unorthodox self:

> The war in Poland is over. . . . [Hitler] was able to say that as
> Poland's cause is lost we have no further excuse for continuing the
> war. Whereupon we threw off the mask of knight errantry and
> avowed flatly that we did not care two hoots about Poland and
> were out, on our old balance of power lines, to disable Germany,
> which we now called abolishing Hitlerism. . . .
>
> Meanwhile we are enduring all the vagaries, from mere discom-
> fort to financial ruin and the breaking up of our homes, of the
> ineptest Military Communism. Powers which no Plantagenet king
> or Fascist dictator would dream of claiming have been granted to

any unqualified person who offered to assume them, including an enterprising burglar. Whatever our work in life may be, we have been ordered to stop doing it and stand by. Wherever our wives and children are they have been transported to somewhere else, with or without the mothers. Our theatres and cinemas have been closed; and our schools, colleges and public libraries occupied by the military bureaucracy.

But, Shaw remarked, we were told that if we did not stop Hitler, he would go on to world conquest.

Stalin will see that nobody, not even our noble selves, will do anything of the sort; and Franklin Roosevelt will be surprised to find himself exactly of Stalin's opinion in this matter. Had we not better wait until Herr Hitler tries to do it, and then stop him with Stalin and Roosevelt at our back?

Something like this did happen, but not before much else had occurred. Shaw ended by drawing attention to a similar letter which H. G. Wells had written to the *Times,* but denying that, as Wells thought, the war would end civilization. It would kill many, including himself and Wells,

but the world will get on without us; and the world will have had an immense gratification of the primitive instinct that is at the bottom of all this mischief and that we never mention: to wit pugnacity, sheer pugnacity for its own sake, that much admired quality of which an example has just been so strikingly set us by the Irish Republican Army [which was then carrying out a bombing campaign in mainland Britain].[15]

How does one judge this letter in the light of history? Mythology has it that, once the war started, all Britons rallied to combat the foe, even though their country might stand alone, that the nation put on its gas mask and marched behind Chamberlain when he went to war, as it had fallen in behind him when he went to Munich. But it was not quite like that, and reading Shaw's letter should remind us that, at the time, it was all much more complex than some versions of history would suggest.

If the decade which began with the Wall Street crash and ended in war did belong to the Devil, what was Shaw's role in it? Certainly he was, as he had always been, something of a demon, prodding his goad into philistines of all persuasions, taunting the smug, distressing the comfortable, always unorthodox, often brilliantly right, frequently brilliantly wrong, always saying what he had to say with elegance and wit, perhaps making some people think. But also he was the permitted revolutionary, the licensed court jester who could be outrageous without having to suffer the consequences of his views. Churchill once rather unworthily taunted him, "His spiritual home is in Russia; but he lives comfortably in England, which he derides and abuses on every occasion."[16] Maynard Keynes could growl, "But Shaw is such a dogmatist by now that it makes but little difference to his enthusiasm whether it is Stalin or Mussolini. He would have a good word for the Pope (as we see in St Joan), if it were not that His Holiness is so mild and broadminded."[17]

Perhaps it would be truer and fairer to say that anyone who in the 1930s simply accepted Shaw's opinions would have been very foolish indeed, but that those who refused to examine their own opinions in the light of Shaw's ideas would have been even more foolish.

Notes

1. *Observer* (London), 2 August 1931, quoted in T. F. Evans, "Myopia or Utopia? Shaw in Russia" in *SHAW 5: Shaw Abroad,* ed. Rodelle Weintraub (University Park: Pennsylvania State University Press, 1985), p. 138.

2. Preface to *The Millionairess, Collected Plays with Their Prefaces,* ed. Dan H. Laurence (London: Max Reinhardt, 1970–74), 6: 880.

3. Preface to *The Apple Cart, Collected Plays with Their Prefaces* 6: 259.

4. Bernard Shaw, *The Intelligent Woman's Guide to Socialism, Capitalism, Sovietism and Fascism* (Harmondsworth: Pelican, 1937; rpt. 1982), p. 481. Subsequent references to *IWG* appear parenthetically.

5. "Further Meditation on Shaw's 'Geneva,' " *Collected Plays with Their Prefaces* 7: 173–74.

6. Quoted in Evans, p. 140.

7. "Stalin-Wells Continued," *New Statesman and Nation* 8 (n.s.) (17 November 1934), 709.

8. "Stalin on Wells: A Comment by Bernard Shaw," *New Statesman and Nation* 8 (3 November 1934), 614.

9. Quoted in Evans, p. 136.

10. All quotations are from the *Listener* 9, no. 265 (7 February 1934). For Shotover, *Heartbreak House,* Act III: "Learn your business as an Englishman. . . . Navigation. Learn it and live; or leave it and be damned" (*Collected Plays with Their Prefaces* 5: 177).

11. Preface to *Geneva, Collected Plays with Their Prefaces* 7: 24.

12. *Authors Take Sides on the Spanish War,* ed. Nancy Cunard (London: *Left Review* pamphlet, 1937).

13. "Telescoping 'Geneva,' " *Collected Plays with Their Prefaces* 7: 171.

14. *Geneva, Collected Plays with Their Prefaces* 7: 152. Subsequent references to *Geneva* appear parenthetically.

15. "Uncommon Sense About the War," *New Statesman and Nation* 18 (7 October 1939), 483–84.

16. *Sunday Pictorial* (16 August 1934), quoted in Evans, p. 139.

17. "Shaw on Wells on Stalin: A Comment by J. M. Keynes," *New Statesman and Nation* 8 (10 November 1934), 653.

REVIEWS AND CHECKLIST

Reviews

Marx versus Shaw

Harry Morrison. *The Socialism of Bernard Shaw.* Jefferson, N.C., and London: McFarland, 1989. 208 pp. $25.95.

The Socialism of Bernard Shaw resonates peculiarly from the outset. By the time one reaches the midpoint of Harry Morrison's book, the feeling is overwhelming. Except that the chronology goes through World War II, it might very well have been published in 1889, not 1989. From first to last Morrison judges Shaw strictly according to the tenets of "Scientific Socialism," a theoretical Marxism that saves some of its harshest comments for the "state capitalism" of the Soviet Union. Born in 1912 and a member of the World Socialist Movement since 1938, Morrison knows his Marx. Given a more balanced approach, such a writer working independently could teach us much about Shaw. But Morrison is no genial scholar avidly pursuing the life of the mind. For him, Shaw's unforgivable failing was not adhering lockstep to Marx's theories. One would never guess from Morrison's account that Shaw's devotion to socialism was ethically based and the result of sophisticated thinking in political economy.

Morrison's asserted aim is threefold: "to present in broad perspective, the basics of (1) Fabian Socialism as promulgated in the essays, books, plays and prefaces to the plays of Shaw; (2) a detailed treatment of him and others on some tangentially related areas as religion and Darwinian evolution; and (3) a running documentation indicating the basis and extent of the Shavian opposition to, rather than acceptance of, Scientific Socialism." Morrison's real aim is to show that Shaw was consistently misled in his politics—misled because he did not follow the path of Scientific Socialism advocated by Marx and Engels, and followed by Morrison—and to censure Shaw for his ignorance of the one true path.

Morrison bases his view of Shaw on isolated passages from several prefaces and plays and some miscellaneous works. Not only does the bulk of Shaw fall outside his purview, he seems to have gleaned the works only for ammunition to use against Shaw. Morrison himself acknowledges the problem, which he sees as Shaw's "outlandish contradictions of himself, by himself, that makes quoting him risky unless one attempts to read *everything* that he wrote—a tough assignment!" Excluded from consideration are editions of Shaw's own political pronouncements, central to any discussion of his politics—his *What I Really Wrote About the War;* Louis Crompton's *The Road to Equality,* and Dan H. Laurence's *Platform and Pulpit.* Morrison does not even include *Fabian Essays* in their entirety—all of which Shaw edited and two of which he wrote, along with his prefaces to the 1908 and 1931 reprints—but only Shaw's "Economic Basis of Socialism," "his contribution to the *Fabian Essays*," according to Morrison. Not reading Shaw, he makes no use of Shaw's commentors, except for some biographical material. There is no mention of Eric Bentley's classic analysis of political economy, now four decades old, in *Bernard Shaw,* or of more recent examinations by Paul A. Hummert and Willard Wolfe. Even more revealingly, from the well-established Marxist critique of Shaw, Morrison excludes the major voices—Alick West, Christopher Caudwell, Maurice Dobb, and Dmitri Mirsky. Where indeed is Leon Trotsky's 1925 study *Whither England?* with its discussion of Shaw? Instead of understanding Shaw, Morrison invokes Marx. Oversimplifications and misunderstandings are inevitable.

Why does the author target Shaw and Fabian Socialism for "debunking" in the first place? According to Morrison,

> The sole justification would seem to be that Shaw, through his extreme volubility to the point of literary diarrhea, has made it necessary. . . . Despite protest by more knowledgeable Marxists, Shaw, by his spate of writings and criticisms, has left a legacy of purported Marxism and criticism of Marxism which should be dealt with by those who would do battle with mass confusion on that subject.

Still Morrison finds it "doubtful that many of those who read his plays bother about his prefaces," and he wonders "how one so seemingly bright could make so many silly errors of judgment and of fact." Morrison feels forced to consider Shaw because of his own more pressing agenda: "to organize politically for world socialism and nothing short of it."

Certainly Marxist insight into Shaw can deepen our understanding. When Morrison explains how Shaw diverges from classic Marxist thought, as in his early discussions of value and commodity, he can be

useful, though covering the same ground marked out by earlier commentators. However, even these brief discussions degenerate into dia-
tribes against Shaw—who variously misunderstood Marx, was fooled
into other postures, or was just plain inconsistent. Throughout, he
blames Shaw for his "unreasonable . . . reasoning. . . . With Shaw, fact
had become so intermixed with fiction in the creation of his prefaces,
plays, and his political and religious speeches that he found it a plain
nuisance to separate truth from the mélange in his brain." Morrison,
whose sense of humor is imperceptible, takes Shaw literally when he
should not.

Morrison devotes a chapter to Shaw's "patriotism," supposedly evidence of Shaw's capitalistic leanings. Morrison asserts that Shaw, though
calling himself an Irishman, regarded himself as British chiefly because
he supported Britain in her wars, including the Boer War and World
Wars I and II. But for Shaw, who thought of himself as "a sojourner on
this planet and not a native of it," the question of homeland was fraught
with complexity and ambivalence, and Morrision does not understand
Shaw's view that in war you side with the lesser evil against the greater.
Far from being hailed as a bulwark of middle-class patriotism, Shaw's
1914 pamphlet *Common Sense About the War* unleashed a barrage of anti-
Shaw vilification so strong that Prime Minister Asquith's son declared
that Shaw "ought to be shot" and former President Theodore Roosevelt
called Shaw "a blue rumped ape."

Misinterpretation is compounded by misreading. According to Morrison, while the social-minded complained about the indignities associated
with the dole for the unemployed, Shaw "was irritated for the opposite
reason," denouncing the recipients. Morrison charges Britain with reducing unemployment only through war and seeking greatness by trying to
destroy European civilization, concluding that Shaw "must have felt it
was a shame that this newly great England was extinguishing those heroic anti-Parliamentarian dictators, Benito Mussolini and Adolf Hitler."
However, the passages that Morrison quotes from *The Intelligent Woman's
Guide to Socialism, Capitalism, Sovietism and Fascism* are wrenched from
context and mean something quite different. Shaw wanted to demonstrate that British money should be kept at home to make jobs; otherwise
a permanent class of unemployed results. Although starving people will
resort to violence, when put on the dole these same people remain doc-
ile, having been demoralized into impotence. Moreover, in the passage
immediately following, Shaw himself draws attention to the problem of
unemployment:

> After the war . . . the capitalists failed to find employment for no
> less than two million demobilized soldiers. . . . If these men had

not been given money to live on they would have taken it by violence. Accordingly the Government had to take millions of spare money from the capitalists and give it to the demobilized men.

Clearly Shaw separates himself from the capitalists.

In *Sixteen Self Sketches,* Shaw asserts that the "professional and penniless younger son classes are the revolutionary element." Morrison sees that statement as Shaw's "belief in the revolutionary potential of the middle class . . . a sort of chosen people," adding that it was "not likely that even Shaw ever regarded those 'penniless' sons of the industrialists and merchants of Britain as having been enslaved." Intent on making Shaw a middle-class capitalist, Morrison completely misses the autobiographical impetus here, and would have dismissed it had it been called to his attention, all such "influences" being too "silly" to consider, according to a prefatory comment. However, in the Preface to *Immaturity,* Shaw, the downstart son of a downstart, sounded a refrain he constantly reiterated—that he endured a kind of poverty worse than the absolutely poor, that talk of the middle class "is meaningless except when it is used by an economist to denote the man of business who stands in the middle between land and capital on the one hand, and labor on the other, and organizes business for both." Furthermore, Shaw separated himself from the middle class precisely because he doubted its revolutionary potential. In an 1890 lecture, Shaw voiced his alarm at the "danger that Fabianism, with its numerous recruits from the middle class, may taint Socialism with the idea of self-sacrifice. The message of Socialism at present is one of rebellion."

Morrison's insistence on Shaw's middle-class identification, apparently necessary for indictment, again shows peculiarly selective reading, as a quoted passage from *The Intelligent Woman's Guide* indicates. Though Shaw identifies the members of the Fabian Society as having middle-class roots, the Fabians "were the first to see that Capitalism was reducing their own class to the condition of a proletariat." Morrison insists that this recognition was based on nothing but a Fabian desire for consumer goods. But in an earlier (omitted) section of the passage Shaw elucidates: "I had to become a clerk at fifteen. I was a proletarian undisguised. . . . I wanted a proletarian party." The rest of the omitted passage is an indictment of capitalism:

. . . the only chance of securing anything more than a slave's share in the national income for anyone but the biggest capitalists or the cleverest professional or business men lay in a combination of all the proletarians without distinction of class or country to put an end to Capitalism by developing the communistic side of our civilization until Communism became the dominant principle in society, and mere owning, profiteering, and genteel idling were disabled and discredited.

Here Shaw explicitly advocates a society that transcends those distinctions of class and country that Morrison accuses the Fabians of supporting.

Given Shaw's disturbing refusal to recognize the plight of Jews in Nazi Germany, Morrison's outrage at what he calls Shaw's "embrace . . . of Fascists and Nazis" at first appears more firmly grounded. Finding support in the Preface to *The Millionairess*, Morrison sees Shaw's repudiation of the "anti-Jewish program of the Hitlerites" as arising exclusively from "sympathy for his friend Albert Einstein who had been forced into exile by Hitler." This is a reasonable reading, since Shaw insists on the difference between Einstein and "the masses." But, however problematic some of Shaw's later pronouncements, it is not reasonable to state that "there was not all that much difference between the stated goals of the Nazis, and those of the Fabian Society and of Shaw, in his political writings."

That the Preface to *The Millionairess* was written in 1935, not 1936, the year Morrison gives, is a small matter, but Morrison's cavalierness with dates (here and elsewhere) is part of a larger pattern of idiosyncratic use of evidence to support a preconceived thesis. Blinded by the beam in his own eye, the author attacks Shaw as an anti-Semite, but Morrison is himself highly incensed when Shaw mentions Marx's Jewish heritage. Thus, Morrison provides two extended fulminations alleged to demonstrate that Marx " 'resigned' from the Jewish cult." Even more distressingly, Morrison indicts "Jewish bourgeois organizations" in Germany for not aiding radical workers, suggesting "had it not been for Hitler's anti-Jewish campaign and his attempt to exterminate Jews *as* Jews, there would very well have been widespread Jewish support for National Socialism." Such unconscionable post-Holocaust accusations forfeit Morrison whatever respect his years and labor for a cause had warranted.

Naturally Morrison's orientation adheres to the Scientific Socialist view in discussing Creative Evolution and religion. Naturally, too, Shaw is found wanting, since Shaw argued against determinism, whether Darwinian causes or Marxist laws of history. It is also predictable that Morrison regards religion as useful "for primitive people" only, while today it functions solely as "a pillar of class society—world capitalism." But must he be scandalized that Shaw would speak in the parish church at Ayot St. Lawrence? Shaw's religious views, including Creative Evolution, are once again evidence only of a "negative attitude toward Socialism." That Morrison's own simplistic brand of Marxism is itself a form of fundamentalism never occurs to him.

The sole value of the book lies in two letters by Shaw that do not appear in the *Collected Letters*. Written in response to an article, "Shaw vs. Marx," by the British Socialist Clifford Allen, they are addressed to the editor of the *Western Socialist* (Boston), a journal that Morrison was associated with for many years and that published Allen's article in the May 1943 issue. That piece, appended to the book with two others, was prompted by Shaw's review of a new edition of Marx's selected works issued on the sixtieth anniversary of his death. Reading Allen is like reading Morrison. Both denounce Shaw's assertion that Marxism "has produced a new civilization in Russia." Allen's aim is publicly to correct and chastise Shaw, who presents "a mumble jumble of ideas," "is outside his sphere" of expertise, and whose "knowledge of Marx's theories is painfully lacking," comments that the less circumspect might turn against Morrison by substituting Shaw for Marx. According to Morrison, "a copy of the article was sent, as a courtesy, to Mr. Shaw—then in his 87th year."(!)

After bombardment by the Allen-Morrison view of the world, one is jolted by the Shaw letters. It is as if the Shavian ghost has risen in righteous indignation to set the record straight, collaborating in this review from beyond the grave. Since no one can speak more eloquently than Shaw on Shaw, eighty-seven years or not, here is the essence of his defense:

> I am much indebted to Mr. Allan [*sic*] for having . . . called my attention to *The Western Socialist*. But I am sorry to have to add that if by some miracle a Socialist government were established in the United States tomorrow, its first painful necessity would be to shoot Mr. Allan. That is the worst of being a thorough-going out-and-out revolutionist. If the revolution is successful they have all to be shot by their old comrades because, as the victorious socialists must take on the government of the country instantly, and the change from capitalist to socialist institutions cannot be instantaneous and its new rulers take some time to learn their business, they are denounced by the thorough-going out-and-outers as betrayers of The Cause, no better than the bold bourgeois rulers. The Possiblist and the Impossiblist may be old friends and comrades; but the Possiblist must shoot the Impossiblist because half a loaf is better than no bread.

Certain that "nature does not make a Socialist world at once with a wave of a Marxian wand," Shaw, the former vestryman, concludes that practical "experience will certainly knock all day-dreaming out of Mr. Allen; and until he gets it he will waste his time and other people's in trying to discredit the better informed Socialists as he is trying to discredit me. However his sympathies are all right. He may have the makings of a good Fabian in him yet."

Despite Shaw's magnanimous close, he soon discovered how wrong he was about Allen, whose second article reiterated his points with greater strength and length (3,500 words), attacking Shaw as an "anti-Socialist" and "a bourgeois thinker" who "has yet to learn the first elementary principles of Socialism." Shaw replied to the editor of the *Western Socialist* with the following:

> The packet of your issues since May with which you threaten me has not yet arrived. I hope it never may. You forget the old precept "No use giving tracts to a missionary."
>
> My time—of which there is so little left—is too precious to be wasted on W.[sic] Allen, whose utter ignorance of the real world created a vacuum into which Marx (what he could understand and misunderstand of him) rushed with irresistible force. Experience alone can drive it out.

The intractable Allen returned the favor with yet another article, "Shaw Evades the Issue." Perhaps the most revealing aspect of the exchange is the portrait of Shaw that emerges, vitally alive, alert, resilient, showing no diminution of powers. He still labors to be understood and is intensely interested in what is written about him. The great wit, the literary facility, and the larger vision are all intact.

Shaw's comments of more than a century ago in the essay "The Illusions of Socialism" summarize his position and account for Morrison's inability to deal with it. Having divided socialists into two groups, "the fanatics" and "the more or less practical men," Shaw states, "Neither in Socialism or anything else is it true that whatever is not white is black." For Shaw exhibited in his socialism exactly the complexity he exhibited in all areas of his life, his own individualism remaining unabated despite his ideological commitment to collectivism. He carried his socialistic convictions with such vigor throughout his long life that he was instrumental in shaping the course of British socialism. Despite Shaw's hyperbolic insistence that he was a "born Communist," he came to Fabianism by a circuitous route, and only by multiple conversions. Converted first to the economics of Henry George, then to Marx, then to Fabianism, his thinking continued its revelatory arc. Once a Fabian, Shaw took pains to separate himself from the other major streams of socialist thought in the nineteenth century—the Utopian, the Christian Socialist, *and* the Marxist. Like Fabius who waited for the right moment to strike, Shaw had a latent militant streak, so that in 1930 he would no longer be certain "that

Morris was not right" in his revolutionary zeal; yet still he shouldered mundane tasks as he appealed for social justice. Since man's perfectability could not be fulfilled in the present society, Shaw's view of contemporary man was essentially gloomy, even as he clung to his vision of a remodeled world.

Morrison's unrelenting worldview results in a repellent, skewed caricature of Shaw. He makes no real attempt to understand Shaw or his socialism in either the artistic or the social and political arena. The author is not concerned to discover why Fabianism attracted Shaw over all other forms of economic ideology, or to trace the origin and growth of Shaw's political thinking, or to consider how more than six decades of socialistic commitment affected the course of the life history. For all these reasons, Morrison's book unfortunately seems far more likely to aggravate than to clear up the "mass confusion" he deplores on the subjects of Shaw, Marx, and socialism. In the duel of Marx versus Shaw, Shaw loses.

Sally Peters

Failures of the Fabian

Michael Holroyd. *Bernard Shaw: A Biography. Volume II, 1898–1918: The Pursuit of Power.* New York: Random House, 1989. 420 pp. Illustrated. $24.95.

In the quest to give Shaw a shape for the world to contemplate, one of Michael Holroyd's predecessors is Rodin, and this account of Shaw's middle years, *The Pursuit of Power,* includes the playwright's comment on the immortality conferred by the sculptor: "at least I was sure of a place in the biographical dictionaries a thousand years hence as: 'Shaw, Bernard: subject of a bust by Rodin: otherwise unknown' " (184). If the entry in the biographical dictionaries should turn out to read "Shaw, Bernard: subject of a biography by Holroyd: otherwise unknown," then what sort of figure would posterity be left with?

One indication is the way in which this second volume, covering the years 1898–1918, begins and ends. The first thing that happens in the book is that Shaw falls downstairs. When the fall occurred, at the beginning of his (apparently unconsummated) marriage, he was already on crutches, and for a time afterward he had to struggle unsuccessfully with a wheelchair. He explained that he could not wheel it, "since when worked with one hand only, it simply spins round & round. . . . I no longer feel any confidence in my ultimate recovery" (3). What we have here is a kind of frontispiece: an image that offers a good idea of what is to come over the next four hundred pages. The volume is full of verbal pictures of its subject falling, in various ways, and spinning round and round instead of heading forward.

A few pages from the end, Shaw is speaking to an audience at King's College, London, when he feels a crippling back pain, "as if my backbone had turned into a red-hot poker" (400). He discovers afterwards that Granville Barker's second wife, Helen, had been sitting behind him and eyeing his backbone with a look of intense hatred. One of the numerous sad events in the final part of the book is the breakup of Granville Barker's marriage with Lillah McCarthy. Shaw, who was close to each, acted as a mediator between them—without success. As Holroyd puts it, he "was now placed in one of those awkward and unrewarding positions for which nature seemed to have intended him" (397).

Altogether the story in this volume ends badly. The final section also tells within its eleven pages of the deaths, in the war, of friends' sons—Alan Campbell, Robert Gregory, Tomarcher, and others—and the wounding of Robert Loraine and St. John Ervine. Even Shaw's reading of part of *Back to Methuselah,* to Granville Barker and Helen, is a depressing failure. The final event is the death of Shaw's sister Lucy, who dies shortly after he has conventionally reassured her that she "will be all right presently" (403). The concluding paragraph describes her cremation.

Shaw's life (in the first two-thirds of the three-volume biography, at any rate) is given the shape of tragedy rather than comedy, and Holroyd's Shaw is for the most part a frustrated, almost pitiable figure: a man who is busy failing at just about everything he undertakes. The strategy of the whole three-volume structure is indicated in the middle of this volume: "The philosophy of violence that makes its appearance in Shaw's later life was a product of his sexual and then his political neutering; and a reaction to having been made to feel as ineffectual as his mother had believed him to be" (237). First volume: sexual neutering; second volume: political neutering; third volume: retreat into fantasy and violence. After the unsuccessful Search for Love comes the equally unfulfilled Pursuit of Power, as a substitute for what has been painfully unattained in the first part of Shaw's life. "To overcome early bitterness he had removed himself from the intimate thing and forced his way into politics—but now felt pessimistically uncertain of his place in public life" (366). Shaw's committee work, which is described at some length, is presented as a substitute for more intimate satisfactions: he "discovered in his commitment to the Society of Authors . . . some of the hopes other men look for and disenchantments they may find, in romance" (224). But all of this work—for the Society of Authors, against the censorship, for a settlement in Ireland, against the drift into war—all of it seems to come to nothing. In all his quixotic efforts to help solve the Irish question, for example, he "united England and Ireland only in their determination to ignore everything he recommended" (387), and his efforts to avert the execution of Roger Casement proved equally futile.

One of the reasons that Holroyd pushes Shaw so far in the direction of tragedy is that he reads Shaw's own expressions of frustration and failure in a literal way. He gives too little weight, it seems to me, to the element of *play* in Shaw's writing, and he does not sufficiently take into account the artist's aesthetic delight in comic exaggeration. He quotes (silently dropping a phrase about "prodigious expenditure of nervous energy") a passage from a letter to Trebitsch describing successful speeches that Shaw had given in Glasgow in 1903:

> I have hardly yet quite recovered from the self-loathing which such triumphs produce. . . . I always suffer torments of remorse when the degrading exhibition is over. . . . I am not at all ashamed of what I said: it was excellent sense; but the way I said it—ugh! All that assumption of stupendous earnestness—merely to drive a little common sense into a crowd, like nails into a very tough board—leaves one empty, exhausted, disgusted. (60)

There is undoubtedly an expression here of some genuine revulsion, but to give the passage simply as an illustration of "the disgust Shaw himself felt at the Shavian publicity phenomenon" is, I think, to miss something of Shaw's tone. Pulling against the sense of failure here is the creative gaiety of the exultant artist in the uttering of such phrases. But Holroyd's emphasis is almost always on the failures of the man, rather than on the gaiety and energy of the comic artist, or on the triumphs of the dramatist whose plays established themselves on the London stage during these years. Holroyd explains the two-year gap between the completion of *Man and Superman* and the beginning of *John Bull's Other Island* by saying that Shaw was "*held back* partly by the business of turning his comedies into books but also by the familiar *difficulty* of seeing them performed" (italics added), and then he introduces the writing of *John Bull's Other Island* with the comment that "London having failed him, he was preparing to return in his imagination to Dublin" (81). The undeniable success of *John Bull's Other Island* at the Court Theatre in 1904 is qualified by the observation that "success and failure . . . lie close together" (100).

Shaw had reservations about Rodin's bust of him. This volume quotes his comment to Jacob Epstein: "I am a comedian as well as a philosopher; and Rodin had no sense of humor. . . . Accordingly, the bust has no sense of humor; and Shaw without a sense of humor is not quite Shaw, except perhaps to himself" (184). Now, I certainly would not want to suggest that Michael Holroyd is lacking in a sense of humor, but I do think his Shaw is rather on the earnest side. The comic detachment is missing, or it is too readily dismissed as a mask which hides the real Shaw beneath. Holroyd's game, one might say, is to find out the man under the pose, and he plays this game with such determination that he under-emphasizes the "true Mozartian joyousness" (Shaw's phrase, in a 1900 letter to Beerbohm, not quoted in this volume) in Shaw's work and life— the energy and exuberance that proclaim themselves in Dan H. Laurence's edition of the *Collected Letters*.

Holroyd is determined to give more than a bust of Shaw. In stressing what he calls "the long shadow of his Dublin childhood" (309), so that the unloved Sonny of the first volume becomes the key to Shaw's life and work, he is striving to strip away the public layers and to get beneath the G.B.S. icon that Shaw offered to the world. He is also determined to get beneath the way in which Shaw wanted to see himself. It is revealing that no fewer than three of the photographs in this second volume display Shaw in some stage of undress. I suspect that Holroyd would like to have written more of a below-the-neck biography than his subject makes possible, and that Shaw's most serious defect, from his point of view, is his failure to be a really appropriate subject for a Holroyd biography.

Paradoxically, the biographer-as-artist declines on the whole to recognize the dramatist-as-artist. Shaw's plays in this biography are not aesthetic constructs but (for the most part) expressions of his own psychic needs. One recognizes that this is a biography of Shaw and not a critical book about his plays, but nevertheless, if Holroyd's work were the only surviving vestige of Shaw, it would be easy to overlook that he was important principally as a playwright, or that he wrote many of his greatest plays during the period covered in this volume. And there is little here that suggests Shaw's place in the drama and theater of his time.

Nor is there much of a focus on intellectual, cultural, social, or historical forces of the early twentieth century as a context for Shaw's work. Holroyd's world is mainly one of individuals, as one might expect of someone who has made a brilliant career as a professional biographer. Thus H. G. Wells is a major figure in this book. His 1906 denunciation of Shaw and the "Old Gang," "Faults of the Fabian," is given more than two pages, and the section on the Shaw-Wells duel in the Fabian Society occupies no fewer than twenty-one pages. There is much more about Wells elsewhere: for example, the story of his last days in the Fabian Society is told at length. Another figure who is given a curiously large amount of attention is Almroth Wright, whose contribution to *The Doctor's Dilemma* would not seem to justify such prominence in a biography of Shaw. Holroyd's interest in people more than in ideas serves him well in telling the stories of Shaw's life, and in discussing his relationships with other people, but it tends to leave out a dimension that is very much a part of Shaw's own conception of things. Intellectual contexts might play a larger part in the biography of a man who was himself passionate about ideas, and who believed that his business (or part of it) was to incarnate the zeitgeist.

And yet *The Pursuit of Power* is well worth reading. There are no surprises or revelations, no apparent archival discoveries, not many fresh insights into Shaw's life and work, but the book is a superbly fluent retelling of the familiar stories of Shaw's middle years: a skillful piece of synthesis, creating a smooth, elegant, highly readable narrative. The sources are mostly the obvious ones—so far as one can tell, that is. Readers must wait for the publication of a fourth, supplemental volume in order to discover just what the sources have been.

Holroyd writes that Rodin told Charlotte, who had arranged for the making of Shaw's bust, "that he would give her 'what is there.' He should more accurately have offered her what he could see was there" (184). Inevitably, Holroyd has given us what he could see was there. One may feel that the image is not quite accurate in representing the original, but one must acknowledge that Shaw has been shaped into a fine piece of biographical art.

J. L. Wisenthal

Shaw as Art Critic

Bernard Shaw on the London Art Scene, 1885–1950. Edited with an Introduction by Stanley Weintraub. University Park and London: Pennsylvania State University Press, 1989. 482 pp. $50.00.

In *Bernard Shaw on the London Art Scene, 1885–1950,* Stanley Weintraub provides 181 examples of Shaw's hitherto uncollected art criticism and presents, in a persuasive introduction, an assessment of the influence of art on Shaw's drama. The volume contains Shaw's art criticism from many sources: newspaper columns, pamphlets, letters to newspapers, unpublished manuscripts, introductions to exhibitions and catalogues, and contributions to magazines and journals. Three of the items are original manuscripts printed for the first time; 170 of the items are reprinted for the first time, most of them from the columns of the *World,* where Shaw held the post of art critic from February 1886 until December 1889. As Weintraub notes, Shaw's art criticism was, "aside from two or three pieces, . . . mostly unsigned, never reprinted, and largely unknown." Now Shaw scholars have available the entirety of that criticism, along with thorough prefatory notes explaining allusions and identifying artists mentioned in the criticism.

Apparently Shaw intended to add a volume of his art criticism to his Collected Edition, for he wrote a Preface for such a volume around 1947. Weintraub's collection begins with this Preface (manuscript in the British Library); in it Shaw disclaims the artistic importance of his youthful criticism except as it illustrates "to some extent the evanescence of fashionable reputations in art, and also the growth of unfashionable ones." Reading the criticism today is like stepping back into the art galleries of the 1880s and early 1890s, observing the received art of the day—epitomized by Royal Academy art—alongside the increasingly accepted Pre-Raphaelites, the newly emerging Impressionists, and the burgeoning Arts and Crafts movement. Through Shaw's sharp eyes one sees the portraits in which subjects are used "as mere clothes-horses," and one laments with Shaw the preponderance of "babies and doggies and pussies" in popular art. One admires the rich colors of John Everett Millais, the "vital glow" of Holman Hunt, the "poetic conception" of Dante Gabriel Rossetti, the "design and color" of Ford Madox Brown. And, finally, one witnesses the challenge to accepted art in the exhibits of the Society of British Artists and of the New English Art Club. Writing of the influence of the "New English Art" in 1888 (the *Star*, 9 April), Shaw notes that "even the scoffers will soon be unable to endure pictures in which there is no attempt to represent any effects of light, air, heat, cold, or weather except such as prevail in a St. John's Wood studio." According to Shaw, the Impressionists, like the Pre-Raphaelites before them, had effected a revolution in English art by "substituting a natural, observant, real style for a conventional, taken-for-granted, ideal one" ("A Degenerate's View of Nordau," *Liberty*, 27 July 1895).

Shaw consistently attacks the cheap sentiment and false effects produced by the "duffers" at the Royal Academy, accusing them of being "gentlemen who do not know how to paint as painting goes nowadays" ("England's Prestige in Art," *Truth*, 24 April 1890, passim). Shaw insists on a fidelity to nature and a truthfulness to the artist's own vision (as distinct from a concern for rules of design). Thus he praises Tissot's Impressionist art as "representing everything as we see it in Nature when our eyes are wide open" (the *World*, 2 June 1886); he compares the realism of Madox Brown favorably with Rembrandt's: "You can all but breathe his open air, warm yourself in his sun, and smell 'the green mantle of the standing pool' in his Dalton picture" ("Madox Brown, Watts, and Ibsen," the *Saturday Review*, 13 March 1897). Time and again

Shaw advises painters to "go to Nature for a lesson," to "imitate Nature"; they must avoid schools of design and trust their own eyes in their search for the real thing.

Not unexpectedly, Shaw also demands "a subject worth painting" and "intellectual power" in art. He complains of "the inanity of British art" while admitting the considerable technical expertise of British painters. Reviewing a winter 1886 exhibition of Royal Institute paintings, Shaw observes that "we have among us some twenty-five score ladies and gentlemen who will be in a position to paint pictures as soon as the necessary subjects occur to them" ("In the Picture Galleries," the *World*, 8 December 1886). Technique is not enough. For example, Millais's "thorough and masterly execution" is marred by a "commonplace" conception and "puerile fancy": he is "as empty in purely intellectual matter as 'Little Miss Muffet' " (*Our Corner*, February 1886; the *World*, 8 May 1889). Conversely, the technically flawed painting of Ford Madox Brown, whose "brush-work is about as clever as the stirring of a basin of gruel," is saved by an imaginative and thoughtful treatment of subject (*Truth*, 17 April 1890). For Shaw, art that does not reflect thought in conception and design becomes mere "ostentatious dexterity" or "facile cleverness."

Shaw's art criticism gives us not only a glimpse into the development of his realistic, idea-oriented aesthetic but also a reminder of the breadth of Shaw's interests. In addition to writing of the London picture galleries which he haunted from 1886 to 1890, Shaw lectures on "Art and Society," protests the demolition of the medieval front of Peterborough Cathedral, debates the purpose of art with Roger Fry in the columns of the *Nation*, contributes to a symposium on theater scene design, complains about the numerous dumpy statues of Queen Victoria scattered about London, questions the exorbitant price of art, and proposes how to support art and artists under socialism. "A Degenerate's View of Nordau," Shaw's open letter to the editor of *Liberty* (printed in July 1895 and revised as *The Sanity of Art* in 1908), defends mutinies against the establishment in morals as well as in art, and provides one of Shaw's most eloquent statements of the purpose of art:

> The claim of art to our respect must stand or fall with the validity of its pretension to cultivate and refine our senses and faculties until seeing, hearing, feeling, smelling, and tasting become highly conscious and critical acts with us. . . . Further, art should refine our sense of character and conduct, of justice and sympathy, greatly heightening our self-knowledge, self-control, precision of action, and considerateness, and making us intolerant of baseness, cruelty, injustice, and intellectual superficiality or vulgarity.

In his "Introduction: In the Victorian Picture Galleries," Stanley Weintraub traces the influence of art on Shaw's career, stating that "to the end, the art of his own formative years remained a catalyst for his playwriting, and his encounters with the visual arts added a unique dimension to his plays." Weintraub points out that Shaw appropriated metaphors from art in his music criticism and in his plays and that art influenced many of Shaw's dramatic settings and incidents. For example, the reading of the will in *The Devil's Disciple* is like a Royal Academy set piece; the cavalry charge in *Arms and the Man* is anticipated by the popular martial works of Elizabeth Thompson (Lady Butler); Shaw's "Mother Play," *Candida*, has Titian's *Assumption of the Virgin* dominating the Morell sitting room. In these and other examples extending to the end of Shaw's long career, Weintraub demonstrates the intimate interconnection of art and drama in Shaw: "perhaps no one else in drama brought so many artistic scenes to life on the stage as Bernard Shaw."

Weintraub's introduction also provides a survey of Shaw's career as art critic, from his earliest reviews in Annie Besant's socialist journal *Our Corner* in 1885 through his final withdrawal as critic for the *World* in December 1889, his columns for *Truth* in 1890 (which he abandoned because of editorial interference from the proprietor and his wife), and his occasional pieces in the early 1890s for the *Star*, the *World*, and other newspapers and journals. The volume demonstrates that Shaw never lost his interest in art criticism, though the art critic was superseded by the music critic and dramatist. And Shaw carried with him throughout his life the images from the galleries of the 1880s and 1890s.

The reader of *Bernard Shaw on the London Art Scene, 1885–1950* is assisted by historical-biographical prefatory notes and by a useful index. "Victorian Pictures: A Select Source List" provides a bibliography for those interested in viewing the works alluded to in Shaw's criticism. The book is a rich addition to Shaw scholarship, providing new and rare material for the serious student of Shaw.

Elsie B. Adams

Shaw on Photography

Bernard Shaw on Photography. Edited by Bill Jay and Margaret Moore, with an Introduction by Michael Holroyd. Layton, Utah: Gibbs Smith, 1989. 146 pp. + xxi. Illustrated. $19.95.

Bernard Shaw occupies a particular, if modest, role in the history of photography. An ambitious amateur photographer, he rarely achieved results beyond the mundane despite his intimacy with such luminaries of the photographic world as Frederick Evans and Alvin Langdon Coburn. Although he continued to take photographs for the rest of his life, by 1909 he had abandoned the arcane mysteries of the darkroom and thereafter turned his negatives over to professional printers. As a photographer, Shaw is thus a figure of marginal interest whose productions have a curiosity value only because he made them. It is as a writer about photography, and as a powerful advocate for its cause, that Shaw is to be honored.

Naturally, Shaw enjoyed the contentious debate about "art photography" in the early years of this century, and in 1901 he confidently asserted the authority of the camera over the other visual arts: "If you cannot see at a glance that the old game is up, that the camera has hopelessly beaten the pencil and paintbrush as an instrument of artistic representation, then you will never make a true critic; you are only, like most critics, a picture fancier." This was to outdo the claims for equality of status with their sister arts which the British Linked Ring (the British photo-secessionist group, which included many American and European photographers and whose exhibitions represented the great strength of the pictorial tradition in photography) and the American Photo-Secessionists made and is perhaps no more than a characteristic piece of Shavian extremism. Yet Shaw was a particularly good reader of photographs and brought to his criticism of them a sympathetic artistry which is both expressive and convincing, as in this famous account of Coburn's portrait of G. K. Chesterton:

> He is our Quinbus Flestrin, the young Man Mountain, a large, abounding, gigantically cherubic person, who is not only large in body and mind beyond all decency, but seems to be growing larger as we look at him—"swellin' wisibly," as Tony Weller puts it. Mr. Coburn has represented him as swelling off the plate in the very act of being photographed, and blurring his own outlines in the process. Also he has caught the Chestertonian resemblance to Balzac, and unconsciously handled his subject as Rodin handled Balzac. You may call the placing of the head on the plate wrong, the focussing wrong, the exposure wrong, if you like; but Chesterton is right; and a right impression of Chesterton is what Mr. Coburn was driving at.

Look at the Chesterton portrait and see how well Shaw has caught the sense of brooding massivity in the image, which seems to be advancing out of the frame which is too fragile to hold it. Shaw's comments appeared in the introduction to the catalogue for Coburn's first one-man

exhibition at the Royal Photographic Society in 1906, an essay in enthusiasm which manages large claims for Coburn with a scrupulous defense
of his techniques. In his final paragraph Shaw anticipates very recent
writing on Coburn in his account of the poetic mood of these photographs, "whether it is a mass of cloud brooding over a river or a great
clump of a warehouse in a dirty street," where Shaw gets near to Mike
Weaver's symbolist reading of Coburn.

The great virtue of this book is the collection here of Shaw's thirteen
articles about photography, which date from 1883 to 1914, although the
bulk of them appeared in the initial decade of this century. The first is an
extract from *An Unsocial Socialist* and, as the editors tell us, demonstrates
that Shaw was knowledgeable about photography ten years before the
onset of his own camera work and his later miscellaneous writings on
photography. Each of these articles is prefaced by a useful commentary
by the editors, setting out its context and summarizing the issues Shaw
dealt with in debates about, for example, pictorialism, as turn-of-the-
century "art photography" came to be known; the orthochromatic process (emulsions sensitive to all colors except red, which expanded the
tonal values of light and shade corresponding to the tones in nature);
and the "fuzzygraph."

On these and other topics, such as "retouching" the negative to improve the image, Shaw's articles show a lively contemporaneity. The
"fuzzygraph" was the unintentional offspring of the theories of vision of
Peter Henry Emerson, the notable photographer of East Anglian rural
scenes, whose *Naturalistic Photography for Students of the Art* (1889) was
widely distributed to camera clubs throughout Britain. Emerson argued
that our field of vision is not uniform, that although the central area is
clearly defined, the marginal areas are more or less blurred. Thus, to
reproduce human vision with the camera, he advocated putting the lens
slightly out of focus. Despite his particular warnings against the excesses
of "fuzziness," the soft-focus blurred image became a common phenomenon of camera-club exhibitions and the public salons, to the derision of
photography's critics. Reviewing the 1902 exhibitions of the Royal Photographic Society and of the Linked Ring, Shaw moves between bluff scorn
for the aesthetic affectation he saw in Edward Steichen's famous series of
nude studies to a feigned surprise at the irregular focus in the work of
George Davison, against the clarity of Reginald Craigie's images, even
those of a "misty softness." This is hard on Davison, whose "Marsh
Weeds," circa 1895, and his yet more famous "The Onion Field" of 1889
are at once powerfully evocative landscapes and precise renderings of
horizontal perspectives in depth, from sharply focused foregrounds to
the solid mass of trees in middle distance which give way to sky: they
have, indeed, an abstract quality in their rendering of space which lives

easily with their realization of specific place. To be fair to Shaw, he
recognized there was something magical in Davison's work, and he was
drawn to it despite his objection that "if I saw the edges of a house blur as
they blur in Mr. Davison's pictures, I should conclude that I was going to
faint." This is the response of a hardheaded realist, which Shaw here
turns into a complaint about Davison's long-range focusing.

Shaw's attack on Steichen's series of nude studies of 1902–3 is wittily
irreverent: "Mr. Steichen's life studies have all been made, apparently, in
coal cellars; why, I do not know." He goes on to read these images as failed
endeavors to imitate Whistler's "subtle local colour in a very low key"
where, he argues, Whistler built up his tones and color from a cold black
foundation "against which a bit of brown fur—say, a muff on the sitter's
hand—came up with a lurking richness that was very seductive. . . . Mr.
Steichen starts with brown, and gets no further than brown." The point is
well made, and difficult to refute, although, as Shaw would have known, it
all depends on the quality of the print you are actually viewing, and who
made it. It was commonly held of Steiglitz's reproductions of other photographers' pieces in *Camera Work* that his photogravure plates were often
finer than the originals made by the artists themselves. Brown on brown is
what you may get if you read these nudes for their tonal values, but there
is at least one other way of seeing them—as studies in form and mass, as
imitations of sculptural qualities—for which Steichen's model was not
Whistler after all, but Rodin: they are contemporary with his 1903 portrait
of Rodin.

However adversarial Shaw is in his treatment of particular images or
photographers, he always writes from an insider's perspective, from the
point of view of one who knows what the photographer is attempting,
understands the difficulties of uniting aesthetic vision with technical
resources, and ultimately appreciates the work before him for what it is:

> I am myself far too sophisticated by long contact with pictures,
> and by the natural insanity which has withheld me from reason-
> able industrial pursuits and driven me into the practice of fine art,
> to be able to say honestly that I do not like these aberrations of
> photography into pseudo-Impressionism. They are so ingenious,
> so difficult, so finely perceived, above all, so direct in their convey-
> ance of the artist's feeling (and the communication of feeling is
> the true diagnosis of fine art), that it is impossible for anyone who
> is not an utter Philistine . . . not to be interested by them.

Notwithstanding that opening self-directed irony—or is it a boast?—this
is well put, the licensed critic's defense of his practice to his own company, and to the unlicensed public.

Bill Jay and Margaret Moore have done a great service in gathering these articles together and in introducing them so instructively. They will fascinate those whose primary interest is in Shaw and will appeal equally to those preoccupied with the language of photography criticism, which is a matter of much debate at present. If his introductory essay to the work of Frederick Evans is essentially biographical, it moves inexorably to the issue that preoccupied Shaw, the disputed status of photography as an art form because of its dependence upon mechanical means of production. He asserts that Evans has decisively resolved the dispute in photography's favor through his gift, "the gift of seeing: his picture-making is done on the screen; and if the negative does not reproduce that picture, it is a failure, because the delicacies he delights in can not be faked." Shaw's reply in the *Amateur Photographer* to Robert Demachy's repudiation of "pure photography," on the grounds of its essentially "antiartistic" character, is again to distinguish between the substantial practice of photography "as a commercial process by men who were not artists" and the work of Coburn, Evans, Käsebier, and the like whose "gift of seeing" provided, in the last analysis, the surety of their aesthetic value.

I wish I could be as enthusiastic about Shaw's own photographs reproduced here, but apart from the fact of them, which is a virtue in itself, very few offer more than momentary interest, and Shaw's abandonment of his darkroom in 1909 seems to me to suggest a realization of his own artistic limitations as a worker in this field. Many of these photographs are no better than the average domestic snapshot, as, for example, an image of a child entitled "Coole 1916," where the background is out of focus and the child's feet are cut off. This is one of the weakest of a series from an album of Irish country scenes, many of which have a nascent picturesque quality which is no doubt native to the subject. But there are moments when Shaw's work suggests a potential which is generally unachieved. An image of a bridge over the Seine, of 1906, seen beyond two powerfully rectilinear trees, has a touch of Coburn about it, and a woodland scene in the Rhda Gorge in Algeria, of 1909, with a path veering away in the center of the image, is suggestive of Frederick Evans's great woodland landscapes. But these moments are rare in Shaw's work. In his portraits, including self-portraits, the sitters have an arch, awkwardly self-conscious pose.

Most of Shaw's photographs reproduced here come from the Shaw collection in the British Library of Political and Economic Science at the London School of Economics, where the National Trust deposited them on permanent loan, though a few come from the Harry Ransom Humanities Research Center at the University of Texas at Austin. The LSE collection comprises fourteen commercially produced albums, some of which are dated and titled, and ten large cardboard boxes of thousands of small unmounted prints: the labor of sifting through this quantity of research material must have been considerable, and the resulting product is ample testimony to these editors' conviction of Shaw's important contribution to the history of photography. Their introduction to this book gives a helpful résumé of Shaw's career and shows how his critical interest in photography survived through the first decade of this century, when Shaw was deeply involved in the debates over the future of the Fabian Society and his work in the theater. The appendices include a selected chronology, a list of major photographic collections which hold work by Shaw, a helpful glossary of technical terms, and brief biographical accounts of photographers and other figures mentioned in Shaw's writings gathered here. This is a most welcome book.

Lionel Kelly

Shaw and Others

Richard F. Dietrich. *British Drama, 1890 to 1950: A Critical History.* Boston: Twayne Publishers, 1989. 308 pp. $21.95.

"There have been two periods of great drama in British history," writes Richard F. Dietrich at the start of his book. As he points out, Shakespeare dominated the first, Shaw the second. A major challenge to anyone writing a book about either of these periods, which are about three hundred years apart, should be to do justice to both the leading figure and to the others.

To Shaw himself, justice might have consisted of paying as little attention as possible to Shakespeare's fellows. He considered them "insufferable bunglers and dullards whose work stands out as vile." The "raving" Marlowe, a "blank-verse beast," is "childish in thought, vulgar and wooden in humor, and stupid in his attempts at invention." Jonson was a "brutish pedant," Webster a "Tussaud laureate," Chapman a "donnish" creator of "sublime balderdash," and Beaumont and Fletcher a "firm" of "humbugs."

Arising from the question of whether Shaw's judgment about Shakespeare's contemporaries is valid is that of placing his own contemporaries. Is D. H. Lawrence a prose beast, adolescent in thought, or do his dramas hold the mirror to nature in a vividly realistic manner? Is Granville Barker a sensitive pedant or is he one of the most underrated playwrights of the period? Is R. C. Sherriff a trench laureate or does his *Journey's End* retain any of what Dietrich says is the "tough anti-war look" audiences felt at the time? Is John Masefield a donnish writer of less-than-sublime balderdash or does he plumb emotional depths? Are Noël Coward, Ben Travers, and Terence Rattigan, who were enormously popular in their time, franchise holders of a firm of humbugs or are they worth the attention some critics and directors are giving them today? Are the plays of James Joyce, Stanley Houghton, and St. John Hankin as absorbing as my memory tells me they are? Are those of J. B. Priestley and James Bridie as pretentious, empty, and ponderous? I looked forward to *British Drama, 1890 to 1950* to learn how the author would treat not only Shaw, on whom he has written perceptively before (and does so now), but also to learn how he would explore the ways in which the comic and noncomic writers I have named, plus others, have followed or departed from traditions Shaw himself followed, departed from, or introduced.

Dietrich does not go nearly as far in appraising Shaw's fellows as Shaw did in assessing Shakespeare's, but the major impression of the book is that Shaw is foremost ("the period's one giant"), the others usually far behind (Barker and Galsworthy are "minor"), sometimes out of sight. One sister, Lady Gregory, is analyzed; another, Clemence Dane (Winifred Ashton), not even named. Also unmentioned are Lawrence, Travers, and Joyce. Rattigan, Priestley, and Bridie receive fewer than a dozen lines each; Sherriff, Masefield, Houghton, and Hankin fewer than five (typically, Dietrich does not explain why he evaluates *Journey's End* as a "slight, sentimental" piece "which strikes us now as very naive and artificial"). Apparently, he considers that he gave these authors their due; but I submit that comic writers who held the stage for so long are worth as much consideration (even if it results in dismissal) as Pinero, whom he discusses at some length (as I would, though I would dismiss him more decisively then Dietrich does) and that attention also be paid to other dramatists whose work was highly regarded in their time. Furthermore, Dietrich does not consistently allocate space on the basis of works he considers important. "With the possible exception of Barrie's *Dear Brutus*," he says, "not a single major new play was produced in the West End during the four years of the war." Yet his treatment of this play consists solely of a two-sentence plot summary.

A large section of the introduction—on naturalism, symbolism, expressionism, and illusionism—introduces little that subsequent chapters develop. Nor does another section, essentially digressive, on William Archer (the book is supposedly on the drama, not its critics). Much of what Dietrich says of the formulaic qualities of the well-made play and the absence of real problems in the problem play is true, but he does not grapple with such issues as why well-made mechanical toys may succeed in comedy, as they do in works by Labiche, Feydeau, and Wilde, and fail in noncomic drama, and the possibility that the failure of most well-made plays derives not from the recipe but from the cooks, who put inadequate ingredients into the pot and mix them unskillfully. (If he were to respond to my assertion that Wilde's formula succeeded in *The Importance of Being Earnest*, as did Jonson's different formula in *Volpone*, with a Shavian counterassertion that both plays were poor jobs, I would ask him to justify Shaw in this matter rather than simply to assume that Shaw was right.)

His treatment of dramatists generally follows a pattern of biography, which is usually irrelevant (Wilde, for example) or unnecessary in a book like this (Shaw, for instance); then, a general statement about significance (often unbuttressed); next, a comment on individual works, which uneasily balances praise (sometimes a quotation from a critic) and skepticism about that statement (sometimes a quotation). The result is bland, seemingly balanced coverage that does not adequately grapple with issues. True, "*The Second Mrs. Tanqueray* was much bolder [than *The Profligate*]," but that statement means little, as Dietrich seems to realize when, in the same paragraph, he writes, "The question about *The Second Mrs. Tanqueray* and the other problem plays that followed is whether they were what they pretended to be." Like Dietrich, I would reply that they were not, but unfortunately the paragraph that follows is less response with justifications than it is plot summary. Soon, instead of arguing his case, he cites Archer's argument. Later, he calls *The Admirable Crichton* "Barrie's first major play and perhaps his best, surprisingly dealing with adult social concerns." At the end of the same paragraph, however, he hedges, shifting into impersonality: with Crichton's refusal to hear a word against England's social system, "critics have found that while *The Admirable Crichton* borders on adult satire in suggesting that the class system is arbitrary and unnatural, the play seems to subvert its challenge to ruling orthodoxy by eventually taking back everything it said, in a last-minute regression." The general effect of such writing, which is representative, is wishy-washiness.

Typical of the deficiencies of his treatment of Shaw's fellow dramatists is his discussion of Barker. More than a third of the nine pages devoted to Barker's drama is biography that, if not irrelevant, is inadequately related to the plays. Perhaps "it is difficult to assess his importance as a dramatist," as Dietrich says, but he seems to have forgotten that he had previously called Barker minor. "Certainly *The Madras House* is a major play," says Dietrich, yet the page devoted to it, chiefly plot summary, does not reveal why (or whether a minor dramatist can write a major play). *The Voysey Inheritance* "may also be important," he says on one page, one of "his major plays," he claims on the next, and then launches into a plot summary and reports on what Eric Salmon says of the play.

Despite the possible magnitude of these works, and of *Waste*, "there's something a little disturbing about the way [Barker] kept revising them." I do not know why extensive revision disturbs Dietrich or what his disturbance has to do with the quality of the plays. He concludes his assessment with the statement "We know that Barker was a leading theater artist and an important critic and theorist; what we need to know is whether he was a major dramatist as well, and only performance will give us an answer to that." If the last phrase in this conclusion is the case (and I am not one to minimize the role of performance), then why does not Dietrich examine Barker's plays in production? Obviously, the (Canada) Shaw Festival's excellent presentation of *The Voysey Inheritance* in the summer of 1988 was too close to printer's deadlines to have made an analysis possible, but this was not the case with the Royal Shakespeare Company's outstanding production of *Waste*, for instance, which transferred from The Pit to the West End in May 1985. Furthermore, apart from the requirement of performance being true of other playwrights whom some critics and audiences have pronounced to be major but whom Dietrich unhesitatingly dismisses, the statement undercuts the value of much of his book's analysis.

Occasionally, he makes provocative observations—for instance, that Jones "had more in common with the dour Norwegian [Ibsen] than he knew"—but he does not follow such statements with reasons to justify them. The perception that in *Lady Windermere's Fan, A Woman of No Importance*, and *An Ideal Husband* Wilde "introduced an element of moral ambiguity and relativity into 'well-made' plots, whose 'well-madeness' depended partly on moral conventions that previously had brooked no ambiguity or relativity" is worth developing in an analysis of these plays. Instead, Dietrich claims that because supposedly villainous characters shine in conversation they "escape any absolute moral condemnation" and observes, "The wit of the 'bad' people in these plays is what redeems them." Among his examples is Lord Goring of *An Ideal Husband*, but Mrs. Chevely, not Lord Goring, is really the "bad" person of this piece, and she is certainly unredeemed. Rather than examine moral ambiguities and relativity, Dietrich simply stops, provides a long quotation by Shaw on *The Importance of Being Earnest*, and then spends more than three pages on *Salomé*. "But what does *Salomé* have to do with Wilde's comedies?" he asks, as well he might, and then fails to answer his question adequately. The space he gives this work could have more profitably gone to another subject, perhaps one of the writers he ignores. "Whether Noël Coward deserves much space in a volume such as this is still debated" begins the section on him. By allocating little more than four pages to Coward, the author reveals his position, but the terms of his debate are shallow; they often employ biography, focus on Coward's homosexuality, quote two critics, call him "a transitional figure who led to both Beckett and . . . Harvey Fierstein," who constitute quite an odd couple, and offer no detailed analysis of a single one of Coward's more than fifty plays.

My generally adverse reaction to this book should not obscure my admiration of many of its sections, particularly those on Shaw. Unfashionably, but in my view accurately, Dietrich points out, "The Ibsen Shaw presents in *The Quintessence of Ibsenism* is a visionary, much akin to Ibsen's own view of himself. His surface realism was a subterfuge, a cover-up and symbolic signpost for the poetic divination that was going on behind the scenes." Dietrich cleverly observes, "A constant complaint of [Henry Arthur Jones's] was the sorry need of dramatists to lower themselves to popular taste, but at times that seemed to be a rationalization for an inability to write much above these tastes." He admirably contrasts Shaw with his early contemporaries: "Pinero, Jones, and Wilde provided escape valves by making everything come out all right, allowing convention to triumph over realism, and the problem to prove unproblematic. Shaw's [unpleasant] plays, though ending happily enough from the Shavian point of view, ended unpleasantly from the conventional point of view." With insight, he calls attention to the "sensuality" in *Caesar and Cleopatra*, "from the gorgeous stage setting to the pretty actresses and handsome actors who dress very becomingly" and how "this sensuality is put in its place: the leading character plays off against it for the moral purpose of showing how the Realist transcends sensuality, not by denying it for himself, but by affirming that it is not necessary to him, it is not the proof of his legitimacy as a hero, true heroism being internal." As Dietrich observes, Shaw did not "*repress* the sensuous and pleasurable" but instead "placed in the background what other playwrights and theater managers had placed in the foreground." Dietrich's analysis of Eliot and his placement of Eliot in relationship to Shaw is fine: "Eliot sought, not to replace the Church, as Shaw did, but to bolster it by bringing the Church and its values to the secular West End." While both would have largely agreed on "the spiritual wasteland of modern life, they would have disagreed on the cure—for Eliot Christianity was the solution; for Shaw institutional Christianity was part of the pollution." Dietrich's account of Synge, O'Casey, and Lady Gregory is perceptive, but except for a passing reference to the Life Force in his analysis of O'Casey, his treatment of Irish drama is insufficiently related to developments in British drama.

Odd errors, oversights, and apparent contradictions sprinkle the book. *Three Plays for Puritans* is Shaw's third, not second, volume of plays. Inaccurately, Dietrich calls both the Greek god and Shaw's Undershaft

"Dionysius," not (as Shaw does) "Dionysos." Perhaps, as he says, *Candida* represents "the questionable Victorian ideal of the angel in the house," but he should explain the latter phrase (how many readers know Coventry Patmore's poem of that title?) and how Shaw's play represents that ideal. *Jitta's Atonement* is not one of "a series of one-act plays" but is a translation or adaptation of a three-act play by Siegfried Trebitsch, who translated Shaw's works into German. Priestley's name is usually misspelled when it appears. "Galsworthy's conversion to drama was far from wholehearted," says Dietrich, but a few pages later he asserts that in two dozen years Galsworthy wrote twenty-seven plays (actually, twenty-eight)—which seems wholehearted enough to me.

In a potentially but not actually important appendix, a Chronology of Plays and Theatrical Events, and of World Events, Dietrich gives both 1898 and 1899 as the year the Irish Literary Theatre was founded; he notes 1890 as the year that movies were first shown in New York but does not note the 1938 *Pygmalion*, the most important film version yet made of a Shaw play, for which Shaw won an Oscar; he cites 1920 as the date of *Heartbreak House* but fails to indicate whether the year is completion, publication, or performance (it is the last). Under Plays and Theatrical Events, he includes Yeats's *The Tower*, which is neither but is a poem, and Shaw's *Intelligent Woman's Guide to Socialism and Capitalism*, which is neither but is a political and economic primer. Among the allegedly significant events this list contains are Coward's *Young Idea*, Barrie's *Shall We Join the Ladies?*, and Pinero's *Enchanted Cottage* in 1922 (the book itself contains a brief comment on the first, none on the others); the birth of "Jellico" in 1928 (actually, Ann Jellicoe, author of *The Knack*—how many remember it?—first produced in 1961, well outside this book's time frame); Priestley's *Time and the Conways* and *I Have Been Here Before*, and MacNeice's *Out of the Picture* in 1937 (the book dismisses both writers as unimportant). And so forth.

In brief, *British Drama, 1890 to 1950: A Critical History* is insufficiently critical or historical. Not only does it fail adequately, sometimes entirely, to address questions I posed in the third paragraph, it also does not address other issues, dramatic and social, such as the greater theatrical viability of D. H. Lawrence's and James Joyce's plays today than when they wrote them, and the Tory values inherent in Ben Travers's farces: notably *Plunder*, which doles out rewards and punishments not on the basis of morality and immorality, virtue and vice, but strictly along class lines—the charming aristocrats get off scot free, while the vulgar plebs are punished. Despite its good qualities, which I have noted, this book is basically a missed opportunity.

Bernard F. Dukore

O'Casey and Shaw, Again

Eileen O'Casey. *Cheerio, Titan: The Friendship between George Bernard Shaw and Eileen and Sean O'Casey.* New York: Charles Scribner's Sons, 1989. 141 pp. $19.95.

Some of the more memorable pages of two previous autobiographical books by the widow of Sean O'Casey have dealt with the kindnesses and loyalties of Bernard Shaw. *Cheerio, Titan* does little more than conflate those pages into a thin, overpriced book with the focus on G.B.S. Even the illustrations are sometimes padding—as with a photo of the Rodin bust of Shaw, executed long before O'Casey had encountered G.B.S.

Shaw first learned of O'Casey in 1919, when the younger Irishman asked that his small book on Irish labor, nationalism, and the Gaelic language, *Three Shouts on a Hill,* be granted the commercial boon of a G.B.S. preface. Typically, Shaw refused, but a relationship arose that was better for the author than a preface.

Eileen O'Casey, who married Sean in 1927, just after the plays that would seal his reputation were written—*Juno and the Paycock, The Plough and the Stars,* and *The Silver Tassie*—knew her husband during the long downhill slide of his career, as self-exile and political radicalism put an end to his bright promise. When O'Casey died at eighty-four in 1964, Eileen became the guardian of his reputation, notably in *Sean* (1972) and *Eileen* (1976). The books told the story of Shaw's encouragement of O'Casey's playwriting, his financial help, including paying the tuition of O'Casey's young children, and his friendship with O'Casey, which was largely epistolary.

A variety of ailments from heart trouble to near-blindness kept Sean in Devon, and it is to the sedentary lives of both men in the 1930s and 1940s that we owe the letters they exchanged. Almost every word of them (on G.B.S.'s part) has appeared in print before, but in this small book they surface in the context of the O'Casey-Shaw connection. Her mobility affected only by her finances, Eileen would visit the Shaws on occasion at Ayot, and she was one of the privileged few permitted to see Shaw in his last years. She was even there close to the end, two days before Shaw died.

Although echoes of Shaw's plays can be perceived in some of O'Casey's own, and Shaw helped make O'Casey's exile years in Devon more comfortable than his own meager earnings could have done, the relationship was more one of respect for the younger man's erratic talents, and a sense of Hibernian camaraderie, than any warm friendship. Without intending to do so, Mrs. O'Casey makes that clear by publishing in an

appendix a letter from St. John Ervine to Ronald Ayling, who had complained to Ervine about his ignoring O'Casey in a 1956 biography of
Shaw. Ervine's response says more than the previous 130 pages of Eileen's book: "You can do a man a kindness, and G.B.S. was incessant in
kindness, without being his intimate. . . . You are not a man's bosom pal
because you do him a good turn."

A rejoinder from O'Casey to Ayling, who shared the letter, follows.
Suggesting more "affinities" than friendship, although a bit of both, it
changes nothing, however full of interest. (A photo of Sean's family was
on Shaw's desk at Ayot, and Shaw once came to tea at O'Casey's house,
arriving after tea, explaining that he did not drink the brew.) If several
of O'Casey's plays were the better for his admiration of Shaw, and if his
life was more comfortable because of Shaw's intervention, the label for
the relationship hardly matters.

Stanley Weintraub

John R. Pfeiffer*

A CONTINUING CHECKLIST OF SHAVIANA

I. Works by Shaw

Shaw, Bernard. *Bernard Shaw on Photography*. Edited by Bill Jay and Margaret Moore. Layton, Utah: Gibbs Smith, 1989. Reviewed in this volume of *SHAW*.

———. "The Emperor and the Little Girl" in *Get Shaw! The Great War News*. Milwaukee Chamber Theatre, 1990, pp. 33–44. A 52-page pamphlet for the 18 May–17 June "8th Annual Shaw Festival" at Stiemke Theatre, 108 E. Wells St., Milwaukee, Wisconsin. The program included *Heartbreak House, Annajanska the Bolshevik Empress, Augustus Does his Bit,* and *The Inca of Perusalem*. The "Emperor" first appeared in *New York Tribune Magazine*, 22 October 1916, and is included in Volume 6 of the Constable *Collected Works*.

———. Extract in *The Longman Literary Companion to Science*. Edited by Walter Gratzer. Harlow, Essex: Longman Scientific and Technical, 1989. Not seen. Other authors of the over two hundred "extracts" mentioned are Conan Doyle, Gustave Flaubert, and Aldous Huxley.

———. Extracts from *A Village Wooing* and *Superman* and postcards and a letter from G.B.S. to Mrs. Louise Rumball. See Rumball, Louise, in "Books and Pamphlets," below.

———. "Granville-Barker, Some Particulars by George Bernard Shaw, Winter 1896." *Drama, The Quarterly Theatre Review* 173 (1989): 30–32. This Shaw reprint appears in a special number of *Drama* for its seventieth anniversary—1919–1989. The number includes as well reprints of H. Granville Barker's "William Archer," "Notes of Rehearsing a Play," and "A Design for a National Theatre"; William Archer's "The Last Two Months"; Gordon Craig's "Henry Irving"; Peter Brook's "Gordon Craig"; and T. S. Eliot's "The Future of Poetic Drama" and "Gordon Craig's Socratic Dialogues."

———. Letters and extracts from letters in Lewis Sawin's *Alfred Sutro: A Man with a Heart*. Niwot: University Press of Colorado, 1989. Four of the six letters referred to concern

*Thanks to Richard E. Winslow III for discovering and supplying copies of at least ten entries in this checklist. Professor Pfeiffer, *SHAW* Bibliographer, welcomes information about new or forthcoming Shaviana: books, articles, pamphlets, monographs, dissertations, reprints, and the like. His address is Department of English, Central Michigan University, Mount Pleasant, MI 48859.

Sutro's role in the Dramatic Authors Society controversy, which began in 1908, and in the formation and conduct of the Dramatists' Club in 1909 and 1910. See Sawin, Lewis, in "Books and Pamphlets," below.

————. Letters and extracts in Harry Morrison's *Socialism of Bernard Shaw*. Jefferson, N.C., and London: McFarland, 1989. The work relies heavily on materials by G.B.S. as evidence. Included are two Shaw letters (1943 and 1944); Fabian Tract numbers 2 and 3; extracts from *Intelligent Woman's Guide, Superman, Androcles, Methuselah, Everybody's Political What's What?*, and *Millionairess*, and material from the *Socialist Standard* and the *Western Socialist*. Reviewed in this volume of *SHAW*.

————. Letters to Sean and Eileen O'Casey in Eileen O'Casey's *Cheerio, Titan: The Friendship between George Bernard Shaw and Eileen and Sean O'Casey*. New York: Charles Scribner's Sons, 1989. Letters date between 1919 and 1929, and include one of 19 June 1928 that has the complimentary close, "Cheerio, Titan," from G.B.S. to Sean. Reviewed in this volume of *SHAW*.

————. *Major Barbara*, an excerpt from the Preface to *Major Barbara*, and "A Doll's House" in *The Bedford Introduction to Drama*. Edited by Lee A. Jacobs. New York: St. Martin's Press, 1989. Not seen.

————. "Mr. Bernard Shaw on His New Play." See *The Once and Future George Bernard Shaw* in "'Books and Pamphlets," below.

————. Quoted from a letter of 1895 in "No Author Is a Man of Genius." *New York Times Book Review*, 3 September 1989, p. 16. "I object to publishers: the one service they have done me is to teach me to do without them. . . ." Shaw's comment is included among those from about twenty-five others, including Wilde, Erle Stanley Gardner, and Shakespeare.

————. Quoted in *Quentin Crisp's Book of Quotations: 1000 Observations on the Life and Love by, for, and about Gay Men and Women*. Edited by Amy Appleby. New York: Macmillan; London: Collier Macmillan, 1989. G.B.S.: "If ever there was a writer whose prayer to posterity might well have been 'Read my works and let my life alone,' it was Oscar [Wilde]."

————. "Reviewer of Forgotten Novelists: Two Early Unsigned Shaw Notices from the *Pall Mall Gazette*." Edited by Stanley Weintraub. *SHAW: The Annual of Bernard Shaw Studies*, Volume Ten, University Park: Pennsylvania State University Press, 1990.

————. See Henderson, Bill, ed., in "Books and Pamphlets," below.

II. Books and Pamphlets

Adams, Carol J. *The Sexual Politics of Meat: A Feminist-Vegetarian Critical Theory*. New York: Continuum, 1990. It is not surprising to find fourteen references to G.B.S. here, including one to *Heartbreak House*.

Anderson, Marston. *The Limits of Realism: Chinese Fiction in the Revolutionary Period*. Berkeley, Los Angeles, Oxford: University of California Press, 1990. Mao Dun in the 1920s, to introduce Western-style realism in China, gave reading lists dominated by Scandinavian and Russian writers: Strindberg, Ibsen, Gogol, Chekhov, Turgenev, Dostoyevski, and Gorky; but the lists also included Zola, Maupassant, Wells, and Shaw.

Berg, A. Scott. *Goldwyn: A Biography*. New York: Alfred A. Knopf, 1989. Goldwyn visited the Shaws at Adelphi Terrace with the hope of doing something by G.B.S. in film around 1920. He asked to do *Arms, Androcles*, and *Pygmalion*, afterward, at different times. Shaw refused: "Goldwyn is after art; I am after money."

Bertolini, John A. *The Playwrighting Self of Bernard Shaw*. Carbondale and Edwardsville: Southern Illinois University Press, 1991. From the dust jacket: "Bernard Shaw claimed that he built his plays from 'atoms of dust.' Showing where these atoms are and explaining how they fit together to form meaning, Bertolini demolishes the conventional argument that Shaw was not a meticulous, self-conscious writer." To be reviewed in *SHAW* 12.

Brand, Gerhard. A review of Michael Holroyd's *"Bernard Shaw, Volume II: 1898–1918, The Pursuit of Power,"* in *Magill's Literary Annual 1990.* Edited by Frank N. Magill. Pasadena, Calif., and Englewood Cliffs, N.J.: Salem Press, 1990.

Brandon, Ruth. *The New Women and the Old Men.* New York and London: W. W. Norton, 1990. Lots of attention to Shaw and Ellen Terry. Includes also discussion of Havelock Ellis, Olive Schreiner, Eleanor Marx, Edward Aveling, the Webbs, H. G. Wells, Amber Reeves, Rebecca West, and Margaret Sanger.

Bromwich, David. *A Choice of Inheritance: Self and Community from Edmund Burke to Robert Frost.* Cambridge and London: Harvard University Press, 1989. One very interesting G.B.S. reference: Bromwich notes the high quality of criticism by Walter Pater and Oscar Wilde, but observes that, even so, there is no sustained critical eloquence to match the great passages of Johnson and Hazlitt until that of Shaw—"an unforced command and ready exuberance of wit, which after a time we cease to look for when we read Pater and Wilde."

Butler, Nancy. "The Shaw Festival Collection." *Collection Update, No. 11.* Guelph, Ontario: University of Guelph Library, 1988, pp. 23–25. A brief account of the disposition of the materials that collect from Shaw Festival seasons, now sent, as much as possible, to the Shaw collection at the University of Guelph Library.

Charlton, James, and Lisbeth Mark. *The Writer's Home Companion.* New York: Penguin Books, 1989. Not indexed. Contains at least five anecdotes involving G.B.S. on pages 18, 45, 65, 102, and 118.

Crawford, Fred D. "Sidelights" in the entry for "Shaw, George Bernard." *Contemporary Authors, Volume 128.* Detroit: Gale Research, 1990; pp. 375–78. The "Shaw" entry here provides the basic facts of his life, a list of the plays with dates of first production, "Letters, Conversations, and Diaries," "Collections," and "Other" (novels, essays on Ibsen and Wagner, "Shaw on Music," "Shaw on Dickens," etc.). "Sidelights" is an information-intensive summary of the reputation and influence of G.B.S., who "has earned almost universal recognition as the chief English-speaking dramatist of the modern age, second only to William Shakespeare in his contribution to the British theatrical tradition."

————. "Ways Pleasant and Unpleasant" (review of Volume IV of Shaw's *Collected Letters*). *SHAW: The Annual of Bernard Shaw Studies,* Volume Ten. University Park: Pennsylvania State University Press, 1990.

Davies, Robertson. "Bernard Shaw and Mrs. Patrick Campbell" in *The Enthusiasms of Robertson Davies.* Edited by Judith Skelton Grant. New York: Viking, 1990. This reprint of a *Saturday Night* (24 January 1953) review of *Bernard Shaw & Mrs. Patrick Campbell: Their Correspondence* finds the Shaw/Campbell correspondence less "glorious" than the Shaw/Ellen Terry letters.

Delaney, J. G. P. *Charles Ricketts: A Biography.* Oxford: Clarendon Press, 1990. Not seen. Margery Morgan, in her review of the book, "Of Learned Italian Things," *TLS,* 22–28 June 1990, p. 660, notes that Ricketts was Shaw's favorite designer.

Eduard Kochergin: A Poet of the Stage. Shaw Festival Theatre Foundation of Canada, 1989. Includes sketches of costumes, photographs of several sets, and reproductions and representations of projection screen set backdrops of Kochergin's designs for the 1989 Shaw Festival production of *Superman* and Christopher Newton's "The Art of Eduard Kochergin" explaining the genius of the simplicity of Kochergin's sets.

Einsohn, Howard Ira. "The Biophile: Frommian and Aristotelian Perspectives on Shavian

Ethics." *SHAW: The Annual of Bernard Shaw Studies,* Volume Ten. University Park: Pennsylvania State University Press, 1990.

Everding, Robert G. "Shaw and the Palaces of Variety." *SHAW: The Annual of Bernard Shaw Studies,* Volume Ten. University Park: Pennsylvania State University Press, 1990.

Finney, Gail. *Women in Modern Drama: Freud, Feminism, and European Theatre at the Turn of the Century.* Ithaca, N.Y., and London: Cornell University Press, 1990. Contains a number of references to Shaw, and a chapter, "The New Woman as Madonna: Shaw's *Candida.*" The play is analyzed to "investigate the complexities of maternal power" as "beneficent," opposed to Strindberg's *The Father,* treated in a following chapter, where maternal power is "malevolent." "Seen against the background of his feminism, the innovative nature of Shaw's depiction of the mother in Candida comes even more clearly into relief. Candida, that engaging amalgam of the Virgin Mary and the New Woman, is a more realistic and convincing representation of maternal power than the idealized mother figures so common in Victorian literature."

Gerzina, Gretchen. *Carrington: A Life of Dora Carrington, 1893–1932.* New York and London: Norton, 1989. One reference: Carrington, a painter who knew the Bloomsbury crowd, played a practical joke on Clive Bell, who had criticized Shaw in a *New Republic* article. With her husband's help she typed a letter to Bell and forged G.B.S.'s signature: "Dear Clive Bell, Thank you for the numerous compliments you have paid me in this week's New Republic. I am sorry I cannot return the compliment that I think you, or your prose, 'Perfectly responsible'. . . . You do not, it would appear, lead a very enviable aesthetic life; to me it seems dull, Yours, Bernard Shaw." Bell believed that it came from Shaw.

Gindin, James. "The Belated Shavian Influence: Wartime Disillusion and Galsworthy's *The Foundations.*" *SHAW: The Annual of Bernard Shaw Studies,* Volume Ten. University Park: Pennsylvania State University Press, 1990.

Gordon, David J. *Bernard Shaw and the Comic Sublime.* New York: St. Martin's Press, 1990. To be reviewed in *SHAW* 12. From the dust jacket: The book "discovers in the imaginative life of the Shavian *oeuvre* a mythology of self, of which the political and social themes are aspects. Understanding 'the sublime' as the modes of self-transcendence sought by an authorial will, and 'comic' as the resistances to these, Gordon shows how their interaction creates characteristic dramatic effects."

Grene, Nicholas. *Bernard Shaw: A Critical View.* New York: St. Martin's Press, 1984. See review by Adams, Elsie B., in "Periodicals," *SHAW* 9..

Hay, Peter. *Broadway Anecdotes.* New York and Oxford: Oxford University Press, 1989. Shaw is mentioned at least seven times. The least familiar item is about Billy Rose, who admired people that he considered "real artists." At a preview of *Heartbreak* at the Billy Rose Theatre, he whispered to Harold Clurman, the director, "This is a play for people who wash every day."

Heberle, Mark A. "The Year in Literary Biography [includes review of the second volume of Michael Holroyd's biography of *Bernard Shaw*]," in *Dictionary of Literary Biography Yearbook: 1989.* Edited by J. M. Brook. Detroit, New York, London: Gale Research, Inc., 1990, pp. 89–95.

Hederman, J., and R. Kearney, eds. *The Crane Bag Book of Irish Studies, Volume Two (1982–1985).* Dublin: Wolfhound Press, 1987. Not seen. From a review by Anthony Roche, *Irish University Review* 19, no. 2 (Autumn 1989), 374–76: "The third section looks at the Irish connection by considering the range of Irish writers who might be classified as 'socialist': Wilde, Shaw, Joyce, Synge and O'Casey."

Henderson, Bill, ed. *Rotten Reviews, A Literary Companion.* New York: Penguin Books, 1987. Includes excerpted negative remarks on *Arms* and *Major Barbara* by William Archer and on *Superman* by Bertrand Russell. Also includes disparaging remarks by G.B.S. on Shakespeare's *Othello, Antony and Cleopatra,* and *Julius Caesar.*

Holroyd, Michael. *Bernard Shaw: A Biography. Volume II, 1898–1918: The Pursuit of Power.* London: Chatto and Windus, 1989. The second of three volumes of Holroyd's official biography. The first is *Bernard Shaw: The Search for Love.* Reviewed in this volume of *SHAW.*

Huckvale, David. "Music and the Man: Bernard Shaw and the Music Collection at Shaw's Corner." *SHAW: The Annual of Bernard Shaw Studies,* Volume Ten. University Park: Pennsylvania State University Press, 1990.

Hughes-Hallett, Lucy. *Cleopatra: Histories, Dreams and Distortions.* Bloomsbury, 1989. Not seen. Reviews indicate that Shaw's interpretation of Cleopatra is treated.

Hugo, Betty. " 'Very Innocent Epistles': The Letters of Elinor Huddart to Shaw." *SHAW: The Annual of Bernard Shaw Studies,* Volume Ten. University Park: Pennsylvania State University Press, 1990.

Hugo, Leon H. *"Punch:* J. M. Barrie's Gentle Swipe at 'Supershaw.' " *SHAW: The Annual of Bernard Shaw Studies,* Volume Ten. University Park: Pennsylvania State University Press, 1990.

Jeffares, A. Norman. *W. B. Yeats: A New Biography.* New York: Farrar, Straus, Giroux, 1989. A number of G.B.S. references, but no new information.

Johnston, John. *The Lord Chamberlain's Blue Pencil.* London: Hodder and Stoughton, 1990. A number of references to censorship, *John Bull, Mrs Warren,* and *Pygmalion.*

Katz, Bernard. "The Dan H. Laurence-Shaw Collection." *Collection Update, No. 11.* Guelph, Ontario: University of Guelph Library, 1988, pp. 7–15. In 1986 the University of Guelph Library acquired the Shaw collection that Laurence had assembled over thirty-five years, probably the largest that remained in private hands, in the course of his work on *Bernard Shaw: A Bibliography* (1983). The article surveys the collection's various holdings, following the sectional divisions of the *Bibliography* and describing breadth, depth, and quality of the materials included.

L'Amour, Louis. *Louis L'Amour: Education of a Wandering Man.* Edited by Daniel J. Boorstin. New York, London, Toronto, Sydney, Auckland: Bantam Books, 1989. No index, but contains a reading-list log headed, "As I expected to reread parts of these books, I wanted their titles available to me. Hence I kept this listing of books read from 1930 to 1935 and in 1937." Of the 731 works listed, 15 are by Shaw, all read between 1930 and 1934: *Man of Destiny, Superman, Disciple, Cashel Byron, Major Barbara, Candida, Bashville, Methuselah, Mrs Warren, Joan, Apple Cart, Black Girl, Androcles, Overruled,* and *Pygmalion.*

Laurence, Dan H. *The Shaw Festival Production Record, 1962–1989.* Guelph, Ontario: University of Guelph Library, 1990. Not seen. Described as a complete record of the productions of the Shaw Festival Company, provided with eight indexes to actors, choreographers, directors, designers, authors, and lyricists, and title indexes to works by G.B.S. and other authors. Also covers, in appendices, the Festival's "Toronto Project" winter productions and a complete record of the annual Shaw Seminars. Order copies from The Shaw Shop, attn: Wendy Mackie, P.O. Box 774, Niagara-on-the-Lake, Ontario, Canada, L0S 1J0.

———. See *Shaw Festival Magazine,* below.

Lederer, Richard. *Crazy English: The Ultimate Joy Ride through Our Language.* New York, London, Toronto, Sydney, Tokyo: Pocket Books, 1989. Devotes two pages (126–27) to a cartoon of G.B.S. and his explanation of a new way to spell "fish"—"G-H-O-T-I."

Lee, Hermione. *Willa Cather: Double Lives.* New York: Pantheon Books, 1989. Between 1895 and 1900 Cather saw "serious" plays by such dramatists as Shakespeare, Ibsen, and Shaw. Later she reviewed *The Perfect Wagnerite* as, "in parts, interesting and brilliant."

London, Jack. *The Letters of Jack London.* Three Volumes: *1896–1905; 1906–1912; 1913–1916.* Stanford, Calif.: Stanford University Press, 1989. Not seen. Peter Kemp's review (*TLS,* 9–15 June 1989, p. 627) indicates that there are letters to G.B.S. included.

MacCarthy, Fiona. *Eric Gill: A Lover's Quest for Art and God.* New York: E. P. Dutton, 1989.

Gill joined the Fabians in 1906 and harangued them on the inadequacies of a socialist view of art. It is "central"—not "supplementary." His journal records a discussion of arts and crafts with Shaw.

Marchand, Philips. *Marshall McLuhan: The Medium and the Messenger.* New York: Ticknor and Fields, 1989. "Insecure students complained that McLuhan spent too little time on GBS—a playwright he had little use for. One recalled, McLuhan 'announced that since Shaw had only three original ideas in his life, we could prepare material on Shaw ourselves. . . . He never even hinted at what the three original ideas were.' "

Mavor, Ronald. *Dr. Mavor and Mr. Bridie: Memories of James Bridie.* Edinburgh: Cannongate, 1989. Not seen. A *TLS* advertisement says that details are given of correspondence with Tyrone Guthrie, Laurence Olivier, Alastair Sim, J. B. Priestley, and Shaw.

McDowell, Frederick P. W. "Holroyd One" (review of the first volume of Michael Holroyd's *Bernard Shaw*). *SHAW: The Annual of Bernard Shaw Studies,* Volume Ten. University Park: Pennsylvania State University Press, 1990.

Meyer, Michael. *Words through a Windowpane: A Life in London's Literary and Theatrical Scenes.* New York: Grove Weidenfeld, 1989. Lots of references to Shaw, whom Meyer met when Meyer was a boy. He knew as well Kenneth Tynan, Philip Larkin, Peter Brook, and Kingsley Amis. He was close friends with Orwell, Koestler, Mervyn Peake, and Graham Greene. He visited G.B.S. and Charlotte in 1942 and records a picture of warm domesticity. Shaw was a most kind and caring person. Sample anecdote: Shaw spoke of how Wells would unexpectedly send him an abusive letter, followed by a "charming one as though the previous letter and the reason or supposed reason for it had never existed."

Miller, Donald L. *Lewis Mumford: A Life.* New York: Weidenfeld and Nicolson, 1989. A number of Shaw references are necessary because G.B.S. was one of Mumford's principal mentors. He read and reread *Superman* in his youth. Later in his life he had to modify his Shavian drift in a conservative direction.

Morgan, Margery. *File on Shaw.* London: Methuen Drama, 1989. This volume in Methuen's "Writer-File" series "intended to assemble essential facts and to make vital but elusive material readily available . . . contains a comprehensive checklist of all the writer's plays, with a detailed performance history, excerpted reviews and, most importantly, a selection of the writer's own comments . . . from essays, interviews, letters and diaries, . . . a chronology of life and work, a checklist of non-dramatic writings and an annotated bibliography." Treats 47 plays. Includes an introduction by the general editor, Simon Trussler.

Morrison, Harry. See "Letters and extracts in Harry Morrison" in "Works by Shaw," above.

Mueller, John. *Retreat from Doomsday: The Obsolescence of Major War.* New York: Basic Books, 1989. To contradict Shaw, Mueller quotes from *Major Barbara:* "Well, the more destructive war becomes, the sooner it will be abolished, eh?" "Not at all. The more destructive war becomes, the more fascinating we find it." Mueller: "Shaw's snappy repartee contains a non-sequitur. The Civil War is endlessly fascinating, but nobody wants to do it again."

Naifeh, Steven, and Gregory White Smith. *Jackson Pollock: An American Saga.* New York: Clarkson N. Potter, 1989. One interesting reference: On 27 May 1929, Pollock began a retreat in Krishnamurti's Star Camp in Ojai, California, where, among other things, he watched plays by Barrie and Shaw.

Nathan, George Jean. "George Bernard Shaw (1856–1950)," in *A George Jean Nathan Reader.* Selected and edited by A. L. Lazarus. Rutherford, Madison, Teaneck: Fairleigh Dickinson University Press, 1990, pp. 116–19. In addition to this celebratory piece on G.B.S., this collection contains nearly fifty references to Shaw by Nathan, who promoted Shaw for decades from New York.

Newton, Christopher. See *Eduard Kochergin: A Poet of the Stage,* above.

———. See *Shaw Festival Magazine,* below.

O'Casey, Eileen. See "Letters to Sean and Eileen" in "Works by Shaw," above.

The Once and Future George Bernard Shaw. Long Island Stage, 1990. A well-produced twenty-four page pamphlet for the April 20–22 symposium, "The Once and Future Shaw," sponsored by the Long Island Stage. Included are an account of the Long Island Stage; a roster of its directors, managers, and trustees; descriptions of the symposium participants; and a "Schedule of Events." In addition there are four short articles. The most important is by Bernard Shaw, "Mr. Bernard Shaw on His New Play [*Getting Married*]," an interview drafted by Shaw for the *Daily Telegraph,* London, 7 May 1908 (C 1641). Of the remaining three, the first is by Stanley Weintraub, "Having It Both Ways: *Getting Married* as Serious Farce," an analysis of the play, a review of Shaw's commentary about it, and a ranking of its place among some of G.B.S.'s other works. The second article, "Shaw and Women," is by Margot Peters, who explains that for all his personal ambiguity about women, "Shaw the artist served women well." The third is by Rodelle Weintraub, "Getting Married? An Edwardian Dilemma." She concludes, "In *Getting Married* [Shaw] challenges us to examine whether women and men could and should undertake marriage and if so under what circumstances. The Edwardian era and its concerns may no longer be with us, except on the stage, but Shaw's question still remains relevant."

Paris, Barry. *Louise Brooks.* New York: Alfred A. Knopf, 1989. For bringing books by Shaw and Schopenhauer to the movie set, the actress became the "Starlet Scorned." Later in her life she explored Goethe, Proust, James, and Shaw, where she found "keys to her own life and family."

Parker, Peter. *Ackerley: The Life of J. R. Ackerley.* New York: Farrar, Straus, Giroux, 1989. A literary editor of the *Listener* from 1935 to 1959, and friend of the Woolfs, Sassoon, Wyndham Lewis, and Stephen Spender, Ackerley had a distinctly Roman profile that once got him a walk-on part in an Aldwych Theatre production of *Caesar.*

Peters, Margot. See *The Once and Future George Bernard Shaw,* above.

Pharand, Michel. "Shaw and the Nonconformist Conscience" (review of J. L. Wisenthal's *Shaw's Sense of History*). *SHAW: The Annual of Bernard Shaw Studies,* Volume Ten. University Park: Pennsylvania State University Press, 1990.

Rumball, Louise. *George Bernard Shaw and Ayot St. Lawrence: Memories and Facts by a Villager 1905–1930.* Louise Rumball, 1987. Includes "Acknowledgements," "Preface," "The Churches," "The Rectories," "The Schools," "The Manor Houses," "Mr and Mrs Cunliffe," "The Post Office," "George Bernard Shaw," "The Story of Their Marriage," "The Years After Marriage," "Happy Memories of George Bernard Shaw from 1905," "Some Close Friends of George Bernard Shaw" (Mr Apsley Cherry-Garrard and T.E. Lawrence), "The Ayot Festival," ". . . Extracts from His Writings" (*Village Wooing* and *Man and Superman*), "From the *Times,* 3 November 1950," "After 1950," and "An Unexpected Visitor." Also included are about twenty-five photos and reproductions of Shaw, the Ayot St. Lawrence buildings and prospects, and postcards and a letter by G.B.S. to Mrs. Rumball, dated between 1922 and 1927.

Sawin, Lewis. *Alfred Sutro: A Man with a Heart.* Niwot: University Press of Colorado, 1989. A well-known playwright in the decade before World War I, and for some years afterward, Sutro has no lasting reputation as a dramatist, but he was influential in the Society of Authors and the Dramatists' Club, and well acquainted with G.B.S. This biography records many of those connections and includes at least seven letters or extracts of letters by Shaw.

Seymour-Smith, Martin. *Rudyard Kipling.* New York: St. Martin's Press, 1989. Two interesting references compare love letters of Kipling to those between Shaw and Mrs. Pat.

Kipling thought Shaw's were "frigid." Seymour-Smith says, "These letters of Kipling's are literary compositions in which all feeling is meticulously kept at a distance. Shaw's letters to Mrs. Campbell are comic as a revelation of their author's ignorance of the real language of sexual love. Kipling's letters to Caroline Taylor are not comic; they are boring exercises."

[Shamshurin, Alexander Andreevich. *You're a Merry Soul, Bernard Shaw.* [*Veselaya Vy Dusha, Bernard Shaw.* Kishinev, Moldavia: "Shtiintsa," 1988.] The brackets here are to indicate this is only a working translation of the Russian-language title.

Its contents include "From the Author," "Bernard Shaw Is Presented," "You're a Merry Soul, Bernard Shaw," "The Other Side of the Pages of Shaw's Plays," "Shaw's Little Adventures," "Shaw Gives an Interview," "Shaw Travels," "Shaw, a Village Dweller," "Shaw, a Guest of the Soviet Union," and "Principal Sources Used." Translation for this annotation is by Professor Roger Freling, Department of English, Central Michigan University.

Shapiro, Doris. *We Danced All Night: My Life Behind the Scenes with Alan Jay Lerner.* New York: William Morrow, 1990. Shapiro became Lerner's personal assistant in 1952 and saw him through four of his eight marriages. She was on hand during the composition of the words for *My Fair Lady.* Alan and Fritz (Loewe) worked "like one expanded person," and the words they made "kept coming out sounding like George Bernard Shaw," to her "delight."

Shaw Festival Magazine. A Companion to the Festival and its Company. Shaw Festival, 1990. A sixty-eight page pamphlet for the 25 April to 21 October 1990 season at Niagara-on-the-Lake, Ontario. Included are Christopher Newton's "*Misalliance,* The Exploding Glass House": "The fragile glass pavilion has, for us, become a structure like the Crystal Palace—something that started as a celebration of new ideas but which, by the early-twentieth century, has become overgrown, entangled with so many ideas that people are losing their way in the profusion"; and "The Academy of the Shaw Festival," a reflection upon the history of the Shaw Festival. Three pieces on G.B.S. by Dan H. Laurence are "*Mrs Warren's Profession,* Victorians Unmasked": "Against the formidable array of Victorian pretensions stands Vivie Warren, the one *vital* character in the play, a self-possessed realist, determined to follow and fulfill the dictates of her own will"; "*Village Wooing,* Ship, Shop & Shaw": *Wooing,* begun on the Empress of India "between Suez and Bombay" ("the traveling shopkeeper apparently was inspired by Mrs. Jisbella Lyth"), has become "the most successful of Shaw's shorter stage works;" and "Shaw's Lifetime: A Chronological History." In addition to articles on the other productions of the Festival season, the pamphlet provides the names and contributions of virtually everyone connected with the Festival.

Sheehy, Helen. *Margo: The Life and Theatre of Margo Jones.* Dallas: Southern Methodist University Press, 1989. A major force in the establishment of the regional-theater movement, Jones was known as the "Texas Tornado." Inspired and influenced by Shaw, she arranged for productions of *Heartbreak, Candida, Misalliance,* and *Pygmalion* in her theater.

Shnayerson, Michael. *Irwin Shaw, A Biography.* New York: G. P. Putnam's Sons, 1989. Shaw is the American author of *The Young Lions* and *Rich Man, Poor Man.* In the late 1940s, as a drama critic, he reviewed *Superman,* saying "it made even the most robust of today's playwrights look as though they were suffering from anemia."

Simon, John. *The Sheep from the Goats: Selected Literary Essays of John Simon.* New York: Weidenfeld and Nicolson, 1989. Reprints Simon's 1975 essay review "The Limits of Intelligence: George Bernard Shaw, *Collected Plays with Their Prefaces* (Definitive Edition)," pp. 172–77.

Taylor, Gary. *Reinventing Shakespeare: A Cultural History from the Restoration to the Present.*

New York: Weidenfeld and Nicolson, 1989. Lots of references to Shaw. The most interesting is in connection with Granville Barker and William Archer. The "new British dramatists redefined Shakespeare between the opposing models of Ibsen and Wagner, between argumentative prose realism and musical myth. Ibsen represented what Shakespeare didn't do and what Shaw and Co. wanted to do. Wagner could be more easily adjusted to" that quality already present in Shakespeare.

Twitchell, James B. *Preposterous Violence: Fables of Aggression in Modern Culture.* New York and Oxford: Oxford University Press, 1989. The "Playground ritual" allows aggression without doing injury. "In *St. Joan* [*sic*], George Bernard Shaw blames Joan for spoiling the ritual. When Joan insists that the French generals stop knocking the English off their horses and get on with the business of killing them, she is effectively doing in the protective routine and, for Shaw, changing the world forever."

Tylee, Claire M. *The Great War and Women's Consciousness: Images of Militarism and Womanhood in Women's Writings, 1914–1964.* Iowa City: University of Iowa Press, 1990. Mentions Shaw three times for his appreciation of the point of view described in the title.

Tynan, Kenneth. *Profiles.* Cornelia and Michael Bessie/Harper Perennial, 1990. Not seen. From a review in *The New York Times Book Review*, 21 October 1990, p. 25. The reviewer contends that "Tynan's theater criticism is still considered second only to George Bernard Shaw's." *Profiles* includes fifty character sketches by Tynan, one of G.B.S.

Weintraub, Rodelle. See *The Once and Future George Bernard Shaw*, above.

Weintraub, Stanley. "Bernard Shaw in Darkest England: G.B.S. and the Salvation Army's General William Booth." *SHAW: The Annual of Bernard Shaw Studies*, Volume Ten. University Park: Pennsylvania State University Press, 1990.

———. See *The Once and Future George Bernard Shaw*, above.

Weiss, Samuel A. "Shaw, *Arms and the Man,* and the Bulgarians." *SHAW: The Annual of Bernard Shaw Studies*, Volume Ten. University Park: Pennsylvania State University Press, 1990.

Whitaker, Thomas R. "Granville Barker's Answer to *Heartbreak.*" *SHAW: The Annual of Bernard Shaw Studies*, Volume Ten. University Park: Pennsylvania State University Press, 1990.

Whitelaw, Lis. *The Life and Rebellious Times of Cicely Hamilton: Actress, Writer, Suffragist.* London: The Women's Press Limited, 1990. Several references to G.B.S. Hamilton wrote plays and appeared as an actress in *Fanny's First Play.*

Woolf, Leonard. *Letters of Leonard Woolf.* Edited by Frederic Spotts. San Diego, New York, London: Harcourt, Brace, Jovanovich, 1989. Woolf read G.B.S. as early as 1903. There are at least eight references here, including Woolf's report in 1943 that "Shaw once told me that the secret of good writing is always to cut out the first paragraph of an article or the first chapter of a book—and there is a lot in it."

Yeats, W. B. *The Collected Works of W. B. Yeats: Volume VI, Prefaces and Introductions.* Edited by William H. O'Donnell. New York: Macmillan, 1989. Subtitled "Uncollected Prefaces and Introductions by Yeats to works by other authors and to anthologies edited by Yeats." Two minor references to Shaw, one of them to *Heartbreak House.*

III. Periodicals

Abel, Betty. "The Long Biography of Bernard Shaw" (review of Volume I of Michael Holroyd's *Bernard Shaw*). *Contemporary Review* 254, no. 1476 (January 1989): 55–56.

———. Review of *SHAW: Shaw Abroad: The Annual of Bernard Shaw Studies*, Volume Five. Edited by Rodelle Weintraub. *Études Anglaises* 42, no. 2 (April–June 1989): 225–26.

Alter, Iska, and William B. Long. Review of the Westside Repertory Theatre production of *Mrs Warren's Profession*. *Stages* 4, no. 5 (October 1989): 29.

Amalric, Jean-Claude. Review of Bernard Shaw's *Agitations: Letters to the Press, 1875–1950*, edited by Dan H. Laurence and James Rambeau. *Études Anglaises* 41, no. 4 (October–December 1988): 490.

Andreae, Christopher. "In Her Own Words, G. B. Shaw." *Christian Science Monitor*, 7 September 1989, p. 14. An interview with Dame Wendy Hiller, whose Shaw roles include the leads in *Saint Joan, Pygmalion*, and *Major Barbara*, on the occasion of her "current" one woman show, "G.B.S. Remembered," based on encounters with and letters from Shaw.

Barr, Alan P. Review of Wisenthal's *Shaw's Sense of History* and *SHAW* 8. *Victorian Studies* 33, no. 2 (Winter 1990): 356–58.

Bembrose, John. "Dramatic Teamwork: Loyal Actors Made the Shaw Festival Shine." *Maclean's*, 25 June 1990, pp. 30–32. This article notices that 1990 is the twenty-ninth season of the Shaw Festival at Niagara-on-the-Lake. Moreover, all the current plays feature actors that have appeared at the Shaw Festival for several years—nine new actors to fifty-six veterans in 1990. The credit for this loyalty is to the Shaw Festival director, Christopher Newton. Rival Stratford has had lots of turnover each year.

Berst, Charles A. "G.B.S.: Oedipal Energies and Love's Artful Dodger" (review of Volume I of Michael Holroyd's *Bernard Shaw*). *English Literature in Transition* 32, no. 4 (1989): 471–75.

———. "Lancing G.B.S." (a review of Volume II of Michael Holroyd's *Bernard Shaw*). *English Literature in Transition* 33, no. 3 (1990): 325–29.

———. Review of *SHAW: The Neglected Plays; Volume VII*, edited by Alfred Turco, Jr. *Theatre Journal* 42, no. 1 (March 1990): 127–28.

Bertolini, John A. "Shaw and History" (review of J. L. Wisenthal's *Shaw's Sense of History*). *English Literature in Transition* 32, no. 3 (1989): 358–60.

———. "Shaw on Photography" (review of Bill Jay and Margaret Moore, eds., *Bernard Shaw on Photography*, 1989). *English Literature in Transition* 33, no. 4 (1990): 478–80.

Brendon, Piers. "A Middle-aged Terror" (review of Volume II of Michael Holroyd's *Bernard Shaw*). *Daily News Tabloid*, 8 September 1989.

Brooks, Harold F. "Shaw and Shelley." *Notes and Queries*, N.S. 36, no. 2 (June 1989): 196. In a *Major Barbara* Undershaft line, "Dare you make war on war?," there may be a debt to *The Masque of Anarchy* by Shelley: ". . . make war . . . on wealth and war and fraud."

Brown, Terence. "Shavian Trinity" (review of Volume II of Holroyd's *Bernard Shaw*). *The New Nation* (October 1989): 21.

Burgess, Anthony. "Saint Bernard and Mrs Pat" (review of Volume II of Michael Holroyd's *Bernard Shaw*). *Sunday Observer*, 10 September 1989, p. 46.

Carpenter, Charles A. "Shaw," in "Modern Drama Studies: An Annual Bibliography." *Modern Drama* 32, no. 2 (June 1989). About twenty-five entries, a number of which have not been mentioned in the *SHAW* Checklists. Carpenter is a former Bibliographer of the *Shaw Review*. His annual bibliographical listing for Shaw is indispensable.

———. "Shaw," in "Modern Drama Studies: An Annual Bibliography." *Modern Drama* 33, no. 2 (June 1990): 199–200. About thirty entries, including cross-references, several of which have not been mentioned in the *SHAW* Checklists.

Carpenter, Humphrey. "Shawly Some Mistake" (review of Volume II of Michael Holroyd's *Bernard Shaw*). *Sunday Times*, 10 September 1989, Books.

Cohen, Edward H. "Shaw," in "Victorian Bibliography for 1988/Section VI." *Victorian Studies* 32, no. 4 (Summer 1989). Seventeen entries, limited to Shaw studies in Victorian contexts, some not mentioned in this Checklist.

Collins, Glenn. "O'Casey's Widow Muses on his Friendship with Shaw" (review of Eileen O'Casey's *Cheerio, Titan*). *New York Times*, 13 November 1989, section C, p. 13.

Corballis, Richard. "Bernard Shaw and Nineteenth-Century Music Criticism." *IRMT Journal* 23 (June 1989): 10–15. "I hope these few examples make the point that Shaw's music reviews are essential reading for anybody interested in his plays [*Superman, Arms,* and *John Bull,* for example]. The fact that he does not get bogged down in the details of the performances he attended means that his criticism provides a better overview than anybody else's of the musical scene in late nineteenth-century London. And his provocative views about the nature and function of music criticism can—I hope—still provoke debate!"

Crawford, Fred D. Review of J. L. Wisenthal's *Shaw's Sense of History. Modern Language Review* 85, no. 2 (April 1990): 424–25.

———. "Shaw on Stage" (review of Aubrey Hampton's *GBS & Company. English Literature in Transition* 33, no. 3 (1990): 361–63.

Crick, Bernard. "Skimping the Tar?" (review of Volume I of Michael Holroyd's *Bernard Shaw*). *History Today* 39 (January 1989): 49.

Curtis, Anthony. "The Mind Behind Superman" (review of Volume II of Michael Holroyd's *Bernard Shaw*). *Financial Times,* 9 September 1989, Books.

Dirda, Michael. "Bernard Shaw: Playwright of the Western World" (review of Volume II of Michael Holroyd's *Bernard Shaw*). *Washington Post,* 24 September 1989, Book World, p. 3.

Dorment, Richard. "Idle Thoughts of an Arrogant Fellow" (review of Stanley Weintraub, editor, *Bernard Shaw on the London Art Scene, 1885–1950*). *TLS,* 8–14 June 1990, p. 614.

Dukore, Bernard. "Alan Ayckbourn's Liza Doolittle." *Modern Drama* 32, no. 3 (September 1989): 425–39. "One of the issues that continues to bedevil *Pygmalion* is that of romance between Henry Higgins and Liza Dolittle. . . ." Ayckbourn's *Intimate Exchanges* has a "Liza" (Sylvie) and a "Higgins" (Toby). "This essay focuses on the various situations and outcomes that result from different circumstances concerning Ayckbourn's Liza and Higgins. Despite their source, Sylvie and Toby are Ayckbourn's own creations. . . . In Ayckbourn's dramatized views, Liza does not necessarily marry Freddy. Neither does she necessarily enter into a romantic relationship with Higgins, and if she does, the results, given the characters of both, do not constitute the unmitigated bliss promised at the conclusions of *My Fair Lady* and the *Pygmalion* film. In part, *Intimate Exchanges* is an elaborate and dazzling set of variations on situations and themes in *Pygmalion.*"

———. "Shaw's Irritating Ways." *American Repertory Theatre News* 10, no. 2 (January 1990): I [*sic*]. "Paradoxically [*Major Barbara*] is a comedy about poverty and the arms industry in which a capitalist dealer in death may lay the basis of societal regeneration, a comic version of the Faust theme in which the Devil may provide a springboard for spiritual salvation. Shaw still requires us to resolve the play's issues. He was optimistic about what we might do to solve our problems, but he was not optimistic that we would do it. Shaw dramatizes his story in a delightful but irritating way, so that we may trouble ourselves about what we find troublesome."

Einsohn, H. I. Review of Volume II of Michael Holroyd's *Bernard Shaw. Choice* (March 1990): 1145.

Evans, T. F. "Shaw: Philanderer, Politician, Playwright." *New Humanist* 103, no. 4 (December 1988): 17–19. The occasion of the publication of Volume 1 of Holroyd's *Bernard Shaw* and Volume 4 of Shaw's *Collected Letters,* edited by Dan H. Laurence, elicit this essay's reflection upon the life and character of G.B.S.

French, Sean. "Pursuing Bernard Shaw" (review of Volume II of Michael Holroyd's *Bernard Shaw*). *New Statesman & Society* 2, no. 67 (15 September 1989): 33.

Friedman, Melvin J. "More on G.B.S." (review of Volume II of Michael Holroyd's *Bernard Shaw*). *Progressive* 54, no. 2 (February 1990): 41–42.

Fromm, Harold. "Holroyd/Strachey/Shaw: Art and Archives in Literary Biography." *Hud-*

son Review 42, no. 2 (Summer 1989): 201–21. "I find that it is the revised *Lytton Strachey* rather than *Bernard Shaw* that comes off as a product of very high art indeed. With its complex, distinctive, narrative voice—a fusion of subject and biographer—and its propulsive emotional energy, it is the sort of event that cannot simply be willed into existence. *Bernard Shaw: The Search for Love* arises from soil that is very fertile but whose circumstances are far from nurturing. Its biographical subject is a rhetorical killer, always threatening to shout down his biographer. A number of previous attempts have already been made at a life, of which St. John Ervine's succeeds by virtue of an artless artistry, a narrative grace, a warmth towards its subject, and a distinction of voice that Holroyd's version so far does not outshine. The materials, while immense and varied, are largely familiar but too diverse to produce a clear effect through any tendency of their own, thereby asking to be cut down to size by means of a unifying narrative persona that came easy to Ervine but that Holroyd does not seem able to supply. . . . The Strachey biography was a Dionysian orgy set off by some explosive conjunction of the planets, and it required both temporal and cultural space in order to domesticate a more properly 'Wagnerian' appreciation. The Shaw biography is cerebral and Apollonian, admittedly the work of a first-order archival authority, and worthy of being the new standard reference. But while violating few sensibilities, as biographical literary art it thus far emanates from a harp imperfectly tuned and with strings that may not lend themselves to precision tightening."

Garebian, Keith. "Eduard Kochergin at the Shaw." *Canadian Theatre Review* 61 (Winter 1989): 13–18. Subtitled "Soviet Designer Tackles *Man and Superman*," the article reports that "when Cameron Porteous, head of design of the Shaw Festival, persuaded artistic director Christopher Newton to invite Kochergin to design *Man and Superman* for the 1989 season, the eventual result was an artistic collaboration which, while never a marriage made in heaven, overturned all the stale preconceptions of the play. . . . There were difficulties with translation, with Kochergin's Byzantine preliminaries (particularly for the *Don Juan in Hell* sequence, which appealed to his strongly Christian temperament), and with the Soviet designer's presumption of autocratic rights. But after the culture-shock of both sides, the Shaw Festival's and Kochergin's, there was, happily, the design itself—a triumph of poetry and pastels." The article gives a good description of the design.

"George Bernard Shaw" in the "1987 Annual Review." *JML* 15, no 2/3 (Fall/Winter 1988–1989): 406–7. The eight entries include two not listed in this Checklist and a review of *SHAW* 7.

Gibbs, A. M. Review of J. L. Wisenthal's *Shaw's Sense of History* and *SHAW* 8 (1988). *The Review of English Studies*, 41, no. 162 (May 1990): 279–80.

Grene, Nicholas. Review of Fred D. Crawford, ed., *SHAW. The Annual of Bernard Shaw Studies*, Volume 9, *Shaw Offstage: The Nondramatic Writings*, 1989. *Notes and Queries*, N.S. 37, no. 2 (June 1990): 237–38.

———. Review of J. L. Wisenthal's *Shaw's Sense of History* and *SHAW* 8 (1988). *Notes and Queries*, N. S. 36, no. 2 (June 1989): 256–57.

———. "Trying to Understand Shaw" (Review of Volume I of Michael Holroyd's *Bernard Shaw*). *The New Nation* (November 1988): 26.

Gross, John. "Shaw and Super-Shaw" (review of Volume II of Michael Holroyd's *Bernard Shaw*). *New York Review of Books*, 21 December 1989, pp. 27–28, 30–31.

Hackett, Francis. "A Change in Shaw" (review of the 12 October 1914 Park Theatre production of *Pygmalion*). *New Republic*, 7 November 1914, p. 25. Included in a 1989 reprint of the entire 7 November 1914 number of the *New Republic*, without, however, 1989 bibliographical data.

Hampton, Aubrey. "Shaw to Please" (review of Volumes I and II of Michael Holroyd's *Bernard Shaw*). *Organica* 8, no. 30 (Winter 1989): 16.

Hartigan, Patti. "Shaw's Silliness, Lyric's Wit Save *Misalliance*" (review of the Lyric Stage, Beacon Hill, production). *Boston Globe,* 11 October 1990, pp. 57, 63.

Henderson, Bruce. "Shaw Offstage" (review of Fred D. Crawford, ed., *SHAW: The Annual of Bernard Shaw Studies.* Volume 9, *The Nondramatic Writings). English Literature in Transition* 33, no. 4 (1990): 487–91.

Hennessy, Michael. Review of Volume II of Michael Holroyd's *Bernard Shaw. Library Journal,* 15 September 1989, p. 112.

Hillier, Bevis. "Alarums and the Man" (review of Volume II of Michael Holroyd's *Bernard Shaw). Spectator,* 23 September 1989, pp. 27–29.

Holder, Heidi J. Review of J. L. Wisenthal's *Shaw's Sense of History. University of Toronto Quarterly* 59, no. 1 (Fall 1989): 131–32.

Hudson, Glenda A. "Modern Critical Interpretations of Shaw" (review of Harold Bloom, ed., *George Bernard Shaw's "Pygmalion"* and *George Bernard Shaw's "Major Barbara").* *English Literature in Transition* 32, no. 4 (1989): 515–18.

Hugo, Leon. Review of Volume II of Michael Holroyd's *Bernard Shaw. Irish University Review* 20, no. 1 (Spring 1990): 194–95.

Hurt, James. "The Canon of Irish Drama." *Eire-Ireland* 24, no. 3 (Fall 1989): 135–38. Hurt suggests that, for the purposes of his essay, the "canon" be defined by the works in Brendan Kennelly's "useful recent collection," *Landmarks of Irish Drama:* Shaw's *John Bull,* Synge's *Playboy,* Yeats's *Baile's Strand,* and O'Casey's *Tassie* are mentioned among several others. However, "Kennelly's landmarks are misleading because—great as they are—they are marginalized in Irish culture, suppressed counter-voices to the dominant discourses." To correct this distortion, he suggests reading more plays and reading *these* plays differently.

Hussey, Susan. "GBS & WWI, An Interview with Dr. Stanley Weintraub." *Organica* 9, no. 33 (Autumn 1990): 11. Weintraub is interviewed on this occasion as project scholar for the April 1990 "Once and Future Shaw" symposium sponsored by the Long Island Stage. See also *The Once and Future George Bernard Shaw* in "Books and Pamphlets," above.

―――. "Shaw in America." *Organica* 9, no. 33 (Autumn 1990): 6–7. The article provides a summary account of the popularity of G.B.S. in America as it reports on the 1990 American Shaw Festival at Stiemke Theatre, Milwaukee, Wisconsin. See "The Emperor and the Little Girl" in "Works by Shaw," above.

Kakutani, Michiko. "George Bernard Shaw and the Urge to Dominate" (review of Volume II of Michael Holroyd's *Bernard Shaw). New York Times,* 15 September 1989, p. C27.

Kauffmann, Stanley. "Ending the Journey" (review of Volume IV of Shaw's *Collected Letters,* edited by Dan H. Laurence). *Salmagundi* 84 (Fall 1989): 232–47.

Kelly, John. "Edwardian Angst" (review of the Cottesloe Theatre production of Granville Barker's *Voysey Inheritance). TLS,* 7–13 July 1989, p. 746.

Kemp, Peter. "The Far, Distant Shaw" (review of Volume II of Michael Holroyd's *Bernard Shaw). Listener,* 14 September 1989, pp. 24–25.

Lahr, John. "Girl Friday Tells All She Can" (review of Doris Shapiro's *We Danced All Night: My Life Behind the Scenes with Alan Jay Lerner). New York Times Book Review,* 11 February 1990, p. 10.

Larson, Gale K. Review of Volume I of Michael Holroyd's *Bernard Shaw. Theatre Journal* 41, no. 3 (October 1989): 426–29.

Leff, Thomas. Review of April–October 1989 Shaw Festival productions of *Getting Married, Man and Superman, Shakes Versus Shav,* and *A Glimpse of Reality. Theatre Review* 42, no. 2 (May 1990): 259–62.

London, Todd. "The Shaw Beneath the Skin" (review of Volume II of Michael Holroyd's *Bernard Shaw. American Theatre* 7, no. 2 (May 1990): 56–57.

Long, William B. See Alter, Iska, above.

Manchester, William. "The Diary of H. L. Mencken" (letter to the editor). *New York Times Book Review*, 4 February 1990, p. 33. Manchester, an old friend of Mencken (dead now for thirty-four years) remembers walks when Mencken recalled how Mencken had introduced America to Bernard Shaw, and how Manchester had read to Mencken from the Prefaces of Shaw.

Markgraf, Carl. "The Neglected Plays of G.B.S." (review of Alfred Turco, Jr., ed., *SHAW: The Annual of Bernard Shaw Studies*. Volume 7, *The Neglected Plays*). *English Literature in Transition* 33, no. 4 (1990): 480–87.

Moore, Mavor. "An Opinion for Every Occasion" (review of Volume I of Michael Holroyd's *Bernard Shaw*). *Books in Canada* 18, no. 2 (March 1989): 23–24.

Murray, Christopher. Review of Volume I of Michael Holroyd's *Bernard Shaw. Irish University Review* 19, no. 1 (Spring 1989).

Nathan, Rhoda. "Author's Query." *New York Times Book Review*, 8 April 1990, p. 28. For a biography of Arnold Daly (1875–1927), the Brooklyn-born actor who helped popularize the plays of G.B.S. in the U.S., looking for letters, memoirs, or other information.

Newton, Christopher. "Artistic Director, The Shaw Festival" in "Surviving the Nineties, a CTR Forum." *Canadian Theatre Review* 63 (Summer 1990): 41–42. "My theatre, The Shaw, is a classic theatre for the modern world. Our plays are the classics of our time, nothing to do with the Renaissance or the world of the Greeks; we deal with railways and Jung and the devastations of war and poverty and the now hidden delicacies of long summer afternoons at the turn of the century. I think we provide a world base on which our indigenous theatre can stand. There will be tougher plays, funnier plays, more desperate plays, and they will be about us and we won't be ashamed. We have always had better actors than anyone else; our trouble has been that we had no means to promote them and because we didn't see them on our videos we couldn't be sure that they were good. But they were; they are; they will be."

———. Review of Volume I of Michael Holroyd's *Bernard Shaw. Queen's Quarterly* 97, no. 2 (Summer 1990): 313–15.

Oliva, Judy Lee. Review of 1988 Shaw Festival productions of *Geneva* and *You Never Can Tell. Theatre Journal* 41, no. 1 (March 1989): 105–8.

Osborne, Charles. "GBS: The Critic as Entertainer." *Weekend Telegraph*, 30 June 1990, p. 13. "It is precisely because Shaw never attempted to separate his creative and critical faculties, precisely because his plays are both creation and criticism and his critical essays and reviews frequently adopt the methods of the novelist, that one tends to compare him with his peers in imaginative literature, even when the subject under discussion is not his dramatic oeuvre but his criticism." The article is accompanied by pictures of G.B.S. at twenty and as the mature metropolitan critic.

Parsons, Melinda Boyd. "The 'Unmechanicalness' of Photography: Bernard Shaw's Activist Photographic Philosophy." *Colby Library Quarterly* 25, no. 2 (June 1989): 64–73. A careful examination of Shaw's "writings suggests that the visual arts were far more central to his thinking on social reform, a position dependent primarily on his belief that the kinds of truth embodied in visual images—especially photographs—could be catalytic both in social reform and in the concomitant spiritual evolution that such reform would foster. The present essay, then, will focus on the inception of one of Shaw's most interesting concepts about art and photography, which was the quality that made the medium suitable as an agent of social reform. We will look first at the development of this idea in his 1883 novel, *An Unsocial Socialist,* where although he did not use the term 'unmechanical,' the basic components of his theory were present. Then we will turn to his transmutation of the idea almost twenty years later in a radical article of 1902, 'The Unmechanicalness of Photography.' . . . It was the job of the artist-genius, Shaw wrote, to try to perceive and express the purposes of the Life

Force, discerning 'the distant light of a new age' and focusing it in the 'magic glass of his artwork,' whence it could be 'flashed back from that into the eyes of the common man.' Thus the 'artist-prophet' could foster the changes in social and political structure that would lead the world into that new age, the new age that was the ultimate goal of the Life Force. . . . The distant light of the new age *had* to be matched by an equally new, modern medium; and for Shaw the most natural, unmechanical, truthful medium was that most 'mechanical' of instruments, the camera."

Peters, Margot. "The Playwright as Terrorist" (review of Volume II of Michael Holroyd's *Bernard Shaw*). *New York Times Book Review*, 17 September 1989, pp. 9–11.

Review of Volume II of Michael Holroyd's *Bernard Shaw*. *Publishers Weekly*, 14 July 1989, p. 66.

Reynolds, Stanley. "Charms and the Man" (review of Volume II of Michael Holroyd's *Bernard Shaw*). *Guardian*, 7 September 1989.

Roberts, Patrick. "Holroyd's Shaw" (letter to the editor). *TLS*, 15–21 September 1989, p. 1003. Corrects John Sutherland's 8–14 September review of Volume I of Michael Holroyd's *Bernard Shaw*, saying that these were the years of brilliant works—hardly representative of "defeat or confusion on all fronts."

Roll-Hansen, Diderik. "Shaw's *Saint Joan* on the Stage: Some Early and Some Recent London Productions Compared." *English Studies* 71, no. 3 (June 1990): 253–60. Shaw wrote *Joan* for Sybil Thorndike, who performed in the role more than two thousand times in the mid-1920s. Roll-Hansen reviews the critics' opinion of the Thorndike interpretation in contrast with productions of four versions of *Joan* mounted from the 1950s to the 1980s. In general he finds that the critics "speak quite favourably about the performances on the stage, which have always been good, or at least interesting, and often excellent, as is only to be expected in a play holding out so many challenges and exciting opportunities for talented actors."

Ruthven, Malise. "A Hero and His Discontents" (review of Jeremy Wilson's *Lawrence of Arabia*). *TLS*, 15–21 June 1990, pp. 635–36. Wilson's book and Malise's review deal with Shaw's allegedly "irresponsible counsel" to Lawrence to publish *Seven Pillars* with Shaw's publisher, Constable. Stanley Weintraub corrects this account in a letter to *TLS*, 20–26 July 1990. p. 775, "The Seven Pillars of Wisdom."

"Shaw Festival" and "Shaw, George Bernard." *Infotrac*. Information Access Co., 362 Lakeside Drive, Foster City, CA 94404, 1986–January 1990. Disc provides about forty items, mostly reviews written in 1988, and a few articles mentioned in this Checklist.

"Shaw, George Bernard." In "Bibliography Bulletin for 1988." *Irish University Review* 19, no. 2 (Autumn 1989): 355–57. More than sixty items listed, only a few not in the *SHAW* Checklist, some items as early as 1985.

"Shaw, George Bernard (1856–1950)." In "Irish Literature/1900–1999." *1988 MLA International Bibliography of Books and Articles on the Modern Languages and Literatures*. New York: Modern Language Association, 1989. Thirty-two entries, several of which have not appeared in this Checklist.

Sisk, John P. "That's Entertainment" (review of Volume I of Michael Holroyd's *Bernard Shaw*). *The American Scholar* 58, no. 4 (Autumn 1989): 597–600.

Smith, Jack. "Ask Not for Whom Shall I Say Is Calling." *Los Angeles Times*, 17 August 1989, Part V, p. 1. Animadversions on the impatience of Prince Charles with British English teachers for leaving his staff so illiterate, and the pedantry of the Higgins of *My Fair Lady*.

Strang, Ronald W. Review of Niloufer Harben's *Twentieth-Century English History Plays: From Shaw to Bond*. *Notes and Queries*, N.S. 36, no. 4 (December 1989): 548–49.

Sutherland, John. "A Poseur's Disappointment" (review of Volume II of Michael Holroyd's *Bernard Shaw*). *TLS*, 8–14 September 1989, p. 965.

302 JOHN R. PFEIFFER

Symons, John. "Licensed Jester" (review of Volume I of Michael Holroyd's *Bernard Shaw*). *London Magazine* 28, nos. 9 and 10 (December 1989/January 1990): 121–23.

Tehan, Arline B. "The Playwright and his 'Mollissima,' in Pursuit of Love." *Smithsonian* 21, no. 8 (November 1990): 154–68; 197. A retelling of the story of Shaw's relationship with Molly Tompkins. No new material.

Trotter, David. "Behaving Naturally" (review of Riverside Studios production of *Heartbreak House*). *TLS*, 1–7 December 1989, p. 1334.

Turco, Alfred, Jr. "Shavian Self-Portrait Complete" (review of Volume IV of Shaw's *Collected Letters*, edited by Dan H. Laurence). *English Literature in Transition* 2, no. 3 (1989): 317–23.

Updike, John. Review of Volume IV of Shaw's *Collected Letters*, edited by Dan H. Laurence, and Volume I of Michael Holroyd's *Bernard Shaw*. *New Yorker*, 2 January 1989, pp. 62–68.

Vaux, Anna. Review of Volume II of Michael Holroyd's *Bernard Shaw*. "Liber," no. 2, p. 18, in *TLS*, 15–21 December 1989.

Von Albrecht, Michael. "Fate or Hate? A Textual Problem in Shaw's *Major Barbara*." *Notes and Queries*, N.S. 36, no. 2 (June 1989):196–97. In Act II, CP 3, 117–18 of *Major Barbara*, the line "To hold a hand uplifted over *Fate*?" is absurd or wrong. Evidence from the manuscript shows that it is almost certainly wrong and should be "*Hate*," with a correction typical of Shaw's handwriting.

Watson, George. "The Return of the Sage." *Encounter* 74, no. 1 (January–February 1990): 53–58. In this "Memoir" of the late Raymond Williams (1921–88), Watson observes, not immediately cogently as he winds up his discussion of Williams as "liberal individualist," that "the avowed racialism of Marx and Engels, Shaw and Wells, is not to be answered by silence concerning those passages in their writings, public as well as private, in which they advocated genocide on Socialist grounds."

Weales, Gerald. "The Life of a Gadfly-dramatist: Act II" (review of Volume II of Michael Holroyd's *Bernard Shaw*). *Boston Sunday Globe*, 17 September 1989, pp. B18, 20.

———. Review of Bill Jay and Margaret Moore's *Bernard Shaw on Photography*. *Georgia Review* 44, no. 3 (Fall 1990): 534–38.

Weintraub, Stanley. Review of Bill Jay and Margaret Moore's *Bernard Shaw on Photography*. *History of Photography: An International Quarterly* 13, no. 4 (October–December 1989): 378.

———. See Ruthven, Malise, above.

Weiss, Samuel A. "Bernard Shaw's Legal Battles in Hungary." *Angol Filológiai Tanulmányok* [Hungarian Studies in English] 20. Debrecen: Kossuth Lajos Tudományegyetem, 1989, pp. 5–14. Shaw was eventually a success in Hungary, but not before legal difficulty with copyrights with the Vígszínház (Comedy Theatre). The basis "of Shaw's action and its outcome . . . can no longer be ascertained. But fortunately, Shaw's files of important business correspondence—now deposited in the London School of Economics—and his correspondence with his Viennese German-language translator, Siegfried Trebitsch, allow us to reconstruct his legal battles with Hungarian producers in 1906 and thereafter."

West, Rebecca. "The Duty of Harsh Criticism" (on *Androcles* and G.B.S. as a "spiritual teacher"). *New Republic*, 7 November 1914, pp. 18–20. Included in a 1989 reprint (without 1989 bibliographical data) of the entire 7 November 1914 number of the *New Republic*.

Worth, Katharine. "Ibsen and the Irish Theatre." *Theatre Research International* 15, no. 1 (Spring 1990): 18–28. Shaw is mentioned, but the essay is also valuable as an explanation of a dramatic vision in turn-of-the-century Irish theater that was a pole away from the Yeatsian one.

The Independent Shavian 27, nos. 1/2 (1989). Journal of the Bernard Shaw Society. In-
cludes "Shaw Against the Alphabet" by Jacques Barzun, "Shaw and the Lone Star
State," "Vox Populi," "Shaw and Mozart" by Ross Parmenter, "Shaw in Academe: the
1950s" by Richard Nickson, "Letter from London" by T. F. Evans, "You Never Can
Choose," "The Search for Love" by Jonathan Rose, "Beatrice Lillie," "Book Review"
by Daniel Leary, "Book Review" by Lillian Wachtel, "Book Review" by Richard
Nickson, "Another Word on Behalf of the Biographee," "From a Well-Used Mind,"
"Verses for Shaw" by Beth-Anne Carroll, "Shaw Signed and Framed," "Check This
One Out," "Arms and the Pen," "Unchallengeable Assertions," "News About Our
Members," "Maurice Evans," "Society Activities," "Kudos from *The Shavian*," and
"Our Cover."

The Independent Shavian 3 [27], no. 3 (1989). Journal of the Bernard Shaw Society. Includes
"Reflections on *Androcles*—Self, Fable, and History" by Alfred Turco, Jr., "Fifty Years
Ago," "Dear Ann Landers," "Letter from London" by T. F. Evans, "Tactless Shaw,"
"Another First for G.B.S.?," "Atrocities," "Book Reviews" by Richard Nickson, "Book
Review" [of *SHAW* 9] by John Koontz, "A Bernard Shaw Evening at the New School
for Social Research" by Lillian Wachtel, "Shaw and Sean: Irish Titans," "Feliks
Topalski," "Alexander Mauro," "Victorian Studies," "The Abusive Cyclist," "Auden
on Shaw," "Shaw's Flow of Comment," "Shaw Returns to Dublin," "Shaw and Barrie,"
"News About Our Members," and "Society Activities."

The Independent Shavian 28, nos 1/2 (1990). Journal of the Bernard Shaw Society. Includes
"From Mystic Betrothal to *Ménage à Trois:* Bernard Shaw and May Morris" by Sally
Peters, "Churchill on the Volcanic Shaw," "Shaw Business," "George Bernard Shaw
and Siegried Trebitsch: A Prolegomenon to Translation Study" by Steve Joyce, "Book
Review" by Daniel Leary, "Letter from London" by T. F. Evans, "Shaw's Impudent
Facility," "It Takes One to Know One: Bridie on Shaw," "Book Review" by Richard
Nickson, "Book Review" by Junius Scales, "Arnold Moss," "Myron Matlaw," "The
Once and Future Shaw," "News About Our Members," "Society Activities," "Corri-
gendum," and "Our Cover."

Organica 8, no. 29 (Autumn 1989). Organic Writings on Science and the Arts. Includes a
cover drawing of G.B.S. by Sue Meadows, "Publisher's Corner: A Vote for the New
Shaw Festival: Shaw on Animal Rights, Economics and the Environment and *GBS and
Company*" by Aubrey Hampton, "Summer in Shawtown" by Susan Hussey, "World on a
String: Ronnie Burkett's Puppet Theatre" by Silvia Curbelo, "Shaw and the Su-
perwoman" by Susan Hussey, "Shaw Shots" by Silvia Curbelo, "Art in Metamorphosis:
A Conversation with Jacques Barzun" by Mitch Hampton," and "Shaw's 'Man and
Superman': The Superman Gets Married" by Aubrey Hampton.

IV. Dissertations

Aston, Elaine. "Outside the Doll's House: A Study in Images of Women in English and
French Theatre, 1848–1914." University of Warwick, 1987. *DAI* 49 (May 1989), 3355-
A. The abstract does not mention G.B.S., but it treats matters familiar to Shavian
studies: "The images are divided into three groups, viz., the 'female outcast,' the 'third
sex' and 'revolting women.'. . . . Overall, the three groups of images represent three
strategies for power and their success and failure is [*sic*] indicated and assessed."

Cosgrove, James Daniel. "The Rebel in Modern Drama." St. John's University, 1988. *DAI*
49 (April 1989), 2864-A. Shaw's *Saint Joan* is treated with six plays by different major
writers: Ionesco's *Rhinoceros,* Anouilh's *Antigone,* Eliot's *Murder in the Cathedral,* Osborne's *Luther,* Brecht's *Galileo,* and Ibsen's *Enemy of the People.* G.B.S. treats Joan

"affectionately," finding "in the irony of her life—condemnation ultimately followed by canonization—perfect material for his satiric wit."

Decker, David John. "The Temptation of Saint George: A Critical Study of the 1880's Novels of Bernard Shaw." University of Washington, 1988. *DAI* 50 (September 1989), 689-A. "The greatest modern English-language dramatist must be seen as an Irish Victorian novelist, and . . . Shaw's drama-of-ideas develops out of the Victorian novel where there are serious issues at stake." These aspects are too much neglected by scholars. "The dissertation re-places Shaw in his proper place and time, as a young Irish novelist in 1880's London, the decade in which the Irish Land War and Fenian violence reach a peak, and the decade of Parnell's triumph at Westminster." The novels reflect the development of G.B.S.'s socialism. In the "cycle of novels, Shaw prepares ground for his theory of Creative Evolution and the Life Force by overturning conventional Christianity, the Victorian Work Ethic, and traditionalist Parliamentary politics, and provides a model in which Work and Art, Religion and Politics become different facets of one thing, a philosophy-in-ovo for modern man."

Fan, Ada Mei. "In and Out of Bounds: Marriage, Adultery, and Women in the Plays of Henry Arthur Jones, Arthur Wing Pinero, Harley Granville-Barker, John Galsworthy, and W. Somerset Maugham." University of Rochester, 1988. *DAI* 49 (January 1989), 1808-A. Of particular interest is the following: "Less influenced by the French *bien-faite* tradition and more influenced by Ibsen, Shaw, and the Russian drama, Granville-Barker and Galsworthy champion the New Woman and call attention to the need for societal reform, especially in marriage, an institution that mirrors the inequities of the larger society."

Harless, Winston Neely. "Characterization in Selected One-act Plays of George Bernard Shaw: A Display of Enthymematic Argument." Ohio State University, 1988. *DAI* 49 (April 1989), 2864-A. Six plays are chosen: *O'Flaherty, Blanco Posnet, Augustus, Six of Calais, Man of Destiny,* and *Overruled.* "The general observations of the study are four in number. First, enthymematic [rhetorical] analysis is demonstrated to be a useful and appropriate technique for the study of the formal structure of thought in Shavian one-act characterization. Second, Shaw's use of enthymematic argument is consistent and complex in pattern and strategy. Third, Shaw's rhetorical strategies are appropriate to the particular contexts of the plays. Finally, Shaw's rhetorical choices are consistent with the didactic dramatic pattern of thought used not only as thought but as structure."

Henderson, Heather Donielson. " 'All Life Transfigured': Structural and Thematic Disillusionment in Shaw's 'Heartbreak House.' " Yale University, 1988. *DAI* 50 (November 1989), 1311-A. "If it is discussed at . . . length and along its own lines of development, *Heartbreak House* emerges as less a parable of the eve of World War I than a consummate Shavian drama of creative evolution. From its title onward, the play asks us to redefine 'heartbreak' as disillusionment, itself a positive process that produces enlightenment about courage, political action, love and communality."

Joyce, Steven James. "Transformations and Text: The Rehearsal Copies of George Bernard Shaw's 'Buoyant Billions' in Critical Perspective." University of North Carolina at Chapel Hill, 1988. *DAI* 49 (March 1989), 2649-A. "The study argues the significance of George Bernard Shaw's last full-fledged play, *Buoyant Billions.* It examines a number of major emendations Shaw made to the early texts of the play as well as discusses the German translation of the play by Siegfried Trebitsch."

Koritz, Amy E. "Gendering Bodies, Performing Art: Theatrical Dancing and the Performance Aesthetics of Wilde, Shaw and Yeats." University of North Carolina at Chapel Hill, 1988. *DAI* 50 (September 1989), 691-A. In Edwardian Britain, dance rose dramatically in status because modern dance was being created and ballet rejuvenated. "The literary treatment of dance was essential to this process because of the renewed interest in the theatre shared by important writers like Wilde, Shaw and Yeats." Working in a feminist and materialist theoretical framework, each chapter of the dissertation integrates literary, critical, and theatrical treatments of dance. "Chapter two investigates how Shaw's writings on acting and dancing reinforce a particular structural positioning of dance in performances. . . . Shaw shared with [Wilde and Yeats] . . . a performance aesthetic that subordinated the dancer to the demands of an artist-governed aesthetic whole. Valorizing this separation between the artist and the performer 'feminized' the performer, reinforcing the gender hierarchy of a separate spheres ideology."

Larabee, Ann E. "First-wave Feminist Theatre, 1890–1930." State University of New York at Binghamton, 1988. *DAI* 49 (February 1989), 2426-A. Major attention is to Djuna Barnes, Susan Glaspell, Edna St. Vincent Millay, Marita Bonner, and Angelina Weld Grimké.

Reynolds, Jean. "Immodest Proposals: The Performer in Shaw's Prose." University of South Florida, 1988. *DAI* 49 (January 1989), 1811-A. "Shaw's 'Immodest proposals'— his non-dramatic prose works—frequently puzzle their readers, who have difficulty determining when Shaw was serious and when he was playing. . . . Masks and role-playing were essential to Shaw's post-Enlightenemnt metaphysics, which denied the existence of a 'serious,' changeless human nature. Rather than pretend to be a godlike, omniscient author, Shaw used exaggerations and other bold rhetorical ploys to take his readers behind the scenes and demystify the whole rhetorical process. . . . Shaw's prose style is both varied and extravagant, challenging three assumptions that limited his readers' ability to think creatively and forcefully: the beliefs that reality can be separated from appearances, that verisimilitude is more honest than style, and that seriousness has greater value than play. In his playful use of words and ideas, and his 'Immodest' challenges to conventional religious, political, and economic beliefs, Shaw both entertained and enlightened his readers."

V. Recordings

Caesar and Cleopatra, Pygmalion, and *Saint Joan.* Available as numbers VV7028, VB6018, and VH3303, respectively, as videocassettes, from Merit Audio Visual, P.O. Box 392-F, New York, NY 10024. Phone: (212) 267-7437.

George Bernard Shaw and His Times. Available from the Institute for Advanced Studies in the Theatre Arts, no order numbers, as 16mm film and Beta or VHS videocassettes, from IASTA, 310 West 56th Street, #1B, New York, NY 10019. Phone: (212) 581-3133. Provides two scenes from *Man and Superman* to address aspects of Shavian and Edwardian theatrical styles. "Shaw" is seen rehearsing his actors with lines taken from *The Art of Rehearsal,* in which Shaw outlined his manner of directing.

NOTICES

Conference: "1992: Shaw and the Last Hundred Years" (4–7 November 1992)

To mark the 100th anniversary of the first production of *Widowers' Houses,* the Department of Theatre Arts and the Center for Programs in the Humanities at Virginia Polytechnic Institute and State University (Virginia Tech) are planning a conference that will bring together theater scholars, critics, and artists from different parts of the English-speaking world. The conference is supported in part by a grant from the National Endowment for the Humanities, an independent federal agency.

The conference will explore such topics as Shaw's influence on drama and theater, a reconsideration of Shaw and Shavianism, the extent to which Shaw speaks to us today, changes in performance of Shavian drama in different countries, reactions against Shavian drama, and the aftermath of the dramatic revolution begun in English by Shaw. The conference will conclude with an attempt to assess the future of Shavian drama.

Speakers will include scholars and critics (Charles A. Berst, Bernard F. Dukore, Nicholas Grene, Holly Hill, Michael Holroyd, Irving Wardle, Stanley Weintraub, J. L. Wisenthal) and artistic directors of Shaw festivals (Montgomery Davis, Christopher Newton). There will also be performances of Shavian plays, a symposium of directors of major regional theaters, panels of refereed papers, and special panels of new Shaw scholars.

For information, write to Bernard F. Dukore, Virginia Tech, Blacksburg, VA 24061-0141, U.S.A.

An Appeal: Shaw Birthplace Museum Trust

The Shaw Birthplace Museum Trust succeeded in purchasing the Shaw house (33 Synge Street) in January 1990 with the aid of some generous local sponsors and a bank loan. The trust is now seeking donations from friends of Ireland and its literary heritage to complete the museum project, which will include Shaw memorabilia, an exhibition/lecture space, bookshop, and visitors' center. It is hoped that the Shaw Birthplace Museum may be opened to the public during the second half of 1991.

The Shaw Birthplace Museum Trust has budgeted for a total funding requirement of $750,000 to cover the initial purchase of the Shaw house ($200,000), acquiring the adjoining house, essential immediate repairs, complete and authentic restoration to the highest standards of craftsmanship, purchase of appropriate furnishings and Shaw memorabilia, and all necessary administrative expenses. The objective of the trust is to restore and furnish 33 Synge Street as closely as possible to the way it was when the Shaw family lived there in the last century.

Please address your donation to the Honorary Treasurer, Shaw Birthplace Museum Trust, 32 Synge Street, Dublin 8, Ireland. If you wish your donation to qualify as tax deductible under the U.S. tax code of 1986, please make your check payable to Irish Georgian Society, Inc., marking the payment as for the Shaw Birthplace Museum Trust (Internal Revenue Service determination of 5.27.1968, ref. M-68-EO-347, Manhattan).

Request For Manuscripts: Shaw 13

SHAW 13, guest edited by John A. Bertolini, will have as its theme "Shaw and Other Playwrights." Contributors should submit manuscripts in three copies by December 1991 to Fred D. Crawford, *SHAW* Editor, Department of English, Central Michigan University, Mt. Pleasant, MI 48859. Contributors should follow the *MLA Style Sheet* format, double-space throughout (including block-indented quotations and notes), and include SASE for return of their manuscripts.

SHAW Forum

Beginning with *SHAW* 12, "SCRAPS AND SHAVINGS: Letters from Our Readers" will provide space for scholarly and serious response to issues raised by articles in the *SHAW*. Letters should be directed to Fred D. Crawford, *SHAW* Editor, Department of English, Central Michigan University, Mt. Pleasant, MI 48859. Letters should be double-spaced throughout.

Milwaukee Chamber Theatre Shaw Festival
(17 MAY–9 JUNE 1991)

The Milwaukee Chamber Theatre's ninth annual Shaw Festival (Artistic Director, Montgomery Davis) will feature performances of *Saint Joan* and *The Doctor's Dilemma* at Helfaer Theater, Marquette University. The festival will also include limited performances of a double bill: *Audience*, by Czechoslovakia's new president Vaclav Havel, a droll view of his own persecution, and *Catastrophe*, Samuel Beckett's moving tribute to Havel. For ticket information, please call (414) 276-8842 or write to Milwaukee Chamber Theatre, 152 W. Wisconsin Avenue, Suite 731, Milwaukee, WI 53203.

Tickets are $16.00 for Friday and Saturday evenings and $14.00 for all other performances. Group rates are available for groups over twenty.

Schedule of Performances

Friday	17 May	7:30 pm	SAINT JOAN
Saturday	18 May	8:00 pm	SAINT JOAN
Sunday	19 May	2:00 pm	SAINT JOAN
Wednesday	22 May	1:30 pm	SAINT JOAN
Wednesday	22 May	8:00 pm	SAINT JOAN
Thursday	23 May	8:00 pm	SAINT JOAN
Friday	24 May	7:30 pm	THE DOCTOR'S DILEMMA
Saturday	25 May	8:00 pm	THE DOCTOR'S DILEMMA
Sunday	26 May	2:00 pm	SAINT JOAN
Sunday	26 May	7:00 pm	THE DOCTOR'S DILEMMA
Wednesday	29 May	1:30 pm	THE DOCTOR'S DILEMMA
Wednesday	29 May	8:00pm	THE DOCTOR'S DILEMMA
Thursday	30 May	8:00 pm	THE DOCTOR'S DILEMMA
Friday	31 May	7:30 pm	HAVEL/BECKETT
Saturday	1 June	4:00 pm	SAINT JOAN
Saturday	1 June	8:00 pm	HAVEL/BECKETT
Sunday	2 June	2:00 pm	THE DOCTOR'S DILEMMA
Sunday	2 June	7:00 pm	HAVEL/BECKETT
Wednesday	5 June	8:00 pm	HAVEL/BECKETT
Thursday	6 June	8:00 pm	SAINT JOAN
Friday	7 June	8:00 pm	THE DOCTOR'S DILEMMA
Saturday	8 June	4:00 pm	THE DOCTOR'S DILEMMA
Saturday	8 June	8:00 pm	THE DOCTOR'S DILEMMA
Sunday	9 June	2:00 pm	HAVEL/BECKETT
Sunday	9 June	7:00 pm	SAINT JOAN

30th Anniversary Season,
Shaw Festival, Niagara-on-the-Lake

The 1991 playbill of the Shaw Festival (Artistic Director, Christopher Newton) will include nine plays, three by Shaw: *The Doctor's Dilemma, The Millionairess,* and *Press Cuttings.* The Festival will run from 19 April (the preview of *The Doctor's Dilemma*) through 10 November (the final performance of Coward's *This Happy Breed*). Those wishing to see all nine plays on a single visit will be able to do so from 8 August through 15 September.

For further information, write to Shaw Festival, P. O. Box 774, Niagara-on-the-Lake, Ontario, Canada L0S 1J0, or telephone (416) 468-2172 (direct from Toronto, call 361-1544).

Schedule of Performances

FESTIVAL THEATRE

THE DOCTOR'S DILEMMA   by Bernard Shaw
Previews 19 April
Opens 22 May, 7:30 p.m.
In repertory until 13 October

LULU   by Frank Wedekind,
Previews 8 May   adapted by Peter Barnes
Opens 23 May, 7:30 p.m.
In repertory until 18 September

A CUCKOO IN THE NEST   by Ben Travers
Previews 27 April
Opens 25 May, 6:30 p.m.
In repertory until 13 October

COURT HOUSE THEATRE

THE MILLIONAIRESS   by Bernard Shaw
Previews 30 June
Opens 11 July, 7:30 p.m.
In repertory until 22 September

HENRY IV   by Luigi Pirandello
Previews 28 June
Opens 12 July, 7:30 p.m.
In repertory until 21 September

HEDDA GABLER   by Henrik Ibsen
Previews 30 July
Opens 8 August, 7:30 p.m.
In repertory until 22 September

ROYAL GEORGE THEATRE

A CONNECTICUT YANKEE   music by Richard Rodgers
Previews 25 April   lyrics by Lorenz Hart
Opens 24 May, 7:30 p.m.   book by Herbert Fields
In repertory until 12 October

THIS HAPPY BREED   by Noel Coward
Previews 1 May
Opens 25 May, 2:00 p.m.
In repertory until 13 October, continuing until 10 November

PRESS CUTTINGS   by Bernard Shaw
Previews 6 July
Press Opening 12 July, noon
Opens 13 July
In repertory until 15 September (Lunchtime production)

For the 1991 season, evening performances in all three
theaters (excluding openings) will commence at 8:00 p.m.

CONTRIBUTORS

Elsie B. Adams, a member of the *SHAW* editorial board, is professor of English at San Diego State University and the author of *Bernard Shaw and the Aesthetes.*

John V. Antinori has a master's degree in English literature from the Pennsylvania State University, where he currently teaches. He is also editorial assistant for the journal *College & Research Libraries.*

Peter Archer, Q.C., M.P., is Labour member of Parliament for Warley West. He was solicitor general in the Callaghan government and, for a time, was Opposition spokesman on Northern Ireland affairs.

Norman Buchan, who died on 23 October 1990, was Labour member of Parliament for Paisley South. He had also been Opposition spokesman on the arts.

Fred D. Crawford, general editor of *SHAW*, is associate professor of English at Central Michigan University. He was guest editor for *SHAW 9: Shaw Offstage* and is the author of *British Poets of the Great War.*

Bernard Crick is Emeritus Professor of Politics of Birkbeck College, University of London. He is the author of *George Orwell: A Life, In Defence of Politics,* and *Essays on Politics and Literature.*

Bernard F. Dukore, a member of the *SHAW* editorial board, is University Distinguished Professor of Theatre Arts and Humanities at Virginia Polytechnic Institute and State University. He has written on Shaw as director, dramatist, and screenwriter and is preparing the first full collection of Shaw's drama and theater criticism, to be titled *The Drama Observed.*

T. F. Evans, guest editor of this volume, was deputy director of the Department of Extra-Mural Studies, University of London. He is editor of the *Shavian* and also edited *Shaw: The Critical Heritage.*

H. J. Fyrth was senior staff tutor in history in the Department of Extra-Mural Studies, University of London. He has written several books on political and industrial history.

C. E. Hill graduated in history in 1981 and was granted a doctorate in the history of political thought in 1985. Both degrees were awarded by the University of London. Since September 1987 he has lectured in political science at the City of London Polytechnic.

Leon H. Hugo, a member of the *SHAW* editorial board, is professor of English at the University of South Africa. He is the author of *Bernard Shaw: Playwright and Producer.*

Lionel Kelly is director of American studies at the University of Reading. He is reviews editor of *The Yearbook of English Studies* and writes on twentieth-century American poetry, fiction, and drama.

David Nathan is deputy editor and dramatic critic of the *Jewish Chronicle* (London).

Sally Peters is lecturer in English at Yale University. She has published articles on Shaw's plays, on Shavian biography, and on dance. She is completing an interpretative study entitled *Bernard Shaw: Fantastic Sojourner.*

John R. Pfeiffer, *SHAW* bibliographer, is professor of English at Central Michigan University.

Michel W. Pharand teaches in the Department of English and Humanities at SUNY College of Technology (Canton, N.Y.). He has published articles on Shaw's affinities with the French writers Eugene Brieux and Henri Bergson.

Patricia Pugh is the author of *Educate, Agitate, Organize: 100 Years of Fabian Socialism.* She is working at present on documents concerning British imperial history in the Bodleian Library, University of Oxford.

Eric Wallis was, until his recent retirement, secretary of the Workers' Educational Association, London and is a graduate of Oxford University.

Stanley Weintraub, general editor of *SHAW* from 1956 to 1990, is Evan Pugh Professor of Arts and Humanities at Penn State University. He has written and edited more than fifty books on Shaw and his times.

J. L. Wisenthal, a member of the *SHAW* editorial board, is professor of English at the University of British Columbia. His most recent G.B.S. book was *Shaw's Sense of History.*

James Woodfield is professor of English and University Secretary at the University of New Brunswick. He has written *English Theatre in Transition: 1889–1914.*